The One Year Josh McDowell's Family Devotions 2

Dickinsons

Enjoy your ongoing
Walk with Jesus!

Love,

The Brunners

January, 2010

The ONE YEAR®

JOSH McDOWELL'S

Family
Devotions
2

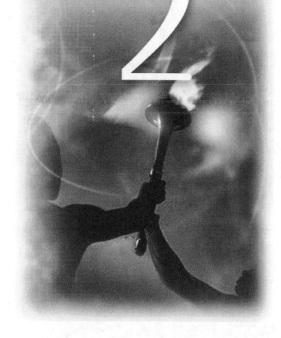

JOSH McDOWELL
KEVIN JOHNSON

Tyndale House Publishers, Inc. • Carol Stream, Illinois

Visit Tyndale's exciting Web site at www.tyndale.com

TYNDALE and Tyndale's quill logo are registered trademarks of Tyndale House Publishers, Inc.

The One Year is a registered trademark of Tyndale House Publishers, Inc.

The One Year Josh McDowell's Family Devotions 2

Cover design by Chris Gilbert

Cover illustration by Kevin Conrad and Jeromy Cox

Edited by Betty Free Swanberg

The Library of Congress has cataloged the first edition as follows:

McDowell, Josh.
  [One year book of family devotions]
  Josh McDowell's one year book of family devotions / Bob Hostetler.
    p. cm.
  Includes index.
  ISBN-13: 978-0-8423-4302-2 (alk. paper)
  ISBN-10: 0-8423-4302-4 (alk. paper)
  ISBN-13: 978-0-8423-5625-1 Vol. 2
  ISBN-10: 0-8423-5625-8 Vol. 2
  1. Family—Prayer-books and devotions—English.   2. Devotional calendars.
I. Hostetler, Bob, date.   II. Title.
BV255.M394   1997
249—dc21   97-17460

Printed in the United States of America

12   11   10   09   08   07
9   8   7   6   5   4

CONTENTS

Acknowledgments
Using This Book

March

April

November

December

A C K N O W L E D G M E N T S

We want to say a special thank you to

- *Betty Free Swanberg* for her editing talents as she molded and shaped each devotion, and
- *Dave Bellis* for guiding this project through the many details to get this work published and released.

Josh McDowell
Kevin Johnson

Here's a deep question: Can you imagine anything ever happening in your family's life that might rattle the trust some of your family members have in God? Or might anyone in your family ever swap his or her Christian faith for another belief that seems to make more sense?

God wants to make unshakable the faith that everyone in your family has in him. He wants all of you to understand the undeniable reasons your beliefs are worth hanging on to. Christianity not only promises eternity in heaven with God, but it also offers the individuals in your family a relationship with God right here and right now. No matter what your family will face, you'll never be alone. When you belong to God, you've got a solid rock now and forever.

In *The One Year® Josh McDowell's Family Devotions 2,* you'll come face-to-face with the truth that all of us need to keep from "forever changing our minds about what we believe because someone has told us something different or because someone has cleverly lied to us and made the lie sound like the truth" (Ephesians 4:14). You'll be able to convince one another that your faith is true. And you'll each know why your faith matters for every moment of your life.

Each page of this book brings your family a short Bible reading and a key verse; a devotional reading; and a brief "Talk," "Pray," and "Act" section to help you apply the truth of that day's lesson. You'll take quizzes and read stories. You'll get true-life accounts and fiction—and some selections that are stranger than fiction. You might laugh or cry. You'll also need to think together, because the goal of each daily adventure is to understand the "God who is passionate about his relationship with you" (Exodus 34:14).

Finally, *The One Year® Josh McDowell's Family Devotions 2* can be used in tandem with *The One Year® Josh McDowell's Youth Devotions 2*. The two devotionals correspond to each other so that a teenage brother or sister will receive reinforcement of the family devotionals in the daily youth readings. At the back of this book you'll find information on many other "Beyond Belief" resources.

Teaching biblical truth to each new generation is a solemn responsibility of godly parents (Deuteronomy 6:4-9). Our prayer is that these devotions will help you better impart godly values and views to your family.

1

No Way? No Way!

Bible Reading: John 14:6-7

I am the way, the truth, and the life. No one can come to the Father except through me. John 14:6

You've thought really hard, and now you've made up your mind. Instead of lazing around next summer doing nothing, you want to hatch an adventure. You want to go where none of your friends have gone before. You want to go visit your cousin.

But there's a problem. Your cousin lives on the other side of the planet, where his scientist parents study insects in the wild jungles of Borneo. You don't know how to get there—or where to find him. So you ask around.

Not all the responses you hear are helpful.

"Go to China and turn south for a few thousand miles. Lotsa luck."

"Don't accept any dinner invitations. I think there are still cannibals in Borneo."

"Haven't you heard of Bornean flying cockroaches? They're as big as grass huts. They eat people."

But finally your search pays off when you meet a professor at a nearby college. "Borneo? You want to get to Borneo? I love Borneo. That's where I was born and raised! And I'm headed back there for the summer. I also happen to know your cousin and the jungle where he lives. I can take you right to him."

Suppose you were actually hunting for a far-off cousin. Which bit of advice would help you most? It's no contest! You want to link up with someone who not only knows where you are going and how to get there, but who also knows your cousin and precisely how to find him. How could a trip to the jungle get any easier?

As Christians, we are already on an all-important quest. God has invited us to come to him. James 4:8 says, "Draw close to God, and God will draw close to you."

God invites us to enjoy that close relationship with him right now.

But how do we get to God?

If we had all the time, money, and cockroach repellent in the world, we could probably find a cousin without the help of someone born in Borneo. But there's no way we can get to God without Jesus. To know our heavenly Father, we have to know Jesus, his Son. He came to earth as a person to show us how we can know God.

Jesus doesn't just *show* the way to his Father in heaven; he *is* the way! He's not a road map; he's our road. As we trust Jesus, his heavenly Father welcomes us because he wants to be our heavenly Father too.

 TALK: How does it feel knowing that Jesus, the Son, cares enough about you to show you the way to God, the Father?

 PRAY: *God, thanks that we don't have to stumble through life to find you. Thank you that you sent Jesus to show us the way to you.*

 ACT: Draw a map or a picture that reminds you that God's Son, Jesus, is the way to God, the Father.

2 Like Father, Like Son

Bible Reading: John 14:8-9

Anyone who has seen me has seen the Father! John 14:9

Kids, answer this question: How would you feel if someone said to you, "You're so much like your dad"?

That all depends on what your dad is like, right? If Dad has the looks of a movie star and the brains of a rocket scientist, you might want to be like him. But if he has wiry hairs sprouting from his ears—like most dads—there's at least one way you probably hope you're *not* like him!

How much are you like your dad? Have each child in your family check (✔) any statements below that describe how you and Dad are alike. (If you want, you can compare yourself to someone else instead—your mother, older sibling, or other relative.) Do you have . . .

(Name)	(Name)	(Name)	
			the same eye and hair color?
			the same body shape and/or goofy face?
			the same musical and artistic talents—or lack of them?
			the same desire to learn more about Jesus?
			the same interests in TV, movies, and music?
			the same food likes and dislikes?
			the same sense of humor?

Here's something really cool to think about: The more you resemble your dad, the better people will know what your dad is like, even if they never meet him.

If you asked Jesus if he was a lot like his Father, he would answer, "Absolutely!" Jesus not only is your way to *get* to his Father, he is also your way to *know* what God the Father is like. You can't see God, but in the Bible you can see Christ, his Son. Jesus is "the visible image of the invisible God" (Colossians 1:15).

The more we know about what Jesus said and did while he was on earth, the more we know about God. When we hear about Christ's kindness, for example, we know God is kind. Or when we read Christ's truthful words, we know God is truth. We might not look or act or talk exactly like our dad, but Jesus perfectly shows us God. When we get to know the Son, we get to know the Father!

 TALK: What great stuff do you see in Jesus that attracts you to God?

 PRAY: *God, you could have made it tough for us to get to know you. We're grateful that Jesus shows us what you are like.*

 ACT: Pick one trait you know is true of God because you've seen it in Jesus—kindness, honesty, and so on—and practice that trait today.

God's Outrageous Gifts

Bible Reading: John 14:12-14

You can ask for anything in my name, and I will do it, because the work of the Son brings glory to the Father. John 14:13

Michael nudges himself over the edge of the steep hill. *Dear God,* he prays as his snowboard gains speed, *help me pull off this blindfolded, double-flip, 360-degree-spin so everyone watching will think I'm cool.*

Ashley lays her hand on the multiplication drill she just completed. Closing her eyes, she prays, *God, I don't expect a perfect paper. But please make enough answers right so I don't have to take the test again.*

What's the most outrageous thing you have ever asked from God? Have you asked for a twenty-pound sack of money to drop from the sky into your lap? for a dog to appear under the Christmas tree? for that terrible haircut you got to miraculously grow out before anyone sees you?

Jesus said we can ask him for anything. Hear it again: He said *anything!*

Could Jesus really mean that? What do you think? Take a minute or two to explain what you think he meant.

John 14:13 says Jesus wants to help us show off God's greatness. Here's how:

> Your prayer for anything in Jesus' name
> + Jesus' perfect answer to your prayer
> = Glory to the Father

Notice what happens when we pray: When we pray *in Jesus' name,* we are saying we want our requests answered *the way Jesus knows is best.* Since Jesus always knows what will show God's "glory" (what will bring him honor for his great wisdom, power, and love), we always get the perfect answer. That perfect answer helps us, and it brings God the praise he deserves.

Think about how that works in real life. We might ask Jesus to miraculously make all our wrong test answers right. But he knows we could grow more and bring greater glory to God if he helped us become strong and smart by studying hard. So he might not bail us out of a bad grade, but our prayer allows him to do what is best for us.

So go ahead—ask for anything. But ask in Jesus' name. Allow Jesus to decide the best way to respond. If you don't get the exact *anything* you pray for, it's because Jesus knows a better way to give God glory through you.

 TALK: How do you like the idea that God always wants to do the best thing for you? And that his best answer to your prayers brings him glory by showing off his greatness?

 PRAY: *God, it's a privilege to be able to ask for what we want—and also to know you will answer our prayers in ways that grow us and give glory to you.*

 ACT: Create a sign for your refrigerator that says, "We want God's best!"

4 What a Way to Go!

Bible Reading: John 14:1-4

I am going to prepare a place for you. . . . I will come and get you, so that you will always be with me where I am. John 14:2-3

You probably don't live in a town with a really weird name.

Then again, maybe you're from Finger.

Or Eyebrow.

Or Coldfoot.

Yes, those are real towns—in Tennessee, Saskatchewan, and Alaska.

You might not have thought about how long you're going to live in your hometown. But wherever you live, if you are a Christian, your hometown is only a short-term home. It's not temporary because you can't wait to get out of Boring (that's in Oregon). Or because you think it stinks like Worms (a place in Nebraska). Or because you want to wash Mud from between your toes (Mud is way off in Iran). Even if you are stuck in Muck (that's in Scotland), you'll be there only for a short time. That's because Christ has gone to heaven to prepare a permanent home where you will live forever with him.

Wherever you live, you're just a-passin' through. Even if you live in one place your whole life, that's just a blink of an eye compared to the eternity you'll spend with Jesus in heaven.

Do you ever wonder how you'll get to your real home? After all, you don't exactly have an atlas or a road map or a Web site that shows the way. Once again, Jesus Christ steps in to show us how to get where we're going.

- Jesus is the way to God, our heavenly Father.
- Jesus is the way to know what the Father is like.
- Jesus is the way to bring glory to the Father as you pray in his name.

But beyond all that, Jesus is also the way to our heavenly home. When his time is right for us—either when Jesus returns to earth or the moment we die, whichever comes first—Jesus promises to take us to where he is.

We need more than a *map* to find our way to God. We even need more than somebody to *tell* us the way. We need somebody to *meet* us where we are. Jesus, the Son of God, left his home in heaven and came into our world to show us the way home. And he came looking for us because he loves us.

 TALK: Jesus came to earth to show you the way home to heaven. How do you think his actions showed his love for you?

 PRAY: *Jesus, thank you for coming to earth to show us our way home. We want to follow you—through life, to heaven.*

 ACT: Tell a friend that you have proof of God's love for us—that Jesus promises to bring us home to heaven.

5 Down in Lonesome Town

Bible Reading: John 15:12-15

The greatest love is shown when people lay down their lives for their friends. John 15:13

"I don't know what my problem is," Tamara blurts through her tears. "I have friends, but I guess they're not the right kind. Or maybe I don't have enough. I never have to sit alone at lunch or on the bus. But I can feel lonely even in a crowd. Sometimes I'm not sure anyone understands me—or wants to. Even my teachers. I raise my hand and it's like I'm invisible. I think that if I never showed up at school again, nobody would even notice I'd left."

If you could grow up without ever feeling lonely, it would be like making it through cold season without getting a runny nose. Sometimes you might get lucky. But sooner or later you're going to feel like a giant drip.

Like a runny nose, lonely feelings tell us something isn't right. But what? Loneliness might seem as if it's all about not being popular or pretty. It actually has more to do with a desire God gives us to be loved and accepted. That's a deep, healthy need—and a need everyone has. When that need isn't met, we're going to feel lonely.

Most folks try to get rid of loneliness in one of two ways.

- Approach #1: **Act like a worm.** Worms try to cure their loneliness by crawling away from the crowds. Here's how this person thinks: *I'm lonely because nobody loves me. The safest thing I can do is burrow underground. So I'm staying down in the dirt. I'm never going to get close to other people.*
- Approach #2: **Act like a puppy dog.** Puppy dogs try to cure loneliness by doing anything to get people to like them. This person thinks, *I'm lonely because nobody loves me. I'm going to try harder. I'll do whatever it takes to get people to like me, even if it means doing something wrong.*

We don't have to act like a worm—or a pooch. Feeling loved and accepted starts with our relationship with Jesus, who is the only one able to meet the deepest needs of our life. Talking to Jesus and reading about him in the Bible are steps to strengthening our friendship with him. He laid down his life for us, so it's obvious that *he* regards us as friends worth dying for (John 15:13). That's the best comfort we can find when we wonder if anyone cares!

 TALK: When you feel lonely, do you act like a worm or a puppy dog? How can knowing that God loves you keep you from acting that way when you are lonely?

 PRAY: *God, when we feel all alone, help us to remember that you love us more than we can ever imagine.*

 ACT: Make time today to be a true friend to someone who feels lonely.

6 A Friend in Need

Bible Reading: Proverbs 17:17
> *A friend is always loyal, and a brother is born to help in time of need.*
> *Proverbs 17:17*

During Christmas vacation, Jacob and Daniel built a fearsome hideout. With their snow fort towering at the top of a hill in Jacob's backyard, the boys dominated snowball fights against the other neighborhood kids. They were a winning team.

Back at school Jacob followed Daniel everywhere. Daniel started to wish he had a few ice chunks to toss at Jacob. Sure, he'd had fun building the fort with Jacob, but he had other friends at school. So he ignored Jacob—and Daniel's coldness left Jacob wondering what had happened to their friendship.

So what's up? Daniel and Jacob ran into trouble because they had different expectations of what it means to be friends.

Take a minute to talk about it: Exactly what is a friend?

Which of these ideas about the meaning of friendship do you think are true?

☐ True ☐ False A friend is any human being I know.
☐ True ☐ False A friend knows me totally and likes me anyway.
☐ True ☐ False A friend is someone with whom I can share my secrets and feelings.
☐ True ☐ False A friend is a person I eat lunch with every day.
☐ True ☐ False A friend has the same hobbies and interests I do.
☐ True ☐ False A friend loans me money for a soda.

That's a bit of a trick quiz, because there are many different kinds of friends. Some are *casual* friends—classmates, neighbors, or adults we chat with but don't know well. Our *close* friends include people we choose to eat lunch with or sit by in class. But what we all need most are *committed* friends who will remain our friends no matter what.

Most people have a crowd—big or small—of casual friends, fewer close friends, and just a handful of committed friends who truly care for us and accept us. We let them see inside us. We trust them with our secrets, hurts, and joys.

We might know loads of people. But if we have no special friends, we'll still feel lonely. God wants each of us to be a committed friend and to let committed friends into our life, because they're the only ones who can take away our loneliness. When you make good friends, say thanks to God. They're a gift from him!

 TALK: Who are your committed friends? How do they show they are committed to you? How do they show God's love to you?

 PRAY: Ask God today to guide you to a few trustworthy friends.

 ACT: Get together this week with someone with whom you'd like to become a better friend.

7 Bad Apples in the Barrel

Bible Reading: 2 Timothy 3:2-5
Bad company corrupts good morals. 1 Corinthians 15:33, NASB

"My parents are always nagging me about my friends," Hailey fussed. "They say I shouldn't hang out with 'kids who look like trouble.' I know my friends aren't perfect. But my dad and mom must think I'm a two-year-old. They want my best friends to be Barney and Mister Rogers."

Ever had your parents get after you because of the people you choose to be around? Maybe you've heard them say things like, "I don't like how you act when you're around so-and-so" or "I don't want you to act like so-and-so just did" or even "I think so-and-so is a bad influence on you."

Parents do *not* have eyes in the backs of their heads. But whether you're four or fourteen years old, parents can spot trouble you don't see. Grown-ups don't just look at what your friends are like right now. They try really hard to peer into your future. And sometimes they see trouble down the road—that someone you're close to is steering into a ditch. You might be sure your parents are wrong, or deep down you might know they're right. But either way, they know that bad friends can slide off the road and take you with them—dragging you away from God, family, and healthy friends (see 1 Corinthians 15:33).

Being smart in choosing our friends helps us become the people God wants us to be. If we're willing to admit that our close friends have a big influence on us—and they do—then we will want to be careful whom we choose as our closest friends.

Talk about it: So how can we tell good friends from ones who might pull us in the wrong direction?

Here's one sure way: Ask yourself how a friend changes your behavior—and don't kid yourself when you answer. Let's assume you're a sweet, kind, obedient, thoughtful, responsible person. Suppose you find a new friend, and after a few weeks or months you're goofing off at school or getting sassy at home. What happened? You might feel that your new friend is just helping you to loosen up. But "friends" who drag you into trouble aren't friends, even if you have fun together.

Do you have a friend who is steering you away from following God? Then it's time to back off and find better friends. That's tough—but in the long run, it's not as tough as staying in a friendship that hurts you!

 TALK: When have you had a friend who tugged you in the wrong direction? With which better friend might God want you to grow closer?

 PRAY: Ask God to give you really good friends who help you get close to him.

 ACT: If you have a friend who has been dragging you down, talk to your parents about whether you need to take a break from hanging out together or break off the friendship completely.

8 Find a Friend—Be a Friend

Bible Reading: Proverbs 18:24

There are "friends" who destroy each other, but a real friend sticks closer than a brother. Proverbs 18:24

Give a thumbs-up or thumbs-down on these hot ideas for getting new friends:

- Throw a party and give away your parents' credit cards as door prizes.
- Hack the school loudspeaker system in the middle of the morning and in your best principal voice announce that school is dismissed early.
- Drag a crate of Twinkies to school and fling them to the crowds at recess.

While those way-out ideas will get you friends, they won't attract friends who will last. Here are some better ideas for attracting friends. As you listen, think of one or two that could work for you:

- *Start with being yourself.* Nikki made friends by pretending to be interested in sports, but she had a hard time keeping that up. When she let people see the things she sewed, she found friends who liked her for who she was.
- *Take the first step.* After moving to a new school, Marc expected people to welcome him. He waited a long time before he figured out that it was okay for him to make the first move.
- *Be adventurous.* Josh was another student who entered a new school. He found some valuable friends when he was willing to try the sports and hobbies that were popular at his new school.
- *Don't be a grump.* Emma always looked like her cat had just been flattened by a truck. Once she started noticing—and talking about—the good things in her life, people saw her as a whole new person.
- *Don't give up.* Most of Blake's buddies had moved away or found new friends. He felt rejected, and he wasn't exactly enthusiastic about trying to find new friends. But as he kept at it, he found two new best friends.

We can try all sorts of wild stunts to attract friends. But think about what we really want in a friend. Sure, maybe we would like to be handed a credit card, let out of school early, or fed a Twinkie feast. But in the long run we would probably like a friend with really cool character—someone who is genuine, easy to talk to, adventurous, positive, persistent. Look for that kind of friend. And be that kind of friend.

TALK: Who in your world might make a good new friend? What can you do to open a door to the great friendships God has planned for you?

PRAY: *God, teach us how to reach out and make new friends. Help us make friends by being friends.*

ACT: Even if you have a bunch of great friends, make a plan to get to know someone new this week.

9 Happy Re-Birthday to You!

Bible Reading: Romans 8:1-4, 11

The power of the life-giving Spirit has freed you through Christ Jesus from the power of sin that leads to death. Romans 8:2

Just minutes after the umbilical cord is cut, their eyes meet. The young husband and wife can't believe that cradled in their arms and looking up at them is a tiny baby boy, their firstborn child. They have never seen anything so beautiful . . . so perfect . . . so wonderful. And they can't remember ever being more happy.

For nine months this pair of new parents dreamed of their child's birth. Now they stare at a scrunchy little thing and look forward to watching him grow up. As they tenderly bundle up the helpless ball of life, tears of joy stream down their cheeks. They expect nothing less than a bright future.

Then their little boy grows up and draws all over the living-room carpet with red permanent marker. And the parents are certain that their happy life has come to an end. Not really. The point isn't that some lives turn out with unhappy *endings,* but that every life starts out with a happy *beginning.*

Few things in life are as awe-inspiring as becoming a mom or dad. But there is one moment that is even more joyful.

Hmmm . . . any guesses what that is?

It's not the day you were finally potty-trained. It's not the day you learned to ride a bike. It won't even be the day you get your driver's license.

There is no way to describe the happiness that happened on the day of our *re-birth,* the day we trusted Jesus Christ as Savior and Lord. (You can read John 3:1-21 for how Jesus describes the rebirth process.)

Just as loving parents eagerly await and welcome a new child, God eagerly awaited our rebirth. The Holy Spirit planted the seed of God's love in our heart. He waited for the day we would believe in Christ. And then an incredible thing happened—something we read about in today's Bible passage. When we trusted Christ, God's Spirit entered our lives to set us free from sin and to help us grow as God's children.

The day we trusted Jesus brought gigantic joy to God and to the people who care about us. Yep, we all have birthdays, and they're a great thing. But our re-birthdays are an even bigger deal. If you have one, celebrate! If you haven't trusted Jesus as your Savior yet, talk to your mom and dad about what that means.

 TALK: If earthly parents are excited when their children are born, how do you think God feels when one of his children accepts his salvation and is reborn?

 PRAY: *God, thank you for the Holy Spirit's work in bringing us to Christ—and helping us grow up as Christians.*

 ACT: Make a plan as a family to celebrate your re-birthdays.

10 Free at Last, I'm Free at Last

Bible Reading: Romans 8:5-9

You are not controlled by your sinful nature. You are controlled by the Spirit. Romans 8:9

Alrika hadn't believed the rumors about people snatched from their huts and abducted to an unknown land until it happened to her. Chained for months in the dungeon-like hull of a ship, the young girl feared she would die in slavery. After she endured years of cruelty and hard labor, the Union army of the northern United States marched into her town. Now an officer in a blue uniform stands before her. "You are no longer controlled by your master," he says. "You are free."

Talk about it: What would it feel like to be a girl or boy in bondage as a slave—and then to be set free?

You didn't come to America chained in the hull of a slave ship, though maybe your ancestors did.

But all of us, the Bible says, have experienced a different kind of slavery. We were born as slaves to sin. All of us are stuck in evil we can't escape on our own. The only way we can get free is to ask for Jesus' help and forgiveness.

It might be hard to believe that we are slaves to sin. But here's one way to be sure: Have you ever noticed that it's easier to do evil than to do good? When your parents find a broken lamp in the living room, it usually seems easier to lie and say you didn't break it than to tell the truth and admit what you did. It's easy to choose wrong because we are slaves to sin.

But the great news in Romans 8 is that Jesus changed all that. When we trusted him, we were set free from slavery to sin. Because of the power of God's Holy Spirit living inside us, we don't have to sin anymore. Yes, we *will* sin from time to time. We *will* still be tempted to do wrong. We *will* sometimes give in because of our own weakness. But we don't *have* to sin. We can *choose* to be controlled by the Holy Spirit—the Spirit of God living inside of us—instead of by sin. We are *free.*

Sin is bigger than a bad habit. We can't break loose by making a New Year's resolution. Sin is a disease we can't cure on our own.

God knew the perfect solution to our problem. We needed a Savior (Jesus) to die for us and a Helper (the Holy Spirit) to live inside us. Thanks to God, we are free from sin. Aren't you grateful?

 TALK: What does it mean to be controlled by the Holy Spirit? What is different about your life because the Holy Spirit is at work inside you?

 PRAY: *Jesus, you died to set us free from sin. We want your freedom in every area of our life.*

 ACT: Learn more about what it meant to American slaves to be set free. Look for books on slavery at your local library.

I'm Your Daddy Now

Bible Reading: Romans 8:14-17
All who are led by the Spirit of God are children of God. Romans 8:14

Amanda had never met her father. He had left her mother before she was born.

Life with Mom was more than okay, and for a long time Amanda didn't worry about not having a dad. Then Scott came along. He started dating Amanda's mom when Amanda was twelve. Now she was fourteen, and the couple had been married for two months. Amanda loved Scott like the dad she never had. She had always thought it was too big of a wish to ask God for a father, but God had given her one. And Scott was incredible. He was kind, fun, and very close to God.

Still, a dark fear lurked in a back corner of Amanda's brain. She worried that one day Scott would leave her too. Why wouldn't he? Her real dad had left. Nothing forced Scott to take any fatherly responsibility for Amanda. He could leave whenever he wanted, and she couldn't do anything to stop him.

Then one day Scott and Amanda's mom took Amanda out for dinner and told her something they had decided even before they were married. They said it was important to them that Scott legally adopt Amanda. The thought both terrified and excited her. If he went through with it, he would be her legal father. She would finally have a real dad. But what if he backed out?

Day after day Amanda awaited news that her adoption was final and official. One day she came home from school and spotted Scott's car in the driveway, earlier than usual. When Amanda walked in the door, Scott and Mom were waiting. Scott stood. "The adoption papers came through today, Amanda," he said. Tears filled his eyes. "I'm your daddy now."

Amanda dove toward him with a gigantic hug. "Thank you for choosing me," she said through her own tears. "Thank you, thank you . . . Daddy."

Scott took a one-of-a-kind step to demonstrate his love for Amanda and his desire to be her father, making their relationship official through adoption. When God makes us his children, he does the same thing. He adopts us. He makes our family relationship with him permanent. We are forever his sons and daughters.

If you've accepted Jesus as your Savior, you're part of God's family. You don't ever have to worry when it comes to your relationship with your heavenly Father. He will never leave you. The adoption papers have come through. He's your daddy.

 TALK: How do you feel knowing that God has permanently adopted you into his family?

 PRAY: *Thank you for choosing us to be your children, God. Thank you for adopting us. Thank you that you will never leave us.*

 ACT: Share with a friend how cool it is to be adopted into God's family.

12 Just a Few More Hours

Bible Reading: Romans 8:22-24
Even we Christians, although we have the Holy Spirit within us as a foretaste of future glory, also groan to be released from pain and suffering. Romans 8:23

For months the mission team from Sara's church had been preparing for this day. In just a few more hours the bus would arrive at a town in northern Mexico. There the team would spend two weeks repairing a church building and sharing the love of Christ with as many people as possible. Sara couldn't wait.

More than six months ago Sara had applied to take part in the mission trip. She had been through grueling fund-raising activities, wacky ways to make money fast. She had attended weekly meetings to prepare and pray. She had spent a half hour at her computer each night learning Spanish. And now she had endured a twenty-hour ride on a school bus. But she knew there was something ahead worth the work and the wait. Soon all her hard work would pay off.

Have you ever poured your heart into something—and then waited for all your effort to pay off? It's like

- practicing the same football play over and over—then finally getting to use it in a game
- rehearsing a solo until you can sing a song backwards and forwards—then finally getting to perform
- studying until your head hurts—then finally getting to show off what you know on a test
- baking all day—then finally getting to eat the cake

Christ calls us to put our whole heart into following him. That can be difficult. But there's something we look forward to that's bigger and better than our dreams! God has promised that there will be a spectacular day when Christ returns to earth and takes us to be with him for eternity. There will be no more pain or suffering. We will live in heaven as God's children. The whole world is waiting for God's plan to come together.

Like a mom waiting to give birth, we can't wait to take hold of the reward of our work. Obeying God can be hard. Following Jesus sometimes makes us tired. But God gives us the Holy Spirit to help us. And the great gifts that will be ours as God's children are worth the wait!

 TALK: Do you look forward to Christ's return? What is the most exciting thing about it?

 PRAY: *God, it's hard to wait for you to fix the things that hurt in our life. Thank you that you send your Holy Spirit to make us strong as we wait.*

 ACT: Encourage each other today to stay strong even when living as a Christian feels hard.

13 God, Please Help My Friend

Bible Reading: Romans 8:26-30
The Spirit pleads for us believers in harmony with God's own will.
Romans 8:27

"Dear God, please help my friend Rochelle."

Emmy wouldn't give up. No matter how sick Rochelle got, no matter how down she got or how many people gave up believing that God could ever heal her, Emmy simply wouldn't stop praying for her friend. Ever since doctors had told Rochelle that she had a rare form of cancer, Emmy had felt a nudge to pray for Rochelle. And as Rochelle's body grew more and more sick, Emmy prayed all the more. "Only God can heal my friend," Emmy told her own parents, "so we've got to pray." And she did pray. No one outside Rochelle's own family knew her problems and needs better than Emmy, and Emmy took her responsibility to pray very seriously.

Isn't it great to have Christian friends who pray for you? Do you sense the special privilege and responsibility you have of praying for your friends? Things happen when you and your friends pray for one another. God responds and acts when you share your friends' needs with him.

You might wonder if you have any friends who talk to God about you. You might worry that you're the kind of kid only a mom or dad would pray for. Well, the Bible guarantees you have a friend praying for you—a friend whose prayers are more powerful than the prayers of any human being. Do you realize that the Holy Spirit prays for you to God the Father?

Whoa. That's huge. The Holy Spirit lives inside Christians and is constantly talking to God the Father about our needs, our hurts, and our struggles. And his prayers are even more effective than anything we can dream up, because no one knows us like the Spirit of God living inside of us—not our friends, not our Sunday school teachers, not even our brothers and sisters or our moms and dads. Because the Spirit peers into our life and spots our needs, he can pray for us better than anyone.

All of us go through times when we feel so hurt or confused or angry that we don't even know how to pray. We bow our heads and sigh, cry, or groan, but we just can't get any words out.

That's when the Holy Spirit takes our sighs and groans and hurts and concerns straight to the Father's throne. He prays, "God, please help my friend." And we can remember this: He takes prayer for us very seriously.

 TALK: What does it mean to you when a friend prays for you? How about when the Holy Spirit joins in with prayers that never stop?

 PRAY: *Father, thank you that even when we can't find the right words to pray, your Holy Spirit is praying for us—and he knows exactly what to say.*

 ACT: Take time today to pray for a friend.

14 The Biggest No-Brainer of Them All

Bible Reading: Romans 8:38-39

Nothing in all creation will ever be able to separate us from the love of God that is revealed in Christ Jesus our Lord. Romans 8:39

Let's take a little quiz. For each statement below, check either true or false.

- ☐ True ☐ False   Fire is hot.
- ☐ True ☐ False   Water is wet.
- ☐ True ☐ False   A rock is hard.
- ☐ True ☐ False   The sky is up.
- ☐ True ☐ False   Pickles are disgusting.

All right, how did you do? If you checked true for each statement, you're pretty smart. Now, the people in your family may have different opinions about pickles—though that doesn't change the fact that they truly are disgusting! But that was a pretty easy quiz, right?

What made it so easy? The statements are all about basic facts and knowledge. Every statement—okay, except maybe the last one—is a no-brainer. Everyone knows these statements are true simply because they are. They really aren't that complicated.

Here are a few more statements. Check true or false for each.

- ☐ True ☐ False   God loves you.
- ☐ True ☐ False   God will always love you.
- ☐ True ☐ False   Absolutely nothing can separate you from God's love.

Do you think those statements are still no-brainers? You should, because they are. In fact, they are more certain than the first set. Even when being a Christian is difficult, God's constant love for you is totally real.

Now let's try one more quiz. Check true or false for each statement.

- ☐ True ☐ False   God's love runs out when you sin.
- ☐ True ☐ False   God stops loving you if you eat too many pickles.
- ☐ True ☐ False   The devil can cut you off from God's love.
- ☐ True ☐ False   God doesn't love you when you think bad thoughts.
- ☐ True ☐ False   You lose God's love if you fall asleep in church.

No-brainers to be sure, because they are all totally false. You might need to seek God's forgiveness for some of these acts, but you will never lose out on his love for you.

 TALK: What do you think about the fact that God's love for you never quits?

 PRAY: *God, thank you that your love for us is total and unending.*

 ACT: Explain to a friend today what it means that God's love for us never ends.

15 Mobilizing a Rescue Operation

Bible Reading: Matthew 9:35-38

The harvest is so great, but the workers are so few. Matthew 9:37

Here's a huge question to talk about: Do you know how you can spot the difference between Christians and non-Christians?

No, that isn't the lead-in to a bad joke. The difference between Christians and non-Christians is really serious. But it isn't totally obvious.

Big devil horns, for example, don't stick out of the heads of non-Christians. And huge angel halos don't circle the heads of Christians.

Lined up on a football bench, believers and unbelievers all wear the same uniform. Sitting at desks at school, they all just look like kids trying to get a good grade.

You probably know unbelievers who are just as nice, just as smart, and just as friendly as believers. But there's still a difference. It's huge. And it matters for all of eternity:

- Unbelievers are cut off from God and eternal life. That means they can't stop sinning. They're slaves to sin (see Ephesians 2:1-3).
- Believers have a friendship with God and the guarantee of eternal life. They have been rescued from their sin and now are part of God's family (see Colossians 1:13).

Maybe you've heard "Non-Christians need to know Jesus" so many times that the hugeness of that fact bounces off you. It's really easy not to care when non-Christians can be so much like you.

But God hasn't forgotten the difference. He aches for the millions and millions of people—possibly thousands just in your school and hometown—who don't know him. He's incredibly concerned for each one—*so* concerned, in fact, that he took the ultimate step for every student, mom, dad, and other person. He became a human being and gave his life for them.

This is serious business to God. He doesn't want anyone to perish—to go to hell because he or she hasn't asked his forgiveness (2 Peter 3:9). He died to rescue the lost, and his rescue operation didn't stop at the Cross.

God gives us the privilege of being a rescuer along with him. There are countless people in our world just waiting for someone to tell them about God's unconditional love. So we want to tell as many people as we can that Jesus has come to set them free!

 TALK: How can you work as a family to reach out the way God reaches out to you—rescuing the lost people around you?

 PRAY: *Father, give us compassion for our non-Christian friends. Help us never to forget that they are lost without you.*

 ACT: Decide as a family how you can show God's love to the lost all around you.

16 Get the Word Out

Bible Reading: Matthew 28:18-20
Go and make disciples of all the nations. Matthew 28:19, NIV

God has a huge rescue mission going on. Do you know what our part in that rescue mission is called? *Evangelism.* That's the job of communicating the Good News of Jesus Christ to people who don't know him.

Do you know what a person who spreads that incredible news is called? An *evangelist.* Here's one more astounding fact: *You* are an evangelist.

How did you get to be an evangelist? Check any qualifications that you think earned you the job of telling others about Jesus:

- ☐ You've formed a family singing group and you're good enough to belt out Christian songs in front of stadiums of people.
- ☐ You mention Jesus at least a dozen times in every conversation.
- ☐ You pray really loudly in restaurants.
- ☐ You've signed up to do your own Christian talk show on TV.
- ☐ You grab strangers on the street and start spiritual conversations.
- ☐ You slick back your hair in an evangelist hairdo.

Do you really think you need to do any of those things to be ready to share Christ with others? Nope. Because it's not a matter of deciding if you have what it takes to be an evangelist. The fact is, you already *are* an evangelist. God has appointed you his ambassador, his official messenger to take the Good News of salvation to others (see 2 Corinthians 5:18-20).

Don't freeze with fear at that thought. The Bible explains that at the heart of real evangelism is one activity: *telling the facts of Jesus* (1 Corinthians 15:1-4). And that's an activity you can do.

The Good News centers on what God has done to free our non-Christian friends from sin and introduce them to his love. Telling the facts of Jesus means explaining to people how his death and resurrection have provided forgiveness for their sins and eternal life with God—and how they must trust Christ to receive what God has done for them. Evangelism is when you spill the facts and urge them to respond.

Because you've trusted Christ, you know the meaning of the Good News. Because someone told you about Christ, you have the privilege of telling others about him. And because God has done a great thing in your life, you can be a part of his great work in someone else's life.

 TALK: What non-Christian friends or family members do you think God wants to reach through you?

 PRAY: Pray for those people by name, asking God to show you how to share Christ with them.

 ACT: Try to start a spiritual conversation with one of those people today.

17 Call Yourself a Rescue Ranger

Bible Reading: 1 Corinthians 9:22-23

I try to find common ground with everyone so that I might bring them to Christ. 1 Corinthians 9:22

Kallie looked puzzled. "Isn't Jesus giving us way too big of a job when he tells us to reach the world? I mean, there are a bazillion kids just at my school. And how can I ever talk to the whole world? Where am I supposed to start?"

Great questions. And here are some questions for you to talk about:

- Think about your best friends. Are any of them non-Christians?
- Think about the people you spend big chunks of your day with at school or work. Are any of them non-Christians?
- Think about the people you live near. Are any of them non-Christians?

If you nodded yes to any of those questions, you can join God in his mission to rescue non-Christians. The people near to you are your place to start!

There are three tips to remember as you share Christ with these people:

1. *Ask God to lead you.* Think about it: God has already placed people all around you who don't know him. When Brent prayed to be able to see nearby non-Christians the way God saw them, he found he cared more about them—and he noticed more chances to share his faith.
2. *Be a friend to non-Christians.* The Bible commands you to stick together with Christian friends because you need them to challenge and encourage you (Hebrews 10:25). But also having some non-Christian friends puts you in a far better position to lead others to Christ.

   Matt used his interest in scouting to build relationships with non-Christians. He couldn't join in everything his scouting buddies did, but like Jesus he worked to be a friend of "sinners" (see Matthew 11:19) without taking part in anything he knew would disappoint God.
3. *Take the first step.* Don't wait for your non-Christian friends to ask you about spiritual subjects—*you* ask *them.* When Sherri told her non-Christian friends about God's love and forgiveness, she saw God work through her words and her example to bring a couple of her friends to Christ. Whether or not other kids agree with you, show them that you're a friend.

   When Jesus asked you to tell others about him, he wasn't giving you an impossible task. You can share him with the people right around you!

 TALK: With which people right around you can you share the love of God by lovingly talking with and serving them?

 PRAY: *God, help us to share your love and forgiveness with people close to us.*

 ACT: Make a plan to reach out to people closest to you.

18 The Liberator

Bible Reading: Matthew 4:18-22
Come, be my disciples, and I will show you how to fish for people!
Matthew 4:19

You probably don't picture yourself as a superhero, ready to do battle with the forces of evil. After all, you're not faster than a speeding bullet, stronger than a locomotive, or able to leap tall buildings in a single bound. Most of all, you probably don't dress in superhero long undies—you probably don't even own a pair!

However, here's an awesome fact: To all the kids in your school and community who don't know Christ, you can be a *spiritual* superhero. When you help others trust in Jesus, you rescue them from the power of sin and Satan.

Most Christians like the idea of following Jesus. We might need a little persuading, however, that telling others about Christ is a great idea. Let me give you three big reasons why this superhero mission is a job you'll want to accept.

Reason Number 1: The non-Christians around you need to be set free. No matter how happy people might look, if they haven't trusted Christ they're separated from God. Jesus felt compassion for the people around him who weren't saved. He said they were "harassed and helpless, like sheep without a shepherd" (Matthew 9:36, NIV).

Reason Number 2: God's rescue plan won't work without you. Jesus told his first disciples to tell others about him—from home (for them, that was Jerusalem) all the way to the ends of the earth (Acts 1:8). And nowadays someone still needs to tell the Good News to people nearby—and not so nearby. God wants you to be that someone! Like the apostle Paul said, "How can [people] call on [God] to save them unless they believe in him? And how can they believe in him if they have never heard about him? And how can they hear about him unless someone tells them?" (Romans 10:14).

Reason Number 3: You want to rescue others because God rescued you. Paul said Christ's love made him want to join God's rescue mission (see 2 Corinthians 5:14-15). Think about this: What would your life be like today without Christ? If you are glad that God lovingly invited you to be his child, then join him in inviting others to trust him. The more deeply you understand God's love for you, the more you will want to help others find him.

Your mission is no secret. God's Word is clear: You're a spiritual superhero. And there's nothing better you can be!

 TALK: What great reasons do you have to tell others about Jesus?

 PRAY: *God, help us to be bold in telling others about you. Help us to remember all the great reasons we have to be spiritual superheroes.*

 ACT: Think about one person who needs to hear about God's love, and make plans today to tell that person about it.

19 Breaking Down the Barriers

Bible Reading: 2 Timothy 1:3-8

God has not given us a spirit of fear and timidity, but of power, love, and self-discipline. 2 Timothy 1:7

"I just know it," Tyler erupted. "If I say anything about Jesus to my friends, I'm going to be an instant reject. Last year a friend of mine from church started witnessing to the guys on the soccer team. By the time they got done making fun of him, I practically had to peel his lips off the floor."

Okay. Let's be honest. Talk about what would happen if you became part of God's rescue team. How would the people in your world react if you talked to them about Jesus? Let's think about the worst things that could happen.

- People could stop being your friend.
- People could talk behind your back.
- People could reject you for taking a stand.
- People could uninvite you to their birthday parties.
- People could laugh at you for believing in God.

I'm not saying that none of those things will ever happen if we tell people about Jesus. But did you know there's a good chance that great things will happen? Let's think about some of those:

- People could become your bigger and better friends.
- People could say thanks to God for you.
- People could respect you for taking a stand.
- People could invite you to their re-birthday parties in heaven forever.
- People could come to know Jesus.

No one likes to be made fun of. But Christians come up with a million excuses not to get personally involved in God's rescue mission. We might worry that we're not good enough, or that we don't know what to say. But our biggest fear is usually of how non-Christians will react. In other words, what people think is more important than the astounding message of freedom we have to share with them. God doesn't want us to be afraid.

Trust God to give you his confidence. Then take a step of faith and talk with others. As you do, you'll discover God's courage in your life—just when you need it. You'll probably even get to keep your lips!

 TALK: How can you boldly share Christ's love—just like Christ boldly stepped into your world to love you?

 PRAY: *God, help us to overcome the fears that keep us from talking to others about you.*

 ACT: Pick a friend you're terrified to talk with about Jesus—and talk! Ask your family to pray for you before you go, and then report back to them how it went.

20 Tough Guy

Bible Reading: John 2:13-16

Don't turn my Father's house into a marketplace! John 2:16

Barely awake, you struggle to your feet in church. You turn to page 473 in your hymnal, open your mouth, and croak these lines: "Gentle Jesus, meek and mild, look upon that little child."

Wait a second! Exactly what kind of picture of Jesus do you get from those lyrics? Do you know what it means to be "meek" or "mild"? You might hear those words and worry that Jesus was so sweet he wouldn't swat a fly. Or that back in his hometown of Nazareth your Lord was the neighborhood wimp.

Well, Jesus was hardly weak. Yet, these facts are true about him:

- He was a poet who spoke beautifully of the birds and the lilies.
- He was a storyteller who spun yarns about women baking bread and fishermen hauling in a catch.
- He was a gentle friend who bounced little children on his lap.
- He was a silent prisoner who stood in humility before kings, suffering bitter insults without uttering a word.

But Jesus was still tough. Listen to these facts:

- He was a carpenter whose hands were rough from the work he did in Joseph's workshop.
- He was an outdoorsman capable of living for long periods in the wilderness alone.
- He was a leader who courageously spoke against the dishonest authorities of his day, calling them "blind fools" and "snakes."
- He chose an excruciatingly painful death on the cross to bring us salvation.

Jesus was gentle. He was meek. But his gentleness and meekness didn't indicate the absence of strength. They showed *strength under control!*

According to the Bible, Jesus stormed into the temple in Jerusalem—maybe more than once—to single-handedly drive out a mob of crooked merchants. *No one* dared to protest or fight back against the red-hot blaze of his anger.

Jesus is gentle. But he is also strong and mighty. His love guards and protects us. And if he storms into our life to challenge our wrong thoughts, words, and behaviors, he does it because he's *for* us, not *against* us, and wants the best for us!

 TALK: Do you think Jesus is a wimp? How do you know that your God is incredibly strong?

 PRAY: *Jesus, thanks for your gentleness. Thanks too for your strength.*

 ACT: Jesus wants you to act boldly against your own sin. Is there anything he wants you to boot out of your life?

21 The Nitty-Gritty Savior

Bible Reading: Mark 6:1-6

A prophet is honored everywhere except in his own hometown and among his relatives and his own family. Mark 6:4

"Listen," Dan said as he shook a wrench in Aaron's face, "you can't tell me that some guy who lived two thousand years ago and spent his time walking around in a white robe telling stories actually matters to me today." He swept his arm around him, waving toward the garage and the cars up on blocks.

"I don't have time to hear about Jesus," he continued. "I mean, Jesus is okay for women and kids who like the stories and might even get something out of them. But for me? I don't think so. Jesus has nothing to do with a guy who has a garage full of wrecked cars to fix."

Dan echoes the way some people think about Jesus—especially guys who think they're tough. They think Jesus is like a plastic statue on a car dashboard—smiling, dressed in a robe, a shiny halo hanging above his bobbing head. "Jesus doesn't work for people like me," they say. They think Jesus has as much to do with real life as that statue on a dashboard.

That's a myth.

Here's the real Jesus: He was a working guy. We can picture him in a shop that opens onto a dusty street in Israel, with a sign over the door that reads, "Jesus, son of Joseph, Carpenter." Imagine him bending over a cedar plank clamped to the bench in front of him. He wears a leather apron. Sweat drips off his face. He wields a knife, then a mallet. The shop is filled with the rough-sawed fragrance of cedar and cypress from the shavings that cover the floor.

Jesus of Nazareth worked as a carpenter for eighteen years or more, growing muscles in his arms and tough skin on his hands. He managed the stresses of business. He knew the pressures of family. When Joseph died, Jesus' younger brothers and sisters became his responsibility. He undoubtedly knew how hard it was to buy clothes for kids and try to barter a fair price out of the merchants at the marketplace.

The world Jesus lived in—like ours—was smelly and dirty. And when his life ended, he suffered a filthy, sweaty, bloody death. But because Jesus lived a nitty-gritty life, he understands the nitty-gritty of our life. He knows about our struggles with life, because he had to deal with them too.

Jesus is our real-world Savior. He was no plastic saint.

 TALK: What in your world might some people think Jesus couldn't understand? How do you know he can relate to you firsthand?

 PRAY: *Jesus, thank you for being tough enough to understand the hardest things in our life.*

 ACT: Explain to a friend how you can be sure Jesus wasn't a wimp.

22 What Color Is Your Jesus?

Bible Reading: Galatians 3:26-28

There is no longer Jew or Gentile, slave or free, male or female. For you are all Christians—you are one in Christ Jesus. Galatians 3:28

Here's a question to talk about: What did Jesus look like?

People have painted pictures of Jesus looking like just about everything but a space alien—and they've probably done that too. But most Americans see Jesus as a youngish Harrison Ford—brown hair, brown eyes, with movie-star looks. And white. Tan, most likely, but definitely white. The kind of white that you might bump into in Seattle or Minneapolis in the dead of winter.

The truth is, Jesus' skin color was probably far darker than the average American's. He was a Jew. His Middle Eastern heritage was starkly obvious when he stood before Pilate, a pale Roman.

So why does this matter? Because some people use Jesus or the Christian faith to justify their hatred of other people—especially non-Christian people, like Muslims from the Middle East.

But Jesus is the best reason why *racial prejudice* (hating groups of people because of their race or skin color) is wrong. Even though Jesus was born as a human being at a specific place and time and had specific racial characteristics, his race and color didn't limit his associations with people. How do we know?

- When Jesus was on earth, the Jews hated the Samaritans and looked down on them because they didn't worship God the same way the Jews did. Jesus was a Jew, yet he spoke freely and respectfully to the Samaritan woman (see John 4:4-30).
- Jewish custom said that Jesus shouldn't enter the home of a non-Jew. Yet when a Roman army officer pleaded for Jesus to heal his servant who lay sick at home, Jesus healed him (see Luke 7:3-10).

Jesus lived in a time and place that decided how to treat people based on their race (Jew or Gentile), social class (slave or free, rich or poor), and gender (male or female). But Paul pointed out in Galatians 3:26-28 that Jesus turned those prejudices upside down. As Jesus' followers, we have the chance to be like him—not because we share his skin color or race, but by accepting and loving people no matter their gender, class, or race.

 TALK: In what ways does Jesus look or act just like you? How is he different?

 PRAY: *Jesus, help us to be like you. Help us to overcome our prejudices against people who aren't the same race, against men or women, or against people who have more or less money than we have.*

 ACT: Eat lunch this week with someone outside your race or social class.

23 Red in the Face

Bible Reading: Colossians 4:6
Let your conversation be gracious and effective. Colossians 4:6

Anna invited over a houseful of girls to her tenth birthday party. Most of the girls were from Anna's class at school, but topping her list was her cousin Felicia. Because Felicia lived across town, Anna knew the situation might be weird for Felicia. But she expected Felicia would quickly get to know all her other friends.

Not so. While everyone else at the party laughed and talked all afternoon about everything from sports to school, Felicia sat like a lump. As everyone gabbed, she curled up in her chair, saying nothing. No one knew if she was bored or scared. She finally bolted out of the house to the swing-set in Anna's backyard. She hoisted herself up to the monkey bar, flung herself upside down—and hung by her knees until she was red in the face.

Talk about it: Have you ever been in a situation that felt so uncomfortable that you just wished you could hide?

New situations don't have to feel awkward. But you won't make friends grunting your way through parties, school, and other get-togethers. Friendships grow only when we get beyond silence. There is, however, an easy trick we can use to make friends: *Ask questions.*

Here are some really good questions you can use to get to know people quickly. Look at the list below and pick out four or five you really like. Memorize them. Practice saying them in your own words.

- How did you become a Christian?
- What's your biggest goal?
- What do you do after school (or work)?
- What's the coolest place you've ever visited?
- How can I help you?
- What do you want to be or accomplish someday?
- What class in school do you like the best? How come?
- What are your hobbies?
- How can I pray for you?

Can you see it? If you can ask good questions, you won't even need to do much talking. You'll just need to practice something that can be even harder than talking: listening!

 TALK: God showed an interest in your world by coming to live on earth. How well do you show an interest in others by asking questions?

 PRAY: *Father, help us pay attention to others—not just to make friends, but to make a difference in their lives.*

 ACT: Go out of your way today to practice talking with someone you don't know well.

24 Becoming Best Buddies

Bible Reading: 1 Samuel 18:1-4
> *After David had finished talking with Saul, he met Jonathan, the king's son. There was an immediate bond of love between them, and they became the best of friends. 1 Samuel 18:1*

If you've ever been hurt by a good friend, you might still be wondering, *Is there really such a thing as best friends?* Your best way to find out is to take a look at two totally committed friends in the Bible, David and Jonathan. The story of their friendship is found in 1 Samuel 18–20. If you read the whole three chapters, you'll discover that best friends do exist—and that a best friend is someone who

- speaks positively about you when others don't (see 19:4)
- listens to your problems (see 20:1-2)
- does things for you, regardless of the inconvenience (see 20:4)
- loves you even when you are unlovable (see 20:17)
- protects you from the bad guys (see 20:19)
- hurts when you hurt (see 20:34)
- understands your deepest feelings (see 20:41)
- is committed to you (see 20:42)

We can only be that kind of friend to a few people—and it takes time and work to develop and keep those friends. Making friends isn't a mystery. There are some skills that help us form friendships that last a lifetime:

- *Like yourself.* If you don't like yourself, it's tough to like others.
- *Accept people.* Each of us is unique. Sometimes we're obnoxious and offensive. You have to look past people's faults.
- *Be positive.* You'll be a breath of fresh air to people if you can avoid criticizing them. Learn to build people up.
- *Keep secrets.* Have you ever said, "So-and-so told me not to tell anyone, but I know she won't mind if I tell you." Stop it! Immediately!
- *Be patient.* It takes time to build close and committed friendships.
- *Be a good listener.* Be interested in the other person. Get more information. And don't feel like you always have to jump in with your own stories.

Can you see one or two skills you want to practice? Get at it—because God can't wait to teach you the kind of friendship shared by David and Jonathan!

 TALK: How are you doing at being a David-and-Jonathan kind of friend?

 PRAY: *God, help us grow in our skills at being great friends.*

 ACT: Pick one friendship skill and practice it today.

25 The Friendship Smashers

Bible Reading: Ephesians 4:31–32
> *Be kind to each other, tenderhearted, forgiving one another, just as God through Christ has forgiven you. Ephesians 4:32*

Imagine a plateful of peas. Then think of what you do when you don't feel like eating those little vegetable yum-yums: You push them around with your knife. You smash them with your spoon. You nudge them off the table. And then you scoot them under your plate—or feed them to the dog.

Just as peas that have been speared, smooshed, or pushed out of sight are still peas, friendships that are badly treated are still friendships. But they aren't very appetizing. To make and keep friends, avoid these friendship smashers:

- *Jealousy.* Why envy a friend's achievements? Celebrate them instead!
- *Gossip.* It's the teeter-totter principle: You try to lift yourself up by saying mean things about other people. Sooner or later *you* end up splattered on the ground.
- *Disloyalty.* You say you're her friend—but you turn on her when someone more popular comes around. Real friendship stays true at all times.
- *Competition.* Friendship isn't a race. You aren't running as competitors. Friends cheer each other on.
- *Negativity.* Misery loves company—up to a point. After that, moaning leaves you minus your friends.
- *Comparison.* If you compare yourself to your friends and try to make yourself look better, you're asking for friendship hassles.
- *Selfishness.* Make time to serve your friends' interests, not just your own. If you turn everything inward, you turn others away.

There's one more huge friendship smasher: *insecurity.* It often sounds like this: "What if he doesn't like me?" "What if I say the wrong thing?" "What if she laughs at me?" "What if I do something dumb?"

Those negative thoughts keep you from going any deeper into a friendship. They make you afraid to do anything—or *not* do anything.

But you can choose to meet your fears head-on. Every time you catch your brain stuck on a *negative fear question,* change it to a *positive faith statement:* "I know he will like me." "I am confident I will say the right thing." "She will accept me." "I will do something intelligent."

When you move out in faith instead of fear, you will be a quality friend.

 TALK: How do you get along with the people around you? Do you have any bad habits that get in the way of good friendships? What would you like to change?

 PRAY: *God, we want to do friendship your way. Help us!*

 ACT: Pick a friendship you want to remake. Aim to get rid of one friendship smasher this week. And choose another to work on next week!

26 Maybe You're an Alien

Bible Reading: Luke 6:37-38

Stop criticizing others, or it will all come back on you. If you forgive others, you will be forgiven. Luke 6:37

Angelica and Renee had been best friends since kindergarten. When their science teacher made them partners on a project, they couldn't wait to get started. But what began as a gleeful partnership nearly stomped out their friendship. Angelica didn't like when Renee told her what to do. And since neither girl did well meeting deadlines, they wound up saying things like "You're lazy!" and "Well, you're stupid!"

Whenever you know a person really well, conflict is inevitable. You've probably had some spats with your friends. Maybe you're in the middle of one right now. In fact, if you've never experienced conflict with your best friend, one of the following is true:

(a) Your best friend exists only in your imagination.

(b) Your best friend is a pen pal and you don't speak the same language.

(c) One or both of you are aliens.

(d) You and your friend aren't as close as you think.

When you have a conflict with a friend, you have a choice: resolve the conflict or dissolve the relationship.

Talk about this: What are some ways to work through friendship difficulties?

God has a huge piece of wisdom for solving friendship problems: Realize that what goes around comes around. If you are angry at your friend, your friend will get angry at you in return. If you treat your friend kindly, chances are you will be treated kindly in return.

That means your goal is to treat each other the way you want to be treated (Luke 6:31). And if you need some ideas for doing that, here are three:

- *Pick the right words.* Think before you speak. Consider your words before you say them and ask if they will help to work out the problem.
- *Study your friend's point of view.* See the conflict through your friend's eyes. Think of how he or she feels instead of how you feel.
- *Don't give up.* Friendships aren't meant to be thrown away. So keep talking. Don't give up until you have worked things out.

And here's one more: *Forgive.* When you forgive like God has forgiven you, you can overcome the biggest friendship conflicts.

 TALK: What conflict are you in right now that you need to deal with?

 PRAY: *God, give us tender hearts and a love for our friends that doesn't give up.*

 ACT: Decide on one step you can take to rebuild or strengthen a friendship today.

27 A World of Friendship Opportunities

Bible Reading: Mark 2:13-17
Healthy people don't need a doctor—sick people do. I have come to call sinners, not those who think they are already good enough. Mark 2:17

Ten-year-old Shavonne became a Christian three weeks ago. Now she's slamming head-on into a tough choice in living out her new life. Last night her new friends at church pulled her aside and told her to dump all her non-Christian friends. "They'll pull you into bad stuff," they insisted. "It's wrong for you to be friends with people who don't know Jesus. Christian friends are all you need."

Talk about it: Should Christians get rid of their non-Christian friends? Why or why not?

Friends pile on pressure—often to do wrong. So people who remind us we need close Christian friends are doing us a favor. Christian friends are so important that the Bible tells us to "try hard to live right and to have faith, love, and peace, together with those who trust in the Lord from pure hearts" (2 Timothy 2:22, NCV). We can count on Christian friends for strength and encouragement while we grow.

But we can't cut off non-Christian friends. Jesus, in fact, spent so much time with a tough crowd that some people called him "a friend of the worst sort of sinners!" (Matthew 11:19). Here are two big reasons to keep up your connections:

Reason 1: You have the greatest chance of winning your non-Christian friends to Christ. You know them best. You love them most. Who could do a better job telling them about Jesus?

Reason 2: If you ditch your non-Christian friends, they could blame Jesus for losing you as a friend. Whenever anyone tells them about becoming a Christian, their response could be "Sure, and trash all my friends? No way!"

But here's where Shavonne's church friends are partly right. If your nonbelieving friends continue to pile on pressure to do wrong, you need to distance yourself enough to play it safe.

Heads up: If you spend time with non-Christians you might catch it on both ends. Non-Christians mock you because you won't join in some of their activities, and Christian friends criticize you because they think you're diving into sin.

But don't let that stop you from having non-Christian friends. Don't get mad at your Christian friends either. Just do what Jesus did. Love everyone!

 TALK: How well does it work for you to have both Christian and non-Christian friends?

 PRAY: *God, help us to love like Jesus did—being friends to both believers and nonbelievers.*

 ACT: Take an inventory of your non-Christian friendships. Are you leading your friends closer to Jesus—or are they pulling you away?

28 Friends in a World of Hurt

Bible Reading: 2 Corinthians 1:3-7

When others are troubled, we will be able to give them the same comfort God has given us. 2 Corinthians 1:4

Here's some tough news: Scan any crowd of kids and you'll see pain all around you. You're almost guaranteed to see people struggling with broken friendships, a serious illness, the death of a friend or family member, or a strained situation at home. You can be sure they face the losses and disappointments of everyday life—earning a bad grade, losing a library book, or being cut from a team.

So what can you do to ease the pain and hurt?

You're on the right track if any of these ideas flutter through your brain: *Be available. Speak encouraging words. Pray for your friend. Do acts of kindness. Point your friend to helpful Scripture passages.*

All of those responses are great. Yet God has one more way to use you to ease the grief or trouble of a hurting friend. Maybe you can understand it best through this illustration:

Suppose you love to skateboard. Yet one day you prove the most basic law of science: What goes up must come down. And even though you soar into the air when you hit the jump and get three whole seconds of hang time, you rudely slam to the ground.

Take a vote: When your best friend rushes to your side to cheer you up, which of the following responses would make you feel better?

(a) Your friend zonks and goes to sleep while you're talking.
(b) Your friend tells you how dumb you were—and how dumb skateboarding is.
(c) Your friend gets steaming mad and threatens to sue the guy who sold you the skateboard.
(d) Your friend listens carefully, then says something like, "I'm sorry this happened to you. I feel bad that you are hurting. I'm here for you, dude."

If you went for that last option, you have a good idea how God wants to involve you in bringing comfort to a hurting friend. Romans 12:15 encourages you to share the sorrow of those who feel sad.

When you identify with the pain and hurt of a friend—speaking kind words and showering your friend with care—God miraculously reduces your friend's pain. And that's a Christlike thing to do.

 TALK: Who around you is hurting? What can you do about it?

 PRAY: *God, give us opportunities to heal the sadness of others by sharing their pain.*

 ACT: Scan that crowd of hurting people around you. Plan to help someone today by offering comfort.

29 A People-Centered Focus

Bible Reading: Mark 2:13-17

I have come to call sinners, not those who think they are already good enough. Mark 2:17

One Sunday morning a guy and girl in their midteens wander into a church and sit down. They're not exactly wearing what most church folk would call their Sunday best. From the top of their spiked hair to the bottom of their clunky army boots they're dressed in chains and black leather.

After the service the pastor greets the couple. Despite their scary dress, their faces glow. The pastor finds out they are new Christians, fresh out of harsh lives of drug abuse. He welcomes them to the congregation and fills them in on places they can plug in to nurture their new life in Christ. He grabs them by the hand and introduces them to the youth director, who heads out to the parking lot to drool over the guy's motorcycle.

The next day the pastor gets several loud phone calls. "Who were those people?" "I sure hope you didn't tell them about youth group." "I don't want them hanging around our church."

Huh? Who would have thought you'd get into trouble if you trusted Christ, quit doing drugs, but forgot to buy a new wardrobe before you went to church?

Those church folk missed the opportunity of the moment—to give a loving welcome to two young friends desperately needing a home in the body of Christ. They made appearances more important than people.

To be a Christian always means to put people first. No one has ever been more people-centered than Jesus. He taught, healed, blessed, lived, bled, and died for people. He pointed out how religious people had turned the Old Testament into cold, impersonal rules instead of directions for loving God and loving people.

Slamming the church doors on strangers isn't the only way Christians forget to put people first. If we have only Christian friends, attend only Christian events, and buy only from Christian-owned stores, we're totally missing the chance to be people-centered like Jesus.

"We don't party with sinful scum," the critics of Jesus seemed to say, "because we don't want their sin rubbing off on us." But look again at your Lord. He saw things from a people-centered perspective. Why did he spend time with sinners? So his love could rub off on them.

 TALK: Are you ever afraid to hang out with non-Christians? Why or why not?

 PRAY: *God, remake our attitude. Help us love the people you died for—whatever they look like.*

 ACT: What do you want to do today to love the way Jesus did?

30 Busted for Taking a Day Off

Bible Reading: Mark 2:23-28

The Sabbath was made to benefit people, and not people to benefit the Sabbath. Mark 2:27

Peter, Andrew, John, and the other disciples were still gnawing on the raw grain they had picked when they saw the red lights and heard the sirens. It was the Sabbath police. The Pharisees were on those disciples like a highway patrol officer after a speeding sports car. "You picked grain on the Sabbath, and that breaks a big-time religious rule," they might have said, flashing their badges of religious knowledge. "You're in deep trouble now. You have the right to remain silent. Should you forfeit that right, anything you say can and will be used against you. . . ."

Well, maybe it didn't go down quite that way. But in Mark 2, Jesus and his disciples *were* accused of breaking some big rules. Over the centuries, the Jews had come up with a long list of rules about what a Jew could and couldn't do on the seventh day of the week. The leaders had their noses so glued into their religious rule books that they had missed the whole goal of God's command about the Sabbath. God just wanted his people to take a day off each week for worship and relaxation (see Exodus 20:8-10). But the rules-centered leaders had made the Sabbath a day of no-no's rather than a day of rest.

To Jesus, people were more important than human-made rules about religious behavior. "The Sabbath is a day to enjoy, not a rule to keep," he seemed to say in Mark 2:27. For his hungry disciples out on a stroll, the Sabbath meant picking handfuls of grain to eat, even though it was unlawful to "harvest" grain on the seventh day.

Lots of Christians today are trapped in following rules rather than putting people first. They throw away an invitation to a birthday party because it's at a non-Christian's house. But unbelievers spot that, and they think that they don't matter to us or to God until they shape up. Wouldn't you be turned off by Christianity if all you saw were "dos and don'ts"?

Here's a topic to talk about honestly: Are you people-centered or rule-centered? Do your non-Christian friends see you as an open and accepting person or as holier-than-them?

Some of the most evil people in Bible times came to Jesus and were transformed because he was open, loving, and accepting. That's the result of people-centered living. Wouldn't you like to be part of that kind of success?

 TALK: Have you ever kept away from non-Christians? How come? What would you like to do differently?

 PRAY: *God, help us figure out which rules really come from you—and which ones keep us from showing people your love.*

 ACT: Watch for ways to show love to a non-Christian today.

31 Putting Your Life in His Hands

Bible Reading: Mark 4:35-41
Why are you so afraid? Do you still not have faith in me? Mark 4:40

The afternoon sun dipped behind the rolling hills as a small boat carrying Jesus and his disciples set out across the Sea of Galilee. After a day of teaching, the Master was dog-tired. So he found a quiet spot in the boat and was soon asleep.

The gentle breeze that had launched their boat quickly grew to a stiff wind that filled the sails and rippled the surface of the water with whitecaps. Within minutes fierce downdrafts howled and huge waves crashed against the side of the boat. The disciples frantically tied down the sail while the boat tipped and rolled over the waves. Water sloshed in by the gallons. But Jesus slept on undisturbed.

The disciples shook Jesus awake and screamed over the roaring wind and crashing waves, "We're going under! Don't you care?" The Master rose and shouted back at the wind, "Be quiet," and to the sea, "Be still." Almost immediately the gale dwindled to a whisper and the vicious waves subsided to a great calm.

"What were you so worried about?" Jesus asked as the trembling disciples stared out over the suddenly tranquil lake. "Haven't you learned to trust your lives to God in such a simple thing as a storm?" The disciples hadn't trusted God. They were too worried about dying.

Take a vote. Do you enjoy any of these activities?

- Slamming your fingers in a car door
- Falling over the lip of a cliff
- Licking a frozen metal light post
- Stumbling to the pavement and scraping off a layer of skin

Chances are you don't do any of them for fun. In case you hadn't noticed, you possess a drive to avoid pain and to stay well. And—like the disciples—you try to avoid flipping out of a boat in the middle of a stormy lake. Your desire to survive tells you to wear a life jacket, put on a bike helmet, and steer clear of expired milk.

You can do all sorts of wise things to keep from getting hurt. But sooner or later in life you will face a situation where all you can do is trust God.

But there's good news. Nothing can ever happen to you that will surprise God. He knows the good and bad things that will happen to you and even how long your life will last (see Psalm 139:16). And as you learn to trust Jesus, you can ride out even the most terrifying storms. He holds you in his hands!

 TALK: How does it comfort you to know that you are in God's hands?

 PRAY: *Father, we trust you to take care of us.*

 ACT: Remind a friend or family member today that God watches over us.

1 Sometimes I Feel So Lonely

Bible Reading: Genesis 2:18-23

It is not good for the man to be alone. I will make a companion who will help him. Genesis 2:18

After an awful day at school Danni flopped on her bed and scribbled these painful words in her diary:

I felt really lonely at school today. At lunchtime Katie made fun of my walk-a-thon T-shirt. She called it a rag. She said it so loud that everyone could hear. I didn't know what to do, so at recess I ran off and hid around the corner of the building. I kept to myself for the rest of the day. Am I ever going to feel like I have a friend?

Not all girls write in a diary when they feel lonely. Many boys would never dare to write about their feelings even in secret. But it's a fact: *All of us feel lonely sometimes.* Even if we like being alone, we don't like feeling left out. We hate it when people make fun of us. We really want friends who let us talk about our ideas, our dreams, and our problems. We like people who make us feel likable and lovable.

That's what you read about in your Bible passage today. After God created Adam, he said, "It is not good for the man to be alone" (Genesis 2:18). Adam must have looked in awe at all the fantastic animals, lush plants, and beautiful scenery God had made. But he still felt alone. Adam needed someone just like him. That's why God created Eve. He made her to be Adam's closest possible friend.

Needing human friends is normal. That's how God built all of us.

But even before Adam had Eve, he had God. And after Adam and Eve were created, God enjoyed coming to the Garden of Eden to talk with them.

People are still the same today. God gives us people who can be our close friends and take away our loneliness. But he doesn't want us to be close friends only with people, because sometimes our human friends let us down. He wants us to be best friends with him.

When we feel lonely, the *biggest* cure for our loneliness is knowing Jesus Christ. God sent Jesus to earth so we could be sure he loves us. Jesus is the friend we can talk to every day, even when no one else is around. And we can trust that Jesus is with us wherever we go each day. (You can check out that fact in Matthew 28:20.)

You need people, but you need Jesus most of all. And Jesus wants to be your closest friend ever.

 TALK: How have people made you feel lonely? How have they made you feel loved? How can you get close to God when you feel lonely?

 PRAY: *Jesus, thank you that when we feel lonely you are always close to us—and are always our best friend.*

 ACT: When you feel lonely today, tell Jesus thanks for being your best friend.

2 You Don't Go through Tough Times Alone

Bible Reading: Isaiah 43:1–3
When you go through deep waters and great trouble, I will be with you.
Isaiah 43:2

Okay: You have three seconds to imagine how you would react if Jesus popped out of thin air and sat down next to you. *One. Two. Three.*

Talk about it: So what would you say? Would you beg for his autograph? Would you tell him about what happened in your life today?

If Jesus is your closest friend in the world, chances are you would have a lot to share. But maybe you've never thought about what Jesus might say to *you* if he showed up at your dinner table or at the table where you do your homework. You know that he is incredibly interested in a close, personal friendship with you. And considering everything that Jesus said to his followers in the Bible, maybe he would say some of these things to you:

- "You might think I don't know what it feels like to be an outsider. At times the crowds wanted to crown me king (see John 6:15). But some of the religious leaders hated me. They lurked around me, looking for something they could use to make me look bad—or worse yet, to have me killed (see Matthew 12:14). Doesn't that tell you I know what it's like to be hated?"
- "The way I looked didn't impress people (see Isaiah 53:2). So I know what it's like to feel average."
- "When I called twelve disciples and started to preach, my own family didn't believe in me (see Mark 3:21). So I know what it's like when people in your family give you a hard time."
- "I was mocked and made fun of when I did what was right (see Matthew 27:27-44). So I know what it's like when people around you don't like you."
- "I spent forty days and nights in the wilderness with no one else around (see Matthew 4:1-2). So I know what it's like to be alone."

You might not have guessed that Jesus knows what loneliness, discouragement, and sadness feel like. But he wants you to know that you aren't alone.

Your Lord made you. He saved you. You are his chosen, special child. And he is with you whether you feel him nearby or not. Just because you can't see or touch him doesn't mean he's not with you all the time. You can count on his promise. He's saying, "When you go through deep waters and great troubles, I will be with you."

 TALK: What are some of the tough things you face in life? How does it help you that Christ has promised you won't go through tough times alone?

 PRAY: *When we feel alone, Jesus, help us remember that you're right here with us.*

 ACT: Make a sign with the words of Isaiah 43:2 and hang it where you can see it!

3 When Friends Go Away

Bible Reading: Matthew 26:36-46

My soul is crushed with grief to the point of death. Stay here and watch with me. Matthew 26:38

Brett felt like he had been hit on the head with a hammer when his best baseball buddy moved with his family to another state. Loneliness haunted Laurel after her friend Samantha died from leukemia. Ryan felt totally rejected when two of his non-Christian friends decided he was too "holy" to be their friend anymore. Kara felt ditched when she wasn't invited to a sleep-over with other girls from church.

Loneliness happens when others move away from us. We think we can count on a friend always being with us. But suddenly—or sometimes over a stretch of time—that friend vanishes. Sometimes friends *choose* to go away—they find a different friend, their interests change, or they just don't like us anymore. And sometimes friends *don't choose* to leave us—they simply don't have a choice—like when they move or die.

Do you know that left-in-the-dust feeling? Jesus does too. Here's what Jesus might say to you about your loneliness:

- "Maybe you have experienced loneliness—or even grief—because someone you love has moved away or died. I know what that's like. My close friend Lazarus died, and I shared the sorrow that his sisters, Mary and Martha, felt. Losing Lazarus cut through my heart like a knife. I cried (see John 11:35)."
- "One of the ugliest experiences of my life happened just before I died on the cross. I had spent three action-packed years with my twelve closest friends. We had eaten, traveled, and helped people together all that time. But my friend Judas betrayed me (see Matthew 26:49). Have you ever stopped to think how I felt when someone so close sold me out?"
- "I took the other eleven disciples with me to pray before I went to the cross (see Matthew 26:36-46). I knew I'd soon be facing a situation worse than I could imagine—dying for the sins of every person on earth. So I asked Peter, James, and John to pray with me. *They fell asleep!* Right when I needed them the most, my best friends let me down."

Jesus knows what it's like to be left by people close to you. His heart is touched when you cry because you are sad and lonely. He feels your loneliness. He lived through the same difficult things you have to, so he understands your hurt.

 TALK: When has a friend left you? What happened? Did you let God comfort you?

 PRAY: *Lord, I believe you care for us and feel bad when we feel bad. Thank you for your comforting arms around us.*

 ACT: Have you felt God's comfort grab hold of you like a huge strong hug? Look for someone today who needs that comfort from you.

4 He Knows Just How You Feel

Bible Reading: Hebrews 5:7-9

Even though Jesus was God's Son, he learned obedience from the things he suffered. Hebrews 5:8

One day when Shane's older brother was riding his bike home from school, a car hit him and hurt him badly. When his brother had to spend long weeks in the hospital recovering, Shane was devastated. "My Sunday school teacher keeps telling me that God is always with me," Shane says, "but I'm so sad for my brother. I'm sure that God can't understand what I feel."

Some Christians can't believe God feels their loneliness and pain. They figure he can't be touched by human emotions. But God isn't way up in the sky somewhere, far removed from our real-life problems. He feels our joy, and he feels our sadness. And here's what he might say to us when we hurt:

- "You can spot in the Bible so many times when my heart spilled over with kindness for lonely, hurting, empty people. I once met a woman from Samaria who came to a well by herself to get water (see John 4). I taught her how my love could satisfy her spiritual thirst."
- "And then there was Zacchaeus (see Luke 19:2-10). Nearly everyone hated him for being a tax collector. But Zacchaeus had another problem. He was a little guy, the brunt of jokes. When I spotted him sitting in a tree as I passed by, I knew he was lonely. I invited myself to lunch at his house because I wanted him to know I cared about him."

God knows what is going on inside of us—even when no one else does. Whether we feel happy or sad, we can't hide from him. Do you doubt that? Listen to Psalm 139:1-2: "O Lord, you have examined my heart and know everything about me. You know when I sit down or stand up. You know my every thought when far away."

So when we say something dumb at school and the whole class laughs, he sees. When a brother or sister says something cruel and unkind, he knows. When we go to bed whimpering into a pillow, he hears. He understands our fear when parents fight. He's always been there for us! And he always will be.

Jesus knows exactly what it's like to feel down. But even more than that, he has already been a part of *your* painful experiences. When you feel the sting of even the biggest hurts in your life, you can be sure he knows and understands—and has been with you all along!

 TALK: Does it scare you to realize that God knows everything about you? Why or why not? How can it help you to know God is with you every moment of your life?

 PRAY: *God, we believe that you're here with us—right now and always—through good times and bad.*

 ACT: God is as close to you as close gets. Who needs that kind of support from you today?

35

5 Fads and Facts about Faith

Bible Reading: Romans 10:9-10, 17
Faith comes from listening to this message of good news—the Good News about Christ. Romans 10:17

Welcome to the imaginary—yet entertaining—Carnival of Faith.

A guy in a shiny suit holds up a jar of slime as he waves you over. "Ladies and gentlemen, is your faith weak? Is it hard for you to trust God? Do you ever wonder if he *really* knows what's best for you? Well, your doubting days are over. Introducing *Faith-amins,* the vitamin guaranteed to fire up your faith."

The next guy offers you a plate of what looks like twigs and bark. "Eat right, believe right—it's as simple as that, folks. That's what the *Faith-Builder Diet* is all about. Attend our weekly meetings, eat from our special *Faith-Builder* menu, then watch your unwanted distrust and disbelief disappear."

A woman in another booth leaps around in neon Lycra. "Hey, get over here!" she barks. "That's right, you with the puny faith muscles. You have flab where you should have faith because you don't work out. Twenty minutes a day on my patented *Faith-asizer* will make your faith amazingly strong."

Guess what? We can't get faith in a bottle. We can't hide faith in a tuna fish casserole. We can't even firm up our faith with one of those weird exercise machines collecting cobwebs in the basement. Faith means believing God. It isn't just knowing Bible facts in our head but trusting God with everything in life.

We can't get along without trusting God day to day: "It is impossible to please God without faith," says Hebrews 11:6. Jesus praised people with "great faith" (Matthew 8:10, NASB) and scolded people with "little faith" (Luke 12:28, NASB). He promised that even mustard-seed-sized faith can move mountains (see Matthew 17:20). No wonder his disciples said to him, "We need more faith; tell us how to get it" (Luke 17:5).

That's the important question! How *do* we get more faith? Our spiritual life would be trouble-free if there were a special pill or plan that would increase our faith. But that's not where faith comes from. That's why the Bible says, "Faith comes from hearing the message, and the message is heard through the word of Christ" (Romans 10:17, NIV).

The more we dig into the Bible—reading, studying, memorizing—the more we know about God. And the more we know about God, the more sure we will be that he's worth trusting with our whole life!

TALK: God gave you the Bible so you can know him. How are you making the most of God's Word to get to know him better?

PRAY: *God, help us to use your Word, the Bible, to get to know you and build our trust in you.*

ACT: Talk to a friend today about how you can get to know God better—together.

6 I Feel the Need for Seed

Bible Reading: Matthew 13:3-9, 18-23

The good soil represents the hearts of those who truly accept God's message and produce a huge harvest. Matthew 13:23

"Welcome to the employment office. What can I do to help you find a job, Mister . . . ?"

"My real name is Germinate, ma'am, but you can call me Nate."

"And you're a seed, is that right, Mister . . . er, I mean . . . Nate?"

"Yes, ma'am, I'm a seed. Anyway, I'm ready to go to work and fulfill my great potential."

"And what is your potential, Nate?"

"Fruit, ma'am. Lots of fruit. Tons of fruit."

"But you're only a seed. You're so small and . . . well, insignificant."

"Yes, ma'am, but plant me in the right environment and watch the fruit fly."

"All right, Nate, let me see what I have for you here. Ah, there seem to be a lot of openings down on the footpath. Very easy work, and you can start today."

"Sorry, ma'am, but to grow a lot of fruit, I have to get deep into the soil. Too many distractions on the surface. Besides, my friend Bud was eaten by a bird down there."

"Mmm, I see. Okay, the foreman in shallow soil is calling for more seeds."

"I can't do my best work in shallow soil, ma'am. Too many rocks. I need to send down deep roots and grow tall to be fruitful. What else do you have?"

"Well, there's always the weed patch, Nate. Things seem to grow well there."

"Are you kidding? Those bad boys choke out the competition before it can get started. Dropping into the weed patch would be asking to be strangled."

"You're being awfully picky, Nate. Do you want work or not?"

"Ma'am, with my potential for growing lots and lots of fruit, I deserve the best environment possible. Don't you have some good, rich soil all plowed and ready for planting? I can't be fruitful without it."

That's the way it is with *spiritual* fruit—not apples and oranges and squash and asparagus, but the positive character qualities like love, joy, peace, patience, and kindness that the Bible talks about in Galatians 5:22-23.

You grow those Christlike qualities by welcoming the "seed" of God's Word into your life—reading the Bible faithfully, listening to it attentively, and thinking about it frequently. As you do, the Word does its amazing work in you. You become the eager disciple that God wants you to be.

 TALK: What do you think it means for you to be "good soil"? How are you going to do that today?

 PRAY: *God, we want to spend time getting close to you today by reading and thinking about your Word. Thanks that you will grow fruit in us.*

 ACT: Share with a friend the things God is saying to you through his Word.

7 Something to Chew On

Bible Reading: Psalm 1:1-6

His delight is in the law of the Lord, and on his law he meditates·day and night. Psalm 1:2, NIV

We butter our toast. We peel gooey pizza cheese off our chin. We gulp milk straight out of the carton—well, maybe not. But answer this: Do we ever think about the brave cow who so kindly provided the raw material for all that good dairy stuff? Do we appreciate all the work old Bessie went through?

Believe it or not, milk doesn't magically appear in the grocery store. So here's far more than you might want to know about how milk and other dairy products make their way from *moo* to *you.*

Dairy products start out as hay or grass. When Bessie eats, she chews her food just enough to swallow it—like we do when we're in a hurry. That blob of soggy grass travels into the first *two* of her *four* stomachs. The larger stomach holds *fifty* gallons of food—like a huge shelf stacked full of milk at the supermarket. When Bessie is full, she rests. But the four-stage milk factory inside her keeps working. Undigested food from the stomachs, called cud, burps back up into the cow's mouth so she can chew it again thoroughly.

When Bessie swallows again, the cud passes into stomachs three and four, where some of it is digested to nourish the cow. The rest is transformed into the makings for butter, cheese, eggnog, ice cream, and all that good stuff.

Bessie's digestion is so important to her that she spends *one-third* of her entire life—about eight hours a day—chewing cud. This process is called *ruminating.* It's the amazing way God designed cows to receive nourishment and to produce the dairy products we love.

God designed us to "ruminate" too—on his Word. When we spend time in the Bible, we fill our mind with God's truth, turning it over in our thoughts and "chewing" on it. That's the kind of "rumination" or "meditation" on the law of the Lord that David wrote about (see Psalm 1:2). When you think about the Bible in this way, God will make your life fruitful (see verse 3).

If we want to get the most out of the Bible, we can't hurry when we read it. Like Bessie, we need to allow time to chew on each word. As we do, we can tell God what we are thinking about. Ruminating on God's Word is one great way we can feel close to God. And as his Word grows in our heart, we will grow and be fruitful.

 TALK: When you read the Bible, do you rush—or ruminate? What do you want to do differently?

 PRAY: *God, help us to slow down and truly focus on what you want to teach us about yourself through your Word.*

 ACT: Chew on God's Word today by memorizing a favorite verse as a family.

8 The One and Only

Bible Reading: James 1:22-25

Remember, it is a message to obey, not just to listen to. If you don't obey, you are only fooling yourself. James 1:22

"You read the Bible? Every day?" Rachel made a face like she had just choked on a brussels sprout.

"I've learned a lot from the Bible," Shannon offered.

"That's dumb," Rachel sneered. "My mom says the Bible is just a bunch of stories. Other religions have books too, you know. There are lots of good books you can read besides the Bible."

News flash: Not everyone in the world respects the Bible like Christians do. Some of them think the Bible is just one of many religious books that will do us good if we read them. To them, the Bible is just another book.

That's a myth. The Bible isn't *one of many* great books. It is *the one and only* great book. There is no other book like it.

The Bible isn't a book we merely listen to or read. It's a book we practice and obey. The good stuff that the Bible does in our life—like building our faith in God and often making our lives safer, happier, and more helpful to others—never happens just by *owning* a Bible or *reading* the Bible or *believing* the Bible or *carrying* a Bible. We benefit from this unique book when we *experience* it by letting it change our thoughts, words, and actions. As James says, "If you don't obey, you are only fooling yourself" (James 1:22).

The Bible tells one amazing message. It was written

- over a period of 1,500 years
- on three continents
- by more than forty authors of different nationalities, personalities, social statuses, and backgrounds

The authors of the Bible were astoundingly diverse, but they delivered one astonishingly consistent message. The Bible tells one unfolding story from front to back: God is working to save humankind.

The Bible is unique. It isn't meant to sit on the shelf alongside encyclopedias and big important books from the past. It's far more than a great work of literature. Its message is life changing. The Bible is God's Word, and it's the one and only book in the world *always* worth listening to and living by.

 TALK: What good is the Bible doing in your life? How does that compare to how you are helped and changed by other books you read?

 PRAY: *God, thank you for giving us your one-of-a-kind book, the Bible.*

 ACT: Make a decision to spend time reading God's one-of-a-kind book each day.

9 What's on Your Wish List?

Bible Reading: Luke 12:13-21
> *Beware! Don't be greedy for what you don't have. Real life is not measured by how much we own. Luke 12:15*

Screech got his nickname from the noise he made whenever he skidded his bike to a stop. He was so obsessed with money that he would speed down the road, darting to examine every shiny thing that might be a coin—and every scrap of paper that looked like a dollar bill.

Screech knew how to work hard too. Between a paper route, baby-sitting, and caddying at a golf course, he had a lot of money. And with the money he raked in, he could buy almost anything his twelve-year-old heart desired.

Unfortunately, when Screech made it his biggest goal in life to pile up money, he didn't have any time left for family, friends, or church. So even though his pockets bulged with cash, he had no one to enjoy it with. Screech thought that buying things would bring him total happiness, but it didn't.

What's on *your* wish list? What sports equipment or clothes or toys would stuff you full? Is it possible that you could ever get everything on your wish list and not want anything more? Or would you just start a bigger list?

In the Bible, Paul sounds like a man who had it made. He had what it takes to be happy. In one Bible book—his letter to the Philippians—he mentions joy or rejoicing *seventeen times!*

But wait a minute! Looking again at that book shows that Paul was in prison when he wrote all those words about joy and happiness (see Philippians 1:12-14). He had no comfortable home, few possessions, and no freedom. But he was happy. Later in his letter he wrote, "I have learned how to get along happily whether I have much or little. I know how to live on almost nothing or with everything. I have learned the secret of living in every situation, whether it is with a full stomach or empty, with plenty or little. For I can do everything with the help of Christ who gives me the strength I need" (Philippians 4:11-13).

Happiness doesn't depend on stuffing ourselves with stuff. As a matter of fact, real joy has nothing to do with how much we have. We can be joyful—whether we're wealthy or needy—because we have Jesus. We can't lose him. He can't be stolen. He never breaks or goes out of style. And knowing him can give us joy that no mere object can bring.

 TALK: How happy are you with what you have? Is Christ your most prized possession?

 PRAY: *Jesus, teach us to be content with what we have. And help us realize how great it is to have you.*

 ACT: Instead of thinking only about all the things you wish you had, pick out a toy, book, or piece of clothing and give it to someone who has less than you do.

10 Nice Guys Finish Last— But Not Always

Bible Reading: Luke 14:7-11

The proud will be humbled, but the humble will be honored. Luke 14:11

It's your turn to make the play of the game. You're ready. You're set. You're going to do your best—and then you glance at your basketball coach. He flashes you a look that says "Play dirty!" You realize that he wants you to trip your opponent.

Maybe you have a coach like Leo "the Lip" Durocher. He played shortstop for several major league baseball teams in the 1930s and 1940s, then became a manager. But he is most famous for saying, "Nice guys finish last."

Durocher expected his players to win at any cost—including kicking, clawing, biting, and bumping. But compare Leo Durocher with another major league ballplayer: Orel Hershiser. He was the pitching ace of the 1988 World Champion Los Angeles Dodgers. He won twenty-three games that year and pitched a record-setting fifty-nine innings with no scores against him. He was voted Most Valuable Player in the World Series—and the National League's best pitcher that year.

Orel Hershiser is a nice guy. And he's a Christian. After setting that scoreless-innings record, he knelt on the mound to thank God. In the locker room after the final World Series game, he told reporters that he had sung hymns to himself during the game to stay calm. On national television that night, he said, "This isn't a religious show, but I want to thank God."

If nice guys are losers, how did Orel Hershiser get to the top of the heap? Listen to the truth:

- Leo Durocher says nice guys finish last. But the Bible says: "God blesses those who are gentle and lowly, for the whole earth will belong to them" (Matthew 5:5).
- Leo Durocher says we should fight our way to the top. But God's Word says, "When you bow down before the Lord and admit your dependence on him, he will lift you up and give you honor" (James 4:10).
- Leo Durocher says we have to step on other people to win. But the Bible says, "God sets himself against the proud, but he shows favor to the humble" (James 4:6).

The truth is that some seasons Durocher's team finished dead last. It's true that sometimes nice guys *also* finish last. But in God's eyes a humble and kind person will always finish first.

 TALK: How do you feel when you win in the best possible way—through hard work and humility?

 PRAY: *God, you know that we like to win. We want to win, though, by doing things your way.*

 ACT: Think of one way you can show good sportsmanship in your favorite sport or recess game—and do it!

11 You Have Friends in Weird Places

Bible Reading: John 15:12-16

Now you are my friends. . . . You didn't choose me. I chose you.
John 15:15-16

Wherever Evelyn looked, she saw two kinds of kids. There was a tiny, tight, popular bunch. And then there was everyone else, a pathetic pool of losers.

Evelyn knew she wanted to be part of the in crowd—and to avoid ever being seen with the out crowd. She was afraid that some of the nerds' nerdiness might rub off on her. Or that she could catch whatever disease made nerds nerdy. Or that someone might snap a photo of her hanging out with a herd of nerds. Evelyn made it her job in life to stay clear of all nerds . . . and dweebs . . . and geeks . . . and dorks . . . and make sure nothing ever ruined her reputation for perfect coolness.

It would be marvelous if Christians never thought about the consequences of making friends with people whom others see as rejects. But often we worry that people will snub *us* if we make friends with people that the crowd snubs. Being seen with the "wrong" people might be one of your biggest fears.

Believe it or not, Jesus battled huge pressure to hang out with the in crowd. As a Jewish teacher, he was only supposed to be seen with other teachers and really religious people.

A group called the Pharisees made up especially tough rules about the right crowd and the wrong crowd to hang with. But Jesus smashed their code. He ate with tax collectors. He touched lepers. He talked to a Samaritan woman—a double no-no, because she was both a foreigner and a woman. He got to know all sorts of people from the wrong crowd. As a result, Jesus was called "a friend of the worst sort of sinners" (Luke 7:34).

But Jesus let the Pharisees' disrespect slide off of him. In the end, it turned out that many of his most loyal friends came from the wrong crowd. Matthew, a despised tax collector, was among his twelve disciples. And Mary Magdalene, a woman from whom Jesus had cast out seven demons, was one of the few who didn't desert him through the crucifixion.

Loving *everyone* like God commands means we open our hearts to people who might be disliked by the crowd. It means befriending others in the way Jesus befriended us. After all, Jesus chose us as his friends—and we're really not perfect, are we?

 TALK: What will it cost you to be like Jesus by making friends outside your current group? What are the possible rewards—for you and for others?

 PRAY: Ask God to help you befriend someone who needs it, no matter what group he or she belongs to.

 ACT: Schedule a time to get together with someone you usually avoid.

12 Seeing Evil

Bible Reading: Psalm 141:4

Let not my heart be drawn to what is evil, to take part in wicked deeds.
Psalm 141:4, NIV

If you were an elephant, you could smell danger on the ground or in the air just by waving your trunk.

If you were a housefly, you could easily spot a flyswatter using the four thousand lenses in your eye.

If you were a fish, you could feel a predator even before you saw it through a special sense organ called a lateral line.

But here's a big question: Can *you* spot spiritual danger when it lurks in your life? Can you sense when a bad situation is developing?

You'll be at home or at school or with your friends, and suddenly you'll be tempted. You'll give in before you even know what happened. Unless you are alert to evil, you'll have a tough time ever spotting and choosing the right thing to do.

There are three very important ways to become more sensitive to spiritual danger—to develop your senses for spotting evil before it catches you by surprise:

1. *Study the Bible.* God's Word shows what right and wrong look like. When LaTonya was confused about how to get along with a difficult friend, she dug into the Bible to see what it had to say about loving others. It helped her spot evil before she acted in a way that would disappoint God.
2. *Listen for the Holy Spirit.* God doesn't leave you to sniff out evil all by yourself. Mitch struggled with hanging around too long when his friends were getting out of control—and into trouble. He often felt as if someone was telling him to get out of a bad situation. But it took him a while to figure out that it wasn't just his own head talking to him. It was God's Spirit nudging him to flee evil.
3. *Give your heart to God.* Temptation is strongest when we haven't made up our minds whether or not we want to obey God. Until Katie decided she truly wanted to treat her younger brother better, she was dulled to danger. She didn't see the difference between right and wrong. Making a big choice to do right made it easier for her to spot evil—and to do good.

God wants you to be alert to evil. Let him teach you to see wrong for what it is—a danger to you!

 TALK: What can you do to be more aware of evil around you? How can you help one another stay alert?

 PRAY: *God, help our hearts not to be drawn toward evil. Help us to spot wrongdoing before it takes over.*

 ACT: Practice being alert to God's warnings that you're about to do something wrong!

13 Love Makes the World Go 'Round

Bible Reading: Philippians 2:1-4

Don't think only about your own affairs, but be interested in others, too, and what they are doing. Philippians 2:4

Love. The word slides into conversations almost unnoticed. Talk about it: How many ways can you think of to use the word *love?*

Here are a few that come to mind:

- "I just rented a great movie. You'll love it."
- "Yeah, I'd love a burger slathered with onions, dill pickles, and guacamole."
- "My mom and dad really love each other."
- "You gotta love those basketball players!"

The word *love* can mean a lot of different things. So when you think about love, it's important to know the difference. For example, if a boy can't spot the difference between loving his dog, loving his favorite baseball glove, and loving his mom, he's in deep trouble—with his mom, not the dog.

From everything the Bible says about love—and it says a lot—we can come up with a definition of true love: *Love is wanting and working for the good of the one you love.*

Listen to that said in a couple of different ways: *Love is making the well-being of another person as important to you as your own.* Or *Love is looking out for the health, happiness, and growth of others the same way you look out for your own.*

Do you like to be healthy? Of course!

Do you like to be happy? Duh!

Do you like to grow? Naturally!

We all work hard at staying happy . . . safe . . . secure . . . and comfortable. We like to grow as Christians, do well in school, have fun with friends, and do whatever we can to improve our life. It's how we're wired as human beings. We not only want to survive but to flourish in every way possible.

But true love demands something more—that you want others to succeed as much as you do. That's what Paul meant in Philippians 2:4 when he said, "Don't think only about your own affairs, but be interested in others, too, and what they are doing."

That isn't the kind of love you usually hear about in the halls at school. But it's the true love that will fulfill both you and everyone you love.

 TALK: God is always thinking of what's best for you. How can you think about what's best for others?

 PRAY: *Father, flood us with your kind of unselfish love—the love that thinks of others.*

 ACT: Make a sign that reminds you to think of others this week—and hang it where you'll see it!

14 What Kind of Love Are You Talking About?

Bible Reading: 1 Corinthians 13:1-13

There are three things that will endure—faith, hope, and love—and the greatest of these is love. 1 Corinthians 13:13

On the count of three, point to the person in your family who most often sings along with the radio. One, two, three. Point!

You're a rare family if you don't have someone who sings in the shower, the car, or right in your ear! I'm guessing that you didn't even wait until the count of three to get your finger in that person's face.

Now answer this question: What songs does your singer sing?

Chances are he or she is singing about love. Because if you turn on the radio or TV at any time of the day or night, you can't get away from love. It's sung about on music stations, dramatized—often *melo*dramatized—in soap operas, humorized in sit-coms, and mocked in trash-talk shows. Here's what you hear:

- "If you can't be with the one you love, love the one you're with."
- "I love what you do for me."
- "If you really love me, show me."
- "I want your love, I need your love (O baby, baby, baby)."

In yesterday's devotion we said that true love means making the health, happiness, and growth of another person as important to you as your own. But what does that look like in everyday life? Can you think of some concrete examples for kids and adults to follow?

Here are a few ideas:

- If you think it's reasonable for your sister to share her toys, books, clothes, or CDs with you, love requires that you do the same for her.
- If you expect your teachers to treat you with respect, love requires that you treat them with respect and not bad-mouth them to other students.
- If you think your parents should drive you everywhere you want to go, love requires that you do your part to lighten their workload.

In most situations the loving thing to do isn't hard to figure out. Just put yourself in the shoes of the person involved and ask, "What's the best I could wish for if I were that person?" When you figure out the answer, love requires you to do the best you can, based on the opportunity and your ability.

 TALK: How does being loved by God help you make the health, happiness, and growth of others a priority in your own life?

 PRAY: *Father, give us a love for others that is like the love you have for us.*

 ACT: Think hard about something kind you would like done for you. Now surprise someone else by doing it for him or her!

45

15 When Love Is a One-Way Street

Bible Reading: John 1:10-13

Even in his own land and among his own people, he was not accepted.
John 1:11

After years of being the only boy on the block, Trent whooped when he found out a boy his age was moving in four houses away. The day Daniel arrived, Trent invited him over. They biked the neighborhood, shot hoops at the playground, and tossed a baseball in Trent's backyard.

Daniel was as big on baseball as Trent was. And he really liked Trent's glove. It was so soft it wrapped around the ball all by itself.

One evening when Daniel had to head home for supper, he asked if he could borrow Trent's glove. "Sure," Trent said.

The next morning Trent ran to Daniel's house to fetch his glove. That's when Daniel admitted he had left the glove out in the rain overnight. Both of them knew that when the glove dried it would be as stiff as a slab of oak.

You don't have to love people for very long to figure out that sometimes your kindness is taken advantage of, ignored, or even tossed back in your face. Like this:

- You volunteer to feed, exercise, and even pick up after a friend's dog when your friend heads out of town. But your friend won't ever look after your big, slobbering, mess-making doggy.
- You spend hours picking out the perfect birthday present for a friend. But your friend totally forgets your birthday.
- You hustle to get all your homework done so you can spend Saturday afternoon with a friend. At the last minute your friend calls to say he spent the morning goofing off. He can't play now.

That's the kind of treatment that tempts us to quit looking for opportunities to love our friends. But genuine love doesn't expect a payback.

God loves us no matter how we treat him. Think about how Jesus showed love for others. He knew Judas would betray him, but he loved him and called him to be a disciple anyway. As he hung on the cross, Jesus said, "Father, forgive these people, because they don't know what they are doing" (Luke 23:34). Christ died for all people, even those who turn their back on him.

Love gives because it cares about others—*period.* Whether or not its actions or words are appreciated, love keeps on giving.

TALK: How has God loved you even when you snubbed him? How can you show that kind of love to others?

PRAY: *Lord, help us to love and keep on loving—like you do—no matter what.*

ACT: When someone is rude to you today, pay it back with an act of love.

16 Loving When It Hurts

Bible Reading: 1 John 2:1-6

Those who say they live in God should live their lives as Christ did.
1 John 2:6

Here's a quiz to take. How many of these actions sound loving?

(a) If a friend shows up at church with a smudge on his face, I quietly let him know so he can clean it off.

(b) I share my glue with friends who like to color, cut, and glue.

(c) Once in a while when I'm bowling with friends I purposely throw a gutter ball so they won't feel bad about being such awful bowlers.

While those might not be the most significant examples of love in the world, at least they're a start. Because love is more than a good feeling. It's an action.

Be aware of this: All of your right, good, loving actions might not be accompanied by a flood of warm, fuzzy feelings of love or affection.

You don't always feel like obeying your parents, doing your homework, or brushing your teeth. But most of the time you manage to do those things because you have made a decision to do what's right.

Love is the same way. It isn't something you always *feel;* it's something you *do.* You might get good feelings when you do loving deeds, but God wants you to love even if you don't. Jesus didn't feel like giving his life to save the human race. He prayed, looking for a way to avoid the cross (see Matthew 26:38-39). But he chose to follow God's plan and sacrifice himself for our sin.

When we wonder if we really love people the way God intends, here's our real-life, real-love checklist:

☐ I make the health, happiness, and growth of my friends as important to me as my own.

☐ I help my friends mature in every possible way—mentally, physically, spiritually, and socially.

☐ I protect my friends from anything that threatens their well-being.

☐ I help my friends love God more.

If we can say each of those statements with total honesty, we're truly loving others. And when we put love into action, we're loving people with the greatest love in the universe. It's the kind of real-life, action-packed love that God has shown to us.

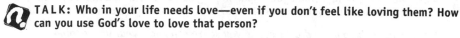 **TALK:** Who in your life needs love—even if you don't feel like loving them? How can you use God's love to love that person?

PRAY: *Jesus, help us to love like you did—not just with big words but with real actions.*

 ACT: Maybe you've intended to do something great for a friend but haven't gotten around to it. Do it today!

17 The <u>Right</u> Right and Wrong

Bible Reading: Proverbs 16:25

There is a path before each person that seems right, but it ends in death. Proverbs 16:25

It's a Saturday morning in mid-October. You're inspired to play a game of football. You only have three people on a team, so you don't want to waste anyone guarding the quarterback after the snap. You resort to the well-known rule of counting to three before the defense can rush in to tackle the quarterback.

Got the picture? You've got a rule. It's what makes the game work.

Everyone understands the rule and plays by the rule.

Except for Brutus, your neighbor. When it's your turn as quarterback, you get the snap. Brutus yells, "One!" Then he runs over the line and grinds you into the ground. Over and over.

Don't you hate it when someone rewrites rules?

Now you might just think of Brutus as a cheat. But if Brutus takes his attitude and applies it to all of life, then he's bigger than a cheat. He's what we can call a *relativist*. And his attitude is called *relativism*.

Relativism has nothing to do with your relatives. It's a way of looking at life that says right and wrong, good and bad are constantly changing. No one—not your parents, not your teachers, not a holy book like the Bible—can say what is right or wrong.

Relativism is an attitude that says:

- God's rules are meant to ruin my fun.
- God's rules don't apply to me.
- I can make up my own rules.

That's the exact opposite of the Bible's attitude:

- God's rules are meant for my good.
- God's rules apply in all times and places to all people.
- God alone makes the rules.

When individual people start picking right from wrong, life ends up like that chaotic football game. Aren't you glad that God gave us commands that don't change—not ones that people can remake to benefit themselves and hurt others?

 TALK: How do you feel when you're playing a game and your opponents ignore the rules? How about when your teammates do? Why does God give us rules to live by?

 PRAY: *Father, help us to draw close to you so we can know your unchanging commands for our life.*

 ACT: Think of one rule or command from God you've been in the habit of throwing out. Make an effort to live within that rule today.

18 You Can't Be Nice Enough

Bible Reading: John 3:1-8

I assure you, unless you are born again, you can never see the Kingdom of God. John 3:3

See if you can recognize these two guys from the Bible. One guy is getting slammed, and another is doing the slamming. Who are they?

"Hey, I might not be the greatest human being in the world, but I'm not as bad as *him!* I could tell you stories about this guy. We grew up in the same neighborhood, so I know enough about him. He was always cocky and arrogant; I kept my mouth shut most of the time. He had a police record; I always cooperated with the authorities. Once he even attacked the high priest's servant!"

Have you figured it out? Let's let him finish:

"Like I said, I might not be a saint or anything, but I'll tell you one thing: My name is Judas Iscariot, and I'm not as bad as Simon Peter!"

The Bible doesn't tell us that Judas used those exact words to try to make himself look good, but everything he says above is true. You probably know that Judas betrayed Jesus. Peter denied Jesus. But Peter repented of his sin, received Jesus' forgiveness, and became one of the greatest leaders the church has ever known.

The words we put in Judas's mouth sound the way some people try to make their bad behavior seem not so bad:

- "Yeah, I swear sometimes, but I don't swear as much as so-and-so."
- "I gossip, but I don't stab people in the back like she does.'"

Making others look bad doesn't make our own faults any better. And this is really important: That isn't how God looks at us when he decides who will enter heaven and live with him for eternity. God doesn't compare Janna to Taylor and decide, "Well, Janna, you weren't quite as bad as Taylor, so come on into heaven. Sorry, Taylor, you didn't do as well as others. You lose."

Jesus explained all this to a man named Nicodemus. Here was a guy who did, said, and believed all the right things. Jesus didn't say to him, "Hey, Nick, you're a better person than anyone else. You'll make it to heaven!" Jesus simply said, "I assure you, unless you are born again, you can never see the Kingdom of God" (John 3:3).

When it comes to spending eternity in heaven, being nicer doesn't get you in. The only thing that matters, according to Jesus, is that you have accepted God's free gift of salvation!

 TALK: How would you explain to a non-Christian friend that God doesn't let us into heaven because of how good we've been? How do we get in?

 PRAY: *Lord, we don't claim to be better than other people. Thanks that Jesus died to bring us close to you.*

 ACT: Who around you needs to know that salvation is a free gift? Make a plan to share that good news!

19 God's Way or the Highway

Bible Reading: Matthew 7:13-14

The gateway to life is small, and the road is narrow, and only a few ever find it. Matthew 7:14

Picture this: You're on a long hike. You've heard that there's an amazing view from a certain rock peak, so you decide to take the path that leads to the top. But the climb gets steeper and rockier. Soon you have to squeeze between narrow rock walls. After a while you begin to wonder if there's an easier path.

Your map says there's only one way up, but you're sure that there must be a shortcut. You whip out your cell phone and holler for the park service. "There's got to be another way to the top," you whine.

Mr. Park Ranger responds right back. "Negative," you hear. "Your map is correct. There's only one route up. Keep going. Just a little bit longer and you'll be there."

It's hard to imagine a place on earth with only one way in. We figure we can crawl in from any angle, drop from a helicopter hanging in the sky, or blast a tunnel from below. But heaven is different. There really is only one way to God's home. And that way is Jesus.

Lots of people nowadays, however, think there are *many* ways we can get to heaven. They argue that different religions—like Christianity, Buddhism, Islam, and Hinduism—are all good paths to God. They claim that we all worship the same Big Being in the sky. Different faiths, they promise, are just different roads to the same destination.

Just because a lot of people believe an idea doesn't make it true. People of all religions don't worship the same God. They aren't just taking different routes to the same place.

Think about it: Through Jesus, God provided a one-of-a-kind path back to himself. Jesus died on the cross so people can find forgiveness and enjoy eternity in heaven. The Bible is clear that no one comes to God except through Jesus (see John 14:6). Jesus is the only way we can be saved (see Acts 4:12).

Christians are the only ones with the truth that shows people how to worship the one true God and live for eternity in heaven. People need the news you have to share. That's why you want to be part of telling your friends *now* the message that Christ is the only way to God!

 TALK: Who—inside and outside of your family—needs to trust Jesus? What can you do to share the truth of salvation with them?

 PRAY: Pray for opportunities to share Christ with the people you put on your list.

 ACT: You might not be able to explain to a friend right away all that it means to be a Christian. But what are the most important things you want to say?

20 Getting to Know You

Bible Reading: Matthew 27:41-44
I am the Son of God. Matthew 27:43

Chad didn't want to forget to do any of his Christian duties. So he made up a list and titled it "Important Stuff to Do as a Christian." He knew he was supposed to go to church, so he scribbled that down first. He kept adding to his list: *Pray. Read my Bible. Obey my parents. Grow together with other Christians.*

The list grew longer and longer. Chad was so busy making his list and checking it twice that by the time he got to the bottom he forgot why he'd made the list in the first place.

Talk about it: Why do we do all the stuff we do as Christians?

Here's a key fact you never want to forget. As important as all the duties of being a Christian are, they all have one goal: to help you get to know God!

Many people assume that Christianity is just a bunch of beliefs—a set of doctrines or rules of behavior. But that's just not true. Christianity isn't a religion. It's a relationship. Christianity isn't a pile of doctrines. It's a person.

When Jesus was put on trial by the religious leaders before his crucifixion, he hadn't been dragged into religious court merely for what he *taught*. He was on trial for *who he was*. The high priest asked Jesus, "Are you the Messiah, the Son of the blessed God?" Jesus answered, "I am" (see Mark 14:61-62). That little scene tells us a lot about our faith. Being a Christian isn't having a bunch of beliefs we pile up in our brain and forget. It isn't making a list of behaviors we can pat ourselves on the back for completing. It's all about Jesus—and how we relate to him every day.

Some of the biggest disputes in the Bible were between Jesus and the Pharisees. The religious leaders thought that sticking to their overly strict rules was the only thing that mattered to God. Jesus said in effect, "You're missing the point. Talking to me and letting me forgive your sins and help you through life is what matters."

Are you growing in your relationship *with* Christ or only in your knowledge *about* Christ? Jesus wants you to study the Bible and understand what he taught, but that doesn't make you a Christian. He wants you to do what's right, but that isn't all there is to Christianity either. He wants you to talk to him and live as his close friend—and grow in faith as you trust him!

 TALK: How are you getting to know Christ himself—not just learning about him?

 PRAY: *Jesus, don't let us make faith into a bunch of rules and ideas and miss out on knowing you. We want to know you personally and follow you totally.*

 ACT: Take time today to tell God for yourself that you want to know him up close and personal.

21 Don't Check Your Brains at the Door

Bible Reading: Romans 1:16-17

I am not ashamed of this Good News about Christ. It is the power of God at work, saving everyone who believes. Romans 1:16

Waldo strolled down the city sidewalk, lost in thought. He had decided he had run from God long enough. *I can't stand it anymore,* he said to himself. *I feel so much guilt. I'm so lonely. I think my life is missing something big.* After walking for blocks, Waldo reached a church and walked in. He stood inside for a moment to let his eyes get used to the dark. "Will you be coming in?" someone asked. The voice startled Waldo. He turned and saw a little old gray-haired lady standing beside him.

"Yes," Waldo answered. "I want to come in."

"Then I'll be needing your brains, please, sir," the woman said.

"My brains?" Waldo was puzzled. Why would she need his brains?

"Haven't you decided to become a Christian?" Waldo nodded yes. "Well, then," she said, "you have to drop off your brains here at the door. You won't be needing them anymore. Christians, you know, don't ever think."

No, there isn't really a guy named Waldo who was forced to hand over his brain. But many people think that believing in Jesus is just for dumb people. That's just not true. Getting to know God doesn't mean you stop thinking. It means you use your mind to understand God's great answers to the biggest questions of life.

The Bible does teach us some challenging facts: that God was born as a human . . . that healings and other miracles really happened back in the Bible . . . that Jesus rose from the dead. Those are some highly unusual happenings, and we're right to test their truth. But plenty of bright people have read the Bible and concluded that it is absolutely true.

Once a very smart British trial lawyer, Frank Morison, tried to prove that our Christian faith wasn't true. He started to write a book showing that Jesus never rose from the dead. He researched, looked at the facts he gathered from the Bible and from history, and worked hard at his task. Finally, all his smarts and research told him that Jesus had risen from the dead! He became a Christian.

Trusting in Jesus doesn't require that you ditch your brains at the door. Actually, it demands that you use all of your smarts until you are fully convinced of your faith: "I am not ashamed of this Good News about Christ. It is the power of God at work, saving everyone who believes" (Romans 1:16).

 TALK: Do you think that you have to check your brains at the door when you become a Christian? Why or why not?

 PRAY: *God, use our minds to help us understand you and your good news.*

 ACT: Do you have a question about your faith that bugs you? Dig into the Bible today to find the answer!

22 The Core of Who You Are

Bible Reading: Psalm 8:1-9

You made us only a little lower than God, and you crowned us with glory and honor. Psalm 8:5

Most of Morgan's fourth-grade classmates walk by the mirror with barely a glance, but she always stops and stares. She pokes her hair. She adjusts her outfit. She twiddles and tweaks until she decides she looks just right. After all, she thinks, how good she looks is what makes her great.

Morgan might be the only one hogging space at the mirror, but she isn't the only one who thinks he or she has found the secret to being special:

- Jason reminds everyone that he's the biggest brain in the grade.
- Jennifer brags about how fast she can whiz a softball.
- Ricky can beat everyone at any video game ever invented.
- Todd lives in the biggest house in town.

As important as those things feel, none of them are what makes us matter. They are parts of who we are. But they're just the outer layers.

Talk about it: If all those things aren't all that important, what really makes you special?

That's a question worth answering, because how you see yourself shapes whether or not you face daily life with confidence. It affects how happy you are, how you treat people, and how you respond to God. You need to know that you are much more than how you look or where you live or what you're good at.

You might work so hard at perfecting your outer layers that you never discover what truly makes you who you are. As a Christian, the thing that makes you incredibly special is this: You're a child of the King.

One girl said this about her friend: "She's one of the prettiest girls in the world, but she thinks she's grotesque. It's as if she's saying to God, 'God, if you made me like this, then you must be a real jerk.'"

That girl doesn't see that God alone knows who she really is, and the fact that she belongs to him is the big deal about her. It's far more precious than how pretty she is, how well she does at school or sports, or how popular she becomes.

You're a person of great value and worth, made to look and act like your Creator. He has crowned you with glory and honor as his child. And when you get close to the King, you'll begin to see yourself as the princess or prince you are.

 TALK: God wants you to enjoy being the person he made you to be. What gets in the way of seeing yourself as God's child?

 PRAY: *God, teach us to see ourselves as you see us—and as the Bible describes us.*

 ACT: Share this great truth with a Christian friend who feels worthless: You are a child of God!

23 There's More to You than Meets the Eye

Bible Reading: 1 Samuel 16:7

People judge by outward appearance, but the Lord looks at a person's thoughts and intentions. 1 Samuel 16:7

When Sam looked in the mirror, scars stared back at him—the result of a childhood auto accident that disfigured his face forever. He felt worse than ugly. His warped self-image told him he was a freak. In school Sam felt constant rejection from his peers, especially girls. To cope, Sam pulled away from people and spent up to twenty hours a week watching movies, escaping into the dark of a theater—a place no one could see the monster he considered himself to be.

Looking good matters hugely in our culture. Each year we spend billions of dollars on clothes, makeup, jewelry, and fitness—and hundreds of millions more to *change* our appearance through tattoos, body piercing, liposuction, and cosmetic surgery. It seems like the closer we get to "picture perfect," the less we like ourselves.

Your true identity isn't determined by your looks. It's a lie that your outward appearance tells who you are, because your identity as God's creation goes far deeper. As the Bible says, "People judge by outward appearance, but the Lord looks at a person's thoughts and intentions" (1 Samuel 16:7).

Talk about it: Does all this mean that how we look doesn't matter?

There's nothing wrong with wearing clothes we like and caring for our body so we look our best. The mistake is when we do those things to *be* someone. As God's unique creations—no matter how we look—we already *are* people with infinite worth.

The Bible verse you just read is part of the story of how God sent the prophet Samuel to choose a king. When David's good-looking older brother strutted by, Samuel was sure he had the right guy. God said to look deeper. That's when David walked in. David labored as a shepherd, and he had fought off both a lion and a bear. You can bet he was tanned and muscled from his work. In fact, the Bible says that "he was ruddy and handsome, with pleasant eyes" (1 Samuel 16:12). But outward appearance isn't what made him fit to be king. It was that he was "a man after [God's] own heart" (1 Samuel 13:14).

So think about this: How do you feel about how you look? Do you have to look good to feel good? God couldn't love you any more if you were the most "beautiful" person on earth. He already loves who you are.

TALK: How does your view of yourself change when you think you look less than your best? How does it encourage you that God is looking at something far deeper than your appearance?

PRAY: *Father, it matters to us what other people think about how we look. But thank you for making us your unique creations.*

ACT: Keep track today: How many times do you judge a person by his or her looks?

24 Know-It-All

Bible Reading: Matthew 23:1-12

The greatest among you must be a servant. But those who exalt themselves will be humbled, and those who humble themselves will be exalted. Matthew 23:11-12

New to her school, Nan was also new to the newspaper club. For years only a handful of kids had worked on the Sunnyside Elementary paper, so club members would have celebrated even if the iguana in the library had decided to join their club. But Nan was even better. She sounded smart. She drew comics. And she gushed ideas to make the paper more interesting.

Nan bragged about the cool newspaper at her old school and rattled off ways to improve the paper. Within a month, everyone was looking to her to lead the paper. And for all the control she was taking, Nan might as well have named herself Princess of the Paper. She was picking all the pictures, rewriting all the stories, and hogging the club's one computer to craft a perfect layout. When she yelled that the fall issue *had* to be on fluorescent orange paper, the adviser asked Nan to back off.

That's when Nan got huffy, wrote a note saying she thought the club was stupid, and joined the chess team. If Nan couldn't be boss, she didn't want to play.

Some people don't feel good about themselves unless they have power over others. They're wrapped up in the status they achieve. And when these folks need a shot of self-worth, they grab leadership in school, church, clubs, and friendships. They aren't content to be available and serve wherever they're needed. They have to flex their muscles to feel like they matter.

So what's so bad about that? If your identity as God's child and your worth to him is based on the importance you achieve, you're likely out of luck. Most people rebel when you try to control them. Most clubs don't want a know-it-all leader. And most countries only need one president.

The Bible is clear: Your identity doesn't depend on the status you attain. God isn't looking for people who want to take over the school newspaper or rule the world. Jesus picked ordinary men and women as his followers—and passed over the religious leaders whose heads were overblown with status and self-importance.

Whether the world thinks you're a somebody or a nobody, you are special to God. Whether you achieve great or small things, you are priceless to him.

 TALK: What does the status or power you attain have to do with God's love for you? Isn't it great that you can let God be God?

 PRAY: *Father, you control the universe. We don't need to control our world to impress you.*

 ACT: How can you share control and include everyone in the clubs and teams to which you belong?

25 Break Free from Those Flimsy Chains

Bible Reading: Ephesians 1:3-8

Long ago, even before he made the world, God loved us and chose us in Christ to be holy and without fault in his eyes. Ephesians 1:4

Have you ever been to a circus and noticed how circus folk keep whole herds of elephants from galloping off? Well, actually, they don't usually have huge packs of these big animals under the big top. But the elephants they *do* have are kept in place with itty-bitty bicycle chains around their legs.

Talk about it and take a guess: How can such a scrawny chain control such a brawny animal?

Here's how. The elephant is locked up by a memory. As a baby, the elephant tried to break loose but wasn't strong enough. Burned into the elephant's brain was the idea that the chain was stronger than he was, and he hasn't forgotten that lesson. Even though the grown elephant could break the chain with a tiny yank, he rarely tries. Yet notice this: Once he *does* break away, he's almost impossible to contain again.

You don't have to wonder why most kids grow up with a warped sense of their worth to God and to others—and as a result, a twisted sense of their true identity. Parents, teachers, the media, advertisers, and even some religious teachers can pummel you with the idea that your identity is defined by how good you look, how well you perform, and how much you succeed.

Even if you know better, you might be chained by that dumb idea. Yet God wants to set you free. His truth is stronger than any chain.

You can't break loose in a bigger way than by getting into your head what God says about who you are in him:

- *First, God says, "You are my child."* John 1:12 says, "But to all who believed him and accepted him, he gave the right to become children of God." Try putting yourself in this verse: "I have believed God and accepted him. He has given me the right to be his child."
- *Second, God says, "You are chosen."* Ephesians 1:4 tells us "For he chose us in him before the creation of the world to be holy and blameless in his sight" (NIV). Personalize that verse too: "I was chosen by God, before he even created the world, to be holy and blameless."

When you let these Scripture truths change the way you see yourself, you figure out that you're way bigger than the chains that bind you.

 TALK: What negative messages do you hear each day that keep you from seeing yourself as God sees you?

 PRAY: *Thanks, God, for making us your children. Help us to remember that fact when lots of other voices try to keep us chained in fear.*

 ACT: Write today's great Scripture words on a card. Tape it to your bathroom mirror. Look at it when you feel put down.

26 Your Inner Self-Portrait

Bible Reading: Jeremiah 31:3

I have loved you, my people, with an everlasting love. With unfailing love I have drawn you to myself. Jeremiah 31:3

Talk about it: What's your all-time ugliest, least favorite, most hideous picture of yourself? Can you describe it? Or go find it? Now explain: Why do you hate it so much?

There's a good chance your most hated picture is one of your school pictures, the photo in your yearbook, or the photo on your driver's license. You might sooner be thrown into a pit of spiders than have that photo flashed in front of a pack of people.

You might not realize that school and Department of Motor Vehicle photographers get paid to capture you at your worst. Really. Well, maybe not. But grab hold of this good news: That picture doesn't even come close to showing what you really look like.

Here's why. Did you know you carry another personal identification photo, one far more important than any portrait in your pocket? It's the picture of yourself you keep in your mind—your concept of who you are. Like your ID photo, your inner self-portrait might or might not accurately represent the real you. But unlike that ID photo, it's the only one you have.

Take Alex, for example. He grew up in a tough home. The big message he heard growing up was, "Alex, you can't do anything right." Was that an accurate picture of Alex? No! It's true, there are some things Alex doesn't do well, just as with any of us. But to say he can't do *anything* right is nasty. Yet that message was burned onto the film of Alex's heart, and that's the distorted self-portrait he carries wherever he goes.

On the other hand, the picture Theresa has of herself is suitable for framing. She grew up in a home where she was cherished and nurtured by loving Christian parents. She learned as a kid that she was God's unique, dearly loved creation. As a result, she's growing up confident—but not cocky—about her worth to God and to others.

Your goal isn't to become Theresa. It's to get God's true view of you—a view that captures your real identity as God's child.

No matter how you see yourself right now, here's one truth that can start to re-arrange your self-portrait into a truer picture of who you are. Jeremiah 31:3 says you are loved by God—*eternally*. That's right. God is committed to love you forever. Try that verse on personally: "God loves me eternally, and in his love he draws me to be close to him." Don't you like that picture?

 TALK: How does God's view of you capture who you really are?

 PRAY: *God, help us get your true view of us.*

 ACT: Today, remind your family members that they can find out who they really are by inserting each of their names in Jeremiah 31:3.

27 Death, Taxes, and Temptation

Bible Reading: James 4:7-10

Humble yourselves before God. Resist the Devil, and he will flee from you. James 4:7

Sasha put her head in her hands and sighed. "I just thought it would be different," she told her Bible study leader. "I thought it would be easier to get along at home once I became a Christian. But I still feel like I'm always fighting not to be bad."

Here's the truth: The only Christians who don't face temptation are the ones in heaven. The rest of us face temptation every single day of our life. The fact that you've become a Christian won't make Satan stop picking at you. In fact, your problems with temptation might hardly even begin until you start responding to God's Holy Spirit.

That's cheery news, isn't it? Actually, knowing Jesus gives you great power to handle temptation. When you face temptation, here's how to fight back:

- *Be on your guard.* Expect temptation. Benjamin Franklin was wrong when he said, "In this world nothing is certain but death and taxes." There's at least one more for-sure fact of life: temptation.
- *Hit back at temptation quickly.* The biggest danger in temptation is telling yourself how much fun evil is instead of dealing with it right away. That's like playing with a lion cub—fun for a while, deadly when it grows up and tears you to pieces. When Jesus was tempted (see Matthew 4) he responded to each temptation quickly—as in immediately!
- *Submit to God.* Wise temptation fighters get to their knees and pray about their situation. It's not enough to turn away from the temptation—you need to turn *to* God. Tell him about your troubles. Ask for his help, the exact help he promises in Hebrews 2:18.
- *Resist the devil.* How? Once you recognize a temptation and ask for God's help in overcoming it, put on your running shoes and get out of there!

And once God has helped you overcome, don't forget to thank him for keeping his promise. After all, he's the one who "will keep the temptation from becoming so strong that you can't stand up against it. When you are tempted, he will show you a way out so that you will not give in to it" (1 Corinthians 10:13).

 TALK: Aren't you glad that God doesn't leave you to battle temptation on your own? How does he help you?

 PRAY: *Father, thank you for your presence and the strength you give us to resist temptation. Help us remember to pray at the first sign of temptation.*

 ACT: What are the biggest temptations you face? How do you deal with them? Talk with a friend or someone in your family about how to make an even better plan!

28 Someone to Watch Over Me

Bible Reading: James 5:16-18

Confess your sins to each other and pray for each other so that you may be healed. James 5:16

Five-year-old Kelli has just finished cleaning her room. She tugs at her mom's leg, eager to get outside and play. "All done, Mommy," she reports.

"If I come and look at it," her mom asks, "what will I say?"

Kelli looks down and twists her toe on the floor. Then she runs off to her room. A few minutes later she scampers back. "All done, Mommy."

"Can I come look under the bed?" asks Mom.

Kelli frowns. But she pulls out her stuffed animal friends and puts them on the shelf where they belong. As Kelli is finishing, her mom walks into the room. Guess what? Kelli's room is spotless.

You might be three, thirteen, or thirty-nine and holding and still try to pull fast ones when it comes to doing what you're told. And you might squirm when others try to figure out the truth.

"Accountability" is a six-syllable word for having someone kindly but persistently check up on you to see if you're doing what you're supposed to. Here's what it looks like:

- Accountability means your *teachers*—people who teach material and assign work—score your work to make sure you are learning. They either pat you on the back or make you do the work again until you understand it.
- Accountability means people like *coaches* and *piano teachers*—people who teach specific skills—make you zoom through wind sprints and scales so you are sure to learn your lessons.
- Accountability means *parents*—people who have the God-given job of raising you—check to see that you obey them because they want you to grow up to be an adult who pleases God and gets along with other people.

Dads and moms, by the way, don't get off the accountability hook. They answer to bosses and pastors and other dads and moms.

Can you see how accountability keeps you on track? It's one of the ways God protects you and provides for your good. And being accountable—without fussing, stomping, or screaming—is a major step of growth in your Christian life!

 TALK: Who in your life holds you accountable? Are you working with—or against—that person?

 PRAY: *God, thanks for putting people in our life who help us be the best that we can be.*

 ACT: Do you have a tough time with accountability? Make a list of all the benefits. Then talk to God and ask him to soften your heart so you respond the right way to those who try to hold you accountable.

29 A Habit You Can Live With

Bible Reading: 1 Timothy 4:11-13

Focus on reading the Scriptures to the church, encouraging the believers, and teaching them. 1 Timothy 4:13

So how are family devotions going?

Talk about it: What words would you use to describe what you get out of doing family devotions? Take a few minutes to chat.

Did anyone use words like "understanding," "enjoyment," "growth," or "closeness to God"?

Getting into a habit of Bible study—either as individuals or as a family—is like getting physically fit. Like physical exercise, reading God's Word *regularly* produces great results—results that show! And after a while you won't like the sluggish feeling you get when you take a day or two off.

If you continue your habit of daily prayer and Bible study, what will you look like spiritually one year from today? What will you look like if you *don't* spend time developing your faith?

God wants to get you close to him. But one huge reason people can find reading the Bible so grueling is they've never learned some simple guidelines for personal study:

- *Start small.* Make a commitment to spend five minutes a day in Bible study. You'll usually find you read longer.
- *Ask the Holy Spirit to help you understand.* As you sit down to read, ask God to teach you.
- *Use a Bible translation you can understand.*
- *Start with the clear, basic parts.* You don't have to plow through the Old Testament first. Start with the book of Mark, John, or Romans.
- *Keep a notebook and pencil close by.* For each section you read, jot notes: What is the main point of this section? What does it teach me about God? What does it tell me about myself? What am I going to do about what I learned?

You can finish by thanking God for what you learned. Pray something like, "Father, thanks that the Bible gives me patience and encouragement. Please help me not just hear your Word but do it. Amen."

 TALK: What makes it hard to get into God's Word daily?

 PRAY: *God, give us the confidence and power to get into your Word every day.*

 ACT: Renew your commitment as a family to study God's Word together!

What Part of Perfect Don't You Understand?

Bible Reading: Romans 3:10-20

No one can ever be made right in God's sight by doing what his law commands. Romans 3:20

It's the last week of school before spring break, and Mia can't wait to see the scores for her fitness tests in gym class. Mia outran, outcrunched, and outscored her whole school in every event. But when her teacher hands her the results, she shrieks in horror. She missed the mark in every single area.

Mia crawls up to her gym teacher, ready to beg for mercy. "Mr. Hammer, what did I do wrong? I thought I would win a fitness award."

"Award?" Mr. Hammer waves his megamuscular finger at Mia. "You didn't win any award. You're not even going to pass my class. Didn't you read the requirements posted by my office? To pass you have to run a mile in under three minutes, hang from a bar for six hours, do the fifty-yard dash in two seconds, and slam a 32-ounce bottle of Gatorade in six seconds while singing our school song. You have to do a thousand sit-ups, five hundred push-ups, bowl a perfect game, and be voted Best Dancer during the square-dance unit."

No wonder they call him Mr. Hammer!

Would you walk out of Mr. Hammer's class feeling a little hopeless? Try *totally* hopeless! This teacher's standards are way out of reach—except maybe the part about guzzling Gatorade. And given a few lifetimes, you might be able to do a thousand sit-ups. But the other requirements are absolutely not doable.

It's obvious that pleasing Mr. Hammer by obeying his rules is impossible.

Hopefully you don't have teachers as tough and unreasonable as Mr. Hammer. But that's what we're up against if we try to please God by obeying his rules. It can't be done. The point isn't that God's rules are *unreasonable,* but that keeping them perfectly is *unreachable.* No one can go through life without committing one little sin, and the Bible says, "The person who keeps all of the laws except one is as guilty as the person who has broken all of God's laws" (James 2:10).

Is God as heartless as Mr. Hammer? No way! God didn't give us his commandments to make us fail. His commandments show what his perfection looks like. But his standards also point out that we aren't perfect—and that we need another way to come to him.

Jesus is the way. He opens the door and welcomes you into heaven—and to a close relationship with your loving God right now. Do you accept?

 TALK: One of the first steps in trusting God is admitting you can't keep all of his rules perfectly. Do you really believe that? Why or why not?

 PRAY: *God, thank you for giving us a way to get to you—through Jesus' death for us.*

 ACT: Remind a friend today that God accepts us because of Jesus—not because we're perfect!

2 Here Comes the Judge

Bible Reading: Romans 3:21-23

We are made right in God's sight when we trust in Jesus Christ to take away our sins. Romans 3:22

A young man found guilty of a serious crime stands waiting to hear a judge announce his punishment. The judge glares at the young man. "Do you admit that your actions were wrong?"

"Yes, Your Honor," the defendant says softly, his head bowed in shame.

"And do you realize that the penalty for your wrongdoing is required by the law—and that it must be fulfilled before you can be set free?"

"Yes, sir."

The judge looks at the young man. "On the basis of the evidence and your admission of guilt, this court sentences you to a fine of $10,000 or one year in jail."

"But, Your Honor," the young man says, choking back tears, "I don't have $10,000."

"Young man," the judge says firmly, "the law requires that you pay the fine or spend a year in jail." Then he raps the gavel once, signaling that court is dismissed.

As the crowd leaves the courtroom, the judge steps down from his bench and approaches the young man. "Come with me," he says.

The defendant follows the robed judge to the cashier where people convicted of crimes pay their fines. As the young man watches, the judge reaches under his robe and pulls out his personal checkbook. He carefully writes a check for $10,000, the full amount of the fine. He signs it and hands it to the court official. Then he turns to the young man with a smile. "You're free to go, Son."

Tears fill the young man's eyes. "I don't deserve this, but thank you, Dad." Then the two embrace.

That's a picture of how God loves you! You can't fully obey God's law. Your sin has earned a heavy punishment you can't pay. And God, who is the perfect judge, can't forgive your sin until the fine is paid. But God—who is also your loving Father—steps down from the bench and pays the fine himself.

All you have to do to receive God's great forgiveness is to accept his generous gift. How? By trusting Jesus Christ to take away your sins. Then all is forgiven—and you can enjoy the fact that you are a much-loved son or daughter of your totally just, totally loving God.

 TALK: What if God hadn't provided Jesus to make things right between you and him? How would you feel if you were still under the penalty for sin?

 PRAY: *God, thanks for sending Jesus as the one way our sins can be forgiven so we can be set free to follow you.*

 ACT: God has kindly forgiven you. Who has done something wrong to you—and needs to know you forgive them? How can you share that great news with them?

3 The Egg and I

Bible Reading: Romans 3:24-26
We are made right with God when we believe that Jesus shed his blood, sacrificing his life for us. Romans 3:25

Here's an astounding way to demonstrate the deep truth that Jesus died for our sins. You'll need a raw egg, an empty tin can (open on one end), a small piece of scrap wood, and a hammer. Then try this in front of your friends and family:

- Place the scrap wood on the table and carefully set the egg on it. Keep the can out of sight for now, but lay the hammer on the table.
- Say, "This egg represents you and me. The Bible says that all of us have sinned, and God's punishment for sin is death."
- Show the hammer. "This hammer represents God's punishment for our sin."
- Wave the hammer above the egg and say, "What is going to happen when I whack the egg with this hammer?" Your witnesses may say something like, "Major splattage!" or "Scrambled egg" or "The yoke will be on us."
- Bring out the empty tin can and cover the egg with it.
- Take a good, hard whack at the top of the can with the hammer. The loud *thunk* will probably make everyone jump.

If all goes well, you'll have one nastily dented can—but when you lift it up, you should find that fragile egg still intact. And here's where you impress everyone with your spiritual insight.

See, Jesus took the hit for us, just as the can took the hit for the egg. The Bible says that by dying on the cross in our place Jesus stepped between us and God's judgment for our sin. We could no more survive God's anger against our sin than an egg could live through a blow from a hammer. But we didn't have to experience God's judgment, thanks to Jesus' willingness to lay down his life for our sin. Escaping God's wrath is a gift we simply receive by trusting Jesus.

Now look at the dented can. Think about what it cost God to forgive your sin. During the last hours of his life, Jesus—who had done nothing wrong—was cursed, mocked, spit on, and beaten. A crown of thorns was forced onto his head. And he was nailed to a cross.

That's the enormous price Jesus paid for your sin. But that's also your amazing worth to God. God loves you so much that he willingly sent his Son to die in your place so that you could be friends with him.

TALK: How do you feel about yourself when you think about the loving sacrifice Jesus made for you? Can you see how incredibly valuable you are to him?

PRAY: *God, when we see what Jesus suffered, we understand your great love for us. Thank you!*

ACT: Do this demonstration for a friend who doesn't know Jesus—and explain how much God loves him or her!

4 Credit Check

Bible Reading: Romans 3:27-28

Can we boast, then, that we have done anything to be accepted by God? No, because our acquittal is not based on our good deeds. It is based on our faith. Romans 3:27

Way back before anyone you know was born—from 1508 to 1512 to be exact—the brilliant Italian painter, sculptor, architect, and poet Michelangelo lay on his back decorating the ceiling of the Sistine Chapel in Rome. He painted nine scenes from the book of Genesis, including the creation of Adam, the creation of Eve, the temptation and fall of Adam and Eve, and the Flood.

When it comes to world class art, Michelangelo is the man. But here's a mouthful you would never hear from Michelangelo: "I take all the credit for my beautiful art. Every piece of my artwork—my famous sculpture of David, my scenes on the ceiling of the Sistine Chapel, and my work as an architect on the stunning church of St. Peter's Basilica in Rome—I did it all myself. I didn't get a bit of help from anyone." You won't find those words in any history book—because Michelangelo never said them.

Lots of us like to tell people about big stuff we do. You don't have to listen long on the ball field or at recess or in the classroom to hear big-time bragging going on. Maybe "Once I kicked a soccer ball so hard it popped!" or "I can beat you across the monkey bars!" or "My dad has a semitrailer full of gold!"

But most people whose accomplishments are truly great admit that they're only partly responsible for their success. Often they give God the credit for their ability, brains, or talent. Late in his life, for example, Michelangelo wrote, "I believe that I have been designated for this work by God. . . . I work out of love for God and I put all my hope in him."

When you accomplish something great—big or small—whom do you pat on the back? Giving credit where credit is due starts with admitting that your skills really come from God. If he hadn't created you and gifted you with all sorts of talents, you could accomplish *nothing*.

And when it comes to the gift of forgiveness, you *really* had nothing to do with it. You didn't create it, earn it, buy it, win it, or think it up. It wasn't your idea. It's not your work of art. Forgiveness is something your loving God did for you. He gives it to you as a totally free gift.

 TALK: How have you said thanks to God for sending Jesus to die on the cross for you?

 PRAY: *God, you deserve all the credit for all the things we can do. And we give you all the credit for giving us your forgiveness.*

 ACT: Give someone some help today—no strings attached.

5 Who's Right about Right and Wrong?

Bible Reading: Genesis 3:1-7
You will know the truth, and the truth will set you free. John 8:32

Your best friend passes you a cigarette. You're shocked. "You smoke?" you protest. "Smoking is wrong. It's *stupid!*"

"Says who?" sasses your friend. "Your mother?"

You stand firm. "Did you sleep through those pictures at school? Smoking makes your lungs look as black as dirt."

Your friend pushes back. "Those pictures are all fake. The only reason adults tell us not to smoke is to keep us from having any fun." Then your friend takes one last shot at you: "Don't you have a brain of your own?"

That's a scene all of us face as we grow up. If the argument isn't about smoking, it's about some other activity "everyone" says is way too fun to pass up. And the temptation grows strongest when others say we're able to make up our own mind.

Back in the Garden of Eden, Satan convinced Eve that God wasn't looking out for her good—and that doing her own thing was the smart way for Eve to get what she wanted. The serpent's sly argument worked, of course. Satan convinced Adam and Eve that they were bright enough to pick right and wrong all on their own.

Know what? Satan still wants to keep us from recognizing God as the only true judge of what's good. He's happy to help us cook up excuses for behavior God says is bad. He makes it sound smart to toss out God's commands and make up our own minds about right and wrong.

That's like a sailor on the ocean who spins himself in a circle and points willy-nilly to decide which way is north. Back in the days before ships had sophisticated navigational systems that showed exactly where they were in the ocean, sailors looked at a certain star—called the North Star—to know which direction was north. When a sailor was surrounded by water and didn't have any landmarks, it was easy for him to get confused, so he couldn't trust his sense of direction. If he didn't chart his course by the North Star, it wouldn't be long before he was lost. If we ignore the fact that God alone gives us direction, we're bound to go astray.

God loves us so much that he doesn't make right and wrong a matter of opinion. He loves us so much that he makes his commands clear and easy to understand. And he doesn't teach us right from wrong to mess up our life. He wants to show us how to make life the best it can be.

 TALK: When have you listened to the wrong person tell you what's right? How do you rely on God to tell you right from wrong? What happens when you don't?

 PRAY: *Lord, you alone know what's best for us. Today and always, we want to listen to you to help us know right from wrong.*

 ACT: Make a list of people or other voices that try to sway you to act a certain way. Talk about which ones are worth listening to—and which ones steer you away from following God's commands.

6 Bending the Rules

Bible Reading: Psalm 9:7-10

The Lord reigns forever, executing judgment from his throne. He will judge the world with justice and rule the nations with fairness. Psalm 9:7-8

Everyone stares when Caroline walks into the party. Her new outfit looks gorgeous, incredibly stylish—and very expensive.

"Go ahead," Caroline says to Mandi. "Ask me where I got it."

Mandi looks stumped.

"It's from that new store uptown," Caroline says, smiling. "Ask me how much I paid."

Mandi shrugs.

"It was free." Caroline winks. "I took it into the dressing room and put my own clothes on over it. Then I just walked out of the store. It's stunning, isn't it?"

"It's beautiful," Mandi agrees. "But, Caroline, it's not yours!"

"That's so judgmental," Caroline protests. "I don't think what I did was wrong. I needed a new outfit, and the store was charging too much."

Thieves don't like being told that stealing is wrong. Bullies don't enjoy hearing that beating people up is bad. People who abuse drugs or alcohol rebel when they are confronted with the hurt they cause themselves and others. People have always wanted others to leave them alone to do the wrong thing.

But these days there's a wild new view of right and wrong floating around. It says that we can each act like Caroline, making up our own rules about right and wrong. It claims we should always accept people's actions, no matter how sinful they are.

That's like saying you should let someone come up and punch you in the nose—just because *that person* says it's okay.

God's commands are for everyone—all people, at all times, and in all places. When we abandon what God says is right, we have a big problem. God is the only Perfect One. He's the only one capable of correctly judging right from wrong. It's silly to applaud another person's bad actions when they clearly violate God's wise rules.

Sometimes the best way you can love a friend is by not letting the wrong she's doing slide by. You can accept her—but you can also warn her that how she's acting is wrong. God cares too much to let bad stuff go on!

 TALK: How would you explain right and wrong to a friend who thinks everything she does is okay?

 PRAY: *God, thank you that you love us enough to tell us when we do wrong. Help us to know how to talk to friends whose behavior is hurting them.*

 ACT: Make a sign listing three ways you can confront someone who is doing wrong, without being rude or mean. Start it with, "When someone is doing wrong, we will . . ."

7 How Do You Measure Truth?

Bible Reading: 2 Thessalonians 2:13-17

We are thankful that God chose you to be among the first to experience salvation, a salvation that came through the Spirit who makes you holy and by your belief in the truth. 2 Thessalonians 2:13

A bank robber rushes up to a teller. "Put the money in the bag, lady," he growls.

"I'm afraid I can't do that," the teller says. "Other people put their money in the bank so we can keep it safe."

"I want the money," he presses. "Hand it over!"

"But why should I give it to you?"

"I've decided I can choose right and wrong for myself. And I've made up my mind that it's a really good thing for me to take money from banks."

"Well, then. Why didn't you say so? You've thought this through—and you've made up your own mind about good and evil. That's so sweet." The teller calls over the guards. "Frank, Charlie—would you help this man load up his car with money?" And then the clerk turns to the bank customers. "Everyone, I'd like you to meet Mister—umm—what's your name?"

"Doe," he stammers. "Joe Doe."

"Joe Doe will be emptying our vaults today. Let's give him a round of applause!"

You wouldn't keep your money at a bank that lets people walk in and demand *your* money just because they think it's the right thing to do. But believe it or not, that's how some people think we should decide what's good and what's evil!

Christians believe that they know the right rules—rules that apply to everyone. Yet it's not enough for Christians to say, "We know the rules everyone should live by." We need to understand where these rules come from and why they are truly best.

We can be sure of the difference between right and wrong because the rules that govern the universe come from one source: God. And they are perfect because he is perfect. God is so righteous, so just, so true that he alone sets the standard for right and wrong, justice and injustice, and truth and lies.

We know love is good and hatred is evil because God is love. Honesty is right and lying is wrong because God is true. Purity is moral and impurity is immoral because God is pure.

What God tells us about right and wrong is *absolute*—true for all people, at all times, in all places. He cares too much for us to command us to do anything less than his best.

 TALK: Why is God's standard of right and wrong the one to use? How would you explain this to a friend?

 PRAY: Lord, the world gives us all kinds of standards to judge actions and ideas. We know you are the perfect judge of what is good and right.

 ACT: Look today for ways that people throw out God's rules of right and wrong. What could you say to change their thinking?

8 Getting to the Bottom of the Rules

Bible Reading: Romans 13:8-10
Love does no wrong to anyone, so love satisfies all of God's requirements. Romans 13:10

You're probably glad not to be in the thick of these sticky situations:

- Eddie tells you he's going to flunk fifth grade if he doesn't start doing better on his tests. He isn't kidding. Do you make him eat your dust as you and all your friends graduate into sixth grade—or do you help him cheat?
- Mona has told you that her dad lost his job and her family is out of money. You're standing in the snack aisle at a grocery store and she says she's starving. She really looks hungry. Do you help her swipe something to eat?

Talk about it: How do you tell right from wrong when you have a tough choice to make?

God began showing us right and wrong with the Ten Commandments. And he packed the Bible full of his commands—not just "dos and don'ts" he made up to be mean, but commands he created to help us live well.

If you want to know whether an attitude or action is right, you can use these three guides.

- *Precept.* A precept is a specific rule. In the Bible God provides some totally clear precepts—or commands. For example, the Bible says, "Don't lie to each other" (Colossians 3:9). Precepts point to bigger principles.
- *Principle.* A principle is the "why" behind a precept. The Bible tells us not to lie, and the principle behind that is that God wants us to be honest. So we know that not only is it wrong to lie, it's also wrong to cheat on a test, because that's not honest.
- *Person.* There's one last test when you want to know if something is right: Compare it to the person of God. How does your choice stack up against what you know about God's caring, loving character? For example, we know that God never lies—so we know that lying is wrong.

Besides helping us know right from wrong through his precepts, his principles, and his person, God also puts mature Christians in our life—parents, pastors, neighbors—to help us gain the wisdom that comes from walking with God for a long time.

 TALK: Think about all that God teaches you through his precepts, his principles, and his person. Do you want to honor God by obeying him?

 PRAY: *God, we want to follow your best for our life. Help us discover what is good and hang tight to it!*

 ACT: Put a sticky situation of your own to the test. What do precepts, principles, and God's person tell you to do?

9 Whose Rules Rule?

Bible Reading: Deuteronomy 10:12-16

He requires you to . . . obey the Lord's commands and laws that I am giving you today for your own good. Deuteronomy 10:12-13

A few months ago fourteen-year-old Christine got the worst Christmas present ever. Her parents announced that they were getting divorced. At first Christine couldn't believe it. Then she cried hard about a situation she knew was real. Right now she's really angry that she's caught in a tug-of-war between her mom and dad. She doesn't know how to respond or what to say.

"You know," Christine insists, "I want to do what's right. But I hear so many things from so many people that I'm not sure what's right anymore. It's like I'm up to bat in a softball game. I've got coaches and teammates and my parents and everyone else behind the backstop all yelling at me at once. This is a bad situation. I need to know what God wants."

Christine feels confused. But she's taken a huge step toward obeying God: *She wants what God wants.*

The truth is, figuring out right and wrong usually isn't very tough. The hardest part of obeying God is *choosing God's way.* It's making up your mind that what God says about right and wrong is smarter and better than anything your little brain could think up. It's deciding that God's ways are far better than what your friends tell you. It's deciding that in your life, God's rules totally rule.

Talk about this: Why is choosing to do what God wants always the best choice you can make? Why is it so great to obey God?

God has a plan for each of our lives. It's what the Bible calls his "will." Some parts of his will apply to everyone. That's the part of his will God makes clear through the obvious commands of the Bible. Other parts of God's will are just for you as an individual. And that's where that big decision enters in. Do you want God's will more than anything else? Do you want what God wants for you?

We have lots of big choices to make in life, but the biggest is deciding whose ideas of right and wrong we will live by. And once we've decided to submit to Jesus as Savior and Lord of our life, we can expect him to give us the power to live according to his ways.

 TALK: Do you want to do God's will? How does that affect your daily decisions?

 PRAY: *God, help us today as we try to follow your commands.*

 ACT: Look for an opportunity today to encourage a friend that following God's rules is the best choice anyone could make.

10 Do Yourself a Favor

Bible Reading: Matthew 22:34-40
Love your neighbor as yourself. Matthew 22:39

Love ourselves, huh? It's what God expects when he tells us to love others just like we love ourselves. So take a vote. Are any of these characters loving themselves the way God likes?

- Trisha picks up her test paper, glances at her perfect score, and dances around the classroom waving her grade in everyone's face.
- Jon pushes to the front of everyone at the locker-room mirror and flexes and poses like he's Mr. World-Champion Sports Guy.
- Melinda tells everyone she's getting out of school early for her first modeling photo shoot—and the next day she's on the playground passing out autographed pictures of herself.

Talk about it: Ever met people like those kids? How are their attitudes and actions goofed up?

There's a healthy kind of self-love, and God wants us to have a good dose of it. But Trisha, Jon, and Melinda don't have a clue what healthy self-love is! Being stuck on our beauty, brains, brawn, or bucks amounts to conceit, not love.

Matthew 22:39 implies that we won't love *others* in the right way unless we love *ourselves* in the right way.

Is loving ourselves really okay? Look at it this way: God loves us, so we can love ourselves. God accepts us, so we can accept ourselves. Loving ourselves isn't just okay, it's great! It's what God wants.

Let's be clear that there are two types of self-image. Seeing ourselves as God sees us—no more or no less—is a *healthy* self-image. That's an uplifting thing. It's also a humbling thing—because we recognize that every gift we possess comes from God.

The second kind of self-image is *unhealthy*. An unhealthy self-image can be either too negative or too positive. People with a negative self-image get down on themselves. People with a positive self-image get high on themselves. Neither kind of unhealthy self-image honors us as God's special creation.

We can be sure we're loving ourselves in the right way when we love others more as a result. And when we make loving others our goal, everything else falls into place. Life—and liking ourselves—makes sense. We put others—beginning with Jesus—smack at the center of our attention. And when that happens, God is pleased.

 TALK: Say it in your own words: What's a healthy self-image?

 PRAY: *Father, teach us to love ourselves in the right way—and to love others as a result.*

 ACT: Do something for a family member today that says "I believe in you."

11 Looking for a Pony

Bible Reading: Philippians 4:6-9
Fix your thoughts on what is true and honorable and right.
Philippians 4:8

A mom and dad were having trouble with their twin boys. One was abnormally happy all the time. The other boy found something bad about everything. After a while the parents decided to take their two sons to a child psychologist.

The psychologist claimed to have an easy cure. He placed the too happy boy in a room filled with horse manure and a pitchfork. Figuring this would cure the boy's overly joyful spirit, the doctor told him to dig. Then he left the boy alone. He took the always crabby boy into a room filled with new toys and candy. He was free to play with it all. "That should cure him of his dark outlook on life," exclaimed the psychologist. "We'll come back in a few hours and see."

When the psychologist and parents returned to the room full of toys and candy, they were shocked to see the little boy sobbing in the middle of the floor. "I might hurt myself if I play with these toys," he cried, "and the candy might give me a tummy ache." All the wonderful things around him hadn't snapped him out of his pessimistic attitude.

"Well, surely your other boy will be cured," claimed the psychologist, trying to sound confident. Peering into the second room, the adults were astounded to see the boy digging through the manure in a fury. The boy's mom tried to get him to slow down, but he was so busy that he only paused to say, "With all this manure, there must be a pony in here somewhere!"

Talk about this: Are you more like the little boy looking for the pony—or the boy afraid of the tummy ache?

We have to admire positive thinking. If we don't have it, we've got to get some!

Negative thinking won't get us anywhere in life. Negative thinking makes us crabby. It also blocks out all the good things God says about us.

Thinking positively, however, draws out the potential—in us and in the people around us. Positive thinking can't make something true that isn't. It can't find a pony in a pile of manure if the pony isn't there. But positive thinking is a great advantage when we focus on what is positively true about us according to God's Word.

If you believe God's Word and what God says about you being his special child, you will discover that God has prepared gifts for you that are even bigger and better than a pony.

 TALK: Are you always crabby about life? Make a list of positive things to think about from Philippians 4:8.

 PRAY: *God, give us a positive outlook on life based on your Word. Help us gain a positive perspective from the Bible.*

 ACT: Pay attention to your attitude today. Are you thinking negatively—or remembering all the positive things God puts in your life?

12 Guess What I Heard about You

Bible Reading: Proverbs 19:19-23

Get all the advice and instruction you can, and be wise the rest of your life. Proverbs 19:20

You sign up for the football team and can't wait to tell your friend. "The football team? Are you kidding?" he snorts. "You're terrible at sports. The only position the coach will let you play is left end—*of the bench!*"

It hurts to get slammed. If we don't deal with the hurts we feel, our self-image starts to wilt. But with God's help we can turn other people's nasty words into helpful advice. Here's how you can make that happen:

1. *Decide if you deserve the criticism.* Do you truly need to take a shower and stop sleeping in your clothes? Do you really need to spend more time on your math homework? If the criticism is right on target, then you just have something to work on.

   When Kristi told Bethany that she was being selfish for always deciding what they were going to play, Bethany thought hard about it. Then she talked with her mom and her older sister, two people she knew would be honest with her. They agreed that sometimes Bethany acted selfishly, and she took some wise advice on being more sensitive to others.

2. *Decide to let undeserved criticism slide off.* Plenty of criticism is way off the mark. If everyone in the world is hurling untrue, ugly remarks at you, it won't work just to think happy thoughts about yourself. But you can help criticism slide off by recalling what God says about you in his Word. No criticism can undo the fact that you are God's much loved child. You are valued, accepted, and gifted.

   Kristi not only said Bethany was being selfish but stomped out of the house screaming that there was no reason she'd ever want Bethany to be her friend. That's when Bethany again turned to her mom and sister. They knew the real Bethany. While they could be honest about her rough spots, they also reminded her of all the times she had been kind to friends.

When you wonder what you should believe about yourself, it's ultraimportant to remember one thing: God is the one who has the truest view of you. And he's put special people in your life to remind you of that precious fact.

 TALK: Have you been criticized recently? How did you react? How did your friends and family help you handle it?

 PRAY: *God, help us to receive criticism. Help us learn from what is true and reject what is untrue.*

 ACT: Decide on one or two trusted, wiser people you can talk to when you get slammed.

13 Credit Where Credit Is Due

Bible Reading: Philippians 1:3-6

I am sure that God, who began the good work within you, will continue his work until it is finally finished on that day when Christ Jesus comes back again. Philippians 1:6

You probably think surviving criticism is tough. So how well do you do when people think you're absolutely *grrrrreat?*

Talk about it: How do you react when people pay you compliments?

You might have noticed that it's easy to slip to one of two extremes. The first is *false humility.* If someone compliments you for singing a solo, you deny your accomplishments by saying something like, "No, no, no, I can't even carry a tune." But everyone who hears you knows that inside you're screaming, "Say it again! Tell me again how great I am!"

The other extreme is *arrogance.* You agree with your complimenters to the point of bragging. They say one nice thing and you remind them of twenty other things you do well. You're like a touchdown-scoring running back who pumps the football to the sky, wiggles his hips, flaps his knees, and motions to the crowd for more applause.

Here's a better way to handle a compliment: Start by asking yourself if you really deserve it. Really. If the credit belongs to someone else, don't be shy about saying it. If you indeed deserve the credit, then simply say "Thank you."

The only thing better than doing something that deserves a compliment is receiving a compliment with grace. Well, except for this: When you receive a compliment, *whisper thanks to Jesus.* You don't have to say it out loud. But in your heart you can tell God that you know he is the source of your stunning gifts, astounding abilities, great looks, and winning personality.

God is the one who deserves the credit for everything you accomplish. And the passage you read tells us why. God is the one who is at work in you, and any good things you've been able to do in your life come from him.

From start to finish you are the handiwork of God. And as wonderful as you are, you haven't reached your fullest potential. God has his hand on your life to make you even better.

God made you like a rose. Left to itself, a rose never reaches its full potential. In fact, untended roses stay small and thorny. But as a master gardener cares for a rose, it grows and becomes even more beautiful. It becomes all that it is capable of becoming. That's God's plan for you!

 TALK: Aren't you grateful that God is always with you to help you grow to your fullest potential? How do you see him at work in you?

 PRAY: *God, thanks that you are at work in us. We want to give you credit for all the good things we do.*

 ACT: Thank God for a good friend today. But go ahead and pass on a warm compliment to that person too!

14 One Gigantic Sign from God

Bible Reading: Acts 17:19-28

For in him we live and move and exist. Acts 17:28

Spring had finally sprung, and Amelia couldn't wait to get her hands back in the dirt. She remembered how last spring her family turned over the hard soil in a patch of their backyard and created a garden. Her mom planted seeds and her little sister watered them. They watched day by day for them to sprout. Warm spring sunlight coaxed green from the moist earth. And then raindrops gently beaded on the leaves in their backyard garden. Later in the summer the garden yielded every sort of taste sensation—tomatoes, zucchini, lettuce, and carrots.

Amelia had to admit that she didn't care much for vegetables. Some of God's gifts were so good for her that she preferred to eat them smothered in an extra blessing of cheese sauce. Even so, she knew that all around her were miracles of God's provision. It's amazing: From dirt, water, sun, and seeds come God's tasty care for us. Daily. And lots of it.

Talk about it: Look around you and name ten things you see that show God's handiwork. Run to a window if you need to. (But then come back!)

Your whole world is like a big blinking sign that says God cares about you. The apostle Paul once told a group of unbelievers that God "has shown kindness by giving you rain from heaven and crops in their seasons; he provides you with plenty of food and fills your hearts with joy" (Acts 14:17, NIV). The green ripeness of a garden, the beauty of a mountain, the intricate design of the tiniest cell swimming in a puddle—they're all signs of God's love.

Paul also wrote that every human being can see enough about God in nature to convince us that God exists. We can figure out that he made us and cares for our needs. Even people who say they don't believe in God can clearly see "[God's] eternal power and all the things that make him God" (Romans 1:20, NCV). He's not a God stuck way up in the sky but one who cares about the earth he made and the creatures who live on it.

Nature sings that God's love is real. Maybe you've never looked at a zucchini as proof of God's care. But every carrot and falling star and snowcapped mountain cry out that God cares for you.

 TALK: When you look at the way God has provided a good world for you, do you feel loved?

 PRAY: *God, thanks for putting beauty all around us. Thanks for showing your care for us by providing for our needs.*

 ACT: Go outside and collect signs of God's provision for us and the other creatures he made. Make a collage or a collection to remind you of God's care.

15 Can You Feel the Love?

Bible Reading: 2 Corinthians 5:11-15
Whatever we do, it is because Christ's love controls us.
2 Corinthians 5:14

Okay, make a quick list in your head of people you love.
Who makes it onto your list?

- ☐ parents?
- ☐ grandparents?
- ☐ siblings—at least a chunk of the time?
- ☐ close friends?
- ☐ a pastor or Sunday school teacher or youth leader?

Here's another question: So who loves you back?
You probably get lots of love from loads of people—and pets. But did you notice anyone important missing from the list above? There's someone else who probably tops your list of loved ones—and your list of those who love you back.
It's God.
Yep, I did ask you to name "people." But even though God isn't a human being, he is a *personal* being. He created you, and he wants you to experience his incredible love for you.
There's a problem: Sensing God's love can be hard. We can't see him and we can't touch him. Lots of times we won't even feel him.
God puts people in our lives for a big reason: to make his love for us feel solid. If we want to know about God's love, human love is a huge hint. It's a gigantic way he demonstrates his love for us. The apostle John put it this way: "Love comes from God. Anyone who loves is born of God and knows God" (1 John 4:7).
Whenever we feel human love, it's God wrapping his arms around us: Parents change messy diapers, referee fights, and provide you with food and clothes and lots more. Husbands and wives commit to love each other through their whole lives. And every time someone runs errands for a shut-in, provides meals for a sick friend, donates money to help the poor, helps a neighbor move furniture, or performs some other loving deed, God's love shines through human behavior.
As a Christian, you're someone who shows God's love to others. He works through you, for "Christ's love controls us" (2 Corinthians 5:14). Love is from God. And people who experience true love from you will sense that God cares.

 TALK: God has surrounded you with human love so you will know he loves you. How do you best see God's message of love to you?

 PRAY: *When people love us, God, help us remember that you are the source of that love. Thanks for showing us your love in solid ways.*

 ACT: Make God's love visible today by showing love to someone who needs it.

16 God Wrote the Book of Love

Bible Reading: Exodus 34:5-7

I am the Lord, the merciful and gracious God. I am slow to anger and rich in unfailing love and faithfulness. Exodus 34:6

Brent looked sadly at his skateboard, destroyed by the most eye-popping trick he had ever pulled. The wooden deck had split in two, and the wheels themselves had launched into space. "It's okay," Brent sighed. "I'll get a new board tonight."

Brent's buddy was amazed. "Tonight? You had a custom deck. And you saved for months to buy those wheels. How are you ever going to get a new board by to-night?" he asked.

"The Skateboard Fairy, of course," Brent said matter-of-factly. "You know, whenever you break a board, you put the broken pieces under your bed and the Skateboard Fairy slips you a new one while you sleep."

Perhaps you're too old to believe in the Skateboard Fairy. But when it comes to God, you might have expectations that are just as wild.

Talk about it: In what spectacular way would you like God to make clear his love for you? By giving you a perfect grade on a test? Making sure you never have to walk in the rain? Making you a front-runner for Miss America or Mr. Universe?

Those could be cool ways to be reassured of God's love. But the fact is, we don't need anything spectacular. We can see his love in the food and other good things he's provided for us. We can spot his love coming through the people he's put all around us. But in case we're still unsure of his love, he's made it clear in his Word.

In the Bible hundreds of verses tell you about God's affection for you. Listen to these words about how your loving God showed himself in the Old Testament: "The Lord's unfailing love surrounds the man who trusts in him" (Psalm 32:10, NIV). "Your love, O Lord, reaches to the heavens, your faithfulness to the skies" (Psalm 36:5, NIV). "The Lord's love never ends; his mercies never stop" (Lamentations 3:22, NCV). "I am constantly aware of your unfailing love" (Psalm 26:3).

And according to Jesus, love is the Bible's big message. He said, "'You must love the Lord your God with all your heart, all your soul, and all your mind.' This is the first and greatest commandment. A second is equally important: 'Love your neighbor as yourself'" (Matthew 22:37-39).

God is all about love. The Bible makes that clear. And we are at the center of his loving heart.

 TALK: Which of those messages in God's Word makes you most sure of his love for you?

 PRAY: Thank God for shouting his love for you through the Bible.

 ACT: Memorize any one of those encouraging verses about God's great love for you.

17 God Wrote the New Book on Love

Bible Reading: 1 John 3:16

We know what real love is because Christ gave up his life for us. And so we also ought to give up our lives for our Christian brothers and sisters. 1 John 3:16

After being kicked around from foster home to foster home, Joleen finally had foster parents who cared about her. She threw tantrums, skipped school, and froze them out of her world by refusing to talk about her interests or her past. As the Murpheys continued to show her love and acceptance, though, Joleen slowly started to respond. But even when she finally felt like people loved her, she still had a hard time believing that *God* loved her.

If the message of God's love is strong in the Old Testament, it's a bone-crushing bear hug in the New Testament. All through the New Testament we figure out that God is crazy about us. These are some words of care we can't live without:

- God's tremendous love is shown in the Bible's most famous verse: "For God so loved the world that he gave his only Son, so that everyone who believes in him will not perish but have eternal life" (John 3:16).
- Jesus said, "The greatest love is shown when people lay down their lives for their friends" (John 15:13).
- Paul was shocked that God would love us while we were still his enemies: "But God showed his great love for us by sending Christ to die for us while we were still sinners" (Romans 5:8).
- God's sacrifice of his Son to save the sinful human race is the maximum expression of love. No wonder John cheered, "See how very much our heavenly Father loves us, for he allows us to be called his children, and we really are!" (1 John 3:1).
- Romans 8:35, 38-39 lists all the things that *can't* separate us from God's love.

And there's more. We see God the Father's love for his Son (Matthew 3:17; Mark 9:7) and the Son's love for his Father (John 14:31). Jesus tells us that his love for us is modeled after the Father's love for him (John 15:9). We are commanded to respond to God's love for us by loving God (Matthew 22:37) and by loving others (John 13:34-35; Romans 13:8; 1 Peter 1:22; 1 John 4:7), including our enemies (Matthew 5:44). And our ability to love comes straight from God and his loving nature (1 John 4:16-17).

You can't read the New Testament and miss God's message of love. God's love for us is everywhere.

 TALK: What do you think of a God who heaps so much love on you?

 PRAY: Pray today for your non-Christian friends who need to know God and his love personally.

 ACT: Memorize one of those incredible Bible verses on love.

18 Three Love Facts

Bible Reading: 1 Peter 4:7–11
Continue to show deep love for each other, for love covers a multitude of sins. 1 Peter 4:8

Jacob ran home after school, feeling like he'd been kicked by his classmates. *If I'm as big of a dirtbag as they say I am,* he thought to himself, *then no one wants to be around me. Fine. If they don't want to be around me, I don't want to be around them.* He went into his room, shut the door, lay down on his bed, and clamped on his headphones. And with the music blasting loud enough to blow his eardrums, he tried hard to think about anything but people.

There's a problem with Jacob's approach to life: We can't resign from the human race. Whether we like the idea or not, God put us here on Earth to have relationships with people. There are three facts about love we can't avoid:

Fact 1: You don't have an option to love. The Bible's biggest command to Christians is to love God and love people. God custom-built us to be involved with people of all kinds—even people who bug us, bother us, or bore us. Even when people make the job look impossible, God created us to try to get along with people.

Once Jacob cooled down, he remembered that all around him were people who needed to experience God's real, life-changing love. He saw every day as a chance to love people who needed it most.

Fact 2: Love is an action. Do you hate hearts, flowers, and drippy love songs? That's okay! Love isn't a feeling. It's a choice.

Once Jacob prayed that God would open his eyes, he saw that God was giving him many opportunities to enjoy people, comfort them, and guide them to Christ.

Fact 3: Love is often hard. Sometimes *figuring out* the loving thing to do is tough. Sometimes *doing* the loving thing is even tougher. Fortunately, God didn't design you to love people and then leave you clueless about how to do it.

Once Jacob read his Bible, he discovered that it *invited* him to experience God's love. It *commanded* him to put love into practice in the real world. And it *instructed* him on what love looks like.

We're made to love and keep on loving. Love never fails, but sometimes we fail at loving God and others. That's when we need to go back and get some of God's fresh love—and while we're at it, we can reread God's instructions on how to show his love to others!

 TALK: When have you wanted to pull away from your world? Why is that *not* a long-term option?

 PRAY: Ask the God of love to keep teaching you what it means to love him and others.

 ACT: Which "love fact" do you have the hardest time accepting and applying to your life? Work on that!

19 The All-Time Right Thing to Do

Bible Reading: Luke 6:27-35
Do for others as you would like them to do for you. Luke 6:31

Chang Ho's life has just twisted into his scariest nightmare. The longer he twiddles the lock on his school locker, the more obvious his problem becomes: Every important scrap of knowledge has vanished from his brain, starting with his ultravital locker combination. In a flash he realizes the only thing he knows is that he no longer knows anything he needs to know, like what classes he has . . . what rooms they're in . . . what time they start . . . who his teachers are . . . what assignments are due. And when he flees to the school office for help, the office assistants will tell him neither his combination nor his schedule if he can't recall his name, which he can't. . . .

You might forget all sorts of facts. But here's a totally right, most basic command you'll want to remember: always love.

God's command to love is one of his *absolutes*. That means it has no exceptions—even if we don't like someone, even if someone is mean to us, even if we think someone's breath smells.

Some people argue that there's no way a command could apply to *all people* at *all times* in *all places*. But we can be sure that the command to love fits whatever situation we face. Have you ever noticed how mean people don't like it when others blast them with the same meanness? They feel okay about ignoring others or starting rumors about people or calling them names. But if anyone does that stuff to them, they feel wronged. That's how we know that anything less than love is wrong.

Think about yourself. You no doubt want loving treatment from people. And you no doubt feel bothered when you fail to receive the treatment you expect. When you help a friend with his homework, for example, you expect him to appreciate your help—and you feel disappointed, hurt, or frustrated when he doesn't say thanks.

All people demand nothing less than to be loved. If you admit that you hope for loving treatment from others, then your job is to love others with the same love you expect for yourself.

Jesus said it right when he spoke the Golden Rule: *Do for others as you would like them to do for you.* That's an easy way to remember God's biggest rule—always love.

 TALK: What's the one command we can't forget? How can we be sure that God's command to love is always right?

 PRAY: *God, we know it's important to love others as we want to be loved. Help us love as you love.*

 ACT: Ever given up loving certain people because you didn't like them? Pick one person and start a new habit of loving that person today.

20 A Love That Is More than Human

Bible Reading: 1 John 4:16-19

As we live in God, our love grows more perfect. 1 John 4:17

Talk about it: Think of someone who is really nice—well, beyond nice. Name someone who is really *good*—and here's the catch—who isn't a Christian. And then answer this: How can someone not believe in Jesus and still be an awesome person?

Here's an example. Nina had been Felicia's best friend for most of their lives. Felicia was nice, but Nina was supernice. Nina always welcomed strangers, always spoke kindly, and always signed up to volunteer at nursing homes, food pantries, and animal shelters. When Felicia became a Christian and promptly announced to her best friend that she needed Jesus, Nina answered that she was just as good of a person as Felicia. She didn't need to become a Christian because she already knew how to love people.

Nina's protests cut to the heart of what it means to be a Christian—and why we need to share Jesus even with the nice but non-Christian people in our world. Here are four facts we can be sure of:

Fact 1: Non-Christians can obey the Golden Rule even though they don't know God. You don't have to be a Christian to live out biblical truth. In fact, sometimes unbelievers work harder to obey the Golden Rule than many Christians! Unbelievers may live out the Golden Rule most of the time because it makes sense.

Fact 2: Obeying the Golden Rule all the time takes God's one-of-a-kind strength. Brute willpower can help you do a lot of good. But to live the Golden Rule when loving gets tough takes the supernatural power only the Holy Spirit provides. The natural thing is to be mean to people when they're mean to you!

Fact 3: You need the Bible to tell you how to act. Non-Christians might say they "listen to their heart" to tell right from wrong. But even if your conscience and common sense steer you right most of the time, they aren't perfect. Your conscience can be affected by pressures outside you and urges inside you.

Fact 4: Being nice doesn't mean you know God. That's really hard to think about—especially about good people we like and admire. But here's the truth: As kind and loving as a non-Christian can be, salvation comes through faith in Christ alone, not through following the Golden Rule. People need more than a commonsense love for others. They need a friendship with God himself, the source of love!

 TALK: How could you answer someone like Nina, who says she doesn't need to become a Christian because she follows the Golden Rule?

 PRAY: *God, there are great people all around us. Show us how to help them see that they still need to know you.*

 ACT: What nice people do you know who still need to know Jesus? Make a plan as a family to kindly and wisely share Jesus with them.

Steve and Snideley

Bible Reading: Romans 8:28-30
For God knew his people in advance, and he chose them to become like his Son. Romans 8:29

When Steve walked in the room, the air reeked of success. The high schooler was everything anyone wanted to be all bundled into one: He was athletic—captain of the school's championship football team. He was hunky—the easy winner for homecoming king. He was musical—first-chair trumpet in the state youth orchestra. And he was brilliant—the guy with the highest grade point average in school.

Snideley wasn't any of those things. He wasn't athletic—in fact, he once fell out of his shoes while talking in speech class. He wasn't good-looking—just ask any girl. He wasn't musical—not after being booted from band for dropping the tuba. And he wasn't smart—his grades slid as low as they could go without flunking. But instead of being himself, Snideley kept trying to do all the things Steve did.

Wanting to be somebody different might be a fun dream for a few minutes, but it's no way to live every day. God made you unique. You're different from every other person on this planet, and he wants you to stay different.

- You're great just the way God made you.
- You don't have to be anybody else.
- You don't have to compare yourself to anyone else.

Face it: You compare yourself to others because you want to know how you measure up. If you're doing well, you soar. If you aren't as gorgeous, brainy, rich, or athletic as the other person, you crash. The trouble with comparing is that you're using the wrong measure—other people. Every person is different, so you're *always* guaranteed to find someone you think is better or worse than you are, filling you with either frustration or pride.

There is, however, someone you *should* strive to be like. It's someone even God wants you to copy. And that's his Son.

God doesn't want you to remake yourself in the mold of anyone but Jesus. He doesn't want you to try to look or dress like Jesus, but he wants you to develop Jesus' character.

Instead of asking, "Am I as good as so-and-so?" quiz yourself on this: "Do I have the character of Jesus, God's Son?" When you can say yes to that question, you'll know you're just like him.

 TALK: Whom do you want to be like? Why?

 PRAY: *Father, thanks that you don't expect us to remake ourselves in the mold of anyone but your Son.*

 ACT: With the Holy Spirit's help, identify one characteristic of Jesus you would you like to put into practice. Then try to do it today!

22 There's a Price on Your Head

Bible Reading: 1 Corinthians 1:26-29

God chose things despised by the world, things counted as nothing at all, and used them to bring to nothing what the world considers important. 1 Corinthians 1:28

Carlie grinned as she counted the change from all the stuff she had sold at the yearly neighborhood garage sale. She could hardly believe how strangers had raced from all over town to show up at the sale and hand her money for toys and books she no longer needed. But her excitement melted when she saw that she still had a big box of things to carry home. Carlie had brought a table full of sale items, but most of it hadn't sold.

Carlie had a problem. *She* didn't want that stuff. Worse than that, *others* didn't want that stuff, even when it was priced at just pennies.

Carlie took her leftovers home. But then she tossed them out with the trash.

Most of us have times when *we* feel like garage-sale leftovers. When we let other people tell us our value, we feel like we're worth even less than small change. When we compare ourselves to people around us, we can wind up feeling puny and weak, ugly and unappealing, even dumb and dumber. We feel like stuff that no one wants—useless to ourselves, to others, and to God.

When you feel that way, don't despair. You're no garage-sale leftover. You're worth far more than the pennies a worn-out toy might fetch. In fact, a huge price far bigger than any amount of money has already been paid for you. Your life has been bought by the valuable blood of Jesus Christ.

Christ died on the cross to bring you to God. And his death means there's no doubt about your incredibly high value. If you want to figure out how much you're really worth, you need to figure out how much Christ's life was worth. First Peter 1:18-19 gives you a hint: "For you know that God paid a ransom to save you from the empty life you inherited from your ancestors. And the ransom he paid was not mere gold or silver. He paid for you with the precious lifeblood of Christ, the sinless, spotless Lamb of God."

You might still feel worthless. But the fact is, you're not. You are exceedingly valuable. You are worth *Jesus!* Ponder that—and when you do, it will radically change how you see yourself. You're no junk!

 TALK: So what are you worth? What does Christ's death have to do with your incredible worth?

 PRAY: *God, sometimes we don't feel very valuable. Thanks for showing us our real worth through Christ's death on the cross.*

 ACT: Share with someone today the fact that he or she is worth the life of Jesus.

23 Hey, You with the Fluorescent Orange Hair!

Bible Reading: Hebrews 13:5-6

God has said, "I will never fail you. I will never forsake you."
Hebrews 13:5

Have any of the following embarrassing situations happened to you? Can we have a show of hands?

- You tried to tint your hair and it turned fluorescent orange.
- You bent over and your pants suffered a revealing rip up the backside.
- You grew a red zit on your forehead that looked like a third eye.
- You were told your clothes must have been cut from your grandma's curtains—and the style doesn't work nearly as well for you as it did for the kids in *The Sound of Music*.
- You discovered that somebody taped a sign to your back that said, "Loser. Kick Me."
- You smelled an awful odor nearby, then discovered it was you.

You wouldn't like walking down a crowded hallway in school in any of those unfun conditions. You would watch friends and enemies alike scurry away. You would hear whispers and worse. You definitely wouldn't feel confidence oozing out of your pores.

When we wonder whether we are going to feel accepted, we feel insecure. When we stare in the mirror and all we see are shortcomings, we start wondering why anyone would ever want to spend time with us.

But you don't have to feel that way. Why? We are accepted by the One who matters most—Jesus Christ. He takes us as his friend just as we are—fluorescent orange hair, red nose, ripped pants, mismatched socks, and all. He's promised never to ditch us or forsake us. He wants to be with us no matter how we might feel about ourselves.

Now think hard about what this means. If Jesus Christ—Creator of the universe—accepts us, what does it matter if nobody else accepts us? That doesn't mean we stop needing people, but we can stop needing their acceptance to make us feel okay.

When you realize that Christ accepts you unconditionally, you don't have to focus on yourself. You can shift your attention to others. Almost all of your friends feel insecure, whether they act that way or not. They need someone to help meet their needs by reaching out to them and pointing them to Jesus. Knowing that Christ accepts you lets you welcome them as friends the way Christ has welcomed you.

 TALK: How does knowing that Christ accepts you make you more accepting of others?

 PRAY: *Jesus, we're grateful that you accept us completely.*

 ACT: Most people won't believe you if you just *say* you accept them. *Do* something today to demonstrate acceptance to someone you've been unkind to in the past.

24 It's Not How Good You Are, It's How Good He Is

Bible Reading: 2 Corinthians 5:21

God made Christ, who never sinned, to be the offering for our sin, so that we could be made right with God through Christ.
2 Corinthians 5:21

Thomas had reason to let out some wild whoops. He should have been celebrating the fact that he made it all the way to the middle of eighth grade without *ever* getting anything lower than an A. But from the nasty face he was wearing about his first B, you would guess he had been sentenced to summer school for the rest of his life.

Thomas had gotten an A-minus—once—way back in the fall of sixth grade. When his parents saw that report card, they didn't brag about the five A's. They nagged about the one A-minus. His parents told him to work for "real" A's, the kind without minuses. After that, Thomas vowed never to get another "bad" grade. It was his only hope of feeling accepted by his parents.

The great thing about belonging to God is that you don't have to be a whiz at everything to get him to like you.

If you never succeeded at another task, in fact, God would still accept you. He doesn't sit up in heaven grading your day. He isn't counting up points you have to get for him to accept you.

Your real worth is already carved in stone. It can't be changed. It doesn't go up or down with how well you do at school or how much other people like you at the moment. God defines your worth, and he says you are as valuable as the life of his Son, Jesus. When you are sure of that truth, several fantastic things happen.

- *You feel okay about failing.* God frees you to try—and to fall on your face! Once you know God won't reject you, you can stretch to reach your full potential and find out what you are capable of.
- *You do better when you succeed.* Realizing your true value lets you put your focus back on God, who loves and accepts you just as you are. You don't have to take credit for what you accomplish. You don't worry so much about getting people to applaud you.

And there's one more thing. *You don't have to pant like a puppy dog to get people to like you.* It's wonderful to do well. But you don't have to excel to win other people's praise. And you don't have to do anything to earn God's love. You already have his approval!

 TALK: God accepts you totally because of Christ. How does that make you feel?

 PRAY: *God, thanks for accepting us just the way we are. Help us to show your kind of acceptance to others.*

 ACT: Pick a friend or family member today. Look for opportunities to compliment the good he or she does rather than focus on the bad.

March
25 A Day in the Life of Whoever

Bible Reading: 1 Thessalonians 5:9-11
So encourage each other and build each other up, just as you are already doing. 1 Thessalonians 5:11

You've never had a day this swell, have you?

7:45 A.M.:	You miss your bus, so your mother has to drive you to school. She lectures about punctuality the whole way.
8:12 A.M.:	You forgot your homework, so your teacher writes your name on the chalkboard under the heading "No Clue."
11:47 A.M.:	You carry your lunch to the table where your friends are sitting, but nobody moves to squish you in.
4:33 P.M.:	Your dad forgets to come to your game—again.

Now if any of us had a day that lousy, we would need a heap of help. But what would encourage us? Vote "yep" or "nope" on these ideas for raising our spirits.

☐ Yes ☐ No A friend says, "You think *you* have problems. Let me tell you about mine. (Blah, blah, blah.)"

☐ Yes ☐ No A friend explains, "Here's why that happened, dummy, and here's what you need to do so it doesn't happen again. (Blah, blah, blah.)"

☐ Yes ☐ No You receive an e-mail from a friend that says, "Sorry to hear about your discouraging day. I'm praying for you."

☐ Yes ☐ No A friend shows up with a hot new Christian music CD. "I heard you had a tough day. I thought we could listen to this together."

From time to time, everybody you know needs encouragement. Encouragement means lifting people's spirits and cheering them up by helping them focus on the positive and good things in life. But only a couple of choices from the list of "friendly" responses really fit that definition, right? The others don't help at all, and they might even make things worse.

According to 1 Thessalonians 5:11, encouraging others is part of what it means to be a good friend. As we let God be our perfect friend and encourage us with his perfect wisdom, we will know how to be a true source of encouragement to our friends—even on their dumpiest days.

 TALK: How do you treat friends who are down? Have you let God help you spot the difference between helping—and hurting?

 PRAY: *God, make us good friends who know how to encourage the people who need it most.*

 ACT: Phone a friend you know could use some encouragement.

26 A Moment-by-Moment Friend

Bible Reading: Ephesians 4:25-29
Let everything you say be good and helpful, so that your words will be an encouragement to those who hear them. Ephesians 4:29

Nadine cried when a broken arm finished off her volleyball season. She had discovered she loved the game more than anything else she had ever tried. So she hated it when friends said, "I know how you feel." They had no idea.

There's a time and a place for every act or expression of friendship. Some cheery thoughts and words, for example, lift a friend's spirits. Some efforts to assist bring real relief. But some things we say or do make our friends want to slug us for our unsympathetic stupidity.

Another translation of today's key verse tells us to be helpful to people "according to the need of the moment" (Ephesians 4:29, NASB). It's important to respond in a way that fits what our friend needs *at the moment.*

For each scene below, pick the response that you feel would best meet your friend's "need of the moment."

Your friend seems discouraged but has said nothing. Your friend needs:
(a) medication   *(b)* to know that no one likes a loser
(c) just to get over it   *(d)* someone to care enough to listen to him or her

Your friend has just suffered a serious loss and is hurting. Your friend needs:
(a) to run off somewhere and hurt alone   *(b)* to have a good cry and get better
(c) to pretend the hurt doesn't exist   *(d)* someone to hurt with him or her

Your friend has to study hard for a big exam. Your friend needs:
(a) to get smarter   *(b)* to settle for low grades
(c) to learn how to cheat   *(d)* someone to help him or her study for the exam

Instead of getting stuck in one way of reacting to a friend—always whipping out a joke, showing insincere sympathy, or going into detail about your personal experience—take a few seconds to think through some better options. Being a loving, helpful friend means being alert to what your friends are going through and figuring out exactly what they need at that moment.

 TALK: How do you usually react to a friend who is hurting? What are some of your other options?

 PRAY: *God, help us know how to be supportive when and how our friends need us most.*

 ACT: Think of a hurting friend—and then think of a creative way to ease his or her pain.

27 Dinner in a Time Machine

Bible Reading: Mark 14:17-26

This is my blood, poured out for many, sealing the covenant between God and his people. Mark 14:24

"Services at church are so boring," Luke whined. "And I don't get why we do that Communion thing. What's up with that?"

Do you ever feel like Luke on Sunday mornings? Do you ever stare out a window wishing you could move to another time and place? Well, every time we do what Luke calls "that Communion thing," you get your chance. In fact, when we participate in Communion—known in many churches as the Lord's Supper—we're like the science-fiction heroes and heroines who get flung to and fro in time.

When Jesus gathered with his disciples in the upper room to celebrate the Passover, they entered a time warp—not exactly of the sci-fi kind, however. The Passover feast reenacted the events of the Old Testament exodus from Egypt. It helped the Jews remember and applaud God's faithfulness to them in the past.

Wherever and whenever we celebrate the Lord's Supper, we enter a kind of time warp too. It's like we blast to the past *and* fly to the future:

- The Lord's Supper thrusts you back in time two thousand years to Christ's sacrifice on the cross for your sin. "Every time you eat this bread and drink this cup," Paul wrote, "you are announcing the Lord's death until he comes again" (1 Corinthians 11:26). In other words, *when you celebrate the Lord's Supper you're remembering what Jesus already has done for you.*
- The Lord's Supper also lets you look ahead to the end of human history. Jesus said, "I will not drink wine again until the day I drink it new with you in my Father's Kingdom" (Matthew 26:29). The day he means is the day he will come again to invite you and all Christians to a celebration feast in heaven. We'll get to thank him personally for his sacrifice, which won our salvation. In other words, *when you celebrate the Lord's Supper you're looking forward to what Jesus promises to do for you.*

It stretches your mind to think back to the Cross and ahead to Christ's return. Both events matter to your life right here, right now. By looking back you say, "Lord, you gave your life for me. Help me give myself back to you." By looking ahead you say, "Lord, you have an awesome plan for me. I want to make my life count for you. And I'm looking forward to meeting you face-to-face!"

 TALK: How can you make every Communion celebration a feast to remember?

 PRAY: *God, help us to see the Lord's Supper through fresh eyes—looking back to your death for us and forward to your return.*

 ACT: Talk through this study again—perhaps the night before your church next celebrates the Lord's Supper!

28 When the Pressure Is On

Bible Reading: Mark 14:32-42

Please take this cup of suffering away from me. Yet I want your will, not mine. Mark 14:36

Neal wanted his little brother Casey to be ready for the blast of evil awaiting him in middle school. "Some kids are heavy into drugs," he said.

Casey's eyes widened.

"It was really hard to do what was right," Neal admitted. "But I did what I knew I had to do. I still hang around with friends who don't pressure me—but I do it at school, in a safe place. And some other friendships I ended. Losing those old friends wasn't any fun at all."

Talk about it: Have you ever felt painfully sad for doing what was right?

If you've suffered for doing right, Jesus knows just how you feel.

As Jesus walked into the Garden of Gethsemane after sharing the Last Supper with his disciples, the terror of heading to the Cross began to weigh on him. He was totally committed to doing the Father's will. He wanted to give his life to save lost humankind. But he still knew his task would be difficult beyond imagination. The battle between wanting to do right and wanting to avoid the pain he would feel led him to the garden and to prayer.

The New Testament was first written in Greek, and the Greek word for "Gethsemane," the place where Jesus prayed, means "oil press." That's a device for squeezing oil out of olives. Think about that picture. Jesus spent the evening before his death in an oil press. Like an olive, he was being crushed.

We can learn how to stand up under pressure by watching Jesus in Gethsemane. What we learn is this: Doing right isn't always easy, even for the Son of God. It cost Jesus plenty to go through with God's plan. In choosing to go God's way, Jesus made the hard choice of going through pain alone.

You're wise if you handle these tough situations the same way Jesus did. He prayed, "Please take this cup of suffering away from me." It's okay to ask God to change the unpleasant circumstances you face. Jesus did. But he also added, "Yet I want your will, not mine." He told God that more than anything he wanted to obey.

Doing right nowadays isn't easy. Sooner or later you'll face a "Gethsemane moment." That's a tough choice to do what's right even when it hurts. Be assured that God is right there with you. And he knows exactly what you're facing!

 TALK: When have you wanted to do what's right—but had huge struggles because of the cost?

 PRAY: Take a tough situation you're in right now and pray about it using Jesus' prayer.

 ACT: Who do you know who is paying a price for doing right? How can you be supportive?

29 Are You or Aren't You?

Bible Reading: Mark 14:66-72
"That man is definitely one of them!" Peter denied it again.
Mark 14:69-70

Mick shows up at church for fun—the same way other kids join the volleyball team or the chess club.

Last summer Mick's church took a busload of youth to fix up a house in a run-down part of his city. Mick heard that he might get to swing a sledgehammer to smash down walls and climb the roof to tear off shingles. So he signed up. But when the work got hot and hard, he snuck off to a gas station down at the end of the block to buy a soda.

The clerk eyed him. "I haven't seen you in here before," he remarked. "Are you with that church group cleaning up the old drug house?"

"Me?" Mick protested. "I'm not one of them. They look like a bunch of dorks."

"Well, I was just about to say that I like what they're doing," the clerk said. "It's good for the neighborhood."

Talk about this: How do you react when other people figure out you're a Christian?

Even the best followers of Jesus have struggled to speak up for their faith. Peter had boldly promised Jesus that he would never ditch him—no matter what (see Mark 14:29). But as Jesus faced his trial, Peter huddled near a fire outside. He hid his face in the shadows, hoping to see what was happening to Jesus without being spotted as his follower.

There in the darkness, three witnesses said they recognized Peter as a follower of Jesus. And three times Peter denied that he was a friend of Jesus: "I don't know this man you're talking about." When a rooster crowed, Peter remembered how Jesus had predicted his denial earlier that night. Peter broke down and cried (verses 66-72).

We each make choices many times a day about being bold or bashful with our faith. A friend of yours needs a Christian friend to pray and give biblical advice. Do you say anything? Or some Christians at your school want you to join them in praying around the flagpole. Do you let yourself be spotted as part of the group?

If you see yourself as someone who loves Jesus totally, don't settle for being known as a Christian only when it's easy. Ask Jesus to give you the power to step forward and speak wisely for him in every area of life. Step by step, word by word, God wants to give you the power to act and speak with holy boldness!

 TALK: Name a situation where you would like to be bolder. How would you like to act and speak differently for Jesus?

 PRAY: *Lord, we face situations almost every day that tempt us to shrink from admitting we know you. Make us fearless and bold.*

 ACT: Have you ever felt an inner nudge to speak up for Jesus—but pushed it aside? Decide today to let God lead you through those nudges!

30 100 Percent Faithful

Bible Reading: Mark 16:1-11

He has been raised from the dead . . . just as he told you before he died!
Mark 16:6-7

"I meant what I said and I said what I meant. . . . An elephant's faithful one hundred per cent!"

If you're a crazed Dr. Seuss fan, you know those words come from Horton the elephant in *Horton Hatches the Egg*. In this story, a mother bird tells Horton how tired she gets sitting on her egg waiting for it to hatch. Good-hearted Horton agrees to take her place on the nest while the mother bird flies off for a short vacation.

Days pass while Horton keeps watch atop the nest. Over and over Horton is tempted to quit his job, but each time he responds: "I meant what I said and I said what I meant. . . . An elephant's faithful one hundred per cent."

Finally the mother bird returns to the nest, Horton's duty is done, and the baby bird emerges. What's the moral of the story? Like Horton, we should faithfully do what we promise.

That can be hard to do. But God keeps his word perfectly.

Mark 16 opens with the news that Jesus "meant what he said and said what he meant" about coming back to life after his death on the cross. From the disciples' point of view, things looked pretty dark. Their loving teacher had been put to death on a cross. And now they hid for fear that they too would be killed.

Nothing in the Bible tells us the disciples remembered or believed Jesus' prediction in Mark 9:31 that he would rise from the dead. They were "grieving and weeping." When some of the women who had followed Jesus arrived at the tomb, they were astonished to find the huge stone rolled away—and Jesus' body missing! Yet an angel told them that the Savior was alive, "just as he told you before he died" (Mark 16:7). When the disciples heard the news from Mary Magdalene, "they didn't believe her" (verse 11).

If we had watched our friend and leader die on a cross, we would have had a hard time believing he was alive. But Jesus meant what he said. He conquered death, burst out of the tomb, and lives today as Lord and King.

Jesus has never failed to keep a promise. We can rest assured that every promise in Scripture is made by the One who keeps his word 100 percent. And Jesus rising from the dead is our proof. That's a great reason to trust!

 TALK: How does Christ's keeping his promise to rise from the dead make all of his other promises more believable to you?

 PRAY: *God, we believe your Word. Help us to trust you even when the world seems dark.*

 ACT: Do you ever have a hard time taking God at his word? Talk to a more mature Christian about your questions.

31 A Reservation for Your Destination

Bible Reading: Matthew 25:31-46

Come, you who are blessed by my Father, inherit the Kingdom prepared for you from the foundation of the world. Matthew 25:34

"We miss Grandma a lot," Melissa whispered. "It's really sad to think we'll never see her here on earth again." Then Melissa spoke up a little louder. "But we're glad she's in heaven. I'm glad we'll get to see her there!"

Melissa's classmate Amy made a face. "Heaven? I don't see what good it does to believe in heaven," she said. "I think that when you die you're just gone. I mean, where is heaven? Up in the clouds? You can't just hang around up in the air. And how could you believe in hell? There's just a bunch of rocks and lava inside the earth. I hate to be the one to break the news, but you just have to admit that your grandma is gone."

For Melissa to hear that from a girl she counts as her friend is really sad. And what Amy told Melissa is also totally *untrue.*

While the Bible doesn't give a specific location for heaven, it's not make-believe. The Bible teaches that both a *real* heaven and a *real* hell exist.

- *Jesus told his followers he was going to prepare a place for them* (see John 14:2). The apostle John provides some details about heaven, describing it as an incredible place in the presence of God where there will be no more death or tears or pain (see Revelation 21:4). It's a place where God's people will serve him, see him as he is, and be with him forever (see Revelation 22:3-5).
- *God's Word is just as clear that the future holds punishment for evildoers in a place called hell* (see Matthew 25:41). John also describes the punishment waiting for the people who don't know God (see Revelation 21:8). The Bible talks about hell over and over in utterly severe terms as a place that is separated from God, his people, and everything good that he has made.

Unfortunately, not enough people heed the Bible's warning of hell or its promise of heaven. That's why we can't just sit around and wait for God to take us home—because real suffering awaits our friends who don't believe in Christ. But if we have trusted Christ, our future is truly heavenly. Heaven is a real place where we will enjoy being with God and his people forever.

 TALK: Say it in your own words: How would you have responded to Amy? And how would you have offered comfort to Melissa?

 PRAY: Pray for your friends who don't believe in heaven—or hell.

 ACT: Pull out a Bible concordance and look up the references for "heaven" and "hell." What does the Bible teach?

1 A Family Affair

Bible Reading: Romans 1:6-7
God loves you dearly, and he has called you to be his very own people.
Romans 1:7

Even after a tiring trip from the United States to the heart of eastern Europe, the husband and wife were excited to have reached their destination. Now at the Romanian orphanage, they moved carefully between rickety cribs and mattresses set on the floor. The room was dimly lit. The walls, floors, and furniture were less than sparkling clean. The smell of a dozen unchanged diapers clouded the air.

As the couple passed each bed, an infant or toddler eager for love gazed at them. Behind each small face was a sad story of neglect. Tears streamed down the couple's cheeks. They already had five sons at home in America, one of whom was adopted. They had come to Romania to adopt another child. They wished they could bring them all home, but they could take only one. But which one?

Then they saw her, a girl only a few weeks old. She stood out from all the needy children in the room, as if God was pulling the couple to her. After days of working with government officials, the couple left Romania with their sixth child. Tiny Andrea was totally unaware of the miraculous change that had begun in her life.

Andrea today is eight years old. She lives in a loving Christian family with five older brothers and two younger sisters. (Her parents have adopted two more girls!) The care and affection of her new home have wiped away her tragic start in life. And it's all because her dad and mom found her and took her home.

We all have something in common with Andrea. Because sin separated us from God, we came into the world alone. It was like being born in an orphanage. We desperately needed care.

Then God came along—not just to visit, not just to drop off gifts and leave—but to take us home to join his family. He loves us so much that he has invited us to be his very own children.

The change that came into our life was even more remarkable than what Andrea experienced. The apostle Peter put it this way: "Once you were not a people; now you are the people of God" (1 Peter 2:10). When we trusted Christ, we went from having no family to being a member of God's family!

Can you imagine how Andrea will feel someday when she grows to understand what her adoptive parents have done for her? Do you have some of those same feelings when you realize that God has adopted you into his family?

 TALK: How might your life be different if God hadn't adopted you into his family?

 PRAY: *God, we are grateful you have adopted us as your children. Thank you for giving us a home filled with love.*

 ACT: Think of someone who feels lonely and cut off from God. Share with him or her the good news that God adopts us as his children!

2 A Knight to Remember

Bible Reading: Romans 1:16-17
This Good News tells us how God makes us right in his sight. This is accomplished from start to finish by faith. Romans 1:17

It's totally your teacher's fault. If she hadn't forced you to write an essay on "What I Want to Be When I Grow Up," it might never have occurred to you how cool it would be to be a knight. But now you've decided you want to be called Sir Cheese Head—or whatever your name is. You want everybody to bow when you walk into the room.

So you log on to the Internet to find out how to apply. You see that very few people become knights. Only after many years of serving the queen of England will she invite you to Buckingham Palace, knock you on the shoulder three times with a sword, hand you a nifty medal, and—*shazzam!*—make you a knight.

But you have a little problem: If you serve the queen, you can't hang out at the mall anymore. And you're way too busy doing homework and playing computer games to do stuff for the queen. So you decide to cut a few corners on the way to knighthood.

You start passing around your own business cards. In bold letters they say, "Sir Cheese Head—Don't Forget to Bow." You buy some cool knight clothes and get a bunch of official-looking medals at the pawn shop. You tell all your friends, "Call me Sir Cheese Head from now on—or else."

The big question is, are you really a knight? You know the big answer is no!

You can dress like a knight, talk like a knight, act like a knight, swing a sword like a knight, and smell like a knight. But that doesn't make you a knight. If you think otherwise, just try getting into Buckingham Palace with a card that says, "Sir Cheese Head—Don't Forget to Bow."

No one is dumb enough to try that.

But lots of people use the same approach when trying to get close to God. The Bible clearly explains that God makes us right—acceptable to him—and "knights" us—makes us his royal sons and daughters—when we confess our sin and trust him for salvation. Faith, believing and trusting in God, is the only way we become part of God's family.

One reason the Good News of the gospel is *good* news is because God has done everything necessary to make you right and keep you right. When by faith you accept what he has done for you, he welcomes you into his family. You can't invent a title to get in!

 TALK: How do you feel toward a God who loves you enough to make you right by faith—not by your effort—so he can be your Father?

 PRAY: Tell God what you're thinking and feeling about being his son or daughter.

 ACT: Make a poster that reminds you that you're a son or daughter of God—and that you don't have to impress anyone.

3 Getting to Know Him

Bible Reading: Romans 1:18-20

The truth about God is known to them instinctively. God has put this knowledge in their hearts. Romans 1:19

The big day has arrived for the family to head down to the local electronics megastore to watch Dad and Mom spill their wallets on a brand-new computer. It's the one everyone wanted: the XL Hyperflash 6000 Super-Plus. This box comes equipped with enough bytes and gigs and megs to keep a computer geek happy for at least six weeks. It can play CDs and DVDs in HD. It can communicate by phone, fax, and e-mail in sixty different languages and dialects, including pig latin.

A few simple modifications let it run every appliance in the house. It can turn all the lights on and off, take the blender for a spin, flip TV channels, boost your parents' electric blanket up to ten, and nuke burritos in the microwave.

Of course, the Hyperflash 6000 also comes loaded with tons of software—like the Encyclopedia Galactica (the entire knowledge of humankind plus a few alien races), Games-a-Gazillion, and a program for accessing your school's grade records.

Computers are technowonders. They arrive at stores with fully functioning brains. Operating systems and a big selection of software are installed at the factory, so all we have to do is pop open the carton and hook up the hardware. Within minutes we can be playing games, e-mailing friends, or writing the world's next best-selling novel.

But the most advanced computer ever created—or yet to be created—will never beat our brains. The gray, spongy "hardware" crammed inside our cranium isn't much to look at, but the factory-installed "software" is fantastic. Every movement we make, every task we complete, starts in the complex system God built into each of us. God equipped us for life even before we were born.

At the core of our internal operating system is a unique feature we rarely stop to appreciate. It's a built-in capacity to know and relate to our heavenly Father. He put it into every human being. Why? Because God wants us to know him as our loving Father. The God who called us into his family wants us to know him thoroughly. Even our marvelous brain couldn't comprehend God unless he gave us that ability. And he did!

And when we turn to him in faith, it's like he activates that inner program and lets us know him even better. Anybody with half a brain would go for that deal.

 TALK: God created you with a built-in capacity to know him. How much of that capacity are you using?

 PRAY: Thank God that you can know him—and tell him you want to know him better.

 ACT: Make a list of the things you know about God and things you would like to know. Try to find the answer to one of those questions today!

4 Is There an Idol in Your Life?

Bible Reading: Romans 1:21–23

Instead of worshiping the glorious, ever-living God, they worshiped idols made to look like mere people, or birds and animals and snakes. Romans 1:23

Yesenia tilted her head to listen closely as a missionary shared tale after tale from a lifetime of adventures telling people about Jesus in far-off countries. Yesenia squirmed when the missionary said she had tromped through rain forests full of snakes and spiders. She squealed when the missionary admitted she enjoyed eating fish eggs and squid. But Yesenia was downright stumped when the missionary said that the people she served worshiped idols, bowing down and praying to statues they believed were gods. That was the strangest thing Yesenia had ever heard.

As Christians we know that God alone deserves our worship. After all, God welcomes us into his family. He invites us to live as his children. Nobody loves us like he does. Because we know the one true God, we don't bow down to statues of people—or birds or animals or snakes—that are supposed to be gods.

But even so, sometimes our worship gets a little confused. So talk about this: What does "worship" mean?

Worship means to *declare the worth* of something. In fact, that's where the word *worthy* comes from. Something is *worthy* if it's worth a lot. We show what a thing is worth to us by how much it fills our thoughts and time and by how it affects the choices we make. We worship God when our life is full of the thoughts, words, and actions he wants us to have. That happens all through the week, but we make it a special focus when we head to church.

Even though we know that God alone deserves our worship, there can be other things in our life to which we "bow down." We might, for example, let playing computer games or watching TV crowd out our special times with God—opportunities to pray, read the Bible, serve, and sing praises.

We love our sports, our hobbies, our music, and all of our other interests. But if we let an activity rule our thoughts and energy, we are guilty of worshiping an idol. That's as bad as bowing to a statue carved from wood or stone.

We can have only one all-important priority in our life, one thing worth our worship. God gives us all sorts of activities to enjoy. But only God gets to be King!

 TALK: What in your life competes with God for your time, energy, and affection?

 PRAY: Talk to God about things that might get in the way of your worshiping him.

 ACT: Sit down with your weekly schedule and clear out anything that keeps God from being your top priority.

5 He Became One of Us

Bible Reading: Romans 1:1-5

It is the Good News about his Son, Jesus, who came as a man.
Romans 1:3

You're in the supermarket checkout line, waiting patiently while the cashier chats on the phone. Take a vote: Which headline would most tempt you to pick up a tabloid newspaper and read the story?

- "Government Scientist Reports That All Parents Are Space Aliens"
- "My Daughter Is from Mars"
- "Ten-Year-Old Receives Million-Dollar-a-Month Allowance"
- "Jesus Has Returned—Living in Orlando"

You might not be surprised by any of those headlines. But here's one more: "Human Transformed into Ant."

That was actually the theme of a Christian film. No, it wasn't about a missionary sent to preach to a colony of ants. Actually, it was a parable about how Jesus was God born as a human being.

At the start of the film, a man and his adult son tend a lush jungle garden at the top of a mountain. From the base of the mountain rise faint cries. The gardener and his son realize the ants far below are living in hatred and war. The father and son long to bring peace to the ant colony, but they decide that they must visit the colony in a form the ants will understand. The gardener's son agrees to leave the beautiful garden, travel to the bottom of the mountain, and enter the ant colony as—you guessed it—an ant.

This one-of-a-kind ant teaches other ants about the gardener's love for them. Many listen, but the gardener's enemies kill the son. He rises from the dead as a winged ant, returns to his father in the garden, and all the ants who believe in him sprout wings like his. They spread his message of the gardener's love and peace.

Crazy, huh? But it shows how important it was for Jesus to come to earth as a human being like us to make us a part of God's family. If Jesus hadn't left heaven and become a man, we couldn't have become members of God's family. His life, death, and resurrection smashed sin and opened the door to new life through faith.

Think about it: If Jesus hadn't entered our world and provided forgiveness for sin, we would have no way to become God's very own children.

 TALK: How does the story about a man becoming an ant help you understand the price Jesus paid for your sins?

 PRAY: *Jesus, thank you for the steps you took to get close to us. We couldn't know God the Father if you hadn't come to earth.*

 ACT: The next time you see an ant crawling down the sidewalk, squat down and think about what Jesus did for you.

6 Clues to the Big Surprise

Bible Reading: 1 Corinthians 15:1-4

Christ died for our sins, just as the Scriptures said. He was buried, and he was raised from the dead on the third day, as the Scriptures said.
1 Corinthians 15:3-4

Can you remember what it was like to be a tiny tyke at Christmastime?

Nathan's dad helped him pick out a simple gift for his mom. Nathan wrapped the present, the numerous lumps making the gift all the more beautiful. The special gift hadn't been under the tree more than a half hour when Nathan's mom said, "I wonder who this wonderful present is for."

Nathan was too bubbly to keep from babbling: "Mommy, it's for you! *And it's a VeggieTales pot holder!"*

A surprise isn't much of a surprise if somebody tells you about it ahead of time. But sometimes a surprise is way too good to keep to yourself.

God, in fact, had a hard time keeping his secret when he was planning to send Christ to earth to die for us and then rise from the dead. It was a secret God had hidden for a long time. His plan to save the world through Jesus was older than Planet Earth. The apostle Paul wrote, "For [God] chose us in [Jesus] before the creation of the world to be holy and blameless in his sight" (Ephesians 1:4, NIV).

God oozed excitement about his plan and the new life we would receive through it. So centuries before Jesus was born, God burst. He just had to start talking about his surprise. The Old Testament contains hundreds of prophecies about Christ. These detailed statements were spoken hundreds of years before he was born. Jesus would

- be born into the family of David (see 2 Samuel 7:12)
- be born in Bethlehem (see Micah 5:2)
- do miracles (see Isaiah 35:5-6)
- be rejected by his people (see Isaiah 53:3)
- be betrayed by a friend (see Psalm 41:9)
- have his hands and feet pierced (see Psalm 22:16)
- suffer and die for our sins (see Isaiah 53:5)
- rise from the dead (see Job 19:25; Psalm 16:10)
- ascend to heaven (see Psalm 68:18)

God had a surprise he couldn't keep, a plan to bring you close to him now and forever. It was good news that wouldn't keep. It was good news for you.

TALK: Do you feel excited about a God who was so eager to share Christ with you that he couldn't keep silent?

PRAY: Express some of your excitement in a prayer of thanks.

ACT: Do you know someone who doesn't know that God spoke these promises about Jesus hundreds of years before his birth? Go share the good news!

7 Eyewitness Account

Bible Reading: 1 Corinthians 15:5-9

He was seen by more than five hundred of his followers at one time.
1 Corinthians 15:6

Ezra P. Waffle walked into the local police station looking spooked. The eyeballs of the farmer from West Overshoe, Nebraska, were half out of his head, and his white hair stood on end. "One of them flyin' saucers just landed in my cornfield again, Officer," Waffle reported.

The officer bit his lip to keep from laughing. He had been through this a few times before. "So what did it look like this time, Mr. Waffle?"

"'Bout the size of my combine, with little Christmas lights inside."

"The last time you said it looked like the USS *Enterprise.*"

"Yes sir, but that was last time," Ezra clarified. "That was when Captain Picard got out and talked to me."

"And did somebody talk to you this time, Mr. Waffle?"

"Sure did," Ezra said. "'Bout six critters, looked kind of like the Muppets."

"What did these Muppets from outer space want, Mr. Waffle?"

"They wanted some of my corn to take home. I said okay, and then Elmo and Oscar picked a couple of my stalks clean and—*whoosh*—they was gone."

The officer leaned forward, looking serious. "Mr. Waffle, did anybody else see this flying saucer or the Muppet creatures? Your wife? Your kids?"

Ezra shook his head slowly. "By the time I got to the house to tell Bessie Lou, they was long gone into outer space . . . just like Captain Picard and the *Enterprise.*"

You gotta wonder why the flying saucers so many people claim to have seen never land in places like downtown New York City—where millions of people could spot them. It's tough to believe in aliens when they show up to only one or two people at a time.

Jesus wasn't so hard to spot after his resurrection. He didn't just show up for a few folks—he appeared to hundreds in his resurrected body! His victory over the grave wasn't intended to be a secret. He *wanted* his followers to see him alive. He *wanted* people to know that his resurrection was fact—not a crazy made-up story. He *wanted* to make it easy even for us today to believe that the Resurrection is real. Aren't you glad Jesus didn't hide out in a cornfield? He allowed many people to see him so we can *know* he really rose from the dead.

 TALK: Why did God make his plan to save the world so easy to see?

 PRAY: *Thank you, Lord, for working out a plan to save us and for letting so many people see you. Open the eyes of our friends who still haven't seen the truth.*

 ACT: Do you have a friend who thinks that the Resurrection is a crazy, made-up story? Share the real facts with him or her!

8 Whatever Happened to Easter?

Bible Reading: 1 Corinthians 15:17-19

If we have hope in Christ only for this life, we are the most miserable people in the world. 1 Corinthians 15:19

Have you ever wondered what your life would be like if Jesus hadn't risen from the dead? Below are several statements describing what life might be like if Christ had never come out of the tomb. Pick the one statement that would make you the most miserable in a life with no Easter:

- There would be no Easter bunny—and probably no Energizer bunny.
- There would be no such thing as Easter break for students.
- Baskets of jelly beans wouldn't play hide-and-seek with you.
- Chocolate bunnies would never have been invented.
- You wouldn't wonder about the difference between "lint" and "Lent."
- Easter Island, in the South Pacific, might cease to exist.
- You and your friends would have absolutely zero hope of having your sins forgiven and spending eternity in heaven with God.

Did the last one catch you off guard? That's not even funny, is it?

But it's true. If Jesus hadn't come back to life as he promised he would, he would still be dead today. People might stare at his mummified corpse in a museum somewhere—as a curiosity, not a cure for the world's sin.

Almost everyone with a couple years of Sunday school under his or her belt can explain the big points of the New Testament's story of Easter: Jesus was crucified and then rose from the dead on the third day. But we sometimes celebrate the Resurrection without really understanding why it matters.

The Bible clearly explains that it took the Crucifixion *and* the Resurrection to provide our forgiveness. Christ's death paid the *penalty* for sin, but Christ's resurrection freed us from the *power* of sin. If the Savior hadn't burst out of the tomb alive, sin's power would have conquered him *and* us. No wonder Paul said we would be "the most miserable people in the world" if Christ were not alive (1 Corinthians 15:19). We would face all the trials, struggles, and sacrifices of the Christian life—and then die with no hope of heaven. Thank God that he had a better plan!

 TALK: Seriously—and personally: What would your life be like if Jesus had never come to save you from your sin?

 PRAY: *Thank you, Jesus, for dying to pay the penalty for our sins and for coming back to life so that sin need no longer control us. We look forward to living with you forever in heaven someday.*

 ACT: Celebrate the Resurrection by coming up with three reasons why Christ's resurrection really matters to you.

9 It's a Matter of Life and Death—and Life!

Bible Reading: 1 Corinthians 15:21-23

All who are related to Christ . . . will be given new life.
1 Corinthians 15:22

Tex was a very wealthy and well-liked man in his town. When Tex died and his will was read, the family found Tex's plans for his own funeral. More than anything else, he wanted to be buried in his prized possession: a gold-plated, diamond-studded Rolls Royce convertible worth over a million dollars. Tex's family loved him dearly, so they followed his funeral plans exactly.

The big day came and the whole town turned out to view the show. The funeral procession through town to the cemetery included marching bands and Cadillacs full of important people. But the main attraction was the gleaming convertible. Just as he wanted, Tex was propped up in the backseat wearing his most expensive suit. His eyes were glued open and his mouth was pasted in a huge smile. As the chauffeur-driven car came into view, the crowds cheered and clapped wildly for Tex.

Meanwhile, down by the railroad tracks, a stranger hopped off a slow-moving freight train hoping to find something to eat in town. Attracted by the noise on Main Street, the man pushed through the crowd. Seeing the marching bands and carloads of important-looking people pass by, he whistled in amazement.

And when the gold Rolls Royce came into view, the stranger's eyes grew wide. Seeing the grand passenger sitting in the expensive convertible and hearing the wild applause of the crowd, the stranger could contain his excitement no longer. Pointing to Tex, he exclaimed to those around him, "Now that's what I call really living!"

Majorly clueless, wasn't he? Tex had all the appearances of living well, but as he paraded along in the Rolls Royce, he could not have been more dead.

As Christians we are related to Jesus Christ, who conquered death. He has a new life planned for us that is way better than being propped up for a parade.

Physical death isn't the end for us. The resurrection of Christ took care of that. When we trusted him, Christ's resurrection power raised us to life *spiritually*—he promised us eternal life with him in heaven someday. But when Jesus comes back to earth, his resurrection power will raise us to life *physically*. Somehow he will find all of the parts that once made up each of us and will change our remains into a glorious body like his own (see Philippians 3:21). Just as surely as Christ came out of his grave alive, we will come out of the grave alive. It's as certain as Easter.

 TALK: What do you really expect to happen to you when you die? How does the resurrection of Jesus reassure you that your own resurrection will be real?

 PRAY: *Thanks, God, for wanting us to live with you after we die. Thanks for Jesus' resurrection power that makes resurrection possible for each of us.*

 ACT: Tell a friend about this incredible truth!

10 Power Struggle

Bible Reading: 1 Corinthians 15:24-28

God, who gave his Son authority over all things, will be utterly supreme over everything everywhere. 1 Corinthians 15:28

When the powerful king of a tiny island in the South Pacific discovered that his enemies on a distant island were planning an attack by war canoes, he was determined not only to defend his life but to protect his most costly possession: a huge, golden throne that sat in the middle of his grass hut. So the king called in thousands of warriors, armed them with spears, and placed them around his hut. He was sure that no enemy army would be able to get through his defenses.

Just to be on the safe side, the king decided to hide his golden throne. On the night before the enemy war canoes were expected to arrive, he had his strongest warriors lift the thousand-pound throne up onto the wooden rafters of his grass hut and cover it with grass. With his army outside and his throne safely hidden above, the king lay down on his mat and went to sleep.

During the night, the king's warriors were awakened by a loud noise from the king's grass hut. They rushed in to find that the rafters had collapsed under the weight, and the throne had crashed to the floor where the king was sleeping. The king, who had planned his defense so well, was dead.

The moral of the story? "People who live in grass houses shouldn't stow thrones." Ouch. What a silly twist to the old proverb that "people who live in glass houses shouldn't throw stones." However, this story teaches us that even the most powerful people in the world can't control everything. Think about it:

- Bill Gates, the cofounder of Microsoft, is one of the richest men in the world, but he can't buy a cure for cancer.
- Tiger Woods might become the golfer with the most wins of all time, but he can't get away from life's toughest sand traps and water hazards.
- Hillary Clinton could someday become the country's first woman president, but she can't stop wars from happening around the world.

There is only one supreme authority in all of creation: God. No thing or no person has the power, wisdom, or wealth that he does.

The Resurrection proved that God rules over both life and death. When you become a member of God's family by trusting Christ, you become the child of the most powerful person in the universe!

 TALK: Is there anything the God of life and death can't do? Do you have any problem he cannot help you overcome? Of course not—the Resurrection proved it!

 PRAY: *God, thank you that you are big enough to handle all the problems we face today. Use your resurrection power to make us strong.*

 ACT: Do you have a friend facing a problem? How can you help him or her trust God?

Love Who?

Bible Reading: Romans 13:8-10
Love does no wrong to anyone, so love satisfies all of God's requirements. Romans 13:10

Quiz time: Which of these people do you think God wants you to love?

(a) The classmate who broke your niftiest mechanical pencil

(b) The cousin who borrowed your favorite Barbie and shaved her hair off

(c) The art-class bully who dipped his hand in nonwashable blue paint—and then put a print on the back of your favorite shirt

(d) The neighbor who came over to play and broke the original edition Rock 'em Sock 'em Robots game you inherited from your dad

(e) The friend who shared Twinkies with you when you forgot your lunch on an all-day field trip

It's easier to love your friends. Especially a friend with whom you've formed a sugary-sweet bond. Yet Jesus didn't say: "Only love the people who toss you Twinkies at lunch." He doesn't allow us to limit our loving to our friends, people we like, or people who are nice to us.

We owe a heap of love to everyone!

The Bible puts it this way: "Pay all your debts, except the debt of love for others. You can never finish paying that!" (Romans 13:8).

And that passage tells us exactly what love looks like: Romans 13:9-10 says we're showing love when other people's happiness, security, spiritual growth, and physical health is as important to us as our own.

Ephesians 5:29 fills out how we can love ourselves and others: "For no one ever hated his own flesh, but *nourishes* and *cherishes* it, just as the Lord does the church" (NKJV, emphasis added). We nourish our body when we watch out for its happiness, security, spiritual growth, and physical health. We cherish our body when we guard it from anything harmful and destructive.

That's the same kind of love God wants you to have for others. If you truly love yourself like God intended, you'll want to grow your body, spirit, brain, and relationships. You'll guard yourself from anything that gets in the way. And if you truly love others, you'll work to make sure nothing hinders the happiness, security, spiritual growth, or physical health of any of the people God puts in your life!

TALK: How can you nourish and cherish your friends God's way?

PRAY: *God, help us to love everyone around us—and to nourish them the same way we nourish ourselves.*

ACT: Do one "nourishing" thing for a friend, family member, or someone you've needed to forgive in the past.

12 What You Do for Love

Bible Reading: 1 John 4:16–21
Perfect love expels all fear. 1 John 4:18

Marty wanted to win the love of all the people in his world. So he came up with this list reminding him exactly what he needed to do to win people's attention and affection:

- His gym teacher would carry him around school on his shoulders if he won the mile run in the school Olympics.
- The school librarian would quit giving him the evil eye if he would return *Pet Tricks for Iguanas,* the book he lost before Christmas.
- His video-game-crazed neighbor would think he was ultracool if he could beat the forty-eighth level of *Snowboarder Mayhem.*
- His language arts teacher would dance on her desk if he scored an A on his grammar assignment.
- His violin instructor would pull out his earplugs if he played in the right key.

Talk about it: Do you think Marty actually needed to do those things to feel loved? Why—or why not?

There's no doubt Marty *felt* he had to do those things to be lovable. But the *fact* is he doesn't have to do any of those things to be loved. God loves him no matter how he looks, what he does, or whether he ever unearths *Pet Tricks for Iguanas.*

When we were newborn babies, we liked to sleep and gulp milk. But we also longed to be held and cuddled. We *ached* to be loved. It's as if we had a "love tank" inside us that needed to be filled. And if our capacity for love wasn't met, we experienced hunger pangs. The more empty we were, the more hungry we became for love.

All of us still have a love tank. We still need it pumped full. But we don't have to wonder how and where to get our love tanks filled.

Hopefully you experience the unconditional love of your family and friends. Unconditional love accepts you for just being you—it squeezes you silly and says, "No matter what you do, I will always love you just for being you!"

But the first source for filling your love tank is the unconditional, perfect love that comes from Jesus. He has the kind of love for you that lasts and lasts. It takes away your fear that no one will ever love you just the way you are. And no matter what, you can count on that love to be there for you.

 TALK: How can we fill up our love tank? How can we help each other feel loved?

 PRAY: *God, fill us with your unconditional, perfect love for each other.*

 ACT: If your love tank is on empty today, open your heart to God's love right now. Spend some time praying and in his Word.

103

13 God on Patrol

Bible Reading: Psalm 16:1-11

You will show me the way of life, granting me the joy of your presence and the pleasures of living with you forever. Psalm 16:11

Quiz time for kids: Name an event you think would put a knot in the stomach of a parent. You have twelve seconds to guess. *Go!*

Your parents could bore you for hours with all sorts of adult worries. But somewhere on their list of uncheerful moments might be this: *getting pulled over by the police for speeding.*

They see the flash of lights in the rearview mirror.

They hear the *whoo-whoo-whoo* of a siren.

They watch the officer walk to the car, one hand holding a pad of tickets.

Parents don't like watching money fly away as they pay the ticket. They hate thinking about the wad of cash they'll lose when the price of their car insurance goes up. Getting a ticket is guaranteed to ruin their day. (Hint: It's not a good time to ask for a raise in allowance.)

If getting a ticket makes a few days miserable, here's something that could ruin your whole life: thinking that God is a big, mean, cosmic cop.

Lots of people think God is like a police officer, always monitoring us with his radar detector, not to keep the roads safe, but to nab anyone who looks like he or she might be speeding over the "fun limit." (And they figure God's fun limit is *really* low.)

They picture him talking like this. "Hey, you!" he snarls. "Yeah, you! You look like you're having fun over there. Well, cut it out! We'll have no more of that. Not while I'm on patrol."

Talk about it: Have you ever thought that God just wanted to spoil your fun?

The same folks who see God as the ultimate bad guy imagine the devil as a fun-loving cartoon who sits on our shoulders and wants us to enjoy ourselves. That's a lie. The devil isn't interested in making sure we have fun. He hates our guts. Peter says that the devil is always "looking for some victim to devour" (1 Peter 5:8).

So don't think of the devil as a fun dude just waiting to fill your life with excitement. Jesus dashed that myth when he said, "The thief's [devil's] purpose is to steal and kill and destroy" (John 10:10).

God's goal for our life is the exact opposite. Jesus said, "My purpose is to give life in all its fullness" (John 10:10). God wants nothing less for us than to experience a life jam-packed with joy.

 TALK: What does it mean to experience the full and joyful life Jesus promised?

 PRAY: *God, we know that you planned for us to have a joyful life. Help us to experience your best, within your wise boundaries.*

 ACT: Think of a way to show someone today that God wants Christians to have a full, fun-filled life.

14 Getting Personal with "The Force"

Bible Reading: Proverbs 8:17-21

I love all who love me. Those who search for me will surely find me.
Proverbs 8:17

Talk about this: When have you heard someone describe God in a way that doesn't match what the Bible says?

Here's one you've probably heard: Remember the first three *Star Wars* movies? Luke Skywalker was the big hero. In the first movie, Skywalker meets Obi-Wan Kenobi and learns that he was the Jedi knight who had fought in the Clone Wars with Luke's father. Obi-Wan gives Luke a light saber that once belonged to Luke's father and, in the course of the conversation, mentions "The Force."

"The Force?" Luke says.

Obi-Wan responds, "The Force is what gives the Jedi his power. It's an energy field created by all living things. It surrounds and penetrates us. It binds the galaxy together."

The idea of The Force sounds spookily familiar—and not just because we hear about it over and over throughout the *Star Wars* movies. The Force is what many people imagine God to be. They picture God as faceless, formless energy.

That's a way-off idea about God. It's a myth. Think hard about these truths:

- God created, surrounds, and guides the universe.
- God is present everywhere.
- God is spirit.
- God is *not* some mysterious, elusive energy force out there somewhere.
- Most importantly, God is not a *thing* or an *it*—he is a person.

Read again Proverbs 8:17 at the top of this page. Notice all the personal pronouns God uses to refer to himself: "I . . . me . . . me . . . me." Does that sound like some kind of cosmic energy talking?

God, the true God, is *personally* interested in you. He knows your name. "See," he said to his people, "I have written your name on my hand" (Isaiah 49:16). "He cares about what happens to you," the apostle Peter said (1 Peter 5:7). Jesus said that "the very hairs on your head are all numbered" (Matthew 10:30). And God promised that "when you pray, I will listen. If you look for me in earnest, you will find me when you seek me. I will be found by you" (Jeremiah 29:12-14). Those are personal promises that could only come from a loving, personal God.

 TALK: The Bible is clear that God is so much more than a force. How would you explain to a friend why it matters that God is personal?

 PRAY: *God, thank you for being a personal God who is involved in each one of our lives.*

 ACT: Jot down a list of other ways you have seen and heard people misunderstand who God is. Talk about how you might answer each misunderstanding.

15 This Machine Is Out of Order

Bible Reading: 1 John 3:21-24

If our conscience is clear, we can come to God with bold confidence. And we will receive whatever we request because we obey him and do the things that please him. 1 John 3:21-22

"Okay, God, I'm going to give you a chance to prove yourself." Mark knelt beside his bed. He really wanted to believe in God. So he bowed his head and prayed hard.

"I really want to believe in you, God. So when I wake up in the morning, if there's a billion dollars under my bed, I'll know you're real. And I'll never doubt you again."

Guess what? Mark didn't get the billion dollars.

Maybe God turned him down because he wanted it in one-dollar bills—and a billion dollars wouldn't fit under the bed with all the action figures, dirty clothes, and dust bunnies taking up so much space.

Maybe not. A more likely reason Mark didn't get the money was because he had a goofed-up idea about God. He thought God was a heavenly candy machine: Deposit a prayer, push the right button, and out pops your wish. All he had to do was pray hard enough, and God would plop down everything he could ever want.

It's not a surprise when a kid thinks that way, because lots of adults also think of God as the Divine Candy Machine.

God loves to answer prayer. He said, "Ask me and I will tell you some remarkable secrets" (Jeremiah 33:3). He even promised, "While they are still talking to me about their needs, I will go ahead and answer their prayers!" (Isaiah 65:24).

But prayer isn't a coin to plunk into a candy machine, and faith isn't a button you bang on. God doesn't answer every human whim and wish.

See, God isn't a heavenly vending machine who passes out gifts and favors. He thinks bigger than our small, sometimes selfish human wishes. God is totally powerful and totally loving, and he longs for his children to return the love he has heaped on us. He wants us to love *him,* not the stuff he can give us. He wants us to want *him,* not answers to our greedy prayers.

This may seem strange, but it's true: When we quit thinking of God as a heavenly vending machine, we can be confident we will receive what we ask from God— not because we've punched a button and can expect him to produce, but because we *obey his commands* and *do what pleases him.* We know how to ask for his very best for us. That's the promise of 1 John 3:22!

 TALK: God always wants to hear about your hurts, needs, and desires. But how can you change your prayers so you don't treat God like a candy machine?

 PRAY: *Lord, we don't want to ask you for anything right now. We just want to tell you that we love you.*

 ACT: Take your mind off your own wishes by taking extra time to pray for a friend today.

Taking a Stand When You Would Rather Take a Seat

Bible Reading: Matthew 5:10-12
God blesses those who are persecuted because they live for God.
Matthew 5:10

When Jamie's Sunday school teacher asked who was sure they would go to heaven—and why—Jamie shot up her hand.

Jamie thought it was a simple question. In a few sentences she explained how Christ had died for her sins and that through faith she had trusted him and begun a forever friendship with God.

When Jamie finished talking, she glanced around. The rest of the class stared at her. Their jaws dropped. They were shocked that she had willingly answered the teacher's important spiritual question.

Suddenly Jamie felt like the only kid in her Sunday school class willing to be known as a Christian. Her face flushed with embarrassment. When her teacher thanked her for the great answer, Jamie's red cheeks looked ready to burst.

If you jumped up on a lunch table at a public school and started to preach while your classmates ate, you could predict you would get laughed at—and chased down by a lunch monitor. Yet sometimes even Christians will give you the evil eye for doing the right thing. Anyone willing to stand up and be counted as a Christian sooner or later will be *persecuted*—treated badly for his or her beliefs.

But God has an unusual response for you to try the next time you get mocked for being a Christian. He wants you to throw a party! How come? You're *blessed*.

That word *blessed*, believe it or not, actually means to be happy.

How strange is that? Being happy for being made fun of—or worse? What sort of weirdo likes to be embarrassed?

But Jesus says we can feel honored if we suffer for him.

When we stand up for God and what's right, we'll get the support of most Christians and even gain the respect of some non-Christians. On the other hand, being blessed won't automatically make life easy. People watch us. Some tease. Others pick us apart if we do the least little thing wrong.

If it comes down to winning a popularity contest or winning the pleasure of Jesus, shoot for pleasing Jesus every time. Sometimes doing the right thing hurts. But be encouraged. If friends reject you because you take a stand, it's not really you they're rejecting. It's Christ.

TALK: Have you ever been made fun of or left out for something you said or did because you were following Jesus? How did God, your family, and good Christian friends help you deal with it?

PRAY: *God, we want to stand up for you. But we need your wisdom to know when and how to do that best. We want you to teach us!*

ACT: Take a chance today: Speak up when your beliefs as a Christian give you something worth saying.

17 Finding the Road to Freedom

Bible Reading: 1 Corinthians 10:12-13

When you are tempted, he will show you a way out so that you will not give in to it. 1 Corinthians 10:13

Okay. Everyone close your eyes—except the person reading, of course.

Picture yourself walking down a road on the way to the beach. The scenery is stunning and the weather is great. As you round a bend, you see a fork in the road. The road to the right is narrow and heads straight uphill. The road to the left is wide and runs downhill. Your map clearly shows that the road to the right is the one that will get you to the beach, but from where you stand the only thing you see up that way is a hard climb. That road on the left looks like you could take a flying leap and slide on your backside all the way to the bottom.

Open your eyes and talk about this: Which road do you pick? How come?

Now listen to how that applies to following Jesus.

As we walk through life, we stand at many forks in the road. Each fork is a choice. When it comes to being a disciple of Jesus, our correct choice is always the path that keeps us doing good and living close to Jesus.

That means we need to recognize when we stand at a point of decision—at a fork. Think about what forks in the road can look like in your own life:

Places. Most of us go to certain places where we get into trouble. Maybe it's the friend's house where we always tease a little sister until she cries. Or the playground where fights happen. Or the store where we're tempted to steal a candy bar. Those are forks in the road. If we know we're in for a bad situation, why go there?

People. God wants us to reach out to everyone. But there are people we might not be able to handle—who parents call "bad influences." Sometimes a friendship is a fork in the road, a choice between God's way and a bad way. If you always get in trouble when you're with a particular friend, it might be time to stop spending time with that person.

Possessions. Books, magazines, clothes, and video games can take us far away from Christ if we play with evil stuff or make good stuff more important than Christ. We're at a fork in the road each time we choose to tune in to good or turn off bad.

Even if you head down the wrong road, it's never too late to turn around and get back on God's path of doing good. But the better choice is to head down the right path as soon as you reach a fork in the road.

 TALK: What people, places, and possessions make it hard for you to follow God? What makes choosing the right road hard? Why should you pick God's path?

 PRAY: *God, help us see the danger areas in our life. Help us to make the right choice when we come to forks in the road.*

 ACT: Keep track today of how many forks you come to—choices between right and wrong. How does God help you make the right choice?

18 Keeping Your Head above Water

Bible Reading: 1 Peter 2:11-12

Be careful how you live among your unbelieving neighbors. 1 Peter 2:12

Last night Amber and three friends had a sleep-over. For six whole hours they bashed one of the girls from school. No, they didn't thump her over the head with bricks. In fact, she wasn't even at the sleep-over. But their words hurt her nonetheless. They slammed this girl's weight, her hair, and her choice of clothes. Oh—they also laughed at her total inability to do long division. In the morning Amber wished she had walked away when the gossip started, but she just couldn't. Now she felt bad about all the hurtful things she said.

What Amber experienced is the feeling you get when you're swept away by a current too strong to resist. Swimming against a current for very long takes more strength than any of us can muster. If you've ever tried to swim in a river, you know it's easier just to relax and go with the flow. The right flow can give you a wildly fun ride. The problem is, the wrong flow can sweep you away—forever—even when your fingertips are just inches from shore.

Friends are like that flow, wearing down even the strongest swimmer. Sooner or later we go the direction our friends are going.

Talk about it: How is hanging out with the wrong people like getting swept away by a bad current? Why is it important that your closest friends pull you in the right direction?

Surrounding yourself with the right kinds of friends—friends who challenge you to live your whole life for Christ—is how you grow as a Christian.

Amber would have felt a whole lot different in the morning if she had made a different choice the night before. If she had stopped talking about her classmate as soon as the slamming started, she might have fewer friends—or maybe they would have decided to do the right thing. Either way, Amber wouldn't have had to get straightened out with Jesus. And those friends would have seen Amber acting out God's love.

If friends pull us in the wrong direction, it's time to get out of that group—as hard as that can be. First Peter 2:12 says that if we keep our behavior excellent, our friends might one day glorify God. If our friends drag us in the wrong direction and we do wrong, our friends won't ever see a difference between our life and theirs. And if they see no difference, they have no reason to become followers of Christ themselves. Wouldn't you like to stay alive in Christ—and help your friends discover life too?

 TALK: How can we pick friends who don't pull us the wrong way?

 PRAY: *God, help us choose friends who keep us safe and strong. And help us show your love to people who need to see it.*

 ACT: Ask your family to name a friend they think is pulling you the *right* way. Spend time with that friend today.

April

19 Deal with It and Keep Moving On

Bible Reading: Psalm 32:3-7

I confessed all my sins to you and stopped trying to hide them.
Psalm 32:5

Suppose that three months ago you chose to live totally for God. And since that day you've lived for Jesus in a no-compromise way. That was before today.

Kicking the stitching out of a soccer ball seemed like a good way to unwind and get rid of your frustration after your horrible day. So you kicked the ball once. Twice. About a thousand times. And with each shot, you took target practice on the tulips growing against the garage of the nice old lady next door.

You blew it. You know it. So what are you going to do about it?

Talk about it: What could you do to make things right if you hammered the heads off your neighbor's prized tulips?

We can't put flowers back together. But we can start by saying we're sorry. We can help pick up the mess we made. And the moment we realize we've blown it, we have another huge job. We need to talk to God about our disobedience.

When we confess our sin, we admit to God that we've done wrong. We tell him we want nothing to do with sinning again. And when we ask for God's forgiveness, we can be sure we receive it. Listen to the promise of 1 John 1:8-9: "If we say we have no sin, we are only fooling ourselves and refusing to accept the truth. But if we confess our sins to him, he is faithful and just to forgive us and to cleanse us from every wrong." Every wrong. Gone!

When we admit our sins to God, we can be sure that everything is right between us and God. Trying to hide sin from God is a bad idea. In the psalm you read today, you saw that King David knew what it was like not only to have done wrong but also to have tried to hide his sins from God. He felt weak and miserable.

Hiding sin is uncomfortable. But a fantastic thing happens when we get our sin straightened out with God. He helps us change! It doesn't honor God for his children to go around trimming other people's tulips with a soccer ball. So when he forgives us, he sends us spiritual power through the Holy Spirit, who helps us overcome our tendency to sin. As Galatians 5:16 says, "Live according to your new life in the Holy Spirit. Then you won't be doing what your sinful nature craves."

When you blow it, admit it and allow God to change you. Then you're really letting Jesus have control of your life!

 TALK: How does God help us when we get sin straightened out with him?

 PRAY: Invite the Holy Spirit today to remake every area of your life.

 ACT: Have you made any messes lately that you haven't cleaned up—with God or other people? Confess your wrongs to God and ask him how to move ahead.

20 Living on the Edge

Bible Reading: Romans 12:1-2

Don't copy the behavior and customs of this world, but let God transform you into a new person by changing the way you think.
Romans 12:2

Several hundred years ago in England, the king was choosing drivers for his royal horse-drawn coach. He asked each driver a question: "If you were driving me on a winding mountain road, how close could you come to the edge of the road without going over?"

The first driver boasted, "I'm an excellent driver, Your Majesty. I could drive your coach within eighteen inches of the edge at top speed and not go over."

The second driver bragged, "My skill and experience are unmatched, Your Majesty. I could drive your coach to within six inches of the edge."

But the third driver responded, "I would take no chances with your safety, Your Majesty. I would drive the coach as far away from the edge as possible."

The king chose the third driver. He was the only one more interested in the king's safety than in showing off.

There's an attitude that shows up in a lot of people, young and old: "I want to see how close to the edge I can get without getting into trouble." The only thing they want to know about school is, "How little can I work?" Their one puzzle about getting along with parents is, "How sneaky can I be?" Their one question about keeping their life organized is, "How messy can my room get?" And when it comes to serving God, they wonder, "How much sin can I get away with?"

People who are useful to God have the attitude of the third driver. They think, "To honor my God, I will see how *far* away from the edge I can stay."

The battle between good and evil takes place inside of us. According to Romans 12:2, your mind is the battlefield. To be different, you have to be renewed in your mind—you have to think the way Jesus does. Lose the war there, and you lose it in your actions. If you let thoughts about doing bad things run through your mind, for example, it becomes easy to give in to the least little pressure to do wrong. But if you fill your brain with thoughts of doing good and following God, your actions will become more and more like Christ's. You'll be transformed!

If you want to live for God you won't just let him change your *behavior*. You'll allow him to remake you from the *inside out*.

 TALK: What do you think of your God—who helps change you from the inside out?

 PRAY: *God, change our life from the inside out. Help us think differently so we act in a way that pleases you.*

 ACT: Do you have areas in your life where you try to see how close to the edge you can get? If you're not sure, your parents or another family member may be able to tell you. Talk with God about how he would like to change that!

21 Your Infinite Value

Bible Reading: 1 Peter 1:18-19

> *God paid a ransom to save you. . . . He paid for you with the precious lifeblood of Christ, the sinless, spotless Lamb of God. 1 Peter 1:18-19*

Several centuries ago, a scholar named Morena was forced from his home. Living in poverty in Lombardy, Italy, Morena became very ill. He was taken to a hospital for the poor. The doctors, assuming that the wretched-looking patient was uneducated, began speaking in Latin among themselves at his bedside. They said, "This worthless creature is going to die anyway, so let us try an experiment on him."

Morena knew Latin almost as well as his native language. Summoning his strength, he raised himself up and said to the surprised doctors, "How can you call 'worthless' someone for whom Christ died?" Right on.

It isn't tough to look around your world and see all the ways people decide how much someone is worth:

- A baseball team decides a player is worth tens of millions of dollars throughout his playing career.
- A soldier in combat discovers he is worth a human life when another soldier takes a bullet to save him.
- A mom with very little money finds she is worth the efforts of volunteers who spend days repainting her broken-down house.

But as Morena clearly understood, our greatest value as Christians comes from the fact that God the Father allowed Jesus Christ—his sinless Son—to die for our sins. In 1 Peter 1:18-19, the apostle Peter said that no amount of silver or gold could compare to that sacrifice. Jesus declared what we are worth when he said, "The greatest love is shown when people lay down their lives for their friends" (John 15:13).

In God's eyes, you were worth the death of his Son. While you were stuck in your sin and at war with God, there was nothing about you to attract God or to cause him to send his Son to die for you (see Romans 5:8). You weren't righteous. You weren't good. You were a sinner, the total opposite of the perfect Lamb. But God saw you as lovable, and your value skyrocketed when Jesus gave up his life for you.

No matter what your value is to others in earthly terms, you are eternally priceless because of the price the Father lovingly paid for you.

 TALK: Why are all people worth treating with respect? What does that have to do with respecting yourself?

 PRAY: *God, give us an understanding of our value to you. Help us to see that you have made each of us more valuable than all the silver and gold in the world.*

 ACT: Think of the people you've looked down on as less than valuable. What can you do for one of those folks today to prove his or her great worth to you and to God?

22 If You Were the Only One

Bible Reading: 1 Corinthians 6:18-20

You do not belong to yourself, for God bought you with a high price.
1 Corinthians 6:19-20

Terese shrugged whenever she heard anyone talk about how Jesus' death for her proved his love. She felt lost in a crowd. "Sure, Jesus died for my sins," she protested, "but he didn't die for me alone. He died for the whole world. I'm just one among bazillions of people who received God's gift of forgiveness."

Talk about it: Do you ever feel like Jesus' death for you doesn't really tell you how much God loves you—because you were one person out of so many?

Yes, you were one believer among millions. But that doesn't make you worth a nickel less to God! And here's why: If you were the only person on the planet, Christ still would have died for you!

The Bible proves that point: When God made his promise to rescue human beings from sin, there were only *two people* on earth. Right after Adam and Eve sinned, God promised to crush Satan's head. (God was talking about the victory Christ's death on the cross would bring—see Genesis 3:15.) Now here's where *you* come in. If you had been the one in the Garden of Eden—instead of Adam and Eve—you too would have disobeyed God. And you also would have received God's great promise to save you. Guaranteed.

Terese knew the Cross was about sin and forgiveness. But she hadn't ever thought about *why* God bothered to send Jesus to die for her—why God thought it was worth the mind-boggling price of his Son for Terese to be forgiven. *It was all because she was lovable.*

That's huge news for all of us, because Terese isn't the only valuable child of God. You too are worth the death of his Son. Do you doubt that? Then listen to the Bible. You can read in 1 Corinthians 6:19-20: "You do not belong to yourself, for God bought you with a high price." Now try that verse on for size in a personal way. Say it aloud to yourself a few times and let it soak into your brain. "I am so valuable to God that he bought me at a high price."

How does it feel to know that God loves you enough to have paid an enormous price for you—not because of anything you have done, but just because he finds you valuable? God says, "You are valuable." What do *you* say about how much you are worth?

 TALK: Explain it in your own words: How do you know that Christ's death says you are highly valuable to him?

 PRAY: *God, we appreciate the value you give us. And we're thankful for the proof of our value you provided by sending your Son to die for us.*

 ACT: You have a friend who needs to hear this good news. Pass it on!

23 Who Gets into Your World?

Bible Reading: Philippians 2:5-11
*Christ Jesus . . . took the humble position of a slave and appeared in
human form. Philippians 2:5, 7*

Little Lucas went bananas when his favorite uncle came to visit. Uncle Miguel practically dove through the door to hit the floor and play with Lucas. Uncle Miguel knew how to build towering Lego skyscrapers. He gave superhero action figures even more superpowers. He made cool army-guy noises and car noises and all sorts of other unique noises. And Uncle Miguel never got tired of playing with Lucas.

No matter how grown up you get, you need adults to show interest in your activities and concerns. Your need for attention is met when a caring adult leaves the grown-up world for a period of time and gets into your world.

God intends for us to get that kind of attention showered on us through our families. When we receive that attention, we know that we matter to others—and to God. We feel significant. We feel like we are worth spending time on.

No matter how much love we feel at home, however, we still need to know this fact: Jesus Christ left his world—heaven—and entered our world—sinful earth—to demonstrate that he loves us. While he deserved to be seated way up high on the throne of heaven, he became a human being so he could crawl around on the floor with us. That's the message of Philippians 2:5-8. God is the One who meets your need for attention.

God is still paying attention to you and your world. Listen to these facts:

- God values you so highly that he sticks with you day by day in the person of the Holy Spirit (see John 14:16).
- God knows every detail about you. He knew you before you were born (see Psalm 139:13-16).
- God knows all about your hassles. He invites you to "give all your worries and cares to God, for he cares about what happens to you" (1 Peter 5:7).
- God couldn't be closer. Moment by moment, he's right here with you. He's so close that one of Christ's names is Immanuel, which means "God with us" (Matthew 1:23, NIV).

As you let these truths flood your mind and heart, you'll have a new view of you. You'll begin to see yourself as you really are: a person of great value and worth.

 TALK: How has Jesus showered incredible attention on you? What does that say about how much he loves you?

 PRAY: Ask God for his help in seeing yourself as he sees you.

 ACT: Memorize a verse that reminds you how much you're worth to God.

24 Forgive and Forget

Bible Reading: Psalm 103:8-13

[The Lord] has not punished us for all our sins, nor does he deal with us as we deserve. Psalm 103:10

When James pried his little brother's fingers off the jungle gym, he had no idea how badly he would hurt Eddie. All he knew was that his squirmy sidekick was not leaving him alone to play with his older friends. But as Eddie dropped from the top of the jungle gym, he struck three bars before landing in sand. A week after his fall, he still has a knot on his forehead and five more weeks in a leg cast.

Eddie won't talk to James. Sometimes Dad and Mom yell at James; sometimes they stare at him silently through squinty, angry eyes. James cries himself to sleep every night, and he's beginning to wonder if anyone loves him anymore. He's even wondering if God can forgive him for what he did.

James is confused. He caused his family and himself some huge hurts. James worries his sin is too enormous for God's love to cover. Yet the truth is that Jesus came into the world to die for James's sins—*all* of them—including hurting Eddie.

If you want to measure the enormous size of God's forgiveness, look at the life of King Manasseh, one of Judah's most evil kings. Manasseh turned his back on God and led the nation into worshiping false gods (see 2 Chronicles 33:1-9). When Judah's enemies captured him along with the rest of the nation, Manasseh humbled himself before God and prayed (see verses 12-13). Despite Manasseh's evil past, God forgave him. Manasseh no doubt returned home seeing himself more as God saw him: worth being forgiven.

If God was able to forgive Manasseh's staggering sins, James can surely count on God's ability to forgive the wrongs he's done.

Sooner or later most of us see ourselves like James—way beyond forgiveness. But what matters is how God sees us. King David sinned greatly. But as David wrote in the passage you read, the size of God's love meant he wasn't beyond forgiveness. David grabbed hold of God's unlimited forgiveness and discovered the worth God saw in him.

God's forgiveness is like a bottomless checking account. When we sin, there's always enough money in God's account to cover any withdrawal. Truth is, we can't empty God's account of forgiveness. When we draw on God's resources, we can't bounce a check. Every sin we confess, he forgives.

 TALK: Feeling bad about your sins is normal. But are you letting bad feelings cloud the fact that God will forgive you? How are you going to grab hold of God's forgiveness?

 PRAY: *God, thanks for forgiving us yesterday, today, and always.*

 ACT: Share the great size of God's forgiveness with a friend.

25 A Safe Place for You

Bible Reading: Psalm 46:1-7
God is our refuge and strength, always ready to help in times of trouble.
Psalm 46:1

Chelsea knew she was in for a tough time when she moved from Alabama to Montana. Sure enough, as the one girl in her school with a Southern twang, she was treated like a new toy for a couple of days—and then tossed aside when people went back to their old friends.

Two months after moving to her new home, she's sitting alone. Her eyes sometimes look angry, but most of the time she just looks sad.

Know it or not, all around you are people drowning in disappointment or the really deep dumps called "depression." They feel lonely, even afraid. They can be family members. Friends. Classmates. Older people. Christians. Non-Christians.

Talk about it: Who do you know who needs a friend who "is always loyal, . . . born to help in time of need" (Proverbs 17:17)? Why do those folks need a friend right now?

If you want to be a friend "born to help in time of need," you start by being one thing: *available*.

So what exactly does it mean to be an available friend? Vote on which of the following phrases tell you someone is there when you need them:

(a) "You got yourself into this mess. Now *you* need to figure a way out."
(b) "I'm really concerned about you. What's going on?"
(c) "Here's a quarter. Call someone who cares."
(d) "I'm going to be here for you, no matter what."

Here's the truth: Being available means you are interested enough in people to take time to listen to them and actually care about what happens in their world.

Jesus is the ultimate example of an ever present friend, and you see his absolute availability best when he helps hurting people. The woman Jesus spoke to at the well in John 4 was a total outcast. The woman caught in sin in John 8 was a nobody to everyone else, but Jesus was available to care for her. Lepers were despised by society, but in Luke 17 Jesus was available to heal ten of them.

God will always be there for you. He will never fail you. And when he shows you that kind of friendship, he makes you able to be that kind of friend to others too.

 TALK: How does it make you feel to know that the God of the universe is available to you when you need him?

 PRAY: *Thanks, God, for always being available to us.*

 ACT: Ask God to show you where and how to be an available friend this week.

26 Being There When Your Friends Are Down

Bible Reading: Galatians 6:1-5
Share each other's troubles and problems. Galatians 6:2

"I'm really frustrated with this friend," Jamal fumed. "His parents are divorcing, but he hardly talks about it. It's like he has to handle his problems totally on his own.

That's a problem you face when you want to be an available friend. People seldom blurt out, "I need help." But you can be sure it's time to be an available friend when someone talks or acts in a way that shows any of these major signs:

- *Disappointment.* Robert was severely disappointed when he didn't make the traveling baseball team but several of his buddies did. You're seeing disappointment when a friend's hopes or expectations aren't met. Many disappointments are small—but they sting.
- *Discouragement.* Kathi's disappointments with her struggles at school piled up until she felt like she was under a mound of discouragement. You're seeing discouragement when a friend's hope and confidence shrink and he or she doesn't seem to care as much about life.
- *Depression.* Simon's discouragement over his family situation slid into long periods of gloominess, sadness, and pulling away from others. Those are all signs of depression.

People weighed down with disappointment, discouragement, and depression might be all around you—yet you still might not spot them.

Why? Well, how good are you at hiding your true feelings? Even if you spill everything you think and feel, many students don't. Like Jamal's friend, they cover up and bottle up. But the more you become known as a caring person available to others, the more those friends will open up and share their feelings. You can learn to spot when someone is down by looking for those signs mentioned above. And you can always ask someone, "How are you *really* doing?"

There's no doubt that God invites your hurting friends to tell him their cares and troubles (see 1 Peter 5:7). Because God cares about our disappointments, discouragement, and depression, he promises to help (see Hebrews 4:16). But God has another strategy to help: putting *you* into the lives of struggling friends.

You won't be able to solve all of a friend's problems. You often will need to ask an adult for help—especially when a friend dips into discouragement, and always when a friend seems depressed. But you can always be a listening ear.

 TALK: Who in your world needs you right now to be an available friend? What can you do for that person?

 PRAY: *God, we want to show your care and love to our hurting friends. We want to be available friends.*

 ACT: Make a concrete plan as a family to reach out to a hurting friend.

April 27 — Be-Attitudes for Friends

Bible Reading: Ecclesiastes 4:9-12

A person standing alone can be attacked and defeated, but two can stand back-to-back and conquer. Ecclesiastes 4:12

"When my mom had cancer, my Sunday school teacher took a lot of time for me," Trisha recalls. "I don't know how I would have gotten through everything without her help. My mom couldn't pay much attention to me, but Sheila listened. She made me feel like I mattered."

Talk about it: When you are hurting, what do you need in a true friend?

Friendship isn't so much about *doing* things as it is about *being* someone. Doing nice things for your friends is important, but doing feels fake unless it flows from who you are as a true friend.

Available friends have three don't-leave-home-without-them qualities:

First, *an available friend shows interest.* You actually care about your friend and what he or she faces—enough to put time into your friendship and get involved in your friend's world. To show interest in your friend, don't make your friend fight for space in your schedule. Speak up. Say to your friend, "I'm here for you, and with God's help we'll get through this together."

Second, *an available friend listens.* That means more than just digging out your earwax. Listening is how you understand what your friend is feeling. If you don't really listen, the time you spend with your friend doesn't mean much. Make sure you understand. Ask questions like, "What do you mean by that?" or "Why is that important to you?" to draw your friend out. Don't interrupt your friend or jump in to finish his or her sentences.

Third, *an available friend is safe.* Friends won't open up if they fear that you'll blab whatever they share. Being safe means keeping information private. Promise your friends you won't share what they tell you unless they want you to. Mean it. And keep your word. If it's something that an adult needs to know, such as if your friend is being hurt by someone, offer to go with your friend to tell an adult. Don't share secrets with others even if you leave out your friend's name. People figure things out.

As you tell God that you want to be an available friend, he will teach you how. After all, he's the one who does friendship best!

 TALK: How can you grow in your skills as an available friend?

 PRAY: Ask God to help you grow where you need it most!

 ACT: If you're shy about being available to a hurting friend, talk as a family about how you can work together to help people.

28 Plugging In to the Power Source

Bible Reading: 2 Corinthians 12:8-10

My gracious favor is all you need. My power works best in your weakness. 2 Corinthians 12:9

Matt thinks he's the world's greatest friend. Got a problem? He's full of advice. Looking for help? He'll lend you a hand—whether you want him to or not. Do you have a need? He'll fill it—even if he isn't sure what it is.

Matt really wants to be an available friend. But he's totally missed the first step. He needs to understand that he is totally, utterly, completely clueless about how to be that kind of friend.

Maybe you figure your friendship know-how can't possibly be as poor as Matt's. Maybe you think you don't need God's help to be a top-notch friend. That's what these kids thought:

Michelle's head was always jam-packed with her own interests—so she had a hard time noticing when others needed help. Her first step to being an available friend was admitting that she didn't have the power to always be a concerned friend to people who were struggling. She's depending on Christ so she can be more caring like him.

Nick thought what other people had to say was boring—so when others finished a sentence, he couldn't even remember what they were talking about. His first step to being an available friend was admitting that he didn't have the strength to always be a good listener. He's depending on Christ so he can be a better listener like him.

Natalie told other people's secrets—so others often suffered as a result of her blabbermouth. Her first step to being an available friend was admitting that she didn't have what it takes to always keep to herself what her friends shared. She's depending on Christ so she can be a safe friend like him.

The secret to being a good friend is admitting that without help from Jesus, you don't have the power to be a friend like him. That truth isn't meant to make you feel bad but to remind you to depend on Christ for the strength to be an available friend.

You *can* be more like Jesus—a better, more loving friend to others. But that only happens with his help! Tell Jesus how you want to grow as a friend. And trust that the Holy Spirit will be God's power source, living and working inside you to make you more Christlike.

 TALK: Why do you need God's help to be an available friend?

 PRAY: *God, help us to be better friends and keep growing at that skill—now and always.*

 ACT: What's the biggest area where you need to depend on Jesus so you can be a friend like him? Ask a family member or Christian friend to speak up when you act in a way that is less than Christlike.

29 The <u>Super</u> Superhero

Bible Reading: Mark 1:21-28

"What sort of new teaching is this?" they asked excitedly. "It has such authority! Even evil spirits obey his orders!" Mark 1:27

Plastic Man is one cool-but-almost-forgotten comic-book superhero. He could stretch, twist, and mold his body into any shape. He could go from paper thin (for sliding under locked doors) to brick-wall solid (for blocking a bad guy's escape).

Talk about it: Who is your hero?

Your childhood hero might have been Superman, Spider-Man, or a Pokemon character. But in reality, there is only one true *super*-man: Jesus Christ. As God in human flesh, he had a special power that made him more super than anyone around him: *his authority*. Even though he looked like an ordinary man, his commanding actions showed who he actually was. He was the Son of God.

Jesus' teaching had power because he knew God the Father personally. He not only taught what God's Word said but also what it meant. He explained how to have a deep relationship with the Father.

Can you think of a time you were reading the Bible and a passage seemed to flash at you like strobe lights? Have you read a verse and suddenly realized it fit a situation you were dealing with right then? That was Jesus, making God's written Word come alive for you, just like he did for those listening in the synagogue. Today Jesus has the authority to work through the Holy Spirit to catch your attention with the Word, teach you what it means, and apply it to your daily life.

Jesus' authority doesn't stop with his teaching. All through the Gospels we can spot Jesus acting with power.

- He cured sickness (see Matthew 8:14-15).
- He commanded waves to be still (see Matthew 8:26-27).
- He forgave sins (see Matthew 9:2).
- He gave sight to the blind (see Matthew 9:27-30).
- He walked on water (see Matthew 14:25).
- He multiplied fish and bread (see John 6:1-14).
- He brought the dead back to life (see John 11:43-44).

Jesus is the all-powerful Lord of the universe. And his greatness means he deserves to be Lord of your life as well!

 TALK: How are you letting Jesus be Lord in your life today? Is there any area where you haven't let him rule?

 PRAY: *Thanks, Jesus, for being stronger than any problem we could ever face. Help us to give you total control of our life.*

 ACT: If you've picked an area in your life where you know you're not letting Jesus exercise his authority, think of a plan for how you can change.

30 Faith like a Hole in the Ceiling

Bible Reading: Mark 2:1-12

Seeing their faith, Jesus said to the paralyzed man, "My son, your sins are forgiven." Mark 2:5

"Hey, what's going on up there?" A scribe in a fancy robe jumps to his feet, interrupting Jesus' teaching. He wags an angry finger at a wooden stick poking through the crowded home's clay ceiling. Other important-looking leaders rise in a huff to watch the stick break a wide hole in the ceiling, spraying clay and dust over the people below.

Onlookers stare through the hole as four pairs of hands break off roof tiles. Soon those hands lower a stretcher into the room—and it's carrying a man who can't move. The paralyzed man is hurting physically. He depends on his family and friends for his every need. He's also hurting spiritually because he's a sinner who needs forgiveness.

If those are the basic facts about the man on the stretcher, who in the world were the four guys who hacked through the roof to put their friend in front of Jesus?

The Bible doesn't give us names, but it's safe to assume that these guys were just ordinary people with a friend who needed Jesus. They were just like us—ordinary people with needy friends.

And these ordinary guys were able to tap into Jesus' power.

Here's how. These men had faith big enough to believe Jesus would do something for their hurting friend . . . big enough to hack a hole in the ceiling . . . big enough to spray chunks of clay and dust on the people below, then peer down expectantly at Jesus as he stood over the paralyzed man. Jesus, who has power over sickness and sin, saw their faith and used his authority to heal the paralyzed man.

Think about it. One minute, a man is flat on his back, unable even to twitch a muscle. He might have been that way for years. Then Jesus speaks: "Stand up, take your mat, and go on home, because you are healed!" (Mark 2:11). And suddenly the man is on his feet and moving around like anyone else in the room. What power!

Jesus has all the power of God. Even so, you don't have to worry that Jesus will crash into your life, muscle in on all your activities, and force his help on you. He's the only being in the universe who has the strength you need to beat all of life's obstacles—physical, mental, social, or spiritual. But he won't push himself on you. He's patient. He stands ready. He's available to apply his authority in your life and in the lives of your friends and family. All you have to do is ask.

 TALK: What tough stuff are you facing right now where you could use help from Jesus?

 PRAY: Take turns praying for one another's needs.

 ACT: Do you have a friend who needs strength from Jesus? You can start helping by praying. Then make a plan to explain to your friend how Jesus is ready to help.

Love and Hell Don't Mix, Do They?

Bible Reading: Luke 16:19-31

Anyone whose name was not found recorded in the Book of Life was thrown into the lake of fire. Revelation 20:15

"You can't say that word!" yelped Micah's friend.

Micah looked puzzled. "What word? Hell? I was just explaining how the Bible says that hell is . . ."

"Don't say that word!" his friend interrupted.

"How come?" Micah asked. "I wasn't using it as a swearword."

Your friends may not mind joking about hell. But if you start talking about it the way the Bible does, explaining that there really is a hell, your friends may get upset. Hey—if God is so totally loving, your friends want to know why he made a place where people will be separated from him forever. And why does he send people to such a terrible place?

Good questions. The Bible says that Jesus—who loved the world enough to die for it—will one day bring "judgment on those who don't know God and on those who refuse to obey the Good News of our Lord Jesus. They will be punished with everlasting destruction, forever separated from the Lord and from his glorious power" (2 Thessalonians 1:8-9). That's the place we know as hell.

Hell can be hard to understand and even harder to explain, but here's the most important thing we can know about it: Hell is a choice.

See, God won't *force* anyone to love him. We *choose* to love or not to love God. His plan for saving people through Jesus is to do everything within his loving power to *invite* us to love him.

Yet when people totally refuse to accept God's welcoming love, he doesn't take away their freedom. He won't force people into heaven if they don't choose to hang out with him for eternity. So hell is the place where a very patient God sends those who refuse to obey him and go his way. He's tried to win them, but in the end he says, "Okay, have it your way!"

Hell is a choice, but the Bible leaves no doubt about how bad it will be. It's a place far away from God, his people, and everything good.

Hell is a choice nonbelievers will have to live with forever. That's why God gives us the task of talking to people around us who don't believe in him. He wants us to help them know that Jesus is God's Son, and he came to be their Savior and King!

 TALK: Is hell real? Is it unfair? How does it actually show us God's great love?

 PRAY: *Lord, don't let us miss an opportunity to share the love of Christ with our unbelieving friends, so they can enjoy heaven with us.*

 ACT: Discuss how you can wisely explain to someone who hasn't trusted Jesus why there needs to be a place like hell.

Too Late for Another Chance

Bible Reading: Hebrews 9:27-28

It is destined that each person dies only once and after that comes judgment. Hebrews 9:27

Micah wanted so badly for his friend to understand what the Bible has to say about hell. After all, hell isn't a bad word. It's a bad place. And Micah really wanted his friend to be with him forever in heaven. So Micah spent months feeding his friend little bits about the love of Jesus and the total coolness of heaven. One day Micah's friend actually started asking questions of his own about hell.

"Hell is forever?" Micah's friend puzzled. "Isn't that like getting sent to the principal's office and never getting out? Won't people feel bad and tell God that they really do love him and want to live in heaven with him? Won't God let those people out of hell and into heaven?"

Lots of people figure that believing in God is like handing in a school assignment late: better late than never.

Not true. And not because God wants to flunk people out of heaven.

God knows that people in hell won't flip-flop how they think about him. If a thousand more chances would have swayed them to choose his way, God kindly would have given them the chances. Remember: He's the God who "does not want anyone to be lost, but he wants all people to change their hearts and lives" (2 Peter 3:9, NCV). But because God knows everything in advance—including when people have totally made up their mind—God lets them go. He says, "It is destined that each person dies only once and after that comes judgment" (Hebrews 9:27).

Unbelievers are like buckets turned upside down under Niagara Falls. They wonder, "Where is God's love?" Yet they won't turn their heart right side up and let the waterfall of God's unlimited love fill their life. God's love is a gushing torrent. But people who are against God don't feel a drop. And hell is where people go when they have decided they don't even want to feel God's love.

Unbelievers are also like rude guests at a banquet. God offered his love on a platter. When people refuse his love, it's as if they've knocked the platter out of his hand and stomped on the best food.

God doesn't give unbelievers more time to choose him because he knows more time will do no good. But we can be assured that even when it comes to something as hard to understand as hell, God's love for us is perfect!

 TALK: The better you know God, the more you will want to share his heart of love with people who don't know him. How are you expressing God's love to non-Christians?

 PRAY: *God, help our non-Christian friends sense your love through us.*

 ACT: Take a bucket, turn it upside down. How much water goes in? How is that like a person who refuses to accept God's love?

3 Bad Things Happen to Good People

Bible Reading: James 1:2-8

When your faith is tested, your endurance has a chance to grow.
James 1:3

When a tornado tore through Justin's small Midwestern town, it tore dozens of houses off their foundations. Justin couldn't see how God could let his home be destroyed—or how God could allow earthquakes, hurricanes, floods, and disease to hurt thousands of people.

Talk about it: When bad things have happened in your life, have you ever wondered if God messed up?

The Bible says that God isn't to blame for the bad things that happen in life. Bad things happen because of human sin and people's wrong choices:

- *Sometimes evil comes from our own bad choices.* If we go to the ocean and swim in riptides, it's not God's fault if we're swooshed out to sea.
- *Sometimes evil comes from choosing to do nothing.* If we let a bully keep threatening a little kid without telling anyone, for example, the little kid might get seriously hurt.
- *Sometimes evil comes from the choices of others.* If someone drives a car while drunk, a family in another car might be hurt or killed.

But how about natural disasters like storms, earthquakes, volcanic eruptions, and tidal waves? Natural disasters also result from human sin, though that might not be as easy to see. Way back at the beginning of the world, the sin of Adam and Eve disobeying God brought a change to earth (see Genesis 3:17-18). Their sin caused chaos and pain to enter our world (see Romans 8:19-22). And that means that diseases and natural disasters can happen to anyone, even someone who loves God.

That's a big thought. And it doesn't change the fact that we wish our all-powerful God would come down and keep evil from happening.

God does sometimes stop bad stuff. But if God put a halt to everything evil in our world, it would take away our freedom to choose. We wouldn't experience the consequences of bad choices. And we wouldn't learn from our troubles.

None of the bad things that happen in life mean God loves us any less. God hasn't promised to shield us from everything evil. But he did say he would be with us through anything and everything (see Matthew 28:20).

 TALK: How can God's love comfort us when bad things happen to us?

 PRAY: *God, we don't blame you for the times when things go wrong in our life. We know you are with us, and we ask you to help us learn from our troubles.*

 ACT: Explain freedom of choice to a friend and talk about why God isn't to blame when bad things happen.

4 Why Does God Let People Be Evil?

Bible Reading: Galatians 6:7-10

Whenever we have the opportunity, we should do good to everyone, especially to our Christian brothers and sisters. Galatians 6:10

"Everyone does it to me. But Shawn is the worst," Megan wailed. "He keeps teasing me in gym class because I can't do a push-up. I'd like to show him how I can push his head clean off."

Megan's mom shot her a look that said, "Honey, I know you're kidding—but that wouldn't be a good choice."

"I won't do anything to him," Megan promised. "I just wish that God would smack him."

Most of us have wished that God would stomp on our enemies and stop them from making us feel sad. At the bottom of that wish is a question: Why does God let people choose to be bad—especially when some of them choose to be *really* bad?

As hard as it may be to hear, giving people the ability to choose between good and evil was the best choice our loving God could ever have made. We really wouldn't like living in a world where God forces us and everyone else to be good. Think how you squirm when a parent or teacher *makes* you be nice to someone. You feel dragged by the nose. You do the least you can to satisfy the adult who made the request. Even if you smile on the outside, you frown on the inside. Worse yet, the other person can tell that your heart isn't in it, and no one likes receiving halfhearted love.

On the other hand, we all like to show love when loving is our own choice. It's how you feel when you pitch in with chores at a friend's house. When no one *requires* you to do something good, suddenly raking leaves or picking up toys can actually be fun.

If God had made us all be good, he might as well have made us robots. Robots don't really love. They just follow their programming. And they never experience the fun of freely choosing to be good or to show love.

God cared for us enough to put us in a world where we could enjoy being his friend. Even though we don't like getting hurt by others who choose not to be good to us, the chance to choose between good and evil is a privilege too good to give up.

When people aren't good to us, we may think that God doesn't understand. But that's not true. Just remember how people treat God. Human beings reject him, mock him, and disobey him to his face. God feels hurt, but he keeps on loving and doing good things for people. We, too, have the chance to keep on doing good.

 TALK: Say it in your own words: Why did a loving God create a world where people can choose to do evil?

 PRAY: *God, help us keep loving others even when they treat us badly.*

 ACT: Lots of people blame God for the evil in the world. Share what you have learned with a friend who struggles with understanding evil.

5 Bringing Out the Big Gun

Bible Reading: Ephesians 6:10-20
Pray at all times and on every occasion in the power of the Holy Spirit. Ephesians 6:18

Maybe you want to share the good news about Jesus with a non-Christian friend. And you figure that starts with explaining all about Jesus' death on the cross and his resurrection. Whoa—back up! There's a step that comes even before that.

Talking to people about Jesus actually begins with prayer.

Prayer doesn't mean we mumble to God using *thee* and *thou* and big words we don't understand. Prayer is talking to God in simple language about our everyday thoughts, feelings, and concerns. And we can be totally confident that God hears us when we pray. In fact, God eagerly waits for us to come to him in prayer. We are his children, and he values every minute we spend with him.

God really wants to hear us pray for our non-Christian friends. How come? There are two huge reasons:

1. *Prayer gets us close to God.* Prayer unplugs our minds from music and Web sites and television and video games; and it plugs us into God. Instead of God being a stranger we barely know, he's an up-close friend. We grow more and more sure he loves us.

   When we've grown to have a close relationship with God, that's when it's time to start talking to him about our friends. As we hang tight with God in prayer, we get hold of his love for the world and the non-Christians he wants to reach through us. And besides that, a close relationship with God is something we can't pass on to our friends unless we have it ourselves.

2. *Prayer is our best weapon in a spiritual battle.* When we pray, God acts! Our prayers for our non-Christian friends smash Satan. God prepares our friends to receive our message. And he gives us strength to speak up.

God has his mind made up to do some astonishing things in your school and neighborhood. When you pray, you get hold of God—and you get tuned in to what he intends to accomplish.

Can you see why God wants to spend time with you in prayer? Are you taking advantage of this powerful weapon? Are you making the most of God's desire to be close to you?

 TALK: What would you like to do to improve the time you spend with God in prayer?

 PRAY: *God, make our prayer life with you deep. Help us to catch your love for the non-Christians all around us.*

 ACT: Spend some time praying today for someone you want to share your faith with. Go for it!

6 Pray Focused

Bible Reading: John 17:1-4

[God the Father has] given [Christ the Son] authority over everyone in all the earth. [Jesus] gives eternal life to each one [the Father has] given him. John 17:2

You want your friends to know Jesus. And yesterday you learned that prayer is your starting point for telling folks about Jesus. But exactly how sure are you that God will answer your prayers?

Check out this scale from 1–10. How confident are you?

1	3	5	7	10
I don't pray much. When I pray, I hide with a fire extinguisher, just in case God doesn't like what I say and smokes me.	I fling a prayer toward heaven once in a while. I worry that when God hears me praying he says, "Whozzat?"	I pray. But I mumble. I figure that God prefers to listen to my sister.	I'm pretty sure God hears me. But I still keep the fire extinguisher handy for my really big requests.	I talk to God with a bold respect. I know that God answers every prayer in a way that is in line with his will.

It's so absolutely important that we become confident as we pray. This is why: God has a plan for working in your world. In fact, he has some wild promises that may be new to you. Try this one on for size: "If you ask me, I will give you the nations; all the people on earth will be yours" (Psalm 2:8, NCV). To hear God's promise hit home even harder, put it like this: "If you ask me, I will give you your baseball team—or the kid who sits next to you in your math or Spanish class. . . ."

God promises to give you people you can talk to about him. Your job is to ask. Time and experience will give you the confidence to be bold when you ask!

There's a secret that will help you ask confidently and take hold of what God has promised: *Pray with a goal.* A lot of Christians pray "bless so-and-so" prayers with no idea of what they're actually asking. God wants you to pray with a focused picture in mind of what you want him to do. Get specific with God as you pray for non-Christian friends, classmates, teammates, or family members.

There's no doubt about God's will for our friends. He wants all of them in heaven (see 2 Peter 3:9). So when we ask that our friends trust Christ and be saved, we can be sure we're asking for something God has announced as his will!

 TALK: How can you focus the prayers you pray for your non-Christian friends?

 PRAY: Ask God to work in the lives of your non-Christian friends, with the goal of them trusting in Christ.

 ACT: Practice your habit of praying for your non-Christian friends.

7 Wishes Aren't Enough

Bible Reading: James 5:16-18

The earnest prayer of a righteous person has great power and wonderful results. James 5:16

With half a dozen friends at his house for a backyard baseball bonanza, Nicholas was all set to serve the Supercheezer from Fazio's Pizza. As his friends piled inside and grabbed chairs around the kitchen table, they all began looking for the food.

After a half hour of moans about hunger pains, one friend finally spoke up. "Hey, dude? Did you ever call to order the pizza?"

Nicholas looked worried. "Um," he finally said, "could you guys go back outside and play another game or two?"

Here's some huge news: Pizza doesn't show up unless you make one very important phone call.

It works the same way with friends you wish would trust Christ. Wishes aren't *prayer.* Until you *pray,* you haven't done that one very important thing that brings people to Jesus.

Talk about this: Got any ideas on times and places to pray for your friends?

Here are some tips for becoming active pray-ers:

1. Set aside a regular time as a family each week to pray for non-Christian friends and family members.
2. Pray alone each day for one or two non-Christian friends.
3. Get a small group of friends together at school or church to pray regularly for non-Christians.
4. Whenever you get together with Christian friends, ask God to grow your group by adding non-Christians who learn to trust Christ.
5. Join with other Christians at school or in your neighborhood for a "prayer walk." Pray as you walk around the areas where kids hang out.

Prayer isn't your only job. You can pray for your friends until you're hoarse—but you'd better not, because you're eventually going to need your voice to share the Good News about Jesus with them.

The most important prayer you can pray is that your non-Christian friends have a chance to hear and respond to the Good News. You can pray that prayer for people near and far. It's that one very important thing you can do to bring people to Jesus!

 TALK: Why has God given you the privilege of praying for friends?

 PRAY: Talk to God about your attitude toward praying for non-Christians. Tell him if you are eager—or finding it tough to do.

 ACT: How can you make praying for non-Christians a regular part of your life? Start at least in a small way today.

8 Brain Transplant

Bible Reading: Philippians 2:5-11

Don't copy the behavior and customs of this world, but let God transform you into a new person by changing the way you think.
Romans 12:2

How would you like to be smart—*really* smart? Picture this: You wake up one morning and find you have suddenly become the most brilliant person alive. Yesterday you were struggling to master fourth-grade math. Today you're being offered jobs around the world as a rocket scientist.

That sudden rise to total smartness is what happens to a guy named Charlie in the story *Flowers for Algernon* (and an old movie called *Charly*). Thirty-two-year-old Charlie is gentle and friendly—but not very smart. He can read and write—well, sort of. He knows he isn't as bright as people around him. In fact, in the story there's a white lab rat named Algernon who in some ways seems more intelligent than Charlie.

When Algernon undergoes an experimental operation, the rat becomes a genius among mice. Charlie Gordon goes through a similar operation and also becomes a genius. But the results aren't all pleasant. Along with superintelligence comes self-centeredness, distrust, and a habit of arguing with others, traits Charlie had never shown before the operation.

When Paul says in Romans 12:2 that God wants to change the way we think, he isn't saying we should have brain surgery. God isn't looking to spike our brain power and turn us into members of a geniuses-only club. He wants to change us into people who think more and more like Jesus.

So exactly how does Jesus think? He thinks like a servant who is willing to give up his own interests, even his own life, for others.

In Philippians 2:5-11, Paul tells us to have the same attitude as Jesus, who left heaven's glory, was born in a human body, and gave his life on the cross for us. Nobody forced Christ to live among us and die for us. He did it voluntarily. He set aside all his rights so we could be forgiven and be friends with God.

So what does Jesus' attitude look like in us? For one thing, it's so different from how many people act that folks will think we've had our brains rewired. We go from whining for our own way to watching for ways to please others. We change from looking out for our own needs to looking out for the needs of people all around us.

That's a loving attitude! It's the attitude of giving that motivated Christ during his entire visit to our planet. And it's the change of mind God wants to do in us!

 TALK: What will your brain look like when God gets done rearranging it—when he has built Christ's attitude of servanthood in you?

 PRAY: *Father, build in us a loving, giving attitude like the one Jesus had.*

 ACT: Do something for someone else today that demonstrates that God has rearranged your brain!

A Body in Need Is a Body Indeed

Bible Reading: Romans 12:3-8

Since we are all one body in Christ, we belong to each other, and each of us needs all the others. Romans 12:5

Your body parts are getting together for a meeting. The chairman, your hand, calls the meeting to order—your hand, after all, is the only one who can grip a gavel. In a surprise first piece of business, your big toes step to the podium. "We quit!" they shout.

"What are you talking about, Toes?" growls your belly.

"We're tired of getting stepped on," your big toes moan together.

"You *are* low guys on the totem pole," injects the funny bone.

Hand raps the gavel. "Order, please!"

"We'll run away," Toes reply. "We can wriggle to wherever we want."

"You won't be able to see where you're going," observe the eyes.

"We'll get by," one toe insists. "We might even take our friends with us. The feet feel the same way we do. They'll probably hoof off with us too."

The forehead wrinkles. Then your mouth speaks up. "Maybe you can get along without us, Toes, but we won't make it without you. We count on you to keep us balanced."

"Because of you," say the hands, "we can put our best feet forward."

The toes wiggle at the attention. "We do get kind of a kick out of hanging out with the rest of you. Well, maybe we need each other more than we realized."

"And that's what I've been thinking all along," the brain concludes.

Here's a question to talk about: Do you ever think like those toes? Do you wish you could get along without other people?

Folk singers Art Garfunkel and Paul Simon sing Simon's famous words about wanting to tough it through life without the help of other people: "I am a rock," they sing. "I am an i-i-i-island."

Lots of us like to sing along with those words when we're mad at the world. But seventeenth-century English poet John Donne wrote some other words that are much closer to the truth: "No man is an island."

As much as you might try, you can't make it through life alone. After all, even Jesus wanted fellowship, friendship, and prayer with his peers. So your friends, family, and others in the church—the body of Christ—have something you need. They've got help, encouragement, and companionship you can't live without!

TALK: Do your family members and friends know that you need them? Are you meeting their need for you?

PRAY: *God, thanks for keeping us attached to the people in the church, the body of Christ, who love us.*

ACT: Go ahead. Tell someone today that you need him or her.

The Thrill of Second Place

Bible Reading: Romans 12:9-13
Love each other with genuine affection, and take delight in honoring each other. Romans 12:10

You're standing in the lunch line at school, wondering what's left to eat. Not only are you assigned to eat during the last lunch period of the day, but today you're last of the last, kept late by your teacher after you made some serious mistakes on your weekly spelling test.

By the time you get to eat lunch, the pickings are often slim. Sure enough, as you scan the food in front of you, the desserts look especially sad. Though there are stacks of nut-filled brownies, just one nutless brownie remains.

There's a problem. You really hate nuts.

There's an even bigger problem. You're not exactly last in line.

Behind you is a classmate, Patrick, who *reeeeallly* hates nuts in his brownies. In fact, he's allergic. If he eats even a sliver of nut his throat swells shut, his face turns purple, and his eyes roll to the back of his head.

That's not your problem. You just like nut-free brownies. So what do you do?

- ☐ Drop your fork. As the fork *clanks* on the floor, grab the non-nut brownie and make your break.
- ☐ Whine at the cooks. Tell them you're perfectly willing to wait in the lunchroom all afternoon for more plain brownies.
- ☐ Poke Patrick's belly button, giggle, and tell him he needs to go on a diet anyway.
- ☐ Say, "I want you to have that last nut-free brownie, Patrick. Enjoy!"

Was that last choice hard to swallow? Did you feel a twinge of pain at the thought of giving up a dessert that had your name on it? Maybe that choice didn't bother you, but there are probably other times you've hesitated to give up something you wanted in order to put someone else first.

Being a servant doesn't always mean picking the worst. But it for sure doesn't mean always hogging the best, especially when our choice might hurt someone else. God wants to transform our thinking to be like Christ's, who put us first by giving his life for us. God calls us to display the same attitude toward people around us. It's called *honoring* each other. God is pleased when we choose to honor others above ourselves like Jesus did.

 TALK: When have you struggled to honor others? How does it help to know that God honors you?

 PRAY: *God, when we see something we want, we struggle to keep others in mind. Help us to honor others like you have honored us.*

 ACT: Take this triple dare: Find three ways today to put others' interests before your own.

Hurting with Those in a World of Hurt

Bible Reading: Romans 12:14-16
When others are happy, be happy with them. If they are sad, share their sorrow. Romans 12:15

The phone ringing in the middle of the night jarred the young pastor awake. "Pastor, our daughter . . ." the voice on the phone choked. "She was in a bad car accident tonight. She's in surgery and . . . we're not sure . . . she'll make it."

The pastor dressed quickly and hurried to the hospital. When he arrived, sad faces told the story. The teenage girl had died in surgery. He tried to say something to comfort the parents, but he couldn't get any words out. He just sat and sobbed with the heartbroken mom and dad.

Not much later the girl's parents moved away, and the young pastor didn't see them for several years. When he ran into them at a conference, he was embarrassed. "I have an apology to make," he said. "The night your daughter died, I failed you as a pastor. I should have read Scripture to you and offered you words of hope. But I didn't. I just cried. I'm so sorry I let you down that night."

"You didn't let us down, Pastor," the girl's dad said. "You felt our hurt and cried with us. What you did brought us great comfort."

That's a deep lesson: The pastor thought he failed. But what he actually did was show the kind of deep sympathy Jesus showed.

When people run into sorrow, do you know what they need right away? It isn't an explanation of why bad things happen. It isn't advice. The first thing people need is *someone to feel sad along with them.* They need *comfort.*

Jesus showed what comfort looked like after his friend Lazarus died (see John 11). When Jesus showed up at the home of Lazarus's sisters, Mary and Martha, they were crying over the loss of their brother. So Jesus cried with them.

Jesus could have told those sisters, "Don't cry, ladies. Give me a few minutes and I'll have Lazarus back from the dead." Yet at that moment they needed someone to cry with them. So Jesus did. Later he performed a miracle that turned their sorrow to joy.

People who are sad find comfort when they know they aren't suffering alone. So when a friend is crushed with sorrow or disappointment, we should do our best to feel what that person is feeling—to be sad along with our friend. And it's okay to say something like, "I'm so sad for you" or "I hurt for you" or "I'm sorry you are hurting." It's what Jesus would do.

 TALK: How can we best comfort our hurting friends?

 PRAY: Pray for your friends who need God's help—and ask God to use you to comfort them.

 ACT: Do you have a friend who needs your presence? Spend some time showing comfort today.

12 It's Payback Time

Bible Reading: Romans 12:17-21
Dear friends, never avenge yourselves. Leave that to God.
Romans 12:19

Ever had any of the following—or something like them—happen to you? Check the boxes by those to which you can relate.

- ☐ A little brother or sister breaks something of yours.
- ☐ A so-called friend tells others something about you that's not true.
- ☐ Somebody gets mad at you and pounds on you.
- ☐ You get left out of the biggest party of the year.
- ☐ An older brother or sister treats you like you're a pain.

Somewhere, sometime, somehow you've probably been wronged in one or more of those very unhappy ways. So what was your first response?

- ☐ Do unto the other person what he did unto you—only twice as bad.
- ☐ Thump your brother's or sister's head.
- ☐ Send a note with "Dear Ex-Friend" as its opening line.
- ☐ Say something really bad about the person who said unkind things about you.
- ☐ Never listen or talk to this person again.

Have you ever noticed that inside our brain there seems to be a payback chip? Whenever we're wronged, a little switch inside of us flips on and tells us to do unto others as they have done unto us—and maybe a little worse. We've all felt at least a momentary urge to get back at someone who has been unkind to us.

Since we're all tempted in this way at times, how should we respond? Once again Jesus, our Savior, shows us the way to go. If anybody deserved to lash back at unfair treatment, it was God's Son. Jesus never sinned—he never did anything wrong and never even thought about it. "When he suffered, he did not threaten to get even. He left his case in the hands of God, who always judges fairly" (1 Peter 2:23). God the Father knew the treatment his Son received was rotten beyond belief. And he knew exactly what kind of payback it required. God is our heavenly Father too, and he will watch out for us and pay back—in his own way and time—any wrongs done to us.

 TALK: When you are wronged, what's your usual reaction? How does your attitude change when you think about the fact that you can trust God to pay back your enemies perfectly?

 PRAY: *Jesus, help us give up our desire to get even. We trust you to help us work through all of our conflicts.*

 ACT: Is there anyone you're at war with? Call a truce today.

13 Have I Died Yet Today?

Bible Reading: Romans 12:1

I plead with you to give your bodies to God. Let them be a living and holy sacrifice—the kind he will accept. Romans 12:1

On September 11, 2001, hundreds of police and firefighters answered a call for help at the World Trade Center in New York City. As they entered the flaming buildings, they had no way to foresee that they would soon sacrifice their lives to save others. With each step up the crowded staircases of the twin towers, they helped more people to safety. But with each step, they also drew nearer to the time when they would give up their own lives, dying to let others live.

Most of us have never had to be rescued from a flaming building. But someone did die for each of us. In fact, we were saved in the most heroic rescue of all time. You know the familiar story: Because we were unable to please a holy God, we faced judgment—eternal separation from the God who created us. But Jesus became a man and died in our place so we could live forever with him.

Here's the wild part. In Romans 12:1 God calls us to do the same thing: to give ourselves as a sacrifice. But there is a key change: He wants a *living* sacrifice. Sounds like one of those weird word pairs, like "pretty ugly" or "jumbo shrimp."

Sacrifice usually means something *dies*. Yet there are lots of great ways to sacrifice ourselves without dying. We become living sacrifices when we serve God and others with our abilities, time, and resources.

Take a vote. Which of the following activities is a way to be a living sacrifice? Thumbs up for yes, thumbs down for no:

- helping an elderly neighbor by doing yard work
- giving some of your money to a youth group missions project
- using your singing ability by joining a kids' choir
- spending a couple hours each week visiting patients at a nursing home
- volunteering to help your parents clean the garage or attic
- spending the summer on a short-term missions trip

Each of those ideas deserves a thumbs-up. And we have an incredible reason to offer ourselves sacrificially in those ways. As Paul wrote, "When you think of what [God] has done for you, is this too much to ask?" (Romans 12:1). Our daily, living sacrifices are acts of worship to the one who gave *everything* for us.

 TALK: Aren't you glad that Jesus was willing to give his life for you? How do you want to offer your life as a living sacrifice?

 PRAY: *Jesus, we want to say thanks for your death for us by offering ourselves as living sacrifices. Show us how.*

 ACT: How can you be a living sacrifice today? Think about it. Then do it!

14 He Just Keeps Loving and Loving and Loving You

Bible Reading: Jeremiah 31:1-6

Long ago the Lord said to Israel: "I have loved you, my people, with an everlasting love. With unfailing love I have drawn you to myself."
Jeremiah 31:3

Shay storms into the house, slamming the door behind him. He mouths off to his parents, then shoves his little brother's face into a bowl of ice cream. Grounded to his room for the rest of the day, Shay kicks the cat and slams his fist into the pillow.

As Shay cools off, it occurs to him that he's been a jerk and that Jesus has stuck with him through it all. So he wonders, *Lord, why do you love me so much?*

Ever blown it big and asked God that question?

Well, he loves you because he created you.

Have you ever watched parents *ooh* and *ahh* over their newborn baby? Some newborns are the ugliest creatures on earth. But to their own parents, they couldn't be cuter. How come? Because mom and dad helped create the little darling.

It's the same way with God. Because he created us, he loves us even when we're unlovely and unlovable. He thinks we're the greatest. And nothing we do can make him stop loving us.

We might wonder how God can keep loving us after we've sinned. Like when we get angry and break a brother's or sister's toy. Or we yell at our parents. Or we talk behind a friend's back.

God wouldn't be thrilled with any of that behavior, but he wouldn't quit loving us for it. In fact, nothing we can do will stop him from continuing to love us. Jesus' death on the cross paid for our sin—past, present, and future. Absolutely nothing can cause God to change his mind and stop loving us. Nothing! Listen to what the Bible has to say about it:

Psalm 103:12 says, "He has removed our rebellious acts as far away from us as the east is from the west."

Romans 5:8 tells us how much God loved us even before we loved him: "God showed his great love for us by sending Christ to die for us while we were still sinners."

Romans 8:38-39 lists all sorts of things that *cannot* separate us from God's love: "Death can't, and life can't. . . . Whether we are high above the sky or in the deepest ocean, nothing in all creation will ever be able to separate us from the love of God that is revealed in Christ Jesus our Lord."

We need to get it into our head: *God loves us.* We can't scare away his love!

 TALK: How do you feel knowing that nothing can separate you from God?

 PRAY: *God, your love for us is incredible. Thank you for your love that never stops.*

 ACT: Have you ever stopped loving someone who hurt you? Love like God does— and do something caring for that person today.

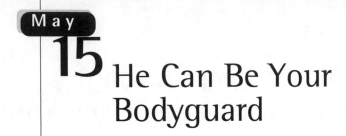

15 He Can Be Your Bodyguard

Bible Reading: Psalm 8:1-9

What are mortals that you should think of us, mere humans that you should care for us? For you made us only a little lower than God, and you crowned us with glory and honor. Psalm 8:4-5

The bulging crowd pressed Adriana up against a rope barricade, but she wouldn't be budged from her front-row seat. She had claimed her spot on the sidewalk five hours earlier, just to wait for a limousine carrying an impressive young man. Together with his royal parents, a teenage prince was making a stop in her hometown.

Adriana had heard this boy was smart, polite, and spoke five languages, so she knew this prince was a one-of-a-kind charming. As his limo swung into view and he waved, Adriana concluded that one glimpse was worth the wait.

Unless you were born into a royal family or have become a professional athlete or pop star, chances are you don't have crowds gathering to honor you, bodyguards gathering to protect you, or people making special arrangements for you.

But did you know that every day of your life you get that special attention from God? God does those exact three things for us, because to him we are more important than any celebrity:

- He honors us with special attention, as Psalm 8:4-5 describes.
- He sends his angels to guard us. Psalm 91:11 says, "He orders his angels to protect you wherever you go."
- He is making amazing arrangements for us. John 14:2 says, "There are many rooms in my Father's home, and I am going to prepare a place for you."

God doesn't think we're great because we're so good. None of us is good enough to deserve that kind of attention. He showers us with honor because of what Jesus Christ did for us, dying for our sins and taking away everything bad that would offend God the Father.

God's great love for us doesn't change even when we act in ways that are less than royal. Our sins make God sad, but he gives us a way to stay a superstar in his eyes. Remember what 1 John 1:9 says? "If we confess our sins to him, he is faithful and just to forgive us and to cleanse us from every wrong."

When you blow it in your relationship with God, get things made right with him immediately. Live like the one-of-a-kind child that you are!

 TALK: How does it feel knowing that God is quick to forgive your sins? How does his acceptance make you want to act?

 PRAY: *God, thanks for treating us as royalty—even when our actions are less than royal.*

 ACT: When you blow it and sin, get it straightened out with God right away!

16 Who's That Looking Back at You?

Bible Reading: Ephesians 1:3-8

How we praise God, the Father of our Lord Jesus Christ, who has blessed us with every spiritual blessing in the heavenly realms because we belong to Christ. Ephesians 1:3

You look in the mirror. How do you react to what you see? Pick the statement that best describes your response:

- ☐ Sigh.
- ☐ Please be patient. God obviously isn't finished with me yet.
- ☐ It's a good thing that beauty is more than skin deep.
- ☐ What potential!
- ☐ I kiss myself!

You can have all sorts of thoughts—good, bad, and ugly—about yourself. Looking at yourself in a mirror is one way to see who you are. But your eyes can't see the whole truth about you. In fact, they can't even spot the most important facts.

A far better way to get to know yourself is to discover how God sees you. If you want a healthy self-image, God's view of you is what you want to get. And Ephesians 1 tells you these truths about you:

- You have been given every spiritual blessing (verse 3).
- You were chosen before the beginning of the world to be without fault in God's eyes (verse 4).
- You were picked for adoption as God's child (verse 5).
- Your freedom and forgiveness were purchased through Christ's blood (verse 7).
- You are marked as God's own by the Holy Spirit (verse 13).

Because of what Christ has done for us, we know, of course, that those great things are true of us. They are truths we can count on. Paul put it like this: "I pray that your hearts will be flooded with light so that you can understand the wonderful future he has promised to those he called. I want you to realize what a rich and glorious inheritance he has given to his people. I pray that you will begin to understand the incredible greatness of his power for us who believe him" (verses 18-19).

You might crack up when you look in a mirror. Or maybe it's the mirror that cracks. But God wants you to see yourself as the incredible son or daughter you are. He wants *you* to see all the great things *he* sees in you!

 TALK: What new fact did you just learn about yourself? How does it make you feel?

 PRAY: *God, thank you that these facts are true about us. Thank you for your goodness to us.*

 ACT: Share one of these absolutely true facts with a friend.

17 Move Over, Mona Lisa

Bible Reading: Ephesians 2:4-10
For we are God's masterpiece. Ephesians 2:10

Your teacher said the artwork you were going to see was "priceless." You thought that meant it was totally cheap and ugly. You were wrong. Every sculpture and painting was beautiful—and valuable beyond imagination. Stone-faced armed guards stood by the most valuable pieces. And throughout the tour your teacher kept flashing a look that said, "Touch anything and you'll never get out of fourth grade."

You don't hang on the wall. You don't have a guard standing by your side day and night. Yet you are God's masterpiece—his cherished, handcrafted creation. Look at what Ephesians 2 says about your worth and value:

- You have been given life (see verse 5).
- You are one with Christ Jesus (see verse 6).
- You have been saved by God's special favor (see verse 8).

And that's only the beginning. If you trust Christ, every one of the following huge truths is a fact about you. Whenever you wonder if you matter to God or anyone else, read this list aloud to yourself:

- I am loved and chosen by God (see Ephesians 1:4).
- I am a child of God (see John 1:12).
- God's Holy Spirit lives in me (see 1 Corinthians 3:16).
- I have access to God's wisdom (see James 1:5)..
- I have a new friendship with God (see Romans 5:11).
- I have been made right in God's sight (see Romans 5:1).
- I have Christ's righteousness (see 2 Corinthians 5:21).
- I am God's ambassador (see 2 Corinthians 5:20).
- I am completely forgiven (see Colossians 1:14).
- God meets all my needs (see Philippians 4:19).
- I am tenderly loved by God (see Jeremiah 31:3).
- I am holy and blameless (see Colossians 1:22).

Paul meant it when he said, "Those who become Christians become new persons. They are not the same anymore, for the old life is gone. A new life has begun!" (2 Corinthians 5:17). When God looks at you, he sees his flawless, awesome masterpiece!

 TALK: How do you like being God's masterpiece?

 PRAY: *God, sometimes it's hard for us to see, but we know that you have made us your masterful works of art. Thank you.*

 ACT: Spend time repeating to yourself any of those Bible facts about you that you have a hard time believing.

18 The Spirit of the Matter

Bible Reading: Acts 1:4-8

When the Holy Spirit has come upon you, you will receive power and will tell people about me everywhere. Acts 1:8

"Fine!" Alissa spat. "Maybe God thinks I'm his masterpiece. But no one else does. Today at school I had to read the grade I got on my reading homework out loud. Everyone snorted when they heard my score. They all know I'm stupid."

Alissa's aunt hugged her and said, "You aren't stupid. Maybe you struggle with reading, but you're learning. And you do other things really well. You know how to do math problems that even I can't do!"

Being sure that God has made you his masterpiece doesn't mean thinking untrue things about yourself. It isn't telling yourself nice lies. It's realizing that God has built into you real strengths you can use in the real world.

Paul wasn't bragging when he said, "I can do everything with the help of Christ who gives me the strength I need" (Philippians 4:13). He just knew he was gifted and equipped to serve God. And that fact is true of you too.

Being gifted by God doesn't mean you'll never flunk a homework assignment or struggle with spelling. But God wants you to be sure of this: He has given you all sorts of abilities—physical, mental, and spiritual—and equipped you to use those abilities successfully. God sees you as capable and useful. And the key to grasping that truth is understanding how the Holy Spirit is at work in you:

- You are born again by the Spirit (John 3:3-5).
- The Spirit lives inside you and will be with you forever (John 14:16-17).
- The Spirit teaches you what you need to know (John 14:26).
- The Spirit guides you (Romans 8:14).
- The Spirit equips you with talents, abilities, and spiritual gifts so you can serve God (1 Corinthians 12:4, 11).
- The Spirit prays for you when you're weak (Romans 8:26-27).
- The Spirit develops his fruit in you: love, joy, peace, patience, kindness, goodness, faithfulness, gentleness, and self-control (Galatians 5:22-23).

God says this: "You are equipped for a successful Christian life." You can read in 1 Corinthians 1:7: "Now you have every spiritual gift you need." God has given everything you need to serve him. That fact doesn't mean you won't fail, but it does mean you have everything you need to succeed.

 TALK: What difference does it make to you that the Holy Spirit lives inside you?

 PRAY: Thank God for valuing you enough to give you everything you need to serve him.

 ACT: Sharing with a Christian friend what you've learned about the Holy Spirit will make you confident—and capable!

19 The Only Way to Go

Bible Reading: Ephesians 5:15-20
Let the Holy Spirit fill and control you. Ephesians 5:18

Skyler whimpered from the couch. *Oooooohh,* he moaned, *I can't believe I ate the whole thing.*

Once again he had consumed a huge turkey dinner just like a Thanksgiving feast: two towers of turkey, three mounds of mashed potatoes, four gobs of gravy, five fluffy dinner rolls, and six glops of green-bean casserole. To top it off he had sucked down seven spoonfuls of sweet potatoes dripping with marshmallows and butter. And later that day when Skyler's mom brought out the leftover Jell-O and started building turkey sandwiches, Skyler mumbled that he didn't ever want to eat again.

Have you ever stuffed yourself so full of food you couldn't move?

God wants to fill us up with something even better than a turkey dinner. It's the Holy Spirit!

Let's grab another look at how the Holy Spirit makes us capable—how he outfits us with everything we need to live the Christian life. How exactly do we get lots of the Holy Spirit in our life?

Fact Number 1: You already have the Holy Spirit in you. From the moment you trust Jesus, the Holy Spirit lives in you, giving you everything you need to live for him. Paul commanded, "Let the Holy Spirit fill and control you" (Ephesians 5:18). This is what Paul was actually saying: "Keep on allowing yourself to be filled with the Spirit." That tells us two things: The Spirit is already inside you—but you can also let more of him into your life.

Fact Number 2: You get "filled with the Holy Spirit" when you let the Holy Spirit fill you over and over again. If you want to serve God day by day, you need to be filled day by day. That doesn't mean you need more of the Holy Spirit to come into you from the *outside.* It means you must let the Holy Spirit control more and more of your life from the *inside.* You can boldly put to work all the power God has put at your disposal, trusting him to make you capable of obeying him and being his witness.

You would probably get sick of turkey if you ate it every day. But the feast of the Spirit *is* something you can enjoy each day. God commands you to be filled with his Spirit, so you can be sure he will load you up whenever you ask him. It's like a fridge that's always full. And God wants you to enjoy him every day!

TALK: Have you invited the Holy Spirit to fill you today? How do you expect him to help you?

PRAY: *Lord, we want your Holy Spirit to control our lives today. Guide us through the Bible, showing us how to live the way God wants.*

ACT: Being filled with the Holy Spirit is a command God wants you to keep every day. Make a poster or a sign to remind you daily of Ephesians 5:18.

20 Are You Power-Packed?

Bible Reading: Job 42:1-5

Job replied to the Lord: "I know that you can do anything, and no one can stop you." Job 42:1-2

Matt tried so hard to behave at his church's Wednesday evening kids' club. But week after week Kirk did stupid stuff to annoy Matt. This week Kirk's trick was poking Matt with a pencil.

Matt's patience was done. When Kirk poked him again, Matt screamed and popped his fist straight at Kirk's nose. For one second Matt was happy he had stopped Kirk. The next second he wished he hadn't.

Matt's dad made him think hard about how he had acted. Besides giving him pointers on better ways to deal with Kirk, his dad told Matt how the Holy Spirit could help him control his temper.

Matt liked that idea. Yet he wondered if God was really there to help him. "If I'm supposed to be filled with the Holy Spirit every day," he complained, "I think I maybe have a leak. I'm not sure if he comes and goes or what." Like most of us, Matt wished he understood a whole lot more about exactly *how* the Holy Spirit works inside of us.

Well, here's a hint: Unlike your heart, which beats whether you ask it to or not, the Holy Spirit does his best work when you *invite* him to do his thing—to make you more like Jesus.

Talk about this: Have you ever invited the Holy Spirit to work in your life? How could you do that?

Inviting the Holy Spirit is like letting a cleanup crew into a messy house. The first step is to open the front door. As a Christian, you've already done that. The Holy Spirit comes to live inside you at the time you trust Christ. So you don't have to ask the Holy Spirit *into* your life. He's *already there.*

But your job is to let him into the rest of your "house." You can ask the Holy Spirit to enter every room of your life. You can invite him to control every area of your life, every hidden crack, corner, and crevice. Honestly tell him where you need help.

That's your first step to truly relying on the Holy Spirit's strength to obey and serve God.

When you have the Spirit's power, you are teamed up with God, who can do everything. Don't doubt that his Spirit is in you. If you believe in Jesus, he is. He will stick with you and do all that he has promised to do. No fooling. And no leaks.

 TALK: How can you allow God to do his great work in you?

 PRAY: Invite God to change whatever he sees inside you that needs changing.

 ACT: Make a sign that reminds you to ask God's Spirit to fill your life. Keep it up until inviting the Holy Spirit to work in you becomes a habit.

It's Not You, but What God Can Do through You

Bible Reading: Philippians 1:3-6

God, who began the good work within you, will continue his work until it is finally finished on that day when Christ Jesus comes back again.
Philippians 1:6

Amelia is an artist. When she was six, her parents rented her a booth at a craft show. She sat with her legs dangling off a folding chair while people talked about that cute little girl and her pretty pictures. By the time she was nine, people started hanging her work in fancy art galleries.

So when Amelia turned twelve and graduated into her church's middle school group, she was an obvious choice to help make posters for the group's spring retreat.

What a disaster.

While everyone else wondered about where to put stuff on the poster and what color markers to use, Amelia barked orders about composition and hues and tints. Instead of seeing the purpose of the posters, she saw a chance to show off her skills.

Talk about it: How could Amelia have better used her gifts—in a way that helped people and pleased God?

God won't say, "Don't use your talents." After all, he's the one who put them there. But when we allow the Spirit to give us power and we tell God we're willing to follow him wherever he wants, he might ask us to serve him in ways we never expected.

God may want us to serve him in an area where we feel uneasy. For example, he may want Amelia to serve him by singing in the choir for a while instead of making posters.

No one can do everything well. But working at a task of which we're a little scared can make us more open to God's help. And as we depend on God, others see God's strength shining through us. Paul wrote, "This precious treasure—this light and power that now shine within us—is held in perishable containers, that is, in our weak bodies. So everyone can see that our glorious power is from God and is not our own" (2 Corinthians 4:7).

When we study the people who serve God best, we notice that real power comes from letting the Holy Spirit take charge and asking God to give us the skills we need to serve him. Being an expert ourselves sometimes gets in the way.

God isn't limited by your age, your weaknesses, or your lack of experience. Just watch what he can do through you when you give his Spirit control!

 TALK: What bold new thing do you think God would like to do through you?

 PRAY: Ask God to lead you wherever he wants you to go.

 ACT: Do you wish you could do something for God—but you feel a little scared? That's a good sign! Ask God to give you his power—then dive in!

22 Potted Plants Can't Answer Prayer

Bible Reading: Acts 16:25-34

Believe on the Lord Jesus and you will be saved, along with your entire household. Acts 16:31

Kelly sat across from her friend Angelica. Even though Kelly and Angelica had grown up in the same church and attended the same Bible camps, Kelly had accepted a new religion that saw Jesus only as a good man among many good teachers.

"Don't worry about me," Kelly told Angelica. "We each have the faith that's right for us. Christianity isn't all there is. The important thing is that you *believe.*"

"I guess," Angelica said. She paused, then started again, speaking slower. "I guess it's not that big a deal *what* you believe, as long as you believe it *enough.*"

Whoops, girls. It *is* a big deal what you believe.

A teacher once said to his class, "I believe in the power of faith. I've seen it change lives." That sounds cool, but it isn't what Christianity teaches. That teacher rightly says how important it is to believe. But he leaves out how important it is to believe in the *right thing* or the *right person.*

Here's a quiz. Take a vote.

You want to hit a home run to win the game. Would you put your faith in
(a) your lucky batting glove?
(b) batting lessons from Sammy Sosa?

You want to cure a cancer that lurks inside you. Would you put your trust in
(a) a sugar pill?
(b) medicine proven to fight cancer?

You want to get to heaven. Would you rather rely on
(a) the potted plant in your living room?
(b) the Savior who died for your sins?

Can you see it? Just having faith in any old thing isn't enough. What counts is believing in a person or thing that actually has the power to do what we need done.

We can have faith no greater than the size of a freckle. But if we put that faith in the right person—Jesus Christ—then faith will bring us forgiveness for sin and a home in heaven. Why? Because it rests in the One we put our faith in.

Christian faith is never fuzzy. It's focused on the real truth of what Jesus did for you. Faith in anything else—no matter how hard you may believe—can't save you!

 TALK: Say it in your own words: What's the difference between having faith in faith—and faith in Jesus?

 PRAY: Pray for friends and neighbors who put their faith in anything other than Jesus.

 ACT: Share the truth of this lesson with a friend who doesn't know Jesus.

23 When Christians Let Us Down

Bible Reading: 2 Peter 3:17-18
Grow in the special favor and knowledge of our Lord and Savior Jesus Christ. 2 Peter 3:18

Mrs. Gustafson had made third grade Carli's best year of Sunday school. First off, she picked Carli to be the donkey in the Christmas play—which doesn't sound so great unless you know that the donkey narrated all the action. Carli still shows off the clay cross she molded that year. And Mrs. Gustafson was the one who helped Carli really understand what it means to trust Jesus. Now that Carli is a little older, she works each week as Mrs. Gustafson's Sunday school helper.

One Sunday when Mrs. Gustafson didn't show up to teach, the children's pastor came to tell her that her teacher needed a week or two off from teaching because a really sad thing had happened in her life. He wouldn't say what. "I'm going to let you talk about that with your parents," he said. "They know."

That afternoon Carli's parents told her that Mrs. Gustafson's husband had decided to divorce her. But he chaired the church council and headed the building committee. When Carli heard the news, she buried her face in her dad's shoulder. "I can't believe he'd leave his wife and kids," she cried. "He's supposed to be a leader. He's supposed to be such a great Christian!"

Talk about this: Have you ever been let down big time by someone you looked up to as a Christian? How did you feel?

Someday you might watch a Christian you respect act in a very un-Christian manner. You're certain to hear someone complain that "all Christians are hypocrites," fakes who pretend to have the right beliefs or behaviors but who don't live up to the message they preach.

The idea that all Christians are hypocrites is a myth. Way back in the first century Peter warned Christians, "There will be false teachers among you. . . . And because of them, Christ and his true way will be slandered" (2 Peter 2:1-2). But one person's hypocrisy doesn't mean all Christians are fakes.

When we learn that someone is a hypocrite, we feel upset. There's one good thing about that: It makes us run to Jesus. He never lets us down. And getting close to him is how we make sure *we* aren't the ones who disobey God and make our faith look foolish. After all, God has the power to "keep you from stumbling" (Jude 24). And that's great news!

 TALK: When have you been disappointed by a Christian leader? Who can you look up to as an example of living close to God?

 PRAY: Pray for the Christian leaders in your life—that they would stay faithful to God.

 ACT: Let your pastor or another leader at church know that you are praying for him or her.

24 Never Believe a Snake in the Grass

Bible Reading: Colossians 1:19-22

Now he has brought you back as his friends. He has done this through his death on the cross in his own human body. As a result, he has brought you into the very presence of God. Colossians 1:22

As Michael stood patiently in the grocery-store checkout with his dad, he couldn't believe what was blaring from the mouth of the woman behind him. With total seriousness she chatted on and on with the next person in line about the amazing healing powers of quartz crystals, pretty little rocks that she hung around her neck, stones that glitter in the sun like diamonds. "I haven't had a sniffle or a headache in over a year," she declared.

The supermarket checkout line isn't the only place you bump into these way-out ideas. You can find that way of thinking in books, newspapers, slick TV shows, and sometimes even at school.

Here are more ways people get involved with unusual miraculous powers:

- A quiet, smart-looking man says he can communicate with animals—whales, dolphins, birds—with musical notes and patterns.
- A TV talk show claims to help people talk to their dead family members.
- An executive uses ancient Chinese principles to make business decisions.
- Kids at a party use horoscopes and a Ouija board to answer questions about their classmates.
- A woman "remembers" being an English princess in the eleventh century.

These are all signs of the mixture of ideas and beliefs called the New Age movement. It isn't an organized religion or group. It's a way of thinking that takes many forms. But people who practice New Age teaching all share a common idea: They say that God is part of everything, so we are all God. It's not hard to spot the problem with that thinking: If everyone were a god, we wouldn't need the God of the Bible.

This mind-set is not new or true. It goes back to the Garden of Eden, where Satan appeared as a serpent and promised Adam and Eve that they would be like God if they ate the forbidden fruit. Satan lied.

The Bible has a one-of-a-kind message. You and I aren't gods. We can't become gods. The one true God became a human in the person of Jesus Christ and died for our sins so we could be friends with him. Isn't that incredible news? You don't have the power to become a god, but you can hang tight to the risen Christ!

 TALK: Have you ever heard people talking about these or other New Age practices? How can you respond?

 PRAY: *God, you alone are God. And we put our trust in you to save us and help us through life.*

 ACT: Do you have friends who believe the false messages of the New Age movement? What wisdom can you share with them?

25 Hey, I Don't Deserve This!

Bible Reading: John 16:31-33

Here on earth you will have many trials and sorrows. But take heart, because I have overcome the world. John 16:33

Jesus couldn't have been more blunt when he said that life would be filled with tough times and sadness. We all face situations that cause us to ask questions only God can answer:

- Nicole, a teenage Christian, drives home late one evening. A car runs through a red stoplight and collides with hers. Nicole spends the next two months in a hospital because of a hit-and-run driver.
- As two-year-old Alonzo toddles down the sidewalk beside his big sister, a mean dog bites him. The doctor has to give Alonzo painful shots to be sure the little guy doesn't get sick.

Most of us would agree on this point: Life isn't fair. And good people who suffer often ask, "Why am *I* going through this bad stuff? I don't deserve this! It's not fair."

People have long asked why bad things happen to good people. Somewhere in the back of our brain we think that good people—especially Christians—shouldn't ever face big struggles, sorrows, and suffering.

God, however, never promised Christians that life would be easy. When Jesus' disciples asked him why people suffer, they pointed to a man who had been born blind. They asked Jesus, "Was it a result of his own sins or those of his parents?" (John 9:2). Jesus responded, "It was not because of his sins or his parents' sins" (verse 3). Then he healed the man.

That's how it is with many of the bad things that happen in the world. Some people suffer because of *their own sin,* like a person who drives drunk and is seriously hurt when he drives off a road. Others suffer because of *the sins of others,* like the girl who was hit by that hit-and-run driver. But some suffering happens just because there is sin in the world. When God created this earth, he set it running with the law of gravity, laws of motion, and so on. Most of the time we benefit from how those laws work. Yet sometimes they make us victims, like when a car misses a curve and flies off an icy road. God doesn't take those laws away for good people.

Accidents, disease, tragedy, death—all of these things happen to both Christians and non-Christians. Your loving Savior never promised you an escape from life's tough stuff, but he did promise to tromp through it with you.

 TALK: Say it in your own words: Why do bad things happen to people? How does God bring hope to bad situations?

 PRAY: *God, thank you that no matter what we face in life, you are with us.*

 ACT: Ask God to help you be kind and understanding as you share this message with hurting friends.

26 Telling What You Know

Bible Reading: Mark 5:1-20

Go home to your friends, and tell them what wonderful things the Lord has done for you. Mark 5:19

Ever heard stories like this?

"I was playing in the park when a kid came over to play with me. We started talking, and soon I asked him, 'Are you sure that you will go to heaven when you die?' He said he wasn't sure. We talked some more, and ten minutes later he prayed and trusted Jesus to be his Savior.

"And the next day a girl in my apartment building came over to watch a video. When I told her I was a Christian, she said she had no idea what a Christian was. So I told her about Jesus, and she also became a Christian.

"Then there was my piano teacher, who . . ."

Talk about it: Do stories like that make you feel guilty because you haven't introduced truckloads of people to Jesus?

Thank God for people who can tell others about Jesus at the park . . . in their neighborhood . . . at school . . . on vacation trips.

But many of us who hear those reports feel like flops as Christians. If you feel unhappy about your abilities as a one-on-one evangelist, the story you read in Mark 5 has a message for you.

As Jesus prepared to sail away, the guy Jesus had helped wanted to join the Lord's disciples. But Jesus gave him an assignment that makes a smart first step in telling people about Jesus. The first part went like this: "Go home to your friends." That seems like the Bible's pattern for witnessing. Start where you live—your family, your friends, your neighbors. (See Acts 1:8. Jesus told his followers to start witnessing in Jerusalem, which was where they lived.)

The second part of Jesus' instructions was to "tell . . . what wonderful things the Lord has done for you" (Mark 5:19). Jesus didn't command this man to come up with a long sermon or to memorize a long list of Bible verses. Instead, Jesus told the man to tell about his own experience with God.

Your first place for one-on-one sharing is right where you live, with people you see every day. And the first thing to share with them is your own experience of learning how Jesus loves you and how he answers your prayers. That's your basic plan for one-on-one witnessing—what Jesus has done for you! Long sermons and memorized verses can work, but the message you know best is the awesomeness of what Jesus has meant in *your* life!

 TALK: How do you expect God can use you to tell others about him?

 PRAY: *Jesus, help us to share you with the people right around us.*

 ACT: What are some things you've learned about Jesus that you can tell someone?

27 On the Outside Looking In

Bible Reading: Mark 6:1-6

A prophet is honored everywhere except in his own hometown and among his relatives and his own family. Mark 6:4

Logan was chubby and brainy. His classmate Olivia was even more chubby and brainy. Unfortunately, their classmates liked to make fun of them.

When Logan and Olivia showed up hand in hand at the last school party of the year, the kids snickered. And when they both tripped and spilled their lemonade, the crowd exploded. Olivia grabbed Logan by the hand and snorted, "Come, Logan. Let's go!" The laughter continued as Logan bumped into the door and dragged Olivia to the ground with him.

Unless you are a very cruel person, you probably feel sad for Logan and Olivia. You might not have the same problems they do, but at some time you may have felt unwanted, unloved, and unwelcomed.

You might think that Jesus never faced that kind of rejection. But the people of this planet had put up a sign for Jesus, the Son of God, that said, "You don't belong here." The apostle John put it bluntly: "Even in his own land and among his own people, he was not accepted" (John 1:11). Jesus was also unwanted by the people of Nazareth, the town where he grew up (see Mark 6).

When you're a Christian, you have to get ready for some rejection. Jesus didn't leave any doubts that at times the world would snub—even hate—his followers: "I chose you to come out of the world, and so it hates you" (John 15:19). It isn't tough to figure out what rejection looks like in our world:

- When you refuse to tease a classmate who doesn't fit in, your buddies might cross you off their list of friends.
- When you won't mess around after the teacher leaves the room, your friends might kick you out in the cold.
- When you won't cheat to get a better score, you might be minus some study partners.

Your loyalty, purity, honesty, and dependability as a Christian will make some people laugh at you just as some of Logan and Olivia's peers laughed at them.

But there's better news. Jesus promised a special blessing for his rejected followers (see Matthew 5:11-12). If you take a stand for what's right, you're in line for eternally significant rewards.

 TALK: As a Christian, you are guaranteed to face rejection. What makes it worth it?

 PRAY: *God, make us strong even when people make fun of our faith.*

 ACT: Do you coast along, hiding the fact that you're a Christian so that no one will make fun of you? How would you like to change that habit?

28 All for Jesus

Bible Reading: Mark 6:14-29

If you want to be my follower you must love me . . . more than your own life. Luke 14:26

On Sunday afternoon, January 8, 1956, five young men stood on the sandy beach of a shallow river. They stared into the jungle, looking for the faces of the Auca Indians of Ecuador. For weeks the missionaries had flown their single-engine plane over the river settlement, dropping gifts in hopes of making friendly contact with the Aucas. On the Friday before, an Auca man and two women had made a friendly visit to the missionaries' beach camp. Now the missionaries waited anxiously for a second face-to-face meeting with the Aucas.

As the five men stood on the river shore, there was a sudden flurry of activity in the undergrowth. Several Auca warriors armed with spears attacked the missionaries. Within minutes the five young men had lost their lives at the river's edge.

The story of Jim Elliot and the other four missionaries was one of the biggest news stories of the 1950s. Five individuals—and the families they left behind—proved that Jesus' command to tell the world about him mattered more to them than their own lives. The families of these men continued working in Ecuador and eventually helped the Aucas learn to follow Jesus Christ.

Talk about it: Why would Jim Elliot and his four coworkers try to make friends with a tribe they knew was hostile?

Living for Jesus means nothing is more important to you than finding out what Jesus wants you to do—and then doing it. For these missionaries, that meant sharing Christ with the Aucas.

Most of us won't ever face a life-and-death test of our faith like the one those five young men met in the jungle. But we can still give our life as a living sacrifice. Do you remember what Paul wrote to the Romans? Read this great verse slowly: "And so, dear brothers and sisters, I plead with you to give your bodies to God. Let them be a living and holy sacrifice—the kind he will accept. When you think of what he has done for you, is this too much to ask?" (Romans 12:1).

Few Christians will ever be called to die bringing the gospel to a jungle tribe. But each of us can keep the command of Jesus to lay down our life by choosing to obey him no matter what he asks us to do or where he leads us!

 TALK: What does it look like to live your whole life for Jesus—even if you're not a missionary?

 PRAY: *God, give us courage to obey you even when we have to give up everything.*

 ACT: Many missionaries still put their lives on the line for Jesus. Ask your pastor if your church supports any Christians working in hostile, "closed" countries.

29 One of God's Great Gifts

Bible Reading: Colossians 3:1-4

Since you have been raised to new life with Christ, set your sights on the realities of heaven. Colossians 3:1

Yesterday you heard about five friends who died bringing God's Good News to the Auca tribe of Ecuador. Take a vote: What's your gut response when you hear about Jim Elliot and his missionary coworkers?

- I want to be just like Jim. Book me an afternoon flight to the jungle.
- I'm hiding behind my couch and not coming out until everyone on the planet is a Christian.
- I think Jim and his buddies would have been safer at home in a church bowling league.
- I want to follow Jesus no matter what, being courageous like Jim in whatever I face.

It's reckless to jump into a situation we don't understand. It's cowardly if all we think about is staying safe at home, not that bowling is a bad thing. But that last choice . . . that's tough. Who knows where Jesus will take us?

Talk about it: What does it mean if we say, "I want to be courageous"? What can happen when we follow Jesus?

Jim Elliot and his friends weren't looking for an early trip to heaven. Their aim in carrying the gospel to the Aucas was to bring life, not death. Yet they were called to give their lives. And without a doubt, they and their families believed the price was worth paying!

Those missionaries had a secret. They knew that for both the Aucas and for themselves, earthly life doesn't last forever. But a relationship with Jesus Christ does. And they traded something temporary for something permanent. As Jim Elliot wrote in his journal before his death: "He is no fool who gives up what he cannot keep to gain what he cannot lose."

Those missionary friends weren't just thinking about earth. They had set their minds on heaven. And they knew that their real life was with Christ.

We can't keep our life or any of the things of earth forever. But the good stuff God promises us will last for eternity. Jim Elliot and friends had hearts set on things that last. They knew exactly where Jesus would take them. Do you?

 TALK: What makes following Jesus worth the price? What benefits of being a Christian do you enjoy right now?

 PRAY: *God, we're inspired by the commitment of those five missionary families in Ecuador. Help us to be courageous wherever you lead us.*

 ACT: Get in touch with a missionary family via e-mail or airmail. Tell them you are praying for them to be courageous—and be sure you do!

Buying into the System

Bible Reading: 1 John 2:15-17

Stop loving this evil world and all that it offers you, for when you love the world, you show that you do not have the love of the Father in you.
1 John 2:15

By the end of his first day at camp, David knew his clothes were all wrong. He said to himself, *I thought only girls have to worry about what they wear. But even the guys have to wear just the right kind of swimming trunks and hiking shoes and T-shirts.*

Talk about it: When have you been tempted go on a spending spree to keep up with the crowd and fit in? How else have you felt pressured to fit into a mold?

The squeeze we all feel to fit in with our surroundings is real. The problem isn't just us. It's even bigger than our peers. It's what the apostle John calls "the world."

In many versions of the Bible, John's warning not to "love the world" sounds confusing. After all, God created this awesome world as a gift to us. He thought up beaches—and then tucked inside some dude's head the idea of a surfboard. The same John who wrote these words also recorded Jesus' wild promise to give us "life in all its fullness" (John 10:10). And James tells us that "whatever is good and perfect comes to us from God above, who created all heaven's lights" (James 1:17).

So the world we're not supposed to love must not just be the stuff we see all around us. The New Living Translation quoted at the top of this page makes the meaning clear. John warned us against loving a different kind of world—an *evil* world. In an evil world we focus on at least three things:

1. Satisfying our sinful nature (making life revolve around ourselves)
2. Grabbing hold of the sinful things we see (being wowed by outward appearances rather than truly good things)
3. Being too proud of what we have (not admitting that everything we own is a gift from God)

That's the "world" we're not to fall in love with. It's a way of living that John said is run by Satan, "the prince of this world" (John 12:31).

You don't have to dress in a paper bag. But whenever you feel you have to make anything more important than God, that's a warning to get away from the evil in the world. That world can't bring you life like God can!

 TALK: Say it in your own words: What exactly is "the world"? When have you felt pressured by it?

 PRAY: *God, help us desire things that last forever. Help us not to get pulled into the attitude of the evil world.*

 ACT: Got that checklist of three characteristics of the world? Spot how "the world" pressures you today. And report back!

The Journey

Bible Reading: 1 John 1:8–2:2

If we confess our sins to him, he is faithful and just to forgive us and to cleanse us from every wrong. 1 John 1:9

"Don't expect me to be a some superstar Christian," Ty protested. "I try to be like my pastor and the missionaries who come to visit my church. They're totally strong Christians. They're so perfect, and I'm not. I'll never be like them."

The mature Christians you know—or know of—might be more than enough to make you feel like a spiritual midget. But grab a look at a few more spiritual giants: Some of our Bible heroes "were tortured, preferring to die rather than turn from God and be free. . . . Some were mocked. . . . Others were chained in dungeons. Some died by stoning, and some were sawed in half; others were killed with the sword" (Hebrews 11:35-37).

Don't think you're immediately and instantly going to be like Abraham or Moses or Ruth or David or Paul. That's the same as wanting to be a baseball hero like Hank Aaron when you're playing T-ball. Or an Olympic skater like Michelle Kwan when you still skate with a pillow taped to your backside. Or a famous golfer like Tiger Woods when you haven't yet learned to swing a fork.

Here's some truth that might shock you—and encourage you. Those Bible heroes were not born spiritual giants. And not one of them was perfect. This is what the Bible says in 1 John: If we claim we never sin, we are just kidding ourselves—and calling God a liar.

Those ultramature Christians also needed to know how to make things right with God: "If we confess our sins to him," John wrote, "he is faithful and just to forgive us and to cleanse us from every wrong" (1 John 1:9). When we get honest about what we have done, God forgives us for every evil deed.

If you can read those verses from 1 John through the eyes of those great heroes, you'll realize that all believers are on a journey. The first step isn't to be totally mature. It's to be totally honest about where we're at. God knows we aren't mature. God knows we sin. But he still loves us. And he wants to take us by the hand and lead us on the path toward heaven.

TALK: Do you get discouraged when you hear about great heroes of the faith? How can those folks bring you inspiration rather than frustration?

PRAY: *God, thanks for taking us on the journey of following you.*

ACT: First John 1:9 is a verse you're guaranteed to need as you walk the journey of faith. How about making a bookmark to keep by that verse? If you say the verse every time you open your Bible to it, you'll soon know it very well. And you'll never forget it!

Busted–or Blessed?

Bible Reading: Psalm 19:7-11

There is great reward for those who obey [the laws of the Lord].
Psalm 19:11

You waited all year long for the note from the school office saying it was your turn to serve on the student discipline committee. Your new job for the last two weeks of the school year, you figure, is to help the principal and teachers hunt down the bad guys and hand out punishments. You're ready to bring down the hammer of justice on your school's bad dudes. With you on duty, if they did the crime, they'll do the time.

You dig through the school rule book, memorizing each and every regulation. "Rule number 802, point 11-B," you read. "Students in the lunchroom may not talk louder than in a normal conversational voice." You stop chewing your liverwurst sandwich and eyeball your peers. At this very instant your entire class is breaking that rule. You could expel them all. Busted!

But when you finally meet with the principal and teachers, you find they're really most interested in finding ways to get students to do right, not just nail them for doing wrong. You thought the rules were all about catching kids being bad. Surprisingly, you find they're more about the great rewards for people who act good.

Talk about this: Why are there rules in life?

Here's some good news about rules: Rules don't just punish bad people; they protect and provide for good people. When we live within the right boundaries, we gain things like freedom, safety, possessions, and other highly prized outcomes.

God's law isn't just a rule book jammed full of reasons to send people to the slammer. Rules, regulations, and consequences aren't the only things we need to know about God's law, because the law isn't just about "thou shalt" do this and "thou shalt not" do that.

Sure, we have to know where God's boundaries are. Psalm 19:11 says that God's laws serve as "a warning to those who hear them." But the next phrase paints the rest of the picture: "There is great reward for those who obey them." Warnings reward us with God's protection and provision–things like peace with God, healthy relationships with others, and eternal life.

The goal of God's Word isn't to hurt us but to help grow us up to be God's happy followers. God isn't out to catch us doing something wrong but to coach us in doing what's right. He loves us so much he wants us to enjoy the rewards of living within his law.

 TALK: Isn't God great for giving us his Word, not to hammer us but to heal us? What good do God's rules do us?

 PRAY: *God, thanks for all the good reasons you give us your commands. Thank you that your rules protect and provide for us.*

 ACT: When you want to wiggle out from under a rule today, write down the rule. Then write down three good reasons that rule exists.

2 Stick with the Game Plan

Bible Reading: Psalm 119:1-8

Happy are those who obey his decrees and search for him with all their hearts. Psalm 119:2

Bruiser Bootkanski was the best. Without question, he was the greatest quarterback ever in the NFL. Cheerleaders adored him, kids idolized him, and all the cereal companies wanted his picture on their boxes. Bruiser was a total football hero . . . at least until the big game.

All his life Bruiser had waited to play in the Super Bowl. Not every player gets that chance, but Bruiser did. He was determined to make the most of it. Bruiser didn't just want to win. He wanted to be the Super Bowl superstar by scoring the winning touchdown.

The game was close because the teams were evenly matched. Every time Bruiser's team got the ball, he threw it with laser accuracy, and it usually paid off with a score. The coach's game plan was for Bruiser to throw, throw, throw—and it worked. Unfortunately, the other team had racked up just as many points.

So the game came down to the last few seconds. Bruiser dropped back to pass, and the final gun sounded. If he didn't throw for a touchdown now, the game was lost. With the goal line only a few yards away and his receiver in the clear in the end zone, all Bruiser had to do was to throw the ball to him. It was the game plan.

Bruiser, though, wanted to score the winning touchdown. So instead of passing the ball to the receiver, he ran for the end zone. He could hear his coach yelling, "Throw the ball, Bruiser! Throw the ball!" But Bruiser wouldn't listen. He darted, he dodged, and he dove for the line . . . and came up one foot short.

Bruiser never became that Super Bowl hero. Instead of experiencing the thrill of victory, he dragged his team to defeat. If he had only stuck with the game plan.

You get the chance to make game-winning choices every day. When you make the right choices, you experience the happiness of success. When you make the wrong choice, well, we all know what it's like to live with the consequences of bad choices. Good outcomes result from good decisions, and good decisions result when you follow God's game plan: his Word.

Psalm 119:2 promises happiness to all who obey God's decrees. That's right—God really wants us to be happy. He gave us his Word so we can know how to obey him and experience the same happiness as the football player who gets to the end zone.

 TALK: How have good decisions led to good outcomes in your life?

 PRAY: *God, thank you for the good things you have made happen in our life.*

 ACT: Remind a friend today why rules are a good idea.

The Instruction Manual

Bible Reading: Psalm 119:9-16

*I have hidden your word in my heart, that I might not sin against you.
Psalm 119:11*

You keep dreaming about the day when you will be sixteen years old. You already feel the breeze blowing through your hair. You picture you and your friends cruising the town in your brand-new SUV as you sit proudly behind the wheel.

You enter your local DMV—that's the Department of Motor Vehicles—and get in line, eager to walk out with a driver's license. Ms. Gearshift, the cheery clerk, hands you a sheet of paper. "Take a seat at the table, answer the questions, and return the sheet to me when you're done." *Sounds simple,* you think. *They just need my name and address and phone number.*

So you sit down and glance at the paper. *Wait a minute! This isn't an application. It's a test!* You start to sweat. Question after question asks about speed limits, signaling, and traffic laws. You recall hearing something about a driver's test, but you never gave it much thought. You get in the car, start the engine, and work the pedals. What's so hard?

You push your way back to Ms. Gearshift. "I've been watching my parents drive all my life. I've taken rides in cars, and once I even sat behind the wheel. I know that green means go and red means stop. I'm sure I can drive, so I don't need a test. Just take my picture and give me my license."

Friendly Ms. Gearshift suddenly glares at you with beady eyes. "If you can't pass the test, you don't know the rules. And if you don't know the rules, you can't drive. Drivers who don't know the rules are dangerous." Then she shoves a driver's instruction booklet at you. "It's your choice, kid. Learn the rules and pass the test, or when you get to be my age you'll be begging your mommy to drive you to work."

You swallow hard. "But these questions are pretty hard," you whine.

"That's the point. There's a lot to know. But the answers are right here." Ms. Gearshift taps the booklet. "Get this stuff down pat, and you won't have a problem with the test—either here or on the road."

Know what? God has given us the Bible as our instruction manual for life. If we don't study the book, we'll likely fail the test—and hurt people because of our carelessness. But if we ponder God's Word, stick it in our memory, and live by its directions, we will know how to safely move through life.

 TALK: God is a lot more friendly than Ms. Gearshift when he says, "Learn this stuff and it will help you pass every test." How are you using God's manual to direct your life?

 PRAY: *Thanks, God, for giving rules meant to steer us toward good things.*

 ACT: If you have never read the Bible on your own, start today by getting your nose into God's instruction manual for life!

4 Which Way Is Up When You're Down?

Bible Reading: Psalm 119:25-32

I lie in the dust, completely discouraged; revive me by your word.
Psalm 119:25

Three years ago, Doug's parents were divorced. He knew, of course, that they were having trouble. He had heard the arguments. Even so, Doug never expected Dad to walk out on him and his mom and not come back. But he did.

Dad promised to call when he could. "You're still my son," his dad had assured him when he left. "That will never change, I promise."

Now those words rattle painfully in Doug's head. Yesterday was Doug's birthday, and Dad didn't call.

Even if we've never been slammed by a bitter, hurtful disappointment like Doug's, we all have faced smaller discouragements. Somebody fails us, something goes wrong, a plan doesn't work, a friend says something unkind, a dream goes unrealized, we get a poor grade. We can't avoid it. Discouragement happens.

So how do you cope? Here's a pretty serious checklist. Which choice best describes what you do when you get down?

☐ I get mad at everyone, including people who didn't cause the problem.
☐ I sulk and want to be alone.
☐ I throw things. If I can't lift something, I punch it.
☐ I stuff my mouth full of food until I feel better.
☐ I get so mad at God that I skip devotions and avoid church.
☐ I zone out with music or use the TV to drown out my pain.

Recognizing that we're down is the first step to getting back up. God doesn't want us to get stuck in discouragement. He has a cure.

It's not a pill. It's actually an exercise.

Here's what you do. You sit down with your Bible, open it, and begin reading. Or you go for a walk and think about a verse you have memorized.

The psalmist wrote, "I lie in the dust, completely discouraged; revive me by your word" (119:25). Discouragement knocks us down—God's Word picks us up. Discouragement leaves us in the dark—God's Word shines new light. Discouragement yanks us away from God and others—God's Word helps us tighten relationships. The Bible is God's way out of discouragement. It's how God gets us up when we're down.

 TALK: How have you used the Bible to help you up when you're down? What has it taught you?

 PRAY: *God, we want to listen to your words of encouragement when we're discouraged. Thanks for giving us your Word.*

 ACT: When you get to know God's encouraging Word, you're better equipped to pass it on. Share a bit of God's Word with a discouraged friend today.

5 Read All about It

Bible Reading: Psalm 119:89-96
Forever, O Lord, your word stands firm in heaven. Psalm 119:89

Courtney took her place in front of the class. She sniffled twice, cleared her throat, and pushed her glasses up on her nose. Then she held her report up within easy view, just as her teacher had shown her. "My report," she said, "is about the rhinoceros."

"Rhinoceroses," Courtney read, "have long necks so they can eat leaves from the top of trees. They have bills like a duck and pouches to carry their babies, tiny hooves to run fast, and spots to help them hide in the jungle. They also have gills to breathe underwater and a big throat and wings so they can fly down and scoop fish to eat from the ocean."

You can't believe everything you hear in a school report. If Courtney's job was to create a silly make-believe animal, she hit a bull's-eye. But if her assignment was to give her classmates accurate facts about the rhinoceros, she missed by a mile.

You don't have to look far in most school assignments to find slipups or even slap-you-in-the-face mistakes. But after your teacher points out your mistakes and you've learned from them, you probably file your paper in a round basket at the back of the room.

The Bible, however, is different. Its message will last forever. It was here before we arrived and will be here after we die. Why? Because it's "God-breathed." It's God's Word.

Not only is the Bible written to last forever, but it is totally without mistakes. We can stake our life on its accuracy and look to it for error-free guidance and inspiration. Dr. Henrietta Mears wrote, "The Bible is a story—it is a revelation, to be begun and pursued and ended as we start and continue other books. Don't trifle with the Bible. . . . Believe that every book is about something and read and reread until you find out what that something is."*

God gives us the Bible as our absolutely reliable guide to life. He is perfect, so we can trust his Word to be perfect. Whenever we open our Bible to read, we find a message from God waiting for us. What he lovingly shows us will be totally true.

 TALK: Why do you read the Bible? What are you looking for? How has the Bible helped you learn to trust God?

 PRAY: *God, we are eager to get to know you better each time we read your Word. Thanks that your Word is trustworthy and true.*

 ACT: Show your eagerness for the Bible by spending some time reading it on your own today.

---

*Henrietta C. Mears, *What the Bible Is All About* (Ventura, Calif.: Regal Books, 1966), 10.

June

6 The Love That You Need

Bible Reading: Daniel 10:10-11, 19

Don't be afraid . . . for you are deeply loved by God. Daniel 10:19

Dimitri had spent a little too much time doing BMX bike stunts—on his video-game machine, that is. He told his parents all about the awesome tricks he could land if he had a real BMX bike of his own. Dimitri pestered his parents to get him the bike *now*. When his parents replied that he would need to save up his allowance, do extra chores, and find ways to work for the neighbors, he handed them his Christmas list— in June. Over and over Dimitri repeated what he thought was the best argument of all: "I *need* that bike!"

Dimitri *wants* a bike, but it doesn't count as a *need*. In fact, even our biggest human needs—for food, air, and water—can't compare to our gigantic need *to love and be loved.*

You might know in your head that you're loved. After all, the Bible makes God's love for you stunningly clear. And someone very near to you—a parent, a grandparent, or a close friend—has probably said those magic little words, "I love you."

But hearing about love isn't enough. The big question is whether we *feel* loved. See, only when our understanding of love hits our brain *and* our heart do we feel we really belong.

We can be sure, for example, that God loves us. John 1:12 declares that when we receive Christ we become God's children. But just *knowing* that fact inside and out doesn't mean we've grasped the truth and *experienced* it. Have you ever thought about everything that God's love means? Take a look at these truths too:

- The God who made the universe wants a close, family relationship with you. If you have trusted Christ, you are his child.
- God welcomes you into his arms as a dearly loved child simply because he wants you as his child.
- God knows all about your weaknesses, your lack of love—and your past, present, and future sins—and he still wants you as his child.

These facts sound too good to be true, but because God is God they *are* true! God wants to grip our heart and mind so we *feel* loved. He says, "You are deeply loved by [me]" (see Daniel 10:19). Take that verse and personalize it: "God loves me deeply. I don't have to be afraid or insecure. I'm lovable." Isn't that incredible?

 TALK: What did you learn about God's love for you?

 PRAY: Spend some time thanking God for what he has shown about himself to you.

 ACT: Share these truths with a friend who isn't sure about God's love.

7 I Love You—Period!

Bible Reading: Ephesians 2:4-10
Salvation is not a reward for the good things we have done, so none of us can boast about it. Ephesians 2:9

Jeremy was one of the most popular boys in his neighborhood. All year long he had a group of guys over playing games, scarfing a feast of snacks, and hanging in front of the wide-screen TV. And a couple of times each summer he invited his best buddies to his parents' cabin, where they ramped through the woods on four-wheelers.

Get the picture? Jeremy had a waiting list of people who wanted to be his friend.

Then Jeremy's dad lost his job—and his family had to sell off almost everything they owned. Gone were the big house full of toys, the wide-screen TV, and the cabin on the lake. Jeremy's family landed in a small apartment nearby so he and his sister wouldn't have to change schools.

A few months after the downsizing, Jeremy had no buddies. "My friends weren't interested in me," he said. "They were my friends only when we had stuff."

Talk about it: Have you ever felt like someone wanted to be your friend because your backyard had a monster sandbox? Or because you got the season's hottest new video game for your birthday?

If all we know is love with strings attached, we might have a hard time believing God loves us just because he does.

Tamera, for example, used to hear about God's love and think, *What's he really want?* She would get suspicious of God's kindness, wondering what the catch was. But now she says she's learned that God does want her to love and obey him. But he loves her whether or not she loves him back.

Jim figures he has to strike a bargain with God. *I need to straighten out my life before God will care about me,* he thinks. But God says, "I already accept you just the way you are. I proved it by sending my Son to die for you while you were lost in your sin" (see Romans 5:8).

Because God loves us unconditionally, we don't have to perform perfectly to get God to accept us. That's what Paul meant when he wrote, "It is by grace you have been saved, through faith—and this not from yourselves, it is the gift of God—not by works, so that no one can boast" (Ephesians 2:8-9, NIV). Our acceptance with God isn't based on our good deeds or great attitudes or on anything snappy we've done for him. He loves us unconditionally because of what *he* has done.

When God shows us his love, there's no catch. He really cares.

 TALK: God loves you unconditionally. What does that mean to your everyday life?

 PRAY: *Father, you love me without strings. Thanks.*

 ACT: Show some love to a friend today—just because you want to.

Wrong Way!

Bible Reading: Isaiah 43:1-4

Do not be afraid, for I have ransomed you. I have called you by name; you are mine. Isaiah 43:1

University of California football player Roy Riegels made Rose Bowl history back in 1929. In the second quarter of the game, he scooped up a Georgia Tech fumble and headed for the *wrong* end zone. He was tackled—by a teammate—just before crossing the goal line. His mistake would have earned Georgia Tech six points. Riegels's team had to punt from their own end zone. Georgia Tech blocked the kick, resulting in a two-point safety that eventually won the game for Georgia Tech.

During halftime, the California players filed glumly into the dressing room. Riegels slumped in a corner, buried his face in his hands, and sobbed uncontrollably. Coach Price offered no halftime pep talk. What could he say? As the team got ready to go out for the second half, his only comment was, "Men, the same team that played the first half will start the second."

The players started for the door, all but Roy Riegels. Coach Price walked to the corner where Riegels sat and said quietly, "Roy, didn't you hear me?"

"I can't do it," Roy protested. "I have ruined you, the university, and myself."

Coach Price put his hand on the player's shoulder. "Roy, get up and go back; the game is only half over." Inspired by his coach's confidence, Roy Riegels went out to play again. After the game, the Georgia Tech players said Riegels played harder in the second half than they had ever seen anyone play.

What you see in Coach Price is just a glimmer of God's accepting attitude toward us. We make mistakes. Once in a while we run the wrong way. And when we stumble and fall, we make the problem worse by shrinking from God in shame. But he comes to us and says, "Get up and keep going; the game is only half over." That's unconditional love for you to receive and enjoy!

In Isaiah 43:1 God promises to love and accept you. He says, "You belong to me; you are mine." Make that verse personal: "The God of the universe has called me by name. He says I belong to him."

God doesn't disown you when you go the wrong way. He never says, "You blew it, so you don't belong to me any longer." Sure, he wants you to turn around and go the right way, and he puts his Spirit inside you to get you going again. But he never says anything but, "You belong to me, you are mine."

 TALK: Think of an area where you've blown it. What does God think of you now that you've messed up?

 PRAY: *God, thanks for believing in us even when we blow it.*

 ACT: Show someone the kind of acceptance that God has shown to you.

9 You're Accepted, Not an Exception

Bible Reading: Romans 15:5-7

Accept each other just as Christ has accepted you. Romans 15:7

You're baffled. You used to think your room was pretty big. But as you look around you realize—well—that you can hardly turn your head. A few months ago you could do gymnastic flip-flops in here. Now you can barely budge an elbow. And while you're trying to figure out how to make your place feel more roomy, you're suddenly squeezed from the comfy home that's been yours for the past nine months.

Bright lights hit your eyes. Loud noises blast your ears. You definitely have room to stretch. And now you have a new job. You have to breathe!

You don't remember the huge change that took place when you were *born*. But think for a moment what happened to you when you were *born again*—that time when you trusted Christ as your Savior and God accepted you as his child:

- You became an heir of God (see Ephesians 1:13-14).
- You were adopted into God's family (see Ephesians 1:5).
- Your heart was filled with God's love (see Romans 5:5).
- You will never be separated from God's love (see Romans 8:38-39).
- You will spend eternity with God in a place he has prepared for you (see John 14:1-4).
- You were welcomed into a new family, and you are a member in good standing throughout all eternity (see 1 Corinthians 12:13, 27).

Some days you might feel as bewildered by life as a baby getting his first whiff of air. But you can be sure of all the truths listed above. They add up to one certain fact: You are accepted by God.

When Jesus took a group of kids into his arms and blessed them (see Mark 10:16), you can bet that they weren't perfect little angels. They were kids—disobedient, disagreeable, sometimes downright bad. Yet Jesus showed God's unconditional love by blessing the imperfect little ones.

God wants us to accept ourselves the way we are—knowing that we have weaknesses as well as strengths, shortcomings as well as abilities. And God challenges us to show the world the same kind of love he shows us. "Accept one another, then," wrote Paul, "just as Christ accepted you, in order to bring praise to God" (Romans 15:7, NIV). And if you want to love like God loves, then start by seeing yourself as God sees you: totally acceptable and totally lovable.

 TALK: In light of all God has done to prove his unconditional love, what keeps you from seeing yourself as lovable?

 PRAY: *God, thanks for accepting us. Help us to see ourselves and others the way you do.*

 ACT: Don't spend your day hiding your flaws and failures. Let people see the real you today.

10 Dad Really Loves Me

Bible Reading: Romans 8:14-17
His Holy Spirit speaks to us deep in our hearts and tells us that we are God's children. Romans 8:16

Addy had never known what it was like to have a stable home. Given up by her mom shortly after she was born, she had spent her whole childhood being shuffled from house to house. For the past two years she had lived in a group home, with an awesome young couple as houseparents. That should have felt more like a family, but the kids who lived there were distant—like they knew they had no hope of finding a real family, and they were just waiting until they turned eighteen so they could leave.

Then the Sampsons came into her life. Addy had always tried to be the perfect child, one that a couple would want to adopt. Yet for the first time in her life, Addy didn't have to wish she was different or struggle to fit someone's mold. The Sampsons actually *wanted* a thirteen-year-old girl. They loved her just the way she was. And right before Christmas, they made her a permanent part of their family by adopting her.

As Christians, we belong to God and his family. Who could enjoy a bigger sense of belonging than God's kids? The apostle John wrote, "See how very much our heavenly Father loves us, for he allows us to be called his children, and we really are!" (1 John 3:1). Something to notice: As soon as John wrote the words "his children," he must have paused as that truth hit him, because he tops off the thought with an exclamation. If John were here today, he might say it this way: "Whoa! We really *are* God's children! That's incredible!"

Maybe you're thinking, "But we're only *adopted*. It's not like we're real children in God's family." Do you think the fact that God has simply adopted us makes us second-class kids?

Listen to how my longtime friend Dick Day views adoption. After having become the parents of five biological children, Dick and his wife, Charlotte, went to Korea and adopted a sixth child, Jimmy. Dick says, "That little guy Jimmy is my son. He has the same rights and privileges as our other five children. He has the same access to our inheritance, our time, and our love." And you know what? Jimmy sees himself just as much as Dick and Charlotte's child as do his siblings.

Our adoption as God's child is a truth worth getting excited about. We can say these words with enthusiasm and awe: "Whoa! I really am a child of God! I really belong!"

 TALK: In your own words tell how you feel about being adopted by God.

 PRAY: *Father, thank you for making us your children.*

 ACT: Take time today to pull out a blank sheet of paper and write a letter to your Father—your *heavenly* Father. Tell him what it means to you to be his child.

Can't Buy Me Love

Bible Reading: 1 Corinthians 12:13, 24-27
All the members care for each other equally. 1 Corinthians 12:25

After five weeks in his new neighborhood, Derrick still didn't fit in. With no friends—no one to hopscotch with, no one to hang on the monkey bars with, and no hope of anyone showing up at his birthday party—he took matters into his own hands. He made a decision: If he couldn't *make* friends, he would *buy* some.

The next day Derrick walked out on the playground with the rolled-up wad of bills he had earned for years of doing extra chores at home. His cash quickly drew a crowd. "Hmmm . . ." he said out loud as he spun around, eyeing his choices. "A dollar for you," he said to a great hopscotch partner. "And a dollar for you," he said to a master monkey-bars climber. "And a five for *you*," he said to the most popular kid on the block. "My birthday is next month. Let's be friends for a *long* time."

Derrick's strategy no doubt won friends for a while. But guess what? His pool of pals dried up the instant his money did.

Talk about it: What kinds of crazy things do we do to get friends?

God has a great plan for us to find the good friendships we all need. He knew we might have a hard time believing how much he loves and accepts us, so he gave us a one-of-a-kind place to find love. You might be surprised to learn the name of this awesomely accepting place. It's the church.

When you believed in Jesus as your Savior and Lord, you became a part of the church—not just *a* church, but the big group of people everywhere who follow Jesus.

The Bible refers to the church as Christ's body. The church—the body of Christ—is made up of Christians from all around the world (see 1 Corinthians 12:13, 24-27). You and I and every other Christian are all closely related to each other. And just like a body can't get along without its various parts, we all need and are needed by the rest of the body.

When you fumble, fail, or feel rejected, God plans for your Christian friends to remind you that you are loved and accepted no matter what. And when someone in your group feels awful, it's your job to come alongside with encouraging words (see 1 Thessalonians 5:11).

You don't have to hand out money to be accepted. Hanging tight with other Christians is God's far better plan for you!

TALK: How are you making the most of being part of a group of loving believers—are you letting God's love touch you through them?

PRAY: *God, strengthen our relationships with our Christian sisters and brothers.*

ACT: Do you need to strengthen your bonds with other Christians? Schedule some time together!

12 Icky Boy Germs?

Bible Reading: Philippians 2:1–4

Don't think only about your own affairs, but be interested in others, too, and what they are doing. Philippians 2:4

Emily has had crushes on boys since she was in first grade. Every evening and weekend she ties up the phone with her calls. She has a buddy list of boys to bug on-line that is as long as her arm. Her brain is bogged down in mushiness and gushiness.

Emily is headed for problems. Kids who start boy-girl craziness early on usually don't make very good choices. They often don't keep their parents clued in to what's going on in their head or heart. And boys or girls like Emily are usually thinking about all sorts of stuff besides asking God to help them make good choices.

Here's a huge question for you kids to ask your parents: "Back when you were our age, could you ever imagine growing up and getting married?"

Kids, maybe you've never thought about two vital facts:

Fact Number One: Growing up is unstoppable. You're maturing. Sooner than you can imagine, you'll look just like your mom and dad!

Fact Number Two: Someday you may get married. Right now you might worry about catching cooties from the guys or girls you know. But sooner or later you'll start noticing how cute somebody is.

Even if you're miles away from ever liking a boy or girl, it's crucial to get into your head *now* what good boy-girl relationships look like. It's the only way you'll get God's best when your parents and you decide you're ready to date.

See, for some growing-up guys or gals the whole world is about *boyfriends and girlfriends*. Like Emily, they're stuck in mush and gush. They make bad choices. Their big goal is to latch on to someone they can call their own.

God has a far better way for you to see the world. Life isn't just about *boyfriends and girlfriends*. It's about *friends*. You know you're on track when your big goal isn't to fall in love but to grow in friendship. You aim to find out what makes another person tick, and you watch out for his or her interests. That's the kind of relationship where real love starts.

When you wonder about your far-off future—like dating and finding a mate—*friendship* is the word you want to keep in the front of your brain. It's how you'll find your best friend for life!

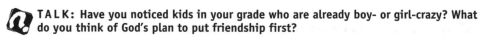 **TALK:** Have you noticed kids in your grade who are already boy- or girl-crazy? What do you think of God's plan to put friendship first?

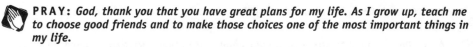 **PRAY:** *God, thank you that you have great plans for my life. As I grow up, teach me to choose good friends and to make those choices one of the most important things in my life.*

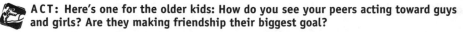 **ACT:** Here's one for the older kids: How do you see your peers acting toward guys and girls? Are they making friendship their biggest goal?

13 Staying within the Lines

Bible Reading: 2 Corinthians 6:14-18

Don't team up with those who are unbelievers. How can goodness be a partner with wickedness? 2 Corinthians 6:14

Did young Noah ever take his future bride on a romantic boat ride?

Did Moses ever take his girlfriend to the Saturday-night chariot races?

Did Jacob and Rachel go out for pizza and Cokes before they were married?

We might never know the answers to those deep questions, because we can't find dating in the Bible. Dating wasn't a part of Bible-times society. Back then, parents usually decided who their children were going to marry.

You've probably never thought of the upside of letting your folks pick your mate. You wouldn't have to worry about dating someday. And you'd be able to tell the google-eyed guy or girl you couldn't stand: "Buzz off. I'm taken."

The arranged-marriage idea has drawbacks, however. When you were just a baby your parents may have signed you up to marry the cutest baby on the block—but in high school that kid might still be sucking his thumb. Besides that, there's a little thing called love. Wouldn't you like to love the person you're going to live with all of your married life?

You're probably glad that someday your parents will let you look for your own mate. You're probably twice as glad that you have a bunch of years before you have to make the ultraimportant decision of which lucky person you're going to marry. Even so, there's something you can decide right now. You want to decide today that when the time comes, you'll look for God's very best for you—a mate who follows God.

When 2 Corinthians 6:14 (NIV) says not to be "yoked" with unbelievers, it's referring to the yoke that oxen wore when they were used as farm animals to pull plows and other farm equipment. It was important for a team of oxen not to pull in different directions. In the same way, Christians shouldn't marry non-Christians, because they want different things out of life. They will try to go in different directions.

If a committed Christian is the kind of person you want to marry someday, then decide today that they are the only people you'll ever date. Then you'll be living by the same wise rule you'll need when you're ready to date or to pick a mate. Getting "yoked" to another Christian is God's most important guideline for finding your best friend for life!

 TALK: How is God's guideline in 2 Corinthians 6:14 meant to make your life great—not miserable?

 PRAY: *God, we want your very best in all of life—including the people we choose to love.*

 ACT: If you're ready, hit Mom and Dad with all your guy-girl questions.

June
14 It's All about Character

Bible Reading: Galatians 5:19-23
When the Holy Spirit controls our lives, he will produce this kind of fruit in us: love, joy, peace, patience, kindness, goodness, faithfulness, gentleness, and self-control. Galatians 5:22-23

Imagine this: You're a girl. (Okay, if you're a guy that's tough to wrap your brain around, but try.) You've been picked as a contestant on the hit game show *Meet Your Perfect Match*. Your job is to pick your perfect marriage partner from three goofy guys sharing the stage with you. By asking and answering several questions, you discover all sorts of significant stuff you have in common. So tell which characteristic makes your guy a great choice for you to marry for life:

(a) You both carry Scooby Doo lunch boxes.
(b) You each think the other is really cute.
(c) You both are exceedingly popular.
(d) You both spend spring break snorkeling with stingrays.
(e) You both are growing Christians who show the character of Christ.

Hmmm . . . not too tough.

But here's something really big to think about. If the goal of going out is to find a best friend with whom to spend the rest of your life, then you aren't looking for how popular someone is, how cute she is, what toys he owns, or the opinions of friends. What makes a winner is the stuff on the inside. Galatians 5:22-23 lists the huge character qualities you need in any good friend—especially your best friend for life.

Actually, that last choice in the list above is the *first* question to ask about someone you like or want to go out with—or someday get hitched to. When you know someone you like is a committed Christian, then you get to start figuring out if you have similar goals and personality as well as a desire to get along—all the things that can help you decide whether God means for you to spend your lives together. (By the way, God won't make you marry someone you can't stand to look at!)

Winning a bride or groom on a bizarre TV game show is not likely God's best plan for you. The person you marry will be someone you choose. If you date losers— like people who fail the Galatians 5:22-23 test—you greatly increase your odds of marrying a loser. But if you pick winners, it's likely you will marry a winner.

 TALK: Would your parents ever ship you to Hollywood to be a contestant on *Meet Your Perfect Match*? How come? Why do you need to keep in mind the standards in Galatians 5 *right now*?

 PRAY: *God, thank you that in your perfect timing you will bring special people into our life—guys or girls that meet your standards.*

 ACT: Here are some giant questions to ask Dad and Mom: When will it be okay to date? On what kind of dates? How will we decide who I should date?

166

June 15

Do You Have That Loving Feeling?

Bible Reading: 1 Corinthians 13:1-3

If I gave everything I have to the poor and even sacrificed my body, I could boast about it; but if I didn't love others, I would be of no value whatsoever. 1 Corinthians 13:3

Six months after Brandon trusted Jesus, he's studying his Bible and getting rid of the rotten stuff in his life. He's feeling pretty cool as a Christian.

I pray thirty minutes a day and I read my Bible for another thirty, he thinks to himself. *I don't watch PG-13 movies anymore—or play T-rated video games, even if the body splats are cartoony. And I never let my boxers show above my belt.*

His mom cuts off his thoughts when she hands him the phone. It's a classmate.

"Help you with math?" Brandon says to the kid on the other end. "Can't do it, dude. I'm too busy with a Bible study. Maybe I could squeeze you in next Tuesday. Let me check my schedule. . . ."

Brandon has a problem. He's patting himself on the back for mastering the basic facts of faith and getting rid of the rude and crude sins in his life. He thinks, *Hey, I believe right and I behave right—most of the time, anyway. So I'm doing just great at being the Christian God expects me to be.*

But God is looking for something more.

Talk about it: Got any ideas? What more could God possibly want from us?

Believing the right things about God, Jesus, and the Bible is important. But that's not enough. Behaving in the right way is also important. But that's also not enough. If you have these two pieces nailed down, that's excellent. Yet you could still be missing something essential—something that just happens to be at the top of God's list!

It's called right *loving.* According to 1 Corinthians 13:1-3, all the right *believing* and right *behaving* we can do means nothing if we don't connect it with right *loving.* God wants us to get along with people just as much as he wants us to believe and do the right things.

Got it? Just because you know that Jesus is your Savior—and you've straightened up the messes in your life—don't stop growing. Loving the people in your life matters just as much to God as keeping the faith and living by his guidelines!

 TALK: Why does God think *loving* right is just as important as *believing* and *behaving* right? What did or could happen if you made the mistake of not loving?

 PRAY: *Lord, we want to believe right and behave right. But help us love right too.*

 ACT: Have you ever used right *beliefs* and right *rules* to convince someone that God is real? Is there something you can do today for that person that shows the importance of *love?*

16 Who's Keeping Score?

Bible Reading: 1 Corinthians 13:4-7

Love . . . keeps no record of when it has been wronged.
1 Corinthians 13:5

Dear God,

It's been three years since my parents' divorce. I have tried to be patient with you on this one. I know you have a plan and that I just can't see it. Still, I wish things were different. I wish my parents were together.

Last month I went to visit my dad. He hasn't changed much. Sure, he likes to buy me things. Doesn't he know that I'll love him no matter what he does? He doesn't have to buy me things. And then he starts yelling about Mom. None of the things he says about Mom are true. He used to tell me that true love could weather any storm. I guess true love couldn't weather his storms. I haven't heard from him since I got home, not even a quick phone call. Give me the strength to love my dad, God, even when he lets me down. I know he needs love as badly as anyone.

And you know that Mom is no easier for me to love. She doesn't care about my life. Whenever I try to talk to her, she doesn't listen. She just keeps right on working. She says she's doing it for me. Yeah, right. If she wanted to do something for me, she would get back together with Dad and listen to me when I talk to her. Oh God, give me the strength to love my mom even when she disappoints me.

You see each time my parents let me down, Lord. Help me to stay faithful to you, and help me to love my mom and dad. I know it is what you want, so I want it too.

Love,
LeShona

You can see in those words the heart of a girl who loves God and others more than herself. How can you tell? Because LeShona is way more concerned about loving her parents than about their failure to love her. That's the kind of love Jesus came to earth to show us. He didn't keep score of the hurts he suffered. He loved everyone just the way they were. He even asked his Father to forgive the people who crucified him (see Luke 23:34).

Your situation might not be as bad as LeShona's. On the other hand, it might be a lot worse. Either way, Christ calls you to love as he loves, focusing on how you can love others—not on how others have failed to love you. If Jesus can love the people who sent him to the Cross, he obviously can help us love people who fail us.

TALK: What would your life look like if you didn't keep track of when people hurt you?

PRAY: Talk to God today about people you have a hard time loving.

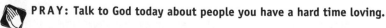

ACT: Is there anyone you've been holding a grudge against? How would you like to show Jesus' kind of love toward them?

June 17

You Want Me
to Build <u>What</u>?

Bible Reading: 1 Corinthians 13:8-12
Now we see things imperfectly as in a poor mirror, but then we will see everything with perfect clarity. 1 Corinthians 13:12

Whack, whack, whack. The sound of hammers echoes across the valley. An old man's neighbors watch him with amusement. They've seen him do strange stuff over the years, but this is the weirdest. They can't help but laugh at him.

The old man and his grown sons ignore the laughter. Instead, they keep on working. A nail here, a board there. Piece by piece they see the creation take shape.

"That crazy old fool!" somebody hoots. "Why is he filling his house with hay? Hasn't he heard of furniture?"

"That's no house," says another observer. "It's a boat! But why would someone need a boat out here? There's no water for miles!"

"Hey! Anyone seen my two elephants?" someone interrupts. "I had a male and female right in my backyard, but they've vanished."

Like the elephants, the other animals come two by two. When the ark is full, God shuts the door. The people outside laugh and point—until the rain starts.

Get the picture? Everyone thought Noah was nuts for obeying God.

Talk about it: Has God ever given you a command you didn't understand? Or has anyone thought you were nuts for obeying God?

God's instructions won't always make sense to us. God gave Noah an assignment: Build an ark. But he was teased as the town idiot because no one had ever seen rain before, let alone a flood. Even so, Noah followed through on God's awesome plan even when he had plenty of reasons to doubt. He did exactly what God told him to do, and only as a flood washed away the ground under the ark did he start to understand God's plan.

Sometimes God sticks us in situations that don't seem to make sense, and we wonder if *God* has gone nuts. He commands us to love people we think are unlovable and to make friends with people who make us crazy. So why should we do the loving thing when it doesn't make sense? That's when we can remember Noah.

Our assignment is clear. God wants us to 1) love him, and 2) love people—even when they don't love us back. It's how Noah loved, and his neighbors laughed at him. It's the way Jesus loved, and his enemies crucified him. But God wants us to love anyway. Someday it will become totally clear to us. In the meantime, let's keep loving as God directs. It's the only way to live.

 TALK: How do you manage to obey God when his commands don't seem to make sense?

 PRAY: *God, we trust you enough that we want to follow you always—even when we don't understand your commands.*

 ACT: When you're tempted to ignore one of God's commands today, remember Noah and dare to believe that God knows what he's doing!

18 Love Lasts Longer than School

Bible Reading: 1 Corinthians 13:8, 13

There are three things that will endure—faith, hope, and love—and the greatest of these is love. 1 Corinthians 13:13

Not too many days ago your school likely set you loose for the summer.

Way back in March, you realized that your school year really would come to an end, but you had months to go. In April, you could number the weeks until you were free. During May, you started counting days. By June you were ticking off hours, minutes, and finally seconds.

In those last moments before you slammed the door on the school year, you entered a time warp—one of the slowest passages of time known to humankind. As you turned in textbooks, scraped glue off desks, and waited for the end, time passed as slowly as if you were watching a dying ant crawl from one end of the white dry-erase board to another. You might even have noticed this startling effect: If you stare at a school clock in the final hour of the year, the hands actually spin *backward*.

Not really. But it's no secret that those final seconds of school seem to last forever.

You know what it's like when *miserable* moments seem to last forever. But the Bible says that there's one *great* thing you'll *want* to last forever—and it will. It's God's love.

There's never been—nor will there ever be—a greater demonstration of love than what Christ did on the cross. Romans 5:8 says, "God showed his great love for us by sending Christ to die for us while we were still sinners." At that point in history, we got a one-of-a-kind demonstration of God's total love for us.

God's love, however, didn't end on the cross. God continues to care for us every moment of every day. And when Jesus rose from the dead, he gave all of us the job of spreading his love throughout the world (see Matthew 28:18-20). When we love someone like Christ loves us, the impact of our action can last as long as God's love. It's like knocking down dominoes. Our love affects someone; that person feels loved and shows love to someone else, who loves still another person. This goes on and on and on.

So are you focusing your life on the one thing that truly lasts—loving God and loving others like Jesus loves you? We can be thankful to God that his love lasts even longer than those last few moments of the school year.

 TALK: If you put love at the top of your to-do list, who might be affected?

 PRAY: *Jesus, help us to put loving you and others at the top of our list of things to do—today and always.*

 ACT: Make a list of all the things you do in life. For each item, ask yourself this question: "How am I using this activity to make a lasting difference in people's lives?"

19 Old Mrs. Headstomper

Bible Reading: Romans 6:20-23

The wages of sin is death, but the free gift of God is eternal life through Christ Jesus our Lord. Romans 6:23

What will the next school year be like? Ellen has heard that the fifth-grade teacher pulls out a yardstick from behind her back and cracks it against the chalkboard. "This is fifth grade," Mrs. Headstomper tells her new students. "Behave like ladies and gentlemen—or else."

This teacher isn't *run-of-the-mill* mean. She is *seriously* mean . . . *headstomper* mean.

Some of the kids who are going into the sixth grade have also told Ellen about Mrs. Headstomper's "penny push-ups." Any student who misbehaves is sentenced to a half hour standing in the corner holding a penny to the wall with his or her nose. Twitch a muscle and the penny drops. The time-out starts over.

Is there really a Mrs. Headstomper? Probably not. But a lot of kids keep thinking that sooner or later they will crash into a wickedly mean teacher. That's sad. What's even sadder is how many people think *God* is a close relative of old Mrs. Headstomper.

Some of your close friends probably picture God as a mean old guy just waiting for them to do something wrong so he can put them under his thumb and crush them. They think God's biggest goal is to trap them, trick them, or hurt them.

But that isn't the God you know.

The Bible's biggest message is that God is love. He loves us so much that he has given us everything we need to spend eternity with him. He's not plotting our misery. In fact, he's planning our good: "'For I know the plans I have for you,' says the Lord. 'They are plans for good and not for disaster, to give you a future and a hope'" (Jeremiah 29:11).

Talk about it: How can we be sure God really loves us and wants to fill our life with good things?

The best and biggest way to be certain of God's love is to examine how he dealt with our major problem: sin. All people rebelled against God. Yet he invented a better way to deal with our wrongdoing than lining us up against a wall and forcing us to do penny push-ups.

You know what God did. He sent Jesus to die and rise again to purchase our forgiveness and make a way for us to be friends with him. That doesn't sound anything like Mrs. Headstomper, does it?

 TALK: How can you explain to your non-Christian friends that God isn't out to get them?

 PRAY: *God, help us to share with our non-Christian friends what you are really like. Help them to understand that your love is for all of us!*

 ACT: Who do you know who needs to hear this message? Share it!

20 A Personal Invitation

Bible Reading: John 1:1-13

To all who believed him and accepted him, he gave the right to become children of God. John 1:12

Steffi practically pressed her nose against the TV the first time she saw a women's downhill ski race. As she watched women barely older than her big sister bust speeds of sixty miles an hour as they carved the hill, Steffi dreamed of learning to ski like that.

Her parents found it was tough to disguise Steffi's gifts under the Christmas tree that year. Steffi had them all scoped out. There was a long package—must be skis. And another long package—poles for sure. Steffi hefted a big, square, weighty box—had to be boots. She figured out that one box was a helmet—good for keeping her head in one piece. In other packages she picked out goggles, a ski jacket, and snow pants—a mind-boggling assortment of everything she needed to launch her downhill career.

On Christmas morning Steffi looked at the wrapped gifts. "Dad . . . Mom . . . I can't believe everything you've given me. Thank you."

Her parents looked at her like she was nuts. "Steffi," they said in unison, "don't you think you should unwrap your presents?"

None of us are as goofy as Steffi when it's time to rip the wrapping paper off of Christmas presents or birthday gifts. But when it comes to knowing God, lots of people leave unopened the valuable gift that God has provided for us.

God has given the whole human race a gift greater than any other we could ever receive. Our sin has separated us from God and left us with no way to pay the penalty. The price of sin, after all, is eternal death! Yet Jesus Christ was God's gift to us. He paid the penalty for our sin. The death of Jesus for our sake guaranteed us life with him now and forever.

As fantastic as that gift is, it doesn't help us until we open it.

Think about this: *The good news isn't really good news until we respond to it.*

Trusting in Jesus is how we open God's gift and enjoy all its benefits. We have opened God's gift only when we admit that we need Christ and the forgiveness he provides. John 1:12 puts it like this: "To all who believed him and accepted him, he gave the right to become children of God."

God has sent you an incredible gift. Don't forget to open it!

 TALK: How have you responded to God's gift?

 PRAY: *God, thank you for sending the most wonderful gift of all—your Son, the one who makes it possible for us to know you and someday to live with you forever.*

 ACT: How would you explain the need to trust Christ to a non-Christian friend? Practice. Then share it!

21 Building Bridges

Bible Reading: John 17:14-19

As you sent me into the world, I am sending them into the world.
John 17:18

When Duncan learned to love Jesus, he knew he had unwrapped a priceless spiritual treasure. Now he wants his friends to love Jesus too.

So Duncan is praying for a list of people who need to know Christ. He plans to pass out tracts at the mall, dangle fish symbols from his book bag, and wear his new "Turn or Burn" witnessing T-shirt to school. Best yet, he's made it his life goal to get on TV holding one of those John 3:16 banners at the Super Bowl.

Those ways of telling people about Jesus may work for some people. But if you really want to get good at sharing the gospel with friends and family, you'll want to practice up on your communication skills. And your hottest opportunities to talk about Jesus are with the people you know well—your friends.

Me? you might be thinking. *How can I know God really wants to use me to tell others about him?* Look at this evidence:

God fills you with gifts so you can serve people. He gives you the supernatural fruit of his Spirit—like joy, love, peace, kindness, and patience (Galatians 5:22-23). But he doesn't fill you full of these gifts just to stuff *you.* He puts those qualities in you so you're equipped to get along with other people and minister to them.

God plopped you down among unbelievers. If God's only goal for your life was to save you, he would have yanked you out of your world and taken you to live with him in heaven the moment you trusted Christ. But after you trusted Christ, God left you right where you were—in the middle of a world full of non-Christians. He wants you where you are so you can introduce others to him.

Your unbelieving friends want to know about God. They might not act like it most of the time, but your non-Christian friends have a gigantic inner desire to know their Maker. God wired that desire into their hearts when he created them. And as you get to know your friends better, you'll spot how God wants to help them.

God put you exactly where you are so you could spread the news about him. And it's so important to him for you to serve others that he puts inside you all the qualities you need for the task. Don't you want to share the good news the way someone shared it with you?

 TALK: How does God help you with the task of telling people about him?

 PRAY: *God, help us to become friends with people around us who need to know you.*

 ACT: Talk to God about any doubts you still may have about sharing Jesus.

June
22 Clamping Shut the Gator's Jaws

Bible Reading: Acts 2:43–47

Each day the Lord added to their group those who were being saved.
Acts 2:47

Here's an easy-to-take test. There's only one question: How excited are you to tell others about Jesus? Rate your enthusiasm on a scale of 1 to 10:

1	3	5	7	10
Your mouth is clamped shut like an oyster determined to hang on to its precious pearl.	You start witnessing by saying, "This is going to hurt me worse than it's going to hurt you."	You think, *Here I am, God. Use me. But do I really have to?*	You're running out of non-Christians to talk to, so you're looking for more.	You talk about Jesus all the time; you will witness to a chair if there's no one to talk to.

Talk about it: What's your answer? Why do you feel that way?

Think about this. If you had to wrestle an alligator, wouldn't you first ask for some helpful hints—like how to clamp a gator's jaws shut before it snaps at you? So here are some helpful hints for sharing Christ. These suggestions won't take the bite out of every nonbeliever, but they can keep you from getting eaten alive:

Tip 1: Meet non-Christians on their turf. Friends do things together, so get involved in a friend's interests. For example, learn what kinds of sports activities your non-Christian friends enjoy.

Tip 2: Show your friends how exciting your faith is. How you act, talk, and think tells your non-Christian friends, "I've found something you really want and need." Ask questions like this: "Do you ever think about God? I do. I think about him a lot."

Tip 3: Ask God for the confidence to share Christ. Just being a friend to unbelievers won't turn them into Christians. They need to understand the Bible's message and respond to it by trusting Christ. Your big prayer should be, *Lord, get my friends' hearts ready to hear and respond to the good news about Jesus. Give me confidence to talk with them about you.*

Your friends are not likely to come crawling up to you asking about God or the Bible. It's more likely you'll have to start the conversation. But if you follow the three tips, you'll be ready!

 TALK: What do you think is the best way you can share Christ with your non-Christian friends?

 PRAY: Pray about that!

 ACT: What do you think is the hardest part about sharing Jesus? Talk with a mature Christian for ideas on how to deal with that problem.

Bible Reading: 1 Corinthians 15:1-9

Christ died for our sins, just as the Scriptures said. He was buried, and he was raised from the dead on the third day, as the Scriptures said.
1 Corinthians 15:3-4

Jorge told his Sunday school class, "I know I'm a Christian. I know God loves me. But I'm just wondering how important it is to believe that Jesus really died and came back to life. Is it possible he just fainted or something?"

Some people have taken Jorge's question a step further. They have tried to make sure everyone knows Christianity is a joke. But they haven't been able to do it because they can't explain away the historical fact that Jesus Christ rose from the dead.

The Resurrection isn't just a teensy part in our Christian belief—an idea we can toss. It's huge! If Jesus didn't rise from the dead, we have no faith at all. If we get rid of the Resurrection, we have to get rid of Christianity. That's why so many non-Christians have tried to prove that Jesus never rose from the dead.

Jorge didn't know that some non-Christians have tried to use an idea like his to explain away the Resurrection. They argue that Jesus just fainted. Everyone thought Jesus was dead, the story goes, but he just woke up, and the disciples imagined he rose from the dead. One author cooked up an even crazier idea, saying that Jesus planned his arrest, trial, and crucifixion, arranging to be drugged on the cross so that he could fake his death.

That's just not true. It's a myth that's impossible to believe when you understand what Jesus experienced on the day of his death.

Jesus was first beaten. What he suffered was so great that he collapsed when he was forced to carry his heavy cross to the place of his death. The death Jesus then experienced—his crucifixion—was gruesome. Jesus was taken down from the cross only after a Roman soldier assured the Roman governor that Jesus was truly dead.

The "Jesus was never really dead" myth is hard to swallow. Don't you think it's easier to believe that Christ died for our sins, was buried, and was raised on the third day?

Jesus was really dead. And now he's really alive.

 TALK: How do you feel, knowing that Jesus endured a horrible death for you?

 PRAY: Ask God to help you make the Resurrection understandable to your non-Christian friends.

 ACT: Say it in your own words: Why is the idea that Jesus never really died so unbelievable? Now explain it to a friend!

24 Room in the Tomb

Bible Reading: Matthew 28:1-10

I know you are looking for Jesus, who was crucified. He isn't here! He has been raised from the dead, just as he said would happen.
Matthew 28:5-6

"I'm telling you, Lizzie, it was the strangest thing! It was me and the other Mary and . . . let's see . . . Salome and . . . give me a minute, I'll remember—"

"Will you get on with it!" Elizabeth urged.

"All right, all right," Mary said. "We found an empty tomb where just the night before we had laid Jesus. Lizzie, it was empty! Nothing there."

Elizabeth stared at her friend. "Are you sure it was the right tomb?"

"If we were at the wrong tomb, don't you think one of us might have figured it out? How stupid do you think we are?

"And what about the angels? I didn't tell you about them, did I? They were at the empty tomb too, shining like lightning! They told us not to be afraid—Jesus was risen, just like he said he would be. I suppose you think the angels showed up at the wrong tomb too, huh?"

"I didn't mean anything by it, I just—"

"And while you are calling me stupid, you might as well call Peter and John stupid too. After all, I ran to tell them, and they ran *straight* to the empty tomb! They beat me back there! And what's more, how many tombs in Jerusalem do you think had the leftovers of a broken seal?"

"Well, I . . . I—"

"And what about the chief priests and the guard? Don't you think they knew which tomb was the right one? If we went to the wrong tomb, wouldn't they have just pointed to the right one and said, 'Ha! Proved you wrong! Here's the body!'?"

Elizabeth said, "I'm sorry; I didn't mean to suggest anything so stupid."

Unfortunately, Elizabeth isn't the only one to make such a suggestion. A guy named Kirsopp Lake argued that the women actually went to the wrong tomb. But, as Mary so strongly protested to Elizabeth, all it would have taken was a fifteen-minute stroll from the palace of the high priest or the Roman fortress in Jerusalem down to the right tomb to quickly shut up for all time any rumors of a resurrection.

But that didn't happen, of course. Because it *was* Jesus' tomb the women had found. And they found it empty.

 TALK: How ridiculous is the theory that the disciples couldn't find the tomb where Jesus was buried?

 PRAY: *Jesus, we're glad you are alive. Thanks that you live in us.*

 ACT: Why does it matter to you that Jesus stepped out of that tomb? Explain it to a friend.

25 Hide-and-Seek

Bible Reading: Matthew 28:11-15
They told the soldiers, "You must say, 'Jesus' disciples came during the night while we were sleeping, and they stole his body.'"
Matthew 28:13

Do you want to hear another fairy tale? How about the one that says the Resurrection isn't true because Christ's body was stolen from the tomb?

Did you know that the Bible itself contains the first version of the Stolen Body myth? After the Resurrection, some of the soldiers who had been guarding the tomb reported to the chief priests what had happened. The chief priests bribed them to say the body had been stolen while they slept (see Matthew 28:11-15).

Some people today still think that the disciples played hide-and-seek with Jesus' body. But a load of facts make that fairy tale impossible to believe.

Think about the stone, for example. The stone that sealed the tomb after Jesus was buried wasn't exactly the kind of pebble you skip across a pond. The five-foot-high circular stone could easily have weighed around *two tons*. When the tomb was first built, a team of workers probably put the stone in place, using a wedge to keep it from rolling down a trench that sloped down to the opening of the tomb. When Jesus was buried, the wedge was removed and gravity did the rest. It sealed the tomb so it could only be reopened with much noisy grunting by a gang of strong men. (That's why the women of Mark 16:3 wondered who would roll the stone away from the tomb entrance for them.)

Then there were the guards, a detachment of soldiers from Pilate, the Roman governor, who stood watch over the tomb. Their unit could have numbered as many as sixteen highly trained soldiers. To think that Jesus' body was stolen you would have to imagine that a group of disciples—the guys who days before had scattered like scared rabbits—confronted a guard of heavily armed, battle-trained soldiers. The disciples would have had to overpower the soldiers or sneak past them in their sleep to heave a two-ton stone up a slope without waking a single man. Then, so the theory goes, the disciples would have hauled off Jesus' body, hid it, and endured ridicule, torture, and martyrdom to spread what they knew to be a lie!

That's ridiculous!

Like the first Christians, you can be sure that the Christian faith isn't based on a fairy tale. It's built on the solid historical fact of the empty tomb and the risen Christ!

 TALK: Why is it impossible that Jesus' disciples stole his body to fake his resurrection?

 PRAY: Thank God that Jesus really rose from the dead.

 ACT: Do you have any doubts that Jesus truly is alive? Get all the evidence you need in Josh McDowell's book *Evidence That Demands a Verdict*.

June
26 Have a Heart

Bible Reading: Mark 6:30-44

He had compassion on them because they were like sheep without a shepherd. Mark 6:34

By the second day of soccer camp, you're sick of being followed. Some little kid thinks you're a soccer pro. "You're my hero!" he squeals. He wants your autograph. And he expects you to teach him every trick you know.

One day as you're crossing a field to your next practice, you spot your little fan. He's up on a goalpost, suspended by his soccer shorts. "I'm so glad you're here!" he shrieks. You study the situation. It's not like he's dangling over a cliff. Sooner or later his shorts will rip and he'll be just fine. So you walk away.

But later you get to thinking. You didn't exactly do what Jesus would have done.

More than once Jesus was followed by a crowd that wouldn't let him go. In Mark 6 the people hunted down Jesus and his disciples, chasing them along the shore and waiting for their boat to pull in. Jesus didn't act annoyed. He was kind, gathering the crowds and teaching them. Late in the afternoon the disciples said the people should get lost—and go find their own supper. Jesus, however, had heard their stomachs growling. He fed the mob a big meal, using a tiny snack—it was a miracle.

Jesus did three loving things in this scene: (1) he gave *time* to the worn-out disciples; (2) he gave *teaching* to the crowd when they needed help to understand God's love; and (3) he gave *physical help* to thousands when they were hungry.

Being a Christian means growing to be more like Jesus so that we have a compassionate heart like his. It means feeling the hurts that other people feel so that we want to help them. To be like Jesus, we can ask ourselves these three questions—and then act on our answers:

Question 1: How can I give my *time* to help people?
Question 2: How can I give *information about God* to people who need to know about him?
Question 3: How can I give practical *help* to people who need something?

Do you ever notice that people around you are sad or upset? It makes you feel sad or upset too, doesn't it? Well, that's the compassion of Jesus showing up in you. Don't let the feeling go away. Take a clue from your compassionate Savior. Show that you care about the way others feel!

 TALK: How do you plan to put into action the compassion that God puts inside of you?

 PRAY: *God, open our eyes to the world all around us. Help us see opportunities to give like Jesus gave.*

 ACT: Answer one of the three questions above and look for a time when you can give in this way today.

27 Time-Out

Bible Reading: Mark 6:45-56
He went up into the hills by himself to pray. Mark 6:46

Okay. It's like this. Every day of your life your parents make you sit still while they flip open a Bible and devotional book—like this one!

You've probably heard how important it is to spend time with God. Your pastor says it. Your Sunday school teacher slides in not-so-small hints. You've maybe even heard this line: "If Jesus needed to spend time alone with his Father, how much more do *you* need to spend time with God?"

Guess what? That's the truth! There's a clear link between Jesus' powerful miracles and the hours he spent alone in prayer.

Spending time with God along with family and friends is fantastic. But do you ever spend time with God by yourself?

"Quiet times" aren't just for older kids. They're not just for old people like parents and pastors. And a time-out with God isn't the kind of time-out you get when you're in trouble. It can be the highlight of your day.

Here's a plan for spending quality time with God. It's three-step simple:

1. *Get alone with God.* Think hard and discover a place where no one will bug you. Head to a bedroom, storage room, attic, garage, or basement. Then get comfortable. If you doze off when you pray lying down, walk around the room. If you're uptight when you sit up, lie down and relax.
2. *Talk to God.* Tell God how you feel: your anger, frustration, happiness, thankfulness—anything, everything. You can even say, "Lord, I don't feel like talking to you today, but I will because I know it's good for me." What you say isn't as important as how honest you are.
3. *Let God talk to you.* Make a point to tell God that you want to hear what he has to say to you. Then read a few verses and think about them for a while. Or listen to some Christian music, read a Christian book or magazine, or just recall what God has done for you.

God probably won't ask you to walk on water, calm the sea, or heal crowds like Jesus did. But God has plans for you, and you will be ready for those plans each day after some quiet time with God!

 TALK: What one or two changes might make the times you spend alone with God more interesting?

 PRAY: *God, use the time we spend with you to get us ready for the cool things you have for us to do.*

 ACT: Take some time to get alone with God today!

28 Lending a Hand

Bible Reading: Galatians 6:1-2

Carry each other's burdens, and in this way you will fulfill the law of Christ. Galatians 6:2, NIV

Your friend Cal asks you to head to the mall with him after school. "Sure," you say, "but I promised Mr. Wong that I would move some benches in the gym first."

Cal says, "Fine. I'll go with you and help out." At the gym, he parks himself in a chair with his handheld video game while you sweat out your chore.

The benches you are to move from the storage room to the gym are eight feet long, and the doorway to the storage room is narrow. "Lift the front end up higher," Cal calls out as he watches you struggle with the first bench. "Now turn the bench on its side. . . . No, the other way."

You swing the bench one way and then the other, banging it against the wall. Cal continues to instruct from his perch on the chair. "Now pick up the back end and move it to the left. . . . Okay, now pick up the front end and slide it around."

You catch your finger between the bench and the door and yelp. The pain causes you to drop the bench, which lands on your foot, and you howl in pain again. You can't believe how *un*helpful your "helpful" friend is.

"C'mon, hurry up," Cal barks. "Move those benches so we can get going." You limp out of the storage room, holding your throbbing finger.

Vote for the words you want to say to Cal:

(a) "Will you find me a Band-Aid and a cup of water, please?"
(b) "This is taking longer than I thought. I'll meet you at the mall later."
(c) "Where did you learn so much about moving benches?"
(d) "Please stop *telling me* what to do and come over here and *help me!*"

Cal wasn't too much help. He may have thought he was being supportive by barking out instructions, but we really don't need that kind of help. To support a friend means coming alongside to lift up a friend in need. Galatians 6:2 doesn't say, "*Tell* others how to carry their burdens" or "*Pray* for someone to help others carry their burdens." It says "Carry each other's burdens" (NIV).

Finding practical ways to help your friends is a cool way to obey Christ's command to love others. When our friends need support, we have a chance to showcase Christ's love—by doing something that actually helps!

 TALK: Who do you know who needs your help right now? What's the best way you can be a supportive friend?

 PRAY: Pray for that friend who needs a burden lifted.

 ACT: Be on the lookout for concrete opportunities to support someone this week.

Bible Reading: Galatians 6:3

If you think you are too important to help someone in need, you are only fooling yourself. You are really a nobody. Galatians 6:3

You need help with a group project. Or you need a friend to stick close when everyone else ditches you. Or you just need someone to hang with because you're feeling a little low.

Talk about it: Have you ever had a friend respond to your needs in a less-than-caring way? What happened? And how happy would you be with each of these responses?

- One friend says, "Not now, I have stuff to do."
- Another friend responds, "Sorry, I can't spare any of my precious time."
- One friend explains, "I can't help you right now; I have my own problems."
- Another friend retorts, "Why would I want to help a dork like you?"

Real friends aren't often blunt or unkind. Neither are you. Yet all of us easily slide into a *me-first* attitude unless we continually work on an *others-first* attitude. God wants to remake our attitudes in two enormous ways:

Makeover 1: *Ditch self-centeredness.* Being supportive means truly caring. As Galatians 6:3 says, "If you think you are too important to help someone in need, you are only fooling yourself. You are a nobody." Alicia caught herself feeling so important and busy that she was above helping others. She worked hard to warm up her chilly attitude toward her friends.

Makeover 2: *Dive into humility.* Philippians 2:3-4 bans the selfish thinking that always puts yourself first. "Don't be selfish. . . . Be humble. . . . Don't think only about your own affairs, but be interested in others, too, and what they are doing." Anthony figured out that he needed to carve out time to find out how his friends were doing and offer help when they needed it. He gulped hard and actually learned to tell his friends he cared about them and wanted to be there for them.

That might sound like a whole lot of giving with no getting. But in Luke 6:38 God says that the more you give to others the more you will receive in return. That's God's promise!

 TALK: So how do you do at caring? What attitude are you willing to let God remake?

 PRAY: *God, help us to become more caring, unselfish, and generous in our support for our friends.*

 ACT: Check out God's promise in Luke 6:38 of the return on your caring.

30 Guess Who You Are Really Serving

Bible Reading: Matthew 25:35-40

When you did it to one of the least of these my brothers and sisters, you were doing it to me! Matthew 25:40

Take this quick true-false test to measure your helpfulness:

☐ True ☐ False   I once sprained my arm at school from waving it so hard to volunteer to help my teacher.

☐ True ☐ False   I excitedly leap out of bed each morning. The first thought to hit my head is this: *Who needs my help today?*

☐ True ☐ False   I'm thrilled to give up the best seat on a long road trip.

☐ True ☐ False   I clean my room without being asked. In fact, I clean the whole house just because I care.

Do those statements sound like anyone you know? Well, maybe not.

Talk about it: What do we do to help one another? Why do we do those things?

Most of us need a kick of motivation to support others. The apostle James must have run into some people like us, because he wrote: "Suppose you see a brother or sister who needs food or clothing, and you say, 'Well, good-bye and God bless you; stay warm and eat well'—but then you don't give that person any food or clothing. What good does that do?" (James 2:15-16).

So how do you get excited about giving your helpful support to the people around you? Well, how would you feel if the friend who needed your support was Jesus himself? Imagine you just finished pitching in around the house or helping a friend solve a problem. Someone taps you on the shoulder. You turn around and see Jesus standing there. He says, "Hey—thanks for taking the time to pitch in. Your help means a lot to me." Wouldn't that make your mind explode?

According to Matthew 25:35-40, Jesus wants his followers to serve others. And whatever we do, it's as if we're actually doing it for him. It's as if Jesus were saying, "I was behind on my homework, and you helped me catch up. My parents told me to clean out the garage, and you helped me get the job done. I had to help my grandparents move all day Saturday, and you came along to haul boxes." Whenever you serve a friend, Jesus applauds that service as if it were done directly to him.

That's an incredible thought! Let this run through your mind when you give your help to other people: "Whatever I do, I do for Jesus."

TALK: Does it boost your desire to help others when you realize your actions are done for Jesus?

PRAY: *God, when we have a hard time doing things for other people, help us picture ourselves doing these things for you.*

ACT: What chore or other act of servanthood have you let slide to the bottom of your to-do list? Do it today!

1

Busted by Jesus!

Bible Reading: Romans 13:1-5
Obey the government, for God is the one who put it there. Romans 13:1

You're riding your scooter down the sidewalk when you bunny-hop the curb and bolt across a busy street in the middle of the block. Faster than you can say the word "jaywalk," a motorcycle cop roars up next to you, lights a-flashing. You freeze.

As the officer approaches, your eyes suddenly bug out. The cop wears the usual leather jacket, helmet, and gun belt. But his bearded, kind face and sandals look familiar. Then it hits you. He looks just like the picture of Jesus in your Bible!

He speaks, and he sounds just like you think Jesus would sound. "Believe it or not," he says, "people get hit right here all the time trying to cross the street outside of the crosswalk. I don't want that to happen to you. That's why there's a law against jaywalking—kids on scooters included." Then he jots out a ticket and hands it to you.

When you spot the initials "J. C." at the bottom of the ticket, your jaw drops. The officer winks at you, like he knows just what you're thinking. Then he says, "Have a safe day," hops on his cycle, and roars away. Could it be that you were just busted by Jesus?

Now, Jesus doesn't have a badge from your hometown police department, but he's definitely pleased with what police officers do. In fact, the Bible says that God has put a number of "authorities" in our life—people who in some way set the rules we must live by.

Talk about it: What authorities do you answer to? Why do you suppose God put them there?

We might be surprised by what God thinks when we ignore these people he meant to do us good: "Those who refuse to obey the laws of the land are refusing to obey God, and punishment will follow" (Romans 13:2). Sounds a little like Christ in a police officer's uniform, doesn't it?

Whenever we spot someone who has the job of keeping us inside lawful boundaries, we're looking at God's representative. Police and teachers and parents might not *know* it, but they truly are God's instruments to protect us and defend us.

We'll probably never get busted by a police officer who looks like Jesus, but we can still spot God caring for us through police, government, and laws. When we obey the authorities he has put in our life, we aren't just being good citizens. We're honoring God.

 TALK: When you obey the authorities in your life, you are obeying God. How does that fact help you do what is right?

 PRAY: *God, help us to respect and obey the people who have authority over our life.*

 ACT: Pay special attention to how you react to authorities in your life today!

2 Do I. O. U.?

Bible Reading: Romans 13:6-7
Give to everyone what you owe them. Romans 13:7

Listen to some of these lines—and see if any of them sound like something you have muttered.

- ☐ "Can I borrow a buck? I'll pay you back tomorrow."
- ☐ "Thanks for the favor. I owe you one."
- ☐ "If you help me clean my room, I'll help you next week."
- ☐ "Can't I get it, Dad? I'll pay you back every week until it's paid off."
- ☐ "I'm going to miss you when you move. I'll write every week!"
- ☐ "Mom, I'll clean up my room as soon as this program is over."

When you make a promise it's like using a credit card. It's painless to plop plastic on the counter, scribble your name, and walk away with something you want. But in a few weeks, a bill shows up from the credit-card company. It's time to pay up. At that point you might not want the DVD as much as you want the fifteen dollars you owe for it. You might even have gotten sick of the DVD and shelved it. You might wish you had never bought it in the first place.

One secret to getting along well in this world is to pay people what you owe them. And not just the buck you borrowed after school yesterday for a candy bar. Paying money you owe is important. But so is taking care of all the other promises you make to friends, brothers and sisters, parents, or strangers. The big question is this: Do you pay what you owe or just blow off your promises?

Here's a great thing: Jesus always keeps his commitments to you.

He promised to "give life in all its fullness" (John 10:10). He's kept that promise to fill your life with good things, hasn't he?

He said, "I . . . have come to seek and save those . . . who are lost" (Luke 19:10), and that's exactly what he did when he became a man and died on the cross.

He promised, "I am with you always, even to the end of the age" (Matthew 28:20), and haven't you sensed he's really there for you?

He promised an eternity in heaven—he said, "I will come and get you, so that you will always be with me where I am" (John 14:3). Is that a promise you look forward to him keeping?

When God says to pay what we owe by making good on our promises, he's asking us to do something he's already done, is still doing, and will always do.

 TALK: Why bother to keep your commitments? How does it inspire you, knowing that Jesus keeps his promises to you?

 PRAY: *Jesus, help us be faithful in keeping the promises we make.*

 ACT: Is there a promise you've let slide? Go keep your promise before you do another thing!

3 Love Is Always Right

Bible Reading: Romans 13:8-10

"Love your neighbor as yourself." Love . . . satisfies all of God's requirements. Romans 13:9-10

Okay. Here's a big question. What is the best, most righteous, most admirable task you could cross off your to-do list? Pick the statement that sounds to you like the biggest, best thing you could ever do:

☐ Read your Bible and pray every day.
☐ Shop ahead of time for your mother's birthday.
☐ Lug a huge Bible to school every day.
☐ Finish all your homework before playing computer games.
☐ Eat something from the four basic food groups every day.
☐ Love others as you love yourself.

Yep, there are loads of good things we can do every day. But if we have to choose just one "most right thing," we're smart to stick with the one Jesus selected and modeled for us: loving others selflessly. Paul explained why that's the greatest thing we can do when he wrote that "love satisfies all of God's requirements" (Romans 13:10).

Think about this: Loving others like Jesus did checks off every item on God's list of right things to do. That's why loving others is the most right thing anybody can ever do.

Our own experiences in life prove that fact. We want to be loved by others. We certainly want to be treated with fairness, respect, courtesy, and honesty. And we like kind, loving treatment in all our relationships. If we don't want those things, we're a little weird. It's normal for people to expect respect and love from others.

Nakita was disappointed when she didn't get the loving treatment she hoped for. She felt slammed when her best friend lied to her. And that's how we all feel. We all go bonkers when we're cheated, ignored, made fun of, or treated with anything less than the love we expect. We want our parents, for example, to pat us on the back for doing things right—and we're disappointed when they take us for granted. We expect our friends to be interested in what *we* like to do—and we get angry when all they want to do is what *they* like to do.

We expect to be loved, so we can be sure it's our job to love others. Loving others is always the right thing to do. It's how God treats us every day!

 TALK: God loves us more than our brain can imagine. Why should you bother to love like God loves?

 PRAY: *Father, help us treat others the way you treat us.*

 ACT: Take this dare: The next time you feel mistreated, return the rotten treatment with loving words and actions.

4 What's the Difference?

Bible Reading: Romans 13:13-14

We should be decent and true in everything we do, so that everyone can approve of our behavior. Romans 13:13

Tom, 11, stands several inches shorter than everyone else in his class. He's always trying to prove he's as big as the other guys. His latest strategy? Acting tough by screaming and cussing his way through every sport he plays.

Chloe, 8, thinks she's dumb. So she almost always copies assignments from her brainy friend, Akiko, who gladly shares her work.

Travis, 9, has a wild temper. He settles arguments by swinging his fists around and inflicting pain.

Leah, 15, has made enemies out of most of her friends. She's known as "The Blab" because she tells the nastiest stories about people—true or not, she doesn't care.

Juan, 10, was lonely after his family moved from Mexico to California. But his new buddies have shown him how to sniff stuff to get high.

Talk about it: From what you just read, how many of these students are Christians? Any of them? Some of them? Most of them? All of them? Can you tell?

Here's another important piece of information to help you answer this question: All of these students attend church and belong to a Bible-club group.

So what do you think now? Which of them are Christians?

Actually, all of them trusted Christ at some point in their lives.

Are you surprised? shocked?

True, how these boys and girls are acting doesn't fit how the Bible says a Christian should live. But we're made right with God by trusting Christ, not by behaving well. Still, you have to wonder about these students. They're supposed to show the world what Christ looks like, but they don't look much like Christ, do they?

That's the point Paul made in today's Bible passage. Even though being God's child depends on faith—not behavior—there should be a difference in how God's children act. Just as Christ lived in obedience to his Father when he walked this earth, we're called to obey God too.

Jesus came to earth in human flesh to show us how to live, and he came to die for our sin. That's called the *Incarnation*—God alive in human form. Jesus has risen from the dead and returned to heaven, so now he wants to live through you. That's another kind of incarnation—God alive in *us*. He wants to show the world through us the huge difference he can make.

 TALK: Isn't it cool Jesus wants to live through you? Will you let him?

 PRAY: Talk to God about your answer to that question.

 ACT: What can you do today so people can see a difference in your life because you belong to Jesus?

5 Time's Up

Bible Reading: Romans 13:11-12

Another reason for right living is that you know how late it is; time is running out. Romans 13:11

Brother William stopped by the log cabin of Brother Frederick so the two of them could walk to church together. There had been reports of wild wolves roaming the woods, so Brother William didn't want to walk to church alone.

When Brother Frederick stepped out of the log cabin, he was carrying a loaded musket. Brother William was shocked because their church didn't believe in carrying weapons for any reason. As they started into the woods, William said, "Brother Frederick, I see that you have a musket with you today."

"That's right, Brother," Frederick said.

"And it looks like your musket is loaded, Brother Frederick."

"Yes, my musket is loaded, Brother William."

William stopped his traveling companion and turned to face him. "Brother Frederick," he said sternly, "don't you realize that when your time is up, the Good Lord is going to take you whether you have a musket to defend yourself or not?"

"Yes, I realize that, Brother."

"Then why are you carrying a musket today?" William pressed.

Frederick smiled. "Just in case I meet a wolf whose time is up."

Someday your stroll on Planet Earth will stop. You might always buckle up in the car and avoid bungee jumping, sky diving, and snow luging. You can do a zillion things to prolong your life, but you can't keep it from ending.

Like it or not, the clock keeps ticking away the hours, days, months, and years for each of us. Since we can't peek at God's giant calendar in the sky, we don't know when our time will be up. It could be eighty years from now, eighty days from now, or eighty minutes from now. God gives most of us lots and lots of years, but all we can say for sure is what Paul said: "Time is running out." There's no time to waste.

Now is the time to start living the way God wants us to live in front of our friends. They need to see Christ alive in our life. Why? Because time is ticking away for them, too. The sinless Son of God became a human being to live among us. It's time to let him live through us so we can show others what he looks like—for all the days we have left, that is!

 TALK: How do you want to use your time on earth? Who do you want to live for?

 PRAY: *God, fill us with yourself. Live through us so others can see what you look like.*

 ACT: Can you think of a friend who hasn't been able to see Jesus through you? What one attitude or action would you like to change to help that friend get a clearer picture of Jesus?

6 Family Feud

Bible Reading: Romans 15:1-6

May God . . . help you live in complete harmony with each other—each with the attitude of Christ Jesus toward the other. Romans 15:5

"Sit up!" Dad barks. "I've told you a hundred times that you look like a caveman when you eat like that."

It's a typical evening meal at the Nelson house. Dad usually sits in silence, wrapped up in his thoughts. Once in a while he looks up long enough to correct Bryce.

"Dad," Bryce says, "would you stop picking at me? Just once I'd like to eat a meal without being yelled at for something I'm doing wrong."

"Honey," Mrs. Nelson breaks in, "I think Bryce is right. You do criticize him a lot."

Dad glares at Mom. "You're taking sides with the kids again," he says. "If you can't support me, then don't say anything."

Bryce's sister, Lara, can't stand family arguments. She tries to calm everyone. "Dad, Mom means well. Please don't get mad at her."

"I've worked hard all day," he shoots back. "When I come home, all I want is peace and quiet."

"It would be a lot quieter if you weren't always jumping on Lara and me," Bryce says, his voice rising. "All you do is yell, yell, yell!"

Do you ever have a hard time getting along as parents and brothers and sisters? It's easy to blame the other family members for our fights. But let's be honest: *none of us are easy to live with.* Like one boy admits, "Sometimes, especially when I have a rotten day at school, I get so mad that I take it out on Mom. I know it's not her fault, but she's just there. I guess I have to yell at somebody."

It's a really grown-up thing when we can own up to our own problems, stresses, and blowups. We can begin by being honest about these three big questions:

1. Can I admit that living with me isn't always a barrel of laughs?
2. Do I admit that sometimes the problem is me?
3. Do I confess my faults to other family members when I've blown it?

Your family will build God's kind of harmony when you make comments such as the following: "I know I've been cranky lately, and I'm sorry about that. I appreciate your patience. I'm working on it."

That's the kind of honesty that builds the closeness you need and want. It's the honesty that might get all of your family members to admit they aren't perfect!

 TALK: How could being honest about our failings bring us closer together?

 PRAY: *God, help us to be honest when we act less-than-our-best at home.*

 ACT: Is there anything you need to say to the other folks in your family about your struggles to get along?

7 Home Is Where He Is

Bible Reading: Psalm 46:1-3

Lord, through all the generations you have been our home! Psalm 90:1

You can be sure you're in deep trouble when your mom or dad hollers for you using your first, middle, and last names. But have you ever gotten any of these hints?

- Your cat's food dish is on the dinner table—and your plate is on the floor.
- Your parents rent out your room to an exchange student from Mongolia—and you still have eight years before you leave for college.
- Your mom short-sheets your bed.
- You get brussels sprouts for dessert—and everyone else gets chocolate mousse.
- Your mom goes on tour as a stand-up comic—and her jokes are about you.
- Your dad is out in the backyard painting your name on the doghouse.

All of us have a need to belong. And despite the fact that once in a while we have a hard time getting along at home, the Lord meant for our needs to be met first in our family. His plan is that no matter how mean the world gets, we can always come home, kick off our shoes, and say, "I can be myself here."

Unfortunately, lots of people don't get that when they go home. And sooner or later all of us feel out-of-joint at home—and not just because we're in trouble. Brothers and sisters can make each other feel unwanted. Sometimes even parents feel unappreciated and unwelcome at home. When we're not getting along with our family, home can feel lonely—or worse.

It might be a surprise that Jesus knew how it felt when the welcome mat was missing at home. His brothers and sisters weren't exactly excited about his ministry (see John 7:5). Besides that, he was homeless as he traveled throughout Israel for the last three years of his earthly life (see Matthew 8:20).

So where did Jesus get that important sense of belonging?

Jesus leaned on the fact that he belonged to his Father. When he lived on earth, Jesus couldn't see the Father any more than you can. But he knew his Father was with him, and that knowledge gave him a peace and security that kept him going. He knew the truth of Psalm 90:1: "Lord, through all the generations you have been our home!"

God, who is with us wherever we are, makes a home for us right where we are. It's the kind of place he wants us to create for one another by making the home where we live a safe, relaxing, and friendly place.

 TALK: How can we make our home a place that feels warm and welcoming for one another?

 PRAY: *God, help us to create a warm home for one another. And thank you that we can always feel at home with you.*

 ACT: Pick a family member and do something today to make your home a welcoming place for that person.

8 Why Did My Friend Go Away?

Bible Reading: Romans 8:35-39

Nothing in all creation will ever be able to separate us from the love of God that is revealed in Christ Jesus our Lord. Romans 8:39

After living for several years in a foster home, Holly had built a close group of friends at her church. One summer Holly went away with a bunch of them for a weeklong church camp. What a week! She couldn't wait to get home and tell her family all about it. But minutes after she arrived back home, her foster parents broke the news that she had to leave *the next day* to live in a home in another state. The authorities in charge of supervising foster children had made up their minds without talking to Holly or her foster parents. There was nothing they could do to fight the decision. So the next day she had to leave.

When Holly was tossed into a strange new place, she felt ripped from her friends and family. For months her heartache was constant.

You've probably formed strong bonds with the people you love—so that when your parents spend a weekend away by themselves, you miss them. Or when you're away from friends and family for a retreat or camp, you get homesick.

Those are small separations that end quickly. But sooner or later we all face a loss or separation that can't be undone. Even if you never face a situation as severe as Holly's, loneliness and sadness can hit you from many directions:

Everyone grows up. Martina found that as she grew up, her friends no longer shared her interests or sense of right and wrong.

People move. Steven had his friends yanked from his life when his dad was promoted and his family moved cross-country.

Families break up. When Brandi's parents divorced, she wound up living far enough from her old friends to make it almost impossible to see them.

Loved ones die. Tim found that there's nothing as painful as the ache of losing a friend to death—and it hurts whether you lose a parent, grandparent, sibling, friend, or even a pet.

Every relationship will someday change. That's not a cheery thought. But here's a thought that puts all of our shifting friendships in perspective: Jesus will always be there for us. He won't move away or die. His feelings toward us won't change.

Not only is Jesus a faithful friend, he goes right beside us when the people we call friends are changing and rearranging. Jesus is the one friend we can never lose!

 TALK: Do you have a lost friendship that is making you lonely right now? How can Jesus help?

 PRAY: *Jesus, we're grateful that you stick with us even when our other friends aren't around.*

 ACT: Be a friend to someone who has recently lost a friend.

9 Turning Losses into Gains

Bible Reading: Romans 8:26-30

We know that God causes everything to work together for the good of those who love God and are called according to his purpose.
Romans 8:28

Until a few months ago Ashley and Morgan didn't even know their Grandpa Hoffman had ever been married to anyone but Grandma Hoffman. But now they have learned that when he was a young man of just twenty-five, his first wife was struck with a rare illness. He took care of her as she grew more and more sick; but after a year of caring for her, his young wife died.

The loneliness you feel when you lose someone you love is worse than having a whole herd of skunks scamper through your life. But Ashley and Morgan learned by talking to Grandpa Hoffman that his loss taught him many lessons.

Do you wonder how anything good can come from losing a friend or a family member you love?

Sure, you get to remind yourself that Jesus never leaves you. And you can practice walking close to him. But is there anything else to learn?

When you start to feel lonely, try hard to think about these three important things you can learn from loneliness:

Losses are a fact of life you have to deal with. Grandpa Hoffman knew all the wishing in the world couldn't change the death of his wife. He knew he needed to learn to raise their son alone—at least for a while.

Grief is a normal feeling when you lose a family member or friend. You expect to grieve when someone dies. But grief is also natural when a special friend moves away or you fight with a friend. The trick is learning to grieve in a healthy way.

God has put Christians in your life to support you. Grandpa Hoffman was surprised that his biggest supporters were some new friends more than twice his age—older Christian men who had also lost their wives. Their solid friendships brought advice and help he could count on.

Sometimes grief will throw us into such a spin that we can't think straight. We think warped things like *God is punishing me!* or *I must be a bad person for this to happen to me!* But God isn't out to get you. He wants to teach you. If you let him, you'll find out that God can cause good to come even from the worst situations. He wants to make you grow strong in him.

 TALK: What are some of the relationship losses you have endured? Can you think of examples from your family history? What did people learn from those losses?

 PRAY: *God, help us to see the positive side of all of our losses.*

 ACT: There's likely someone in your world who has suffered a loss lately. Make a plan as a family to help that person.

10 Who Will Be Your Everything?

Bible Reading: 2 Thessalonians 2:13-17

May our Lord Jesus Christ and God our Father, who loved us . . . comfort your hearts and give you strength in every good thing you do and say. 2 Thessalonians 2:16-17

It's Saturday afternoon and the high sun of summer pounds down on the play lot across the street from Rachel's house. Rachel can see two old friends playing. The big word there is "old." As in "not anymore." She would run over and try to play, but she's sure Kaitlin and Jenni would leave her out once again.

A couple years ago all six girls who lived on the block were great friends. Then Shaniqua and Erin moved away. Natalie splits her time between two homes since her parents divorced. The other two girls love sports. Kaitlin is into gymnastics. Jenni plays soccer. They both make Rachel feel like a reject.

Rachel wonders if God would be mad at her if she begged him to hit the park with a storm cloud—or maybe even a lightning bolt. She sighs and shoots this thought toward God instead: *Friends are such a hassle. Why bother?*

The truth is that God has built into each one of us a need to have deep friendships. He puts people in our life as one way to meet that need. But answering that ache starts and ends with Jesus. He has everything we could ever want in a special friend.

Let's get some basic facts straight.

Jesus wants a friendship with you. Jesus stands waiting and ready to have a tight, personal relationship with you.

Jesus thinks you're amazing. Jesus thinks you're one-of-a-kind special. You're not ordinary, boring, or anywhere near average.

Jesus likes you. When you feel dumpy, Jesus cares. When your life is a thrill, he enjoys every minute with you. He shares your happiness and sadness.

Jesus invites you to open up to him. No one knows your most locked-tight thoughts and feelings the way Jesus does. He's glad when you unlock what you hide from everyone else to share your most hidden thoughts with him.

Just like everyone else, you will have days when you stare out a window and wonder if you have any friends. That's when you can pour out your heart to Jesus, sure that he's listening and knows how to keep a secret. Let him in on your dreams and longings and believe that he understands what you mean. Jesus is the one friend who will *always* be there for you.

 TALK: When you're looking for friendship, where do you start? What can God do for you that human friends can't?

 PRAY: *God, be our unfailing friend. You're the most important person in our life.*

 ACT: There's no better time than now to choose to make him the most special person in your life. Tell God you want to live closer to him!

Mirror, Mirror on the Wall

Bible Reading: Psalm 139:13-14

Thank you for making me so wonderfully complex! Your workmanship is marvelous—and how well I know it. Psalm 139:14

Here's a wild question for you kids to ask your parents: "Think way back to when you were a kid. Can you remember what you thought about the reflection you saw in the mirror? (There were mirrors back then, weren't there?) Or when you look at pictures of yourself as a little kid, what do you think?"

Lots of us have stood in front of the mirror and said something like this: "God, you messed up when you made me!"

Maybe you're a girl and you have to run around in the shower to get wet—you're so skinny the water spray misses you. Or you're a guy and you're missing the muscles all the other guys seem to own. When you really start growing up, you might not even recognize that person staring back at you in the mirror. One minute you'll have a plastic-perfect complexion. The next you'll discover that a Godzilla-like pimple has taken the end of your nose hostage.

Listen carefully. You aren't alone. All of us have had moments of unhappiness as we looked in the mirror. But the truth is that God doesn't make mistakes. He didn't goof on you or anyone else. Whether you feel too tall, too short, too big, too little, or even too ugly, God made you just as you are. He thinks you are perfect.

God loves variety. That's why no two flowers are exactly the same, no two snowflakes are duplicates, and no two people are identical. He didn't want you to be just like everybody else because to him, you're a standout. He made you different because you deserve to be different. You deserve to be interesting and unique.

We do, of course, have some options in how we look. We can't change how tall we are, but we can somewhat control how we fill out that height. How we eat (several slabs of pizza washed down with a liter of cola every day for lunch will impact how you look—duh!) and how we exercise (working out with the chess team doesn't really count) will make a difference. And a doctor can help us solve some appearance problems with our weight, skin, or overall wellness.

But the basic genetic formula that stares back at us in the mirror is God's masterpiece. You are special because God made you special, different because God made you different. If you looked like everyone else, you wouldn't be you.

TALK: God hand-made you as his masterpiece. How are you unique from other people?

PRAY: *God, you didn't make any mistakes when you made us. Thanks for making each of us unique!*

ACT: Make a sign to hang on the mirror that reminds you that God did a marvelous job when he made you.

12 The Coolness Chase

Bible Reading: Psalm 139:15-18
How precious are your thoughts about me, O God! They are innumerable! Psalm 139:17

Of all the people you know, Alex oozes cool. He never wears the same thing twice. And his clothes always look like they came straight off a dummy in the most popular store in the mall. He has the hippest shoes, hippest shirts, and hippest watch—not to mention the coolest bike, snowboard, cell phone, and MP3 player.

One day you figure out how Alex got so hip. "I didn't get cool by accident," he says, waving toward a basement wall covered with computers and jumbo-sized monitors. "This is how I find out *exactly* what's hot and what's not.

"I study ads in the world's coolest magazines," he brags. "I get information from three major TV channels and half a dozen cable stations. I feed all the data in here. And over here I get the coolness quotient of anything and everything." Suddenly a computer beeps. "See? It says I need to switch toothpaste. And use a different dental floss. I've gotta keep up with the coolest brands."

Alex's mom appears with cheeseburger Tasty Meals for your lunch. "The stock for McDaisy's is up today," Alex says. "Had you noticed?"

"And there's more," Alex gushes. "My current project is tracking the most popular college to go to and the hottest car and job to get when I graduate. It's several years away, but you can never be too cool."

It's tough to get dressed these days without the advice of TV, magazines, movies, and commercials. From your friends to your enemies, everyone wants to tell you what's hot and what's not. So talk about this: Is it wrong to try to look the way everyone else says we should?

Trying to be trendy isn't such a big deal if you're aiming to keep up with easy-to-swap styles. If one day you break into a sweat because you just noticed your clothes or hairstyle went out three years ago, it's okay to change. But being cool at any cost takes huge money. And loads of kids do wrong things just to fit in.

The Bible gives you the biggest reason not to make being cool the most important part in your life: You are already the product of God's perfect design. God was your master artist when you were put together in your mother's womb. He watched it all happen to make sure you turned out just right. And he still thinks you're just right. You are his masterpiece!

 TALK: How much do you try to keep up with trends? When does that get in the way of appreciating the way God made you?

 PRAY: *God, thanks for making us unique—your special creations.*

 ACT: Celebrate your uniqueness by picking a hot fashion trend you're *not* going to follow.

13 Image Is Everything

Bible Reading: Genesis 1:26–28

Then God said, "Let us make people in our image, to be like ourselves."
Genesis 1:26

Image is supposedly everything. So what's a self-image?

Think of it this way. Around your house you probably have loads of photos. Baby pictures, vacation snapshots, school portraits, and family photos all give you a fair idea of what you look like.

Did you know that you have another picture of yourself? It's not a shot snapped with a camera and downloaded to a computer or run to a photo shop for processing. It's a picture you carry in your mind. This picture is your self-image.

Here's a question to help you recognize the mental picture you have of yourself. Talk about this: What are the first three words that come to your mind that describe yourself?

Your self-image is incredibly important. It affects everything you do, including how well you get along with people.

If you have a totally *negative* self-image, you don't think well of yourself. It's not a happy way to be. If you have a negative self-image, you're often pessimistic, lack confidence, cringe at what others think of you, worry about how you look or perform, wonder what people think of you, have a tough time accepting love, depend on possessions to make you happy, and talk negatively about yourself or others.

Wow. If that's what a negative self-image does, maybe you want a perfectly *positive* self-image—a totally high view of yourself. But that's not a good way to be either. You might think you're the greatest because of the way you look or how smart you are or some other outstanding feature. You might put other people down because they don't measure up to your greatness. And you might shatter into a bazillion pieces when you find out that the real you isn't quite as perfect as the picture you carry in your mind.

So if those are both bad, what do you want?

God wants you to have a *healthy* self-image. He wants you to see yourself as *he* sees you—no more, no less. If you have a healthy self-image, you *will* think highly of yourself—but that's because God thinks highly of you. You'll also be willing to admit to—and work to change—your weaknesses. You'll accept the reality that God created you in his own image as someone with infinite value and worth. And that's a picture of yourself worth carrying around!

 TALK: How do you see yourself today? Would you see yourself differently if you saw yourself through God's eyes?

 PRAY: *God, build in each of us a healthy self-image. Help us to see ourselves as you see us.*

 ACT: Draw a picture of yourself that reflects who you think you are. Talk about your picture with your family or a friend.

14 Who Are You Anyway?

Bible Reading: Romans 12:1-3

Be honest in your estimate of yourselves, measuring your value by how much faith God has given you. Romans 12:3

It's always good for a chuckle to take a stack of pictures of yourself and line them up for a year-by-year look at how you've changed. There's that goofy haircut you had to have. The outfit that was so stylin' you insisted on wearing it every day. And there's a major thing you can spot as you scan those snapshots: The person you see in those year-by-year pictures keeps getting bigger.

However, it's possible for your self-image to be shrinking.

Your self-image comes from what people tell you. As you grow up, you see yourself according to how parents, teachers, friends, brothers, and sisters talk, think, and act toward you. These opinions feed your young mind. Maybe you're getting fed nutritious, accurate information about yourself. Maybe you've lived on junk food filled with calories—being told you could do no wrong. And maybe you've been getting rotten leftovers—being fed a totally negative view of you.

So answer this: Do you ever get fed negative statements like these, even in fun?

- "You're in the stupid-kid reading group."
- "What's your problem, retard?"
- "Can't you ever help? You are so worthless around here."
- "Why can't you behave like your sister does?"

What happens when you hear statements like that about yourself? You start to believe what people say.

First, you hear it: "You're stupid."

Next, you think about it: *Is he right? Am I really stupid?*

Then an experience drives it home. You make a big mistake and someone laughs at you and says, "That was a stupid thing to do."

Then you begin to feel it: *That was so dumb. I really feel stupid.*

Finally, you believe it: *I am told that I'm stupid; I act stupid; and I feel stupid. It must be true. I am stupid.*

See why it's so important to know what God says about you? As you read the Bible, you find out how God values you. The more you see yourself as God sees you, the more you get a real view of you. And it's God's view of you that is true.

 TALK: How have other people shaped how you see yourself? Have they given you a true view—or a warped, ugly one?

 PRAY: *God, we want your Word to fill us with your view of us. Thanks that your view is the one that's true.*

 ACT: Build up a family member's self-image. Tell that person something good—and true—that you see in him or her.

15 Is There a Way to God's Plan?

Bible Reading: Jeremiah 29:11-14

If you look for me in earnest, you will find me when you seek me.
Jeremiah 29:13

Jennifer's dad sat at the kitchen table poring over bills, with his brow scrunching together the way it does whenever he worried. Jennifer walked up behind him, wrapped her arms around him, and gave him a huge hug. Jennifer knew that money was tight and that her dad struggled to not let her see.

"I appreciate you, Dad," she said. "You're always making big decisions."

Jennifer's dad smiled back at her and said, "Honey, I've actually made most of my big decisions. Now it's usually just a matter of living those out. You still have all those big decisions ahead of you."

Huh? How can thirteen-year-old Jennifer have bigger decisions to make than a parent trying to lead a family? In a way, it's true. Think of the big decisions you will make in the next decade or so of your life.

1. You'll decide who will guide your life—who will be your *master*. Maybe you have already settled that issue by trusting Jesus Christ as Savior and Lord. If so, you intend to live according to his Word and his will as he shows it to you. You're headed in the right direction.
2. You'll decide what to do with your life—your *mission*. You'll have to figure out what preparation you need to accomplish your goals.
3. You'll decide *if* you will marry and *whom* you will marry—your *mate*. It's doubly difficult to make this decision, because it takes two to tie the knot. You both have to sense the same guidance from God.

If you have decided to follow Christ, you have a great advantage in finding answers to every other decision you face. God loves you and has a great plan for your life. Jeremiah 29:11 declares, "'I know the plans I have for you,' says the Lord. 'They are plans for good and not for disaster, to give you a future and a hope.'" God also promises, "I will instruct you and teach you in the way you should go; I will counsel you and watch over you" (Psalm 32:8, NIV).

I hope you have already made a decision about your *master*. You're maybe dreaming about your *mission*. And choosing a *mate* is a long time away. But you can be confident that in each of these things God wants what is totally good for you—and there's nothing you could ever want that's better than to follow God's plans for you!

 TALK: What kind of plans does God have for your life? Do you think they're good—or what?

 PRAY: *God, we want to make decisions that please you. Help us to make the right big choices so all the little ones fall into place.*

 ACT: Spend some time talking with a parent about one of those big life choices—your master, your mission, or your mate.

16 Finding God's Will

Bible Reading: Jeremiah 33:3
> *Ask me and I will tell you some remarkable secrets about what is going to happen here. Jeremiah 33:3*

Mac wished he could sit in class hooked up to a heart monitor. Then he could prove to his parents that if school was any duller, his pulse would stop—and he would die of boredom.

Doing something big was all that Mac dreamed about. Every afternoon he climbed up in his tree house to plot his course toward becoming an astronaut . . . or president . . . or ruler of Planet Earth.

Mac had a lot of ideas about his future. But he was missing out on the world's hottest secret for living a cool life. All he needed to do was *figure out God's will for his life*. Without God, he was missing the best way to plan his future—and to make life fun now.

God *wants* to show you his will—his perfect plan for you. But it's easy to get stuck in several wrong attitudes. Get bogged down in any of these, and you won't escape your confusion.

Wrong Attitude 1: God keeps his will a secret. Felipe thinks that finding God's will is like hunting for Easter eggs. God hides his answers to our big questions—and if we can't find them, too bad! But the Bible shows us that God doesn't tease us. He's glad to show his will to any who want to find it.

Wrong Attitude 2: God's will won't be any fun. Sarah figures God will make her grow up to marry an ugly guy or spend her life doing something she doesn't want to do—like being a missionary in the jungle. But God has no interest in making us miserable. God wants to graciously give us all things that will fulfill our deepest desires.

Wrong Attitude 3: God's will isn't something I want. Joseph acts like a driver who steps on the gas and the brake at the same time. One moment he's saying, "Lord, show me your will," and the next moment, "I don't want to do *that* part of your will." Our job is to do the total will of God.

Those are mixed-up attitudes. But check out this great attitude:

I am willing to do God's will whatever it is. God blesses us when we're willing to obey him even before he shows us what he wants us to do. It's the attitude expressed in Psalm 40:8: "I take joy in doing your will, my God, for your law is written on my heart." God is eager to share his plans—*if* we are eager to obey!

 TALK: How do you feel about your great God who wants to show you his great will?

 PRAY: *God, we want your will for our life. Show us your will so we can obey it.*

 ACT: Is there an area of your life where you want to understand God's plans? Spend some time with a mature Christian, talking about God's will for that part of your life.

Wrap Your Brain around God's Will

Bible Reading: Proverbs 3:1-7

Seek his will in all you do, and he will direct your paths. Proverbs 3:6

Jordan wants to go on a mission trip this summer, but it means missing two volleyball camps he's been handpicked to attend. He's decided to talk to his ultrawise Sunday school teacher about it.

"My parents told me to pray about the decision," he explains. "They said that God has a plan for me and my summer and that he wants to show me what it is—but I'm having a hard time. How am I supposed to figure out what he wants me to do? It's not like he's dropping me any hints."

Jordan's teacher begins, "Have you trusted Christ as your Savior?"

"Sure. Back when I was six."

"Good. Are you obeying your parents?"

"Um—most of the time."

"And are you spending time reading your Bible and talking to God in prayer?"

"Sure," Jordan says. "But I'm trying to figure out God's will for my summer."

"I know, Jordan," his teacher responds. "But when it comes to following God's will, we have to start with obeying his clear commands to everyone. Then we can start figuring out what he wants just for you and your summer plans."

Can you wrap your brain around that idea? When we're looking for God's will, we want to find two things: The first is God's clear will for everyone—what some people call God's "universal will." The second is God's will for each individual—his "specific will."

God's universal will is the can't-miss-it, can't-get-around-it, can't-make-excuses plan for all people. It's what we learn from God's clear commands and principles in the Bible. We know, for example, that God wants all of us to know Christ as our Savior. To obey our parents. To spend time soaking up the Bible and praying.

If we're ignoring God's will in the big choices of life, there's no point looking for what he wants in the details of life. When we've set our heart on obeying God's commands for everyone, we're in the right place to find God's will for our own future—like whether to head out on a world-changing mission trip or take the awesome challenge of showing the world who God is while attending volleyball camps.

So are you into doing God's universal will? And do you want to find out his specific will? Go for it!

 TALK: Answer in your own words: What is God's "universal will"? What's his "specific will"? Why does it matter?

 PRAY: Talk to God about your desire to do his will.

 ACT: Practice explaining to a friend the difference between God's universal will and his specific will.

18 First Things First

Bible Reading: Romans 12:1-2

Let God transform you into a new person by changing the way you think. Then you will know what God wants you to do. Romans 12:2

If you listen for long to Christian teens and young adults talking about God's will, you'll notice they're usually looking for help in the mind-boggling major decisions of life. They're trying to answer questions like these:

Career: Should I major in golf—or underwater basket weaving?
Transportation: Is it better to buy a car without a muffler—or without brakes?
Friendships: Am I supposed to room with the girl who snores when she
    sleeps—or the one who drools when she eats?
Work: Does God want me to wash dishes—or scrub toilets?
School: Should I go study in the library—or go take a nap?

You don't have to wait until you're older and come across complex puzzles like those to solve. God has a plan for your life that starts today. And the bulk of his will is stuff you can know for sure right now.

Do you remember what God's "universal will" is? It's the part of his will that's for everyone. It's clear. It's beyond argument. It's spelled out in his Word.

Let's be clear on four of the big points God expects all of us to follow:

Trust Christ. The most crucial piece of God's will for all of us is that we trust Christ as Savior and Lord. God wants everyone to be saved and to understand the truth (see 1 Timothy 2:3-4).

Submit totally to Christ. Once we trust Christ, God's will for us is to submit our life to him. He wants us to be living sacrifices (see Romans 12:1).

Obey parents. God's no-doubt-about-it will for every son or daughter is that we live in obedience to our parents (see Ephesians 6:1).

Share our faith. God has told us he wants us to go and make disciples in all the world—not just across the ocean but with those across the hall and the lunch table at school (see Matthew 28:19).

Whatever other puzzles we need to solve in life, these are just a few of the things we know are always right to do. When we want to do God's will, those are the places God wants us to start. Figuring out his universal will is no sweat. God has made the biggest points of his will totally clear!

 TALK: Can you think of some other examples of God's universal will—commands he expects all Christians to follow?

 PRAY: *God, thanks for making so much of your will absolutely clear. Help us to live up to what we know.*

 ACT: Do you have a tough time obeying any of God's obvious commands? Talk to God about it.

19 God's Will, Your Desires

Bible Reading: Psalm 37:1-7

Take delight in the Lord, and he will give you your heart's desires.
Psalm 37:4

"I'm doing all that big universal will stuff," Cheri says. "I obey God as best I know how. But how do I figure out all the specific little things God wants each day?"

Cheri is in a great spot! When you're committed to following God's clear, universal will, it's time to dig in and discover his specific will.

God gives us four ways to search out his plans:

Step 1: Look for God's will in the Bible. Knowing Scripture is our starting point for zeroing in on God's will. We don't have to wonder, for example, if it's okay to swear to fit in with friends. Ephesians 5:4 says, "Coarse jokes—these are not for you." If our idea of God's specific will doesn't match up with Scripture, then it's not God's will.

Step 2: Look for God's will in prayer. Jesus taught his disciples to pray for God's will to be done on earth (see Matthew 6:9-10). God wants us to ask for the guidance we need—as often as we need it!

Step 3: Look for God's will in the advice of others. God puts wise, mature Christians in our life to help us spot God's specific will—people like parents, grandparents, youth leaders, Sunday school teachers, and pastors. They have experience we lack.

Step 4: Look for God's will in your circumstances. God can direct us by opening and closing doors in life. You might be good at languages and want to attend a pricey, monthlong language camp. Well, being offered a scholarship might mean God has opened the door for you. Missing out on one might mean the door is shut. But circumstances are tricky. There might be other ways to get to camp, so it still might be God's specific will for your life.

Being sure of God's will happens when we make the most of all four ways God wants to guide us. But how do we settle on a final choice?

Here's where God makes it easy. If you're *doing God's universal will* and *seeking his specific will*, here's how you make your choice: *Do what you want to do.* When you put God first in your life, he promises to give you the desires of your heart (see Psalm 37:4). And guess what? If what you want doesn't line up with God's will, he makes it his job to kindly point that out to you.

 TALK: How does it make you feel to know that God cares about you enough to show you his specific plan for your life?

 PRAY: *God, thanks for having a plan specific to each of us. We want to do your will in every detail.*

 ACT: Think about a big choice you made in the last few months. Knowing what you do now, how could you have done a better job of looking for God's specific will?

Love without Strings

Bible Reading: John 15:9-17
I command you to love each other in the same way that I love you.
John 15:12

The scratch on Alondra's face sparked a lot of good conversations. For six days of her spring break, Alondra baby-sat inner-city children while their moms attended Bible classes. While her friends lounged on the beach, she burped babies. And when they came back to school to show off their tans, Alondra wondered if the scratch dug into her cheek by an angry five-year-old would leave a scar.

Have you heard of *agape* love? Agape (rhymes with "uh-sloppy") is a Greek New Testament word that English Bibles translate simply as "love." Agape is love that's from God. It's the love that gives without expecting anything in return. It's the love that makes the health, happiness, and growth of others as important to us as our own. And it's the kind of love that motivates students like Alondra to give up time, treasures, and perfect tans to do countless kind deeds.

A famous Christian author, C. S. Lewis, called agape "gift-love." When God sent his Son, Jesus, to die for us on the cross, that was the world's biggest demonstration of gift-love. John wrote, "This is real love. It is not that we loved God, but that he loved us and sent his Son as a sacrifice to take away our sins" (1 John 4:10).

Talk about it: When have you received gift-love? When have you given it?

The Bible makes totally clear how powerful gift-love is—and how important it is:

- "Love your enemies!" (Matthew 5:44).
- "Love your neighbor as yourself" (Matthew 22:39).
- "Love each other in the same way that I love you" (John 15:12).
- "Everything you do must be done with love" (1 Corinthians 16:14).
- "Live a life filled with love for others, following the example of Christ, who loved you and gave himself as a sacrifice to take away your sins" (Ephesians 5:2).
- "Let us continue to love one another, for love comes from God. . . . Since God loved us that much, we surely ought to love each other" (1 John 4:7, 11).

Showing God-powered agape love is the only way we can ever love people we don't find lovable—like enemies, misfits, and grimy toddlers. Gift-love is the kind of love Jesus has for us. And it's the love he puts in us for others!

 TALK: How are you doing at loving people with the gift-love God puts in you? Or is your agape a little sloppy?

 PRAY: *Jesus, you have an incredible love for us. Help us to pass that love on to others.*

 ACT: Who in your life needs some gift-love today? What do you want to do about it?

21 You're No Doormat

Bible Reading: John 2:13-17

The Lord disciplines those he loves, and he punishes those he accepts as his children. Hebrews 12:6

You know what agape love is all about. It's gift-love. It's the love that God has for us and that he wants us to pass on to other people. It's sacrificial—we may have to give up something. But we expect nothing in return from those we love.

Now that you have that down pat, vote "yup!" by checking any statements that describe what true agape love looks like:

- ☐ You lie down in the doorway at school or work on a snowy day so people can wipe their boots on you.
- ☐ You invite the guy who copies the front page of your homework to copy the back too.
- ☐ You let your friends order you around and always pick what to do.

When our biggest goal is to love others, we might think we have to do some crazy things. But that's sloppy agape. Agape love doesn't turn us into someone others can abuse. Check out these huge points about agape.

Love involves discipline. Look at God. He's a loving Father, yet his love doesn't mean he creates brats. He "disciplines those he loves, and he punishes those he accepts as his children" (Hebrews 12:6). Love doesn't go soft on wrongdoers by letting bad behavior slide. It helps them grow up.

Love can be tough. Jesus—God's love in human form—unleashed anger at his opponents (see Mark 3:5). He verbally blasted hypocrites, who say one thing and do another (see Matthew 23). He chased greedy merchants out of the temple (see John 2). Love can mean calling attention to evil—or taking a time-out from a friendship when your friend continues to hurt you.

Love can fail. You may remember from some wedding sermon the 1 Corinthians 13:8 phrase, "Love never fails" (NIV). Actually, the right way to translate that is, "Love will last forever." The sad truth is this: While God's love is perfect, humans do not perfectly show that love.

God wants us to show his love, his care, and his best for others. But doing what's best for others doesn't mean letting them take advantage of us. The most loving thing we can do is be a better example—and, if necessary, to point them toward better attitudes and actions. That's real love.

 TALK: Have you ever thought that agape love meant you had to be a doormat? What does it really mean?

 PRAY: *God, help us to love wisely. Show us what true agape love looks like.*

 ACT: Talk together about one way you can show real agape love today—without letting anyone take advantage of you.

22 Close on the Couch

Bible Reading: 1 Thessalonians 4:4

Each of you should learn to control his own body in a way that is holy and honorable. 1 Thessalonians 4:4, NIV

Talk about sloppy agape. Or maybe it was slobbery agape. Four-year-old Megan thought it was just plain slobbery.

A herd of relatives had piled into Megan's house for Thanksgiving. Megan's older cousin, Stacy, even came home from college, bringing her boyfriend, Jared. Stacy snuggled in on the couch next to Jared to watch a football game. He smiled and slid his arm around her. Megan didn't like that one bit. She bounced onto the couch and tried to pry open a spot between Stacy and Jared.

Mom picked up Megan and took her to the kitchen. A minute later Megan ran back into the room. She squealed. "You're in *luuuuuv*. Mommy says so."

Sometimes Christians make it sound like being "in love" is bad.

The Bible doesn't bash romance. Listen how positively the story of Jacob and Rachel paints it, even in a culture in which parents arranged marriages and a husband paid for his wife with cows and camels: "Rachel was beautiful in every way, with a lovely face and shapely figure.... Jacob was in love with Rachel.... So Jacob spent the next seven years working to pay for Rachel. But his love for her was so strong that it seemed to him but a few days" (Genesis 29:17-18, 20).

Jacob thought Rachel was kind of cute. And as you grow up, you'll discover that the magnetic pull between guys and girls is normal. It's how God designed you. But like Paul told the Thessalonians, that attraction needs to be pursued within the boundaries of honor and holiness.

Romance is wonderful when it's built on agape love. It looks like this:

- You like each other for much more than your looks.
- You stay pure, keeping physical closeness for marriage. (If you need more info than that, ask your parents!)
- Your parents approve of your relationship.
- Your relationship doesn't get in the way of school or other friends.
- Your friendship with each other helps you both move toward Jesus.

"Hey," you might say. "I don't even like boys [or girls]." That's fine! But when you do get interested, these are some of the big rules. Any questions?

 TALK: Is romance bad? When is it right?

 PRAY: *God, thanks for giving us hearts that get excited about each other. We're glad you created love.*

 ACT: How can you put agape into action right now in how you treat boys and girls?

23 What the World Needs Is Love, God's Love

Bible Reading: Luke 19:1-10
The Son of Man came to seek and to save what was lost.
Luke 19:10, NIV

As Paul left the movie theater with some friends from his swim team, he almost crashed into another group of friends—boys from church. When Paul said hi to his church buddies, they hit him with a look of disgust that felt like a punch in the face. Paul shrugged and kept walking, puzzling over the weird looks. *They couldn't have been mad about the movie,* he figured. *They were in line to see the same thing.* The more he thought about it, the more sure he was. *It had to be who I was with.*

Talk about it: Have you ever bumped into Christians who think it's wrong to have good friends who aren't Christians? Perhaps you feel that way. Is that the right way to think?

As a Christian you are to make the health, happiness, and growth of *anyone* and *everyone* within your reach as important to you as your own. When it comes to showing agape love, the Bible says, "Pay all your debts, except the debt of love for others. You can never finish paying that! If you love your neighbor, you will fulfill all the requirements of God's law" (Romans 13:8).

Christians who think it's wrong to be good friends with unbelievers point to James 4:4. That verse says, "Don't you realize that friendship with this world makes you an enemy of God?" But think hard about this: That verse warns against accepting the world's *attitudes* and *actions,* not being friends with the world's *people.*

And look at Jesus. He spent so much time among unbelievers that he was mocked as a friend of sinners (see Luke 15:2). His openness to outcasts like Zacchaeus was all part of his mission to seek and save people who are lost—who have not let Jesus find them and save them from sin (see Luke 19:10).

Jesus' mission to save unbelievers gives us a huge clue about what's right or wrong in the way we get along in the world. Here's the test: If we can be friends with a non-Christian and help that person understand what it means to follow Christ, the relationship might be right. But if we get sucked into doing wrong things, we probably need to pick a different friend.

God wants you to be friends with non-Christian people in your world—at school or work, on sports teams, in your neighborhood, among your relatives. Without your friendship, they may never feel Christ's real-life love. And without feeling that great love, they will have no reason to want to become friends with God.

 TALK: What do you think about your Savior's willingness to reach out to sinners? How can you imitate that?

 PRAY: *Lord, we pray that our love for the non-Christians in our life will lead them to a loving relationship with you.*

 ACT: Pick a non-Christian you think you can befriend in a positive way—and plan how to further your friendship.

24 Putting on a Show

Bible Reading: Luke 12:1-3

Beware of the yeast of the Pharisees—beware of their hypocrisy.
Luke 12:1

Quiz time. Vote for the behavior that you think makes God shout, *"Wa-hoo!"*

(a) Every Sunday on the way to church you have a slugfest in the backseat. But when you and your siblings arrive, you act all huggy-kissy.

(b) You cuss and scream with your baseball buddies. But when your Christian friends show up to watch the game, you cut out the swearing.

(c) You agree to never smoke, drink, or do drugs. But you light up when you think God or your Sunday school teacher can't spot you.

Whoops. None of those behaviors wins a round of applause from God. In fact, if that phony behavior becomes a habit, it's called "hypocrisy." From the way Jesus talked, we know that hypocrisy is an awful thing. It's pretending to be better than we are—like bragging that we're totally good when we're terribly bad.

The "hypocrite" label that Jesus flung at the Pharisees comes from a Greek word that means "playacting." It first referred to Greek actors, who were famous for their masks. The Pharisees were the Bible's Oscar-winning hypocrites. They looked religious in front of people, but they were playacting. Their relationship with God was fake.

So what is God looking for? The opposite of a mask. This is what he expects from us: WYSIWYG—what you see is what you get. "Transparent" is a good word for what he wants. We can see through transparent people like glass. They show a completely honest face to themselves, to others, and to God.

God doesn't expect us to show our worst side to the whole world. But he also doesn't think it's cool to show off our scrubbed-up outside when our inside is still a mess. He wants us to clean up what we're really like inside so our goodness will last longer than Sunday school.

All of us do bad things—we sin. But the answer is not found in hiding behind a mask. It's found in being transparent—admitting to God and our Christian brothers and sisters that we're less than perfect and need forgiveness.

Is that easier said than done? Yes. But taking off the mask is the only way you allow God to work in your life. And it's the only way people can get to know and love the real you!

 TALK: Have you ever hidden behind a mask? How does that hurt you? Others?

 PRAY: *God, help us let you clean us up on the inside. We don't want to keep hiding wrongdoings behind a mask. Please help us to become transparent.*

 ACT: Take some time alone with God today to talk to him about any areas where you might be feeling like a fake.

Bible Reading: Mark 9:2-13
This is my beloved Son. Listen to him. Mark 9:7

The knot in Jacki's stomach tied tighter and tighter during the long ride back to reality from the weeklong summer camp put on by her church. "I want to stay up there," she moaned. "It's so easy to be a Christian. It's so cool there. The mountains look like heaven. The Bible lessons are great. Everyone tries to get along. Jesus is so real up there."

If you've ever been to a Christian camp, you know how hard it can be to go home. When Bible lessons, quiet times, and Christian friendships happen so easily, who would ever want to go home?

Peter, James, and John got a taste of church-camp high in a big way. As Jesus' three closest disciples stared at him in amazement, they saw a bright glow. Then Elijah and Moses showed up. It was a touch of heaven, just like camp. Then God's voice shook from the clouds and the mountaintop experience ended.

Isn't that the way it is when you get away to a Christian camp or retreat? Great music, a God-charged atmosphere—Christianity couldn't be easier. On the ride home you might sing camp songs until you're hoarse. Everything is rosy and bright. But then, *thud!* Your alarm clock nags you out of bed, the clothes you want are still dirty from camp, and your mom once again feeds you oatmeal for breakfast. You hate oatmeal—though you happily ate it up on the mountain.

Face it: Life is back with all its realities, good and bad.

But wait! Look back at Mark 9:9. There are *four* figures winding their way back to the valley from that peak experience. Peter, James, John—and *Jesus!*

That's a truth you might forget when you slide down from camp, vacation Bible school, or any other spiritual high. Jesus isn't chained to a mountaintop lodge, a woodsy chapel, or even the youth room in your church basement. He travels with you into everyday life to help you with nagging alarm clocks, grungy clothes, and gloppy oatmeal.

The disciples were no doubt glad to climb the mountain and glimpse Jesus' glory. Those rare experiences can charge your spiritual batteries—and even permanently change you. The bad news is that everyday life isn't lived on the mountaintop. The good news is that if you just look around the valley, you'll find Jesus— hanging out with you, helping you live out the mountaintop glow!

 TALK: What can you and your Christian friends do to make everyday life at home a little more like heaven?

 PRAY: *Jesus, thanks for being with us at home. We want you to hang out with us on the mountaintop—and in the valleys of life.*

 ACT: Are you headed to a Christian camp or a week of vacation Bible school, or have you recently been to one? What's your plan for keeping Jesus close?

26 1 Believe—Kind Of

Bible Reading: Luke 17:5-6

If you have faith as small as a mustard seed, you can say to this mulberry tree, "Be uprooted and planted in the sea," and it will obey you. Luke 17:6, NIV

Kim believes that God can work in the life of her friend Robin so that she will trust Christ in the future, so she prays often for Robin and invites her to a before-school Bible club.

Ian believes he can learn a lot about trusting God by spending time alone with him, so he takes ten to fifteen minutes each morning to read his Bible and talk to God in prayer.

You maybe think of "faith" as the decision a person makes to trust Jesus as Savior. But faith is broader than that. Faith includes all the things we believe about God and all the ways we learn to put our trust in him. Faith is what allows Kim and Ian to see what God is up to in their world.

But faith can be shaky. If you've followed Jesus for a while, you probably know the feeling: "Lord, I really believe in you and your power. But I'm having trouble trusting you in this mess."

Mark 9 shows how a father with a troubled son felt unsure in his faith. He begged Jesus to heal his son. "Have mercy on us and help us" (Mark 9:22), the father cries helplessly. Jesus encourages the man to believe in him, because "anything is possible if a person believes" (verse 23). But the confused father sobs piercing words: "I do believe, but help me not to doubt!" (verse 24). Is that dad confused? How can he believe and doubt at the same time? But the statement is reality!

And in Luke 17 the disciples told Jesus they wanted bigger belief in God. They pleaded, "Increase our faith!" But Jesus hinted they didn't need huge faith. Faith as small as a mustard seed would work, so long as it was faith in him. Then their faith would do the impossible, like uprooting a large tree and flinging it into the sea.

So how do you gain more faith—the faith that recognizes what God is doing in your world? You start by soaking up Scripture. Romans 10:17 says, "Faith comes from listening to this message of good news—the Good News about Christ." The more you read and remember God's Word, the more clearly you will see what God is doing. And your faith will grow as a result!

 TALK: When have you felt torn between believing—and knowing you needed to believe more?

 PRAY: Pray those words to God: "I do believe, but help me not to doubt!"

 ACT: God wants to challenge your faith. Think of a way you would like him to work in your life or the life of a friend or family member. Tell God about it. Exercise your faith by praying daily for your request. And watch what happens!

27 The Faith Factor

Bible Reading: Hebrews 11:1-6

Faith . . . is the confident assurance that what we hope for is going to happen. Hebrews 11:1

Remember Kim? She's the one who finds it easy to see God at work in her friend Robin, nudging her closer to becoming a Christian. But get this: Kim has a hard time seeing how God can help her with her homework, so she constantly worries about her grades.

And Ian? He sees God changing his life from the inside out as a result of his spending time reading the Bible and talking to God. But often he thinks that he alone gets the credit for the money he earns mowing lawns and sweeping driveways. So he seldom gives any of his hard-earned cash to God in the church offering.

What kind of faith is that?

The normal kind! It's the kind of faith that most of us have most of the time.

Faith is like the pitcher on a baseball team—you can't have much of a game without one. The Bible uses strong words to describe the role of faith in the Christian life:

- "It is impossible to please God without faith" (Hebrews 11:6).
- "It is through faith that a righteous person has life" (Romans 1:17).
- "Everything that does not come from faith is sin" (Romans 14:23, NIV).

The apostle Paul said faith is one of the three great qualities in the Christian life—along with hope and love (see 1 Corinthians 13:13).

You can't get along without faith. But faith doesn't start out strong. It doesn't start out like a pitcher who can hurl a fastball over home plate at a hundred miles an hour. It's more like a baby who has trouble just trying to lift her head off the bed.

So sometimes your faith is strong. You can look at a situation and see God at work. Other times doubt, worry, or spiritual ignorance make it difficult to trust God. Sometimes you can say, "I do believe!" But other times you beg God to help you trust him. If you ever feel stuck between belief and unbelief, you're normal.

Jesus' disciples—even though they watched their master up close and personal for three years—were often short on faith. Can you imagine? With their own eyes they saw Jesus raise the dead, heal the sick, calm the storm, and cast out demons— and they still struggled with faith.

When you wish you had bigger trust in God, pray these words straight from the mouths of Jesus' closest disciples, and be confident God will grow your faith in him: "We need more faith; tell us how to get it" (Luke 17:5).

 TALK: How are you going to grow in faith? What is God's plan to help?

 PRAY: *God, thanks for sticking with us even when our faith isn't full grown.*

 ACT: Strengthen your faith by spending some time reading Scripture today!

28 Serving God Hands Down

Bible Reading: Mark 9:43-47

If your hand causes you to sin, cut it off. Mark 9:43

This next story actually happened.

Really.

Two police officers spotted a young man staggering along the road with a Bible under one arm. His other arm was tucked tightly under the Bible in an attempt to stop some heavy bleeding—bleeding caused when the man whacked off his own hand!

Yes, you read that right.

The guy had cut off his own hand. He said he lopped it off to obey Mark 9:43: "If your hand causes you to sin, cut it off." Apparently his hand had touched something or taken something it shouldn't have, so he took Jesus' words literally and removed the misbehaving hand. The story did have some good news. The police officers found the severed hand in a trash can. Doctors were able to sew it back on.

It's *really* important to know what the Bible *means,* not just what it *says.* But Jesus really did speak those words about cutting off a hand. If we read Jesus' commands in this section without understanding what he meant, we would all need to get in line for several amputations! Who hasn't ever sinned with their eyes, hands, or feet?

Jesus was exaggerating for effect and emphasis. People do this all the time: "I've told you a million times." "I was so embarrassed I could have died." "I could eat a horse." "Don't have a cow." The statements aren't literally true but are meant to drive home the point that we were *really* annoyed, embarrassed, hungry, and so on.

Jesus doesn't want us to whack off body parts, like a hand that snuck into a cookie jar. But he does want us to know that we have two ways to use our physical body—*for* God's purposes or *against* God's purposes. If our goal is to serve God and we let our body do things that don't please him, our body has become our enemy.

Jesus wants you, his follower, to give to him not just your soul but your eyes, hands, feet, and every other part of you. Paul put it this way: "I plead with you to give your bodies to God" (Romans 12:1). God isn't interested in watching you chop yourself up until you can't sin anymore. But he does want you to take charge of your physical body and live for God's purposes. It's not a lot easier, but it's a lot less bloody!

 TALK: How are you using your body to serve God?

 PRAY: *God, we want to honor you with our body. Help us use our eyes and our hands and our feet to glorify you.*

 ACT: What are some ways you may have used your body to sin? Can you see the seriousness with which Jesus is saying, "Stop it!"? Make a plan to avoid sin and use your body to do good.

On Your Way to Disneyland

Bible Reading: Galatians 5:16-17

Live according to your new life in the Holy Spirit. Then you won't be doing what your sinful nature craves. Galatians 5:16

Suppose you're dying to get to Disneyland. You've figured out how to reach the pedals and see over the steering wheel—don't try this anywhere but in your imagination—so you hit the road. In the tangled mess of freeways known as Los Angeles, you see a sign that says "Disneyland Next Exit." The sign looks real. It's standard government issue. But the exit isn't anywhere near where you thought it would be, and you're sure you know a quicker way to the happiest place on earth.

You have two choices—which get you two very different results.

- Option One: *Trust the sign and stay on the route.* And here's what happens: As you follow the marked route—even though it goes against your instincts—you ride past fantastic new sights you never could have found on your own. And you shoot straight into the park's front gate.
- Option Two: *Ignore the sign and take your own shortcut.* And here's that result: The shortcut that looked smart at the start takes you farther and farther from your happy destination, and in the end your car plunges over one of those unfinished freeway overpasses so famous in movies.

While you may not be able to hop in the car and drive to Disneyland, at least not for a couple of years, you face similar choices almost as often as you breathe.

Inside each of us is "sinful nature," a drive or desire or wish to do wrong. It's the instinct that makes taking shortcuts sound smart. But as Christians there's a battle raging in our heart as we decide which way to turn, because we also have the Holy Spirit living in us. He's the one urging us to stick to God's paths and do right.

Here's a guarantee: When you follow the desires of your sinful nature, you wind up on roads that won't get you where you want to go. You travel farther and farther from your destination—and you wind up in a place called destruction. But listening to the Spirit brings benefits you can't foresee. It puts you on the route to the destination of your dreams (Romans 8:13; Galatians 5:19-23).

Can you see it? Every choice you face puts you at a fork in the road. You can follow the way of the Holy Spirit—or the way of sinful nature. Which road would you rather take?

 TALK: What good results come when you follow the Spirit? Does that mean obeying the Spirit is easier? Explain your answer.

 PRAY: *God, thanks for giving us your Spirit to guide us. We trust that you know how to get us to good places.*

 ACT: You can hear what the Spirit is saying by learning from God's Word. Are you facing a choice where you feel torn between good and bad? Get some guidance and encouragement by seeing what the Bible says about your struggle.

30 Get Smart

Bible Reading: Proverbs 2:1-5

Listen to me and treasure my instructions. . . . Then you will understand what it means to fear the Lord, and you will gain knowledge of God. Proverbs 2:1, 5

Let's assume you want to get smart—so smart, in fact, that you'll know how to do what's right all the time. What are the best ways to learn right from wrong? Score the following options between 1 and 10 (1 means *a lousy place to learn,* 10 means *the best place to get brainy*):

___Search the Internet—someplace other than your favorite joke page

___Rely on your younger brother—after all, he's surely learned from watching your mistakes

___Ask your older sister—she says she's so much smarter than you

___Ask your parents—your built-in fountain of wisdom

___Read the Bible—the wisdom God thought was important enough to write down for you

God puts many sources of wisdom in your life. But of all those choices, one source trumps all the others. Do you remember all the qualities of God's Word that David rattled off in Psalm 19? "The decrees of the Lord are trustworthy, making wise the simple. The commandments of the Lord are right, bringing joy to the heart. The commands of the Lord are clear, giving insight to life" (verses 7-8).

The wisdom you want for life is plain in the Bible. But it doesn't fly off the page and into your life without some effort on your part.

Talk about it: What does today's Bible passage say to do if you want God's wisdom? Did you find the following six things to do?

1. Listen to God—you see him as your best source for wisdom
2. Treasure his instructions—you hang on to what he teaches you
3. Tune your ears to wisdom—you pay attention
4. Concentrate on understanding—you think hard
5. Cry out for insight—you tell God you want his good sense
6. Search for wisdom—you hunt for it as if looking for buried treasure

When you do these things, there's a promise. You'll find God's wisdom—and understand why it's great to follow God!

 TALK: How do you feel knowing that God has so much wisdom he's willing to share with you?

 PRAY: *God, we cry out for your wisdom! Teach us what is right and good!*

 ACT: How hard are you trying to get smart God's way? Which of the six things to do will you work on today—and how do you want to do that?

July

31 Unbeatable Brains

Bible Reading: Proverbs 2:6-11

You will understand what is right, just, and fair, and you will know how to find the right course of action every time. Proverbs 2:9

Pedro, who was two, glared at his mom. "Cookie!" Pedro's mom held him and explained why he couldn't have another cookie. She didn't want him to get a tummy ache. And his body needed good food. Even though Pedro didn't understand everything, he knew his mom cared about him. He took the carrot she offered him and happily went back to pulling pots and pans out of the cupboards.

God's Word doesn't just toss us a bunch of "dos and don'ts." God holds us tight. As best as our brain can manage, he tells us *why* it's good to obey him.

You don't have to read far in God's Word to spot incredible promises to those who look for God's wisdom and learn how to follow it. In today's Bible passage alone you hear how he gives good sense to the godly. He puts a shield of protection around everyone who follows him.

But one of the best features of God's wisdom is that he doesn't drag you fussing and screaming into obedience. He aims to persuade your mind and win your heart. He desires that you walk in his ways because you *want* to.

Listen again to the promises:

- Wisdom will capture your heart.
- Knowledge will make you joyful.
- You will be able to pick the right course of action every time.

God wants you to use both your mind and heart to take an active role in figuring out his wisdom. He wants you to understand the reasons for his rules.

So try this: Write a private note to yourself. On the left half, spell out a specific command from God you really want to keep—like obeying parents (see Colossians 3:20), telling the truth (see Ephesians 4:25), being kind to a brother or sister (see Ephesians 4:32), or doing your best on your homework (see Colossians 3:23). On the right side, write down all the reasons for keeping that command.

You can't count on having clear, creative thinking when you're not sure why doing something is right. But working through your reasons ahead of time is a fantastic way to get wisdom to enter your heart. And when you do that, God has another promise for you: "Wise planning will watch over you," he says. "Understanding will keep you safe" (Proverbs 2:11).

 TALK: How does God work in you so you are happy to obey him? Would you rather have him force his rules on you?

 PRAY: *God, show us how we can take hold of your wisdom and let it convince our mind and heart.*

 ACT: Try writing that note described above. Really!

1 Call Them "The Ten Freedoms"

Bible Reading: Exodus 20:1-17

I lavish my love on those who love me and obey my commands.
Exodus 20:6

Herman the crab stormed across the ocean floor and under the family rock. "I want to be free!" he screamed. "I don't see how you can expect me to wear this stupid shell twenty-four hours a day. It's confining. It's cramped."

His father, Fred, placed a claw on Herman's shoulder. Herman rolled his eyes. "Son," he said, "let me tell you a story."

"Dad, not another—"

"It's about Harold the human," Fred continued. "Harold insisted on going barefoot to school. He complained that his shoes were too confining. Finally, his mother gave in to him. Harold skipped out of the house—and stepped on a broken soda bottle. His foot required twenty stitches, and some other guy got his spot on the football team."

"That's a dumb story, Dad," Herman said.

"Maybe, Son, but the point is this: Every crab has felt life would be a lot better if he could wiggle free from the shell. Well, your time will come soon." The young crab looked surprised. "That's right. It's called molting, and all crabs do it as they grow up. But when that happens, you will be in more danger than at any other time in your life. Until your new shell hardens like the one you have now, you have to be more careful than usual. Without this shell, you'll be less free—not more."

"That's weird, Dad," Herman said. "Some things seem to limit freedom, but really they make greater freedom possible, right?"

Fred draped his claw over Herman's back. "How did you get so smart, Son?"

Some people think the Ten Commandments and the teachings of Jesus rob us of freedom. They see God's rules as confining, like Herman viewed his shell. Actually, though, God's directions bring true freedom to those who follow them. For example, obeying the fifth commandment, "Honor your father and mother" (Exodus 20:12), brings the promise of living long and well with God's blessings.

All through the Bible we find that God's commands give us incredible freedom if we respond to them. Try this test: Pick any commandment from God, and you're sure to think of benefits that come to you and other people as a result of living within God's wise boundaries.

 TALK: Do you sometimes feel confined and restricted as a Christian? How is that just the opposite of how God wants you to feel?

 PRAY: *Father, thank you that your commandments give us freedom.*

 ACT: Do you have a hard time obeying any of God's commands? Pick a command that seems tough to obey and list all the benefits God provides you when you obey that command.

2 Training for the Ironman

Bible Reading: Ephesians 5:25

You husbands must love your wives with the same love Christ showed the church. He gave up his life for her. Ephesians 5:25

"I don't ever want to get married," Monica declared.

At twelve years old, she had seen as much marital unhappiness as she could handle. Her dad left when she was three. Her mom remarried when she was five. Her mom and stepdad get along okay, but Monica knew they worked hard at it.

Despite the tough marriage stuff we see all around us, the Bible paints an incredibly positive picture of marriage. It was created by God to take away our loneliness (Genesis 2:18). It brings the future generation into this world (Genesis 1:28). It's given for our enjoyment (Proverbs 5:18).

Yet the Bible never hides the rough side of marriage. The Ephesians verse from the pen of the apostle Paul makes it clear that marriage is huge work. He couldn't have made the demands any more obvious than telling husbands to love their wives just as Christ loved the church—the people who believe in him. Exactly how did Christ love us? He died for us! And Paul wasn't just talking to husbands. The love required of a wife for her husband is just as big.

Marriage takes long-distance endurance. But there's a secret to having a long and happy marriage. It's *preparation.*

Suppose you want to run the Hawaii Ironman triathlon. Piled on top of a 26.2-mile marathon run are a 2.4-mile ocean swim and a 112-mile cycle race through blistering tropical heat. So how do you get ready for the Ironman? Competitors train an average of 7 miles a week swimming, 48 miles running, and 232 miles riding.

You can't wake up one morning and decide to do the Ironman. You would die trying. And race officials wouldn't even let you near the course.

Marriage is the ultimate endurance event. The decision to enter the race is only one step. It also takes a training routine rigorous enough to carry you to the end. If you want to cross the finish line of marriage still smiling, getting ready starts *now.*

Every relationship you are part of prepares you for marriage—from your family relationships to your peer friendships to the guy-girl relationships you will someday experience. You can prepare now by learning to live like Jesus did. While it's unlikely that you'll be expected to lay down your life for the ones you love, you *will* be expected sometimes to give up things in your life to express your love.

 TALK: How are you training to be ready for marriage? Why bother?

 PRAY: *God, give us the endurance we need to make all of our relationships great. Help us put in the hours of training we need so we will get the results we want.*

 ACT: The heart of married life is the sacrificial love that caused Jesus to lay down his life for the world. Sacrifice something—time, money, desires—to do an act of love for a friend or family member today!

3 The People Solution

Bible Reading: Acts 4:12

There is salvation in no one else! There is no other name in all of heaven for people to call on to save them. Acts 4:12

Ridge and several friends from his youth group had just finished performing mime in a park pavilion of a large city. During a chat with a nice-looking couple, Ridge explained that the whole point of the mime was to help people know that they need Jesus.

"So that's what you kids are here for," the woman responded. "Well, we don't need Jesus to solve our problems. We just need to come together. People are the real solution to the troubles facing the world."

Ridge just bumped into a way of looking at the world that opposes the Bible, Christians, and the church. It's an idea that's called secular humanism. It says that human beings are so superpowerful that we can solve all the problems of our planet.

At first that sounds smart. After all, we aren't looking to the dolphins, whales, baby seals, or endangered microscopic insects to save the world. And all of us—Christians and non-Christians alike—can work in ways that help people. But can we as humans really solve all of the world's problems all by ourselves?

Perhaps you have spotted that this plan leaves God out. There are folks who argue that God can't save the world, because he doesn't exist.

But solving our problems by ourselves is a fantasy that misses some major facts. Human history is jam-packed with examples that show we can't solve our own problems. Just think of people and groups like Adolf Hitler, Joseph Stalin, the Khmer Rouge, Idi Amin, the KKK, and Osama bin Laden!

Some people think that the only hope we have of a better world is dumping all religions and trusting human brainpower to bring peace and happiness to the world. (When you hear about people working to remove any mention of God from school or public life—like the Pledge of Allegiance—this is the thinking that drives them. They take the idea of "separation of church and state" to an extreme.)

The apostle Peter stood and proclaimed that Jesus—not humankind—is the world's only hope for salvation. Of all the people on earth—including all of us working together—only Jesus has the power to save.

Of course, as humans we need to do our part to erase war and famine, to fight disease and injustice. But in the end, we can't rescue ourselves. We need Jesus!

 TALK: Say it in your own words: What's wrong with thinking people can solve all the planet's problems?

 PRAY: *God, guard our mind from ever thinking that we can live without you.*

 ACT: Explain what you learned about secular humanism to a friend—and explain our real hope as well!

4 The Basic Equipment

Bible Reading: 2 Timothy 3:16-17
All Scripture is inspired by God and is useful to teach us what is true.
2 Timothy 3:16

Caleb wakes up on the morning of his tenth birthday and stumbles into the kitchen for breakfast. His mom is wearing a big smile. "There's something in the family room for you!" she says.

Racing downstairs with his mom right behind him, Caleb stops a few feet from the TV set and stares at the empty carton on the floor.

"You're kidding, right? Where's the video-game deck?" Caleb asks.

"Game deck?" his mom asks. "You said you wanted a box for your birthday."

"You got me . . . a box?" Caleb says.

"Yes, I sure did!" Mom announces proudly. "Pretty neat, huh?"

"I said I wanted an *Xbox* for my birthday," he cries. "Where are all the parts? I can't play video games with *a big box of nothing!*"

Caleb's mom is, of course, kidding. You can't expect a cardboard box to run video games. Without a game console, cables, controllers, power supply, and games, all you've got is a piece of trash.

It's the same with finding a trustworthy way to help you know how to live your life. If you want to decide issues of right and wrong, you need some standard equipment. You need a standard to follow. But if that standard doesn't have some basic parts, it's just junk. Ponder this:

A true standard is bigger than our feelings. It's *objective*. It doesn't depend on what you or any other person thinks or feels. If you think stealing is wrong but your neighbor doesn't, how can you say she shouldn't swipe your big-screen TV?

A true standard applies to everyone. It's *universal*. It applies to all people in all places. You may consider it wrong to hit children, but if another culture in the world disagrees, who can say they are wrong?

A true standard doesn't change. It's *constant*. It doesn't change over time. If standards can be rewritten, how can you know what the rules are?

Someone totally loving and smart knew that we would need an objective, universal, and constant standard to teach us the truth and help us tell right from wrong. God didn't plop us on this planet without the stuff we would need for making right choices. He gave us the Bible as our perfect standard to follow, with all the proper equipment built right in. That's way better than an empty box.

 TALK: Why did God give you flawless standards of right and wrong? Is he out to annoy you—or do you feel his love?

 PRAY: *Thank you, God, for loving us enough to teach us right from wrong.*

 ACT: Explain to a friend what it means that our standard for right and wrong is bigger than our feelings . . . applies to everyone . . . doesn't change.

5 May I Have Your Autograph?

Bible Reading: John 1:1-5, 14

The Word became human and lived here on earth among us. John 1:14

Sixteen-year-old soccer fanatic Lucy Chavez had ruled her age group every year in the park league. Now she was dreaming that someday she would play soccer in the Olympics. But the competition kept getting tougher, and Lucy knew she had to play smarter if she wanted to stay ahead.

She discovered that her idol, soccer star Erin Dupree, had just written a book about soccer. In a snap Lucy ordered the book on-line for overnight delivery. It was huge, the most detailed soccer book Lucy had ever seen. It was so hard to understand that Lucy almost gave up trying to read it. The information was there, but she wasn't getting it.

One day during soccer practice, her coach called out to her from the sideline. "Lucy," she hollered, "plant your foot more ahead of the ball." The advice worked.

When Lucy turned to thank her coach, she couldn't believe her eyes. Erin Dupree was standing next to her coach! "Erin and I grew up together," Coach explained as Lucy approached in awe. "She's in town on a book-signing tour. That advice I just gave you came from her."

"Your coach has told me a lot about you," the soccer star said. "I like what I see. Can we get together after practice to talk about your game?"

Put yourself in Lucy's cleats. Would you ever say something like, "Thanks for the offer, Ms. Dupree, but I can't meet with you. I have to hurry home from practice to study your book."

No way. Unless Lucy has taken one too many headers, that girl will jump at the chance to get to know her hero. What better way to understand a book than to have the author explain it? Lucy, of course, accepted the invitation. Erin's book came alive for her.

Understanding the Bible and having its truth leap alive for us happens the same way. We need a personal relationship with the author, the one John calls "the Word." That's right—the Bible *and* Jesus Christ are *both* called the Word of God.

Whenever we open the Bible, we connect with God's written Word *and* his living Word—Jesus, his Son. Jesus is eager to help us understand and put into action what he wrote. He is the one who really makes "personal devotions" personal!

 TALK: How can you take advantage of God's offer to teach you firsthand from his Word? As you read the Bible, are you meeting with him—or just flipping pages in a book?

 PRAY: *Lord, we're glad that when we open your Word, you are right there with us to teach us.*

 ACT: Take a new attitude with you this week to the time you spend in the Bible. Expect to meet Jesus!

6 There'll Be Some Changes Made

Bible Reading: John 17:9, 17

Make them pure and holy by teaching them your words of truth.
John 17:17

Pa and Ma had spent their whole lives raising five sons on a little place out in the middle of nowhere, completely out of touch with modern culture and its technological advances. But one day Pa reckoned it was time to see what city life was like. So he and the family headed for the bright lights and skyscrapers of the big city.

Arriving in the heart of downtown, Pa and Ma and the boys couldn't believe what they saw. They wandered the streets, mouths a-droop. While Ma explored a dress shop, Pa and the boys stepped into the lobby of a ritzy hotel.

Pa's attention was immediately drawn to a tiny little room with shiny brass doors. He watched with interest as a frumpy old lady walked up to the doors and pushed a button. Soon the brass doors slid open, the old lady stepped in, and the doors closed again. Pa watched curiously as lighted numbers flashed above. Then the doors opened and a gorgeous young woman in a tailored suit stepped out.

Pa's eyes bugged with astonishment. He watched the beautiful woman walk away, then looked back at the little room with brass doors. "Boys," he said to his sons excitedly, "go and get your mother."

Don't you wish it were that easy to change something about yourself—not just the way you look, but maybe an ugly habit? Or perhaps you have wrong attitudes and actions, and you wish these would magically disappear. It would be nice to step into a little room, push a few buttons, and step out completely changed.

God wants all of us to be good. As Christians we would like to follow God's instructions, but by the end of practically every day our actions and attitudes slap us in the face, reminding us how unholy and impure we are. *If getting pure and holy is up to me,* we might figure, *it's never going to happen.*

King David knew that getting good wasn't all up to him. He wrote, "How can a young person stay pure? By obeying your word and following its rules" (Psalm 119:9).

Every time we dig into God's words of truth, Christ's prayer for purity is being answered in us. Purity happens when we daily welcome God's Word into our life. The change might not be as quick and dramatic as the change Pa thought that little elevator room could work. But we *are* being transformed, changed to be like Jesus, because that's what Jesus prayed for.

TALK: How does it make you feel that Jesus would pray for your purity—and that God would send his Word so it could happen?

PRAY: *God, as we read your Word, make us pure.*

ACT: Don't miss taking time alone with God, reading his Word today.

7 No Pain, No Gain

Bible Reading: Hebrews 4:12-13
The word of God is full of living power. It is sharper than the sharpest knife, cutting deep into our innermost thoughts and desires.
Hebrews 4:12

"How bad is it, Doc?" the patient asks. "Tell me the truth."

"I'm afraid it's bad—very bad," the doctor replies. "If I don't perform major surgery and remove the tumor, you will die in a matter of weeks."

"I don't want surgery, Doc. It will hurt."

The doctor smiles. "You won't feel a thing. You'll be asleep during the surgery."

"But there will be pain after the surgery, maybe for weeks, right?"

"We have medications to reduce the pain."

"But the incision will still hurt a little; taking out the stitches will hurt."

"Well, yes, there is always some pain involved in a major—"

The patient interrupts. "No surgery then. I don't like owies."

Talk about it: What things do you do to avoid experiencing the owies of life?

If we're anything close to normal, we make it a rule to avoid pain whenever possible. We wear seat belts so we don't fly through the windshield. We put on shoes so we don't step on glass. We wear skid-lids when we bike so our noggin doesn't knock against the pavement.

But no sane person shies away from the surgeon's lifesaving knife because of being scared it will cause an owie. We know that pain sometimes produces something good, whether it's the pain of a must-do medical procedure, the effort of a sweaty fitness workout, or the agony of attending a little brother's tuba recital when we would rather be hanging with our friends.

Did you know that God's Word can sometimes hurt us? I'm not talking about the pain we feel if we drop a ten-pound study Bible on our toes. The writer of Hebrews pictures God's Word as a surgeon's knife. God, the master surgeon, knows exactly where tumorlike growths of wrong thoughts and desires are lurking. And he knows that those growths will destroy us if they aren't sliced out. His Word is the instrument he uses to expose those growths, bringing them to light and showing us how to get rid of them.

So whenever you read the Bible and feel the pain of God's knife poking at you to correct you, don't pull away. The Great Physician allows the hurt only because he loves you and wants to give you spiritual health.

 TALK: How is God using his good Word like a knife in your life? Are you pulling away or letting him do his healing work?

 PRAY: *Thank you, Lord, for sending your Word to heal us.*

 ACT: Pick a Bible command that makes you hurt inside because you don't want to hear it. Write it on the front of an index card. On the back, list the benefits of obeying. Put your card where you can see it often.

8 Make Yourself at Home

Bible Reading: Colossians 3:12-17

Let the words of Christ, in all their richness, live in your hearts and make you wise. Colossians 3:16

Robert Stroud spent more than fifty years of his life in prison for violent crimes he committed in his youth. In fact, he spent forty-three of them in solitary confinement.

Yet people don't remember Stroud for his crimes. Early in his prison career, Stroud became interested in birds, supposedly when a stray canary flitted into his prison cell. With the prison warden's permission, he began raising birds in his tiny living space. When birds became sick, he requested books on bird diseases and doctored them back to health. As the years passed, he continued to study birds and bird diseases and eventually became one of the world's biggest authorities on the subject—all while serving a life sentence for murder.

Robert Stroud's life story was dramatized in a 1962 film starring actor Burt Lancaster. Since Stroud served part of his sentence in Alcatraz prison in San Francisco Bay, the film was titled *Birdman of Alcatraz*.

How did a murderer from Alaska become the Birdman of Alcatraz? It all began when he turned his prison cell into a home for little birds. As he cared about these creatures and dedicated his life to curing them, he changed. Providing a safe haven for birds, he became a bird lover. And even though he spent most of his life in prison paying for his crimes, he is most famous as a birdman, not a criminal.

That's a story cool enough to make into a Hollywood movie, but it has a huge spiritual point: Whatever you create a home for in your life will influence you bigtime. If you entertain yourself with music or videos or Web sites that aren't appropriate . . . if you hang on to friends who pull you away from Jesus . . . if you spend your whole life on hobbies and leave nothing for God . . . then that is what will roost in your life.

And like it or not, whatever you start spending time with eventually starts bossing you around. An old proverb states, "You can't keep the birds from flying over your head, but you can keep them from making a nest in your hair." You have complete control over the things you allow to be part of your life.

According to Colossians 3:16, the Word of God is a good choice to let nest in us. When we let God's Word into our life as a permanent resident, it changes us. Then, no matter what we were when we began, at the finish of our life we will be more like Jesus.

 TALK: How are you letting God's Word nest in your heart? How is it changing you?

 PRAY: *God, we want your words to live in us and change our life.*

 ACT: Make a plan to make more time for God's Word in your life—even starting with five minutes a day.

9 Yesterday, Today, and Forever

Bible Reading: 1 Peter 1:21-25

The grass withers, and the flowers fall away. But the word of the Lord will last forever. 1 Peter 1:24-25

As Danielle's dad pulled their family van to a stop in Sequoia National Park, she jumped out and hugged one of the biggest of the giant trees. She was sure that it stretched to the top of the sky.

Danielle's mom did some quick math. "It would take thirty of you to reach around that tree," she said. "And about thirty of you stacked on top of each other to reach the top. My book says that tree is almost four thousand years old. It may be one of the oldest living things on earth."

We've all seen grass turn brown in the heat of summer. The other plants in your backyard might be a few seasons old—or they may have lived for a few decades. Yet there's a good chance they will die before you do, grown ragged with old age or eaten up by bugs or blown over by storms. A forest of giant sequoias seems as endless as anything.

Even the long life of those great trees, however, is nothing compared to the span of time God's Word will be around. God's Word, in fact, is the oldest thing we know. And it will last longer than anything else.

How do we know this? The Bible says, "In the beginning the Word already existed" (John 1:1). God's Word was here before anything. It's true that God's *written* Word has only been around since the Bible first appeared on scrolls several thousand years ago. But God's *living* Word has always been around, because Jesus Christ is "the Word" who has always existed. And not only do God and his Word have no beginning, but they will have no end. Like today's Bible verse says, "The word of the Lord will last forever" (1 Peter 1:25).

It's true that even though you might pass your Bible on to your grandchildren someday, that book will eventually fall apart and turn to dust. However, the message written in those pages—the Good News about Christ—will stick around beyond the end of time. Like God himself, his Word is eternal.

God's Word was changing lives and healing hearts for thousands of years before you were born, and it will be here long after you leave Planet Earth. God has given us his Word, and it will always be the right answer for all the big questions of life.

 TALK: God loves you so much that he made sure you would have his Word today. How does that make you feel?

 PRAY: Tell God now how you want to respond to his eternal Word.

 ACT: Make today's Bible verse endure in your brain. Memorize it!

10 The Jesus Question

Bible Reading: 1 Timothy 2:1-6

There is only one God and one Mediator who can reconcile God and people. He is the man Christ Jesus. 1 Timothy 2:5

Talk about this: Have you ever been in a fight where you wrestled to the ground or popped someone? And the bigger question: What was the fight about?

We fight over silly stuff. We settle differences in stupid ways. But it might surprise you that people throughout history have fought over the question "Who is Jesus Christ?" How can anyone get into a battle over Jesus? Why would mentioning his name make people mad?

Maybe you've noticed that you can mention "God" and nobody minds. But as soon as you say "Jesus," people often want to stop the conversation. They might even say something goofy like, "I don't mind talking about religion, but I don't want to talk about Jesus."

How is Jesus different from other religious leaders? Why don't names like Buddha, Muhammad, or Confucius get people upset?

Well, there's a huge difference between Jesus and all those founders of other faiths. The others didn't claim to be God. Jesus did. That's what makes him utterly different from other religious leaders. It's why people fight over him.

Jesus clearly claimed to be God himself. He presented himself as the only way to a relationship with God the Father, the only source of forgiveness for sins, and the only way of salvation.

For many people, that's too big to believe. Yet the issue isn't what we think but rather who Jesus claimed to be. What does the New Testament tell us?

His name is a great place to start. "Jesus Christ" is actually both a name and a title. The name *Jesus* comes from a word meaning "the Lord saves." The title *Christ* comes from a word for Messiah and means "anointed one." So "Jesus Christ" tells us that Jesus is both Savior and anointed King.

Jesus let people worship him (see Matthew 14:33; 28:9). That's an honor only God should receive. Sometimes Scripture actually commands us to worship Jesus as God (see John 5:23; also Hebrews 1:6; Revelation 5:8-14).

Maybe you have heard the phrase "the deity of Christ." This phrase means that Jesus is divine—he is God. He's the Creator of the universe who came to earth as a person, Jesus of Nazareth. He's the God who created you, and his power keeps you alive. Jesus is your best friend, but he's even more than a good friend. He's God.

 TALK: How would you answer a non-Christian friend who asks, "Who is Jesus?"

 PRAY: You can enjoy Jesus, relate to Jesus, learn from Jesus—but don't forget to worship Jesus. Do that now.

 ACT: Share with a non-Christian friend the true identity of Jesus.

11 Those Who Knew Him Best

Bible Reading: Acts 4:8-12

There is salvation in no one else! There is no other name in all of heaven for people to call on to save them. Acts 4:12

Suppose a roving reporter with a TV news crew hunted down all the people who know you, asking each to describe you. What exactly would you want them to say? You wouldn't be thrilled to hear everyone dig down deep and unearth all your ugliest secrets. You would definitely want them to say supernice things. You might even think about flipping your friends a few bucks to make sure they gush something kind.

You can get huge clues about anyone by checking with that person's friends and acquaintances.

That's especially true of Jesus. See, Jesus didn't have to bribe any of his friends. In fact, they were willing to risk their lives to spread the truth about who he was—God in human form. Listen to these descriptions of Jesus straight from the mouths of just a few of those who knew him best:

When Christ asked Peter to tell him who he was, Peter said this: "You are the Messiah, the Son of the living God" (Matthew 16:16). Jesus said Peter's description was true—and that his knowledge came from God: "You are blessed, Simon son of John, because my Father in heaven has revealed this to you" (verse 17).

Jesus' good friend Martha said to him, "I have always believed you are the Messiah, the Son of God, the one who has come into the world from God" (John 11:27).

Then there was Nathanael, who thought nothing good could come out of Jesus' hometown of Nazareth. He acknowledged that Jesus was "the Son of God—the King of Israel" (John 1:49).

While Stephen was being stoned for believing in Jesus, he recognized Jesus as God when he prayed, "Lord Jesus, receive my spirit" (Acts 7:59).

Then of course there's the declaration of Thomas. After seeing the risen Christ and touching his wounds, Thomas said, "My Lord and my God!" (John 20:28).

Can you see it? Those who knew Jesus best had figured out that he was more than just a man. They accepted him as the Savior, as God come to earth—the Messiah that the Old Testament Scriptures had predicted. They were so sure about this that they worshiped him. They obeyed him. And like Stephen, many of them died for the One who had died for them. We can trust that these witnesses spoke truthfully about Jesus—and, like them, we can trust our life to that truth!

 TALK: There's an old saying that Christ isn't Lord *at* all unless he's Lord *of* all. Today, how can people see that he is Lord of all the areas in your life?

 PRAY: *Jesus, you are what your friends said you are—our Lord and our God.*

 ACT: Explain to a non-Christian friend what Jesus' friends said about who he is.

12 He Is Who He Says He Is

Bible Reading: John 10:22-33
The Father and I are one. John 10:30

Roberto sat at the dinner table with his parents and the new boy in the neighborhood, Eric. As soon as Roberto's dad ended grace with "in Jesus' name we pray, amen," Eric dove in with all sorts of things *he* thought about Jesus.

"My parents said we don't have to pray to Jesus," he started. "There are lots of other religions to follow. Did you know Jesus never said he was God?" Roberto and his family were surprised at how many mixed-up ideas about Christianity Eric and his family had.

Despite what people like Eric say, it isn't tough to spot in the New Testament places where Jesus clearly claimed to be God.

For instance, take the Bible event described in John 5. Some Jewish leaders were upset that Jesus healed a lame man on the Sabbath—the weekly day of rest. Jesus told the man to roll up his sleeping bag and take a celebration hike. Carrying the sleeping bag was considered work, which was not allowed on the Sabbath.

We would think that a healing would cause everyone to live happily ever after. But the leaders wanted to kill Jesus. So what made them blow up? Follow these facts:

John 5:18 sums up what Jesus did: "In addition to disobeying the Sabbath rules, he had spoken of God as his Father, thereby making himself equal with God."

Jesus had said "*my* Father," not "*our* Father," and then added "never stops working, so why should I?" (verse 17). Jesus' use of these two phrases made himself equal with God, on a par with God's activity. The Jews never referred to God as "my Father," only as "our Father." By claiming that God was his Father, Jesus identified himself as one with God. By saying that he was working just as the Father was working, Jesus boldly implied that he was God's Son.

Those sound like tricky word games to us, but to his peers the claims of Jesus were shocking—so shocking that the religious experts wanted to do him in.

Later, Jesus didn't just claim *equality* with God. He said he was *one* with the Father (see John 10:30). The religious leaders again began rock collecting right then and there, getting ready to stone him—all because, as they said, "You, a mere man, have made yourself God" (John 10:33).

People might say that Jesus never claimed to be God. But they don't have their facts right. Jesus didn't hide the fact that he was God. His claim was clear. He was no ordinary man. He was God's Son. And he wants the world to recognize that fact!

 TALK: What did Jesus claim about himself? Are you clear on that?

 PRAY: *Jesus, you are more than a mere human being. You are the Son of God.*

 ACT: Explain to a non-Christian friend how we know Jesus was more than a man.

13 Testing Jesus

Bible Reading: Mark 14:53-65

I am [the Messiah], and you will see me, the Son of Man, sitting at God's right hand in the place of power and coming back on the clouds of heaven. Mark 14:62

Picture yourself with a wallet jammed with money—say, a hundred thousand dollars. The only way you're allowed to spend your cash is by picking out and purchasing the automobile of your dreams.

Here's the big question: How should you decide if a particular vehicle is all that you hope for? Would you

- beg the car dealer to let you sleep overnight in your favorite model on the showroom floor?
- park yourself in a lawn chair on a street corner—and gawk as the car you want drives by?
- memorize all the meaty reviews in *Road & Track* magazine?
- get hold of a test car, fasten your seat belt, and take that baby for a ride?

When you're picking out a car, there's no substitute for putting it to the test. Likewise, when you're trying to figure out if Jesus really claimed to be God, there's no better place to look than the trial he faced before his crucifixion. It was a test that shows beyond a shadow of a doubt that Jesus was more than a mere human being.

The high priest running the trial put the big question to Jesus point-blank: "Are you the Messiah, the Son of the blessed God?" (Mark 14:61). Jesus replied with to-day's verse, "I am, and you will see me, the Son of Man, sitting at God's right hand in the place of power and coming back on the clouds of heaven."

The Jewish officials didn't miss Jesus' meaning. The high priest tore his clothing—a public demonstration of his horror at Jesus' claim to be God. And Christ's judges saw the issue clearly—so clearly, in fact, that they crucified him and then taunted, "He trusted God—let God show his approval by delivering him! For he said, 'I am the Son of God'" (Matthew 27:43).

The trial of Jesus should be enough to convince any of us that Jesus didn't just see himself as any old religious teacher. He claimed to be God.

His enemies denied the truth about who he is. So who do you say Jesus is?

 TALK: Are you convinced that Jesus is God? What persuades you? What do you need to learn more about?

 PRAY: *Christ, we understand your claim to be the Son of God. We believe you. You are God come in the flesh. We welcome you as Lord.*

 ACT: Can you explain this sort of complicated stuff in your own words? Practice quizzing each other with this question: How do we know Jesus is God? Looking for some verses to read? Peek at 1 Peter 1:18-19.

14 Plant Yourself Where You Flourish

Bible Reading: 1 Thessalonians 3:9-13

May the Lord make your love grow and overflow to each other and to everyone else. 1 Thessalonians 3:12

Just as Brian bursts out the door from school, his volleyball coach swoops down and not-so-gently breaks the news that he wasn't voted team captain.

Brian feels rotten—bad enough that he considers skipping his Bible-club meeting and numbing his pain with a gallon of ice cream. But somehow he knows that rolling bellyfirst into a lump of self-pity won't solve anything.

When he mumbles to his friends at Bible club what a loser he is, they not only make him stop trashing himself but remind him how talented and helpful he is both at school and in the group. He leaves the group knowing he's liked, appreciated, and needed. He goes away with a better picture of who he is.

Sound silly? Not really. Admit it: Having friends who pick you up when you're down is better than getting beat up by insults and sarcasm.

The Bible says that God sees us as lovable, valuable, and capable—and we have every right to see ourselves that way. Along with getting those facts straight from God's Word, getting around the right people is an unbeatable way to drive those facts home.

Get away from people who treat you like a dirtball—and find some people who believe in you big-time, like God does. Here are some ways to make that happen:

Find friends who accept you for who you are. You aren't shopping for people with the fastest mouths or the coolest clothes, but people who let you be yourself because they are comfortable with themselves.

Find adult friends and leaders who let you dream and try big new things—like volunteering, doing ministry, stretching your brain, or mastering physical challenges. It's easy to spot grown-ups who want to help you discover the strengths God has built into you.

Be consistent in attending a Sunday school class or midweek church group where the atmosphere isn't charged with sarcasm and verbal slams.

Join a small group of Christians where you can be up front about your struggles. Let them love and care for you.

Got the picture? Wherever we find it, an environment that can help us get rid of a self-image not worth wallowing in is the best spot we can be!

 TALK: How can you get tight with a group of Christian friends who express love to one another, value one another, and serve one another in practical ways?

 PRAY: *God, lead us to friendships where we can feel welcomed and built up as people who are lovable, valuable, and capable.*

 ACT: Check your calendar. When are you making time to get built up by your Christian friends this week?

15 Take Two Steps

Bible Reading: Acts 2:42-47

They joined with the other believers and devoted themselves to the apostles' teaching and fellowship, sharing in the Lord's Supper and in prayer. Acts 2:42

No matter how Armani compared himself to others, he fell short. He wasn't as strong as William. He wasn't as smart as Emmy. He didn't live in as nice a house as Megan. He had nowhere near as many friends as Gabriel. Even though Armani thought long and hard, he couldn't think of a single kind thing to say about himself.

One day Armani drew a self-portrait. He pictured himself with scraggly hair and crooked teeth. Big blemishes covered his face from chin to forehead, and a huge hairy mole topped off his nose. And in his picture, Armani was totally alone. At the bottom, he labeled his drawing "The Total Loser."

That was three years ago. Since then Armani has found Christian friends who are into studying the Bible. They're also nuts about just being friends. Armani's new friends have helped him recognize what he is really like. Armani has discovered that God sees him as a wonderful, gifted person inside and out.

God has a simple two-step program for you to get his true view of you:

Step 1: Get into God's Word. You study all day long at school. So the last thing you might want in your life is more study time. Yet if you want to uncover what God thinks of you, your first step is to get into God's Word. The Bible is God's book of absolutely true facts about you.

Step 2: Get godly friends. God's family is where we can learn to treat each other as lovable, valuable, and capable. Getting together with other believers is how we experience the truths of God's Word day by day.

See, God wants to use his Word and other Christians to make us doubly sure we are loved, valued, and useful. There's no better way to discover how God sees us than to dig into his Word. And there's no better way to pound that truth home than to have caring believers remind us how God sees us. It's one thing to learn the truth about God and ourselves in the Bible or a sermon or a Sunday school lesson. The truth is even more real when we experience it through believing friends.

God wants you to grow more and more sure that you are lovable, valuable, and capable. But it's your job to put yourself in the right spot. He's given you his Word to teach you and his people to reinforce that message. When you get those two things, you'll get his view of you!

 TALK: Are you in a Sunday school class, youth group, or Bible club where you get the wise teaching and godly friends you need to grow in God's view of you?

 PRAY: *God, help us do what we need to so we can grow in our understanding of who you say we are.*

 ACT: Do you need to latch on to godly teaching—or godly friends? Go for it!

16 Seeing Yourself with $^{20}/_{20}$ Vision

Bible Reading: Ephesians 4:11-17
Instead, we will hold to the truth in love, becoming more and more in every way like Christ. Ephesians 4:15

Deena spends her whole life figuring out what other people think of her. Before she goes to school each morning she calls to check her outfit with a few friends—so she can fit in without looking like a copycat. Before Deena says a word about anything, she listens to what everyone else in the room is saying—and then parrots their opinions. And when she wonders about her worth, she judges herself through the critical eyes of everyone in her life.

Deena knows in her head that *God* has the only opinion of her that really matters. Why? Because what God thinks is more than opinion. It's fact.

Test your memory from last time: What two things does Deena need to do to grow in what God thinks about her?

If you remember God's two-step plan, you know what Deena needs to do. But she's not budging. Even though she wants God's vision of herself, she doesn't want to work at it. She doesn't make time with her Bible to soak in God's truth. Even though she goes to church, she's nervous about letting people get too close. She sounds like someone with bad eyes who wants to see more clearly but won't wear glasses.

The fact is, you can't change how you see yourself without diving into God's Word. This is what helps you focus on the truth that you are:

Lovable. God loves you just as you are and wants you for his child.

Valuable. God would have sent Jesus to die for you even if you were the only person on earth.

Useful. God trusts you to reach out and help others see who he is.

God's Word is the number-one agent in renewing your mind to think like he thinks and see as he sees (see Romans 12:2). But if that's what you're supposed to learn from the Bible, how do you dig out that truth?

Grabbing hold of the facts God wants you to know beyond any doubt starts with opening his book. And it happens when you study the Bible with your self-portrait in mind. Whenever you sit down to read, ask God to help you see yourself as he does. As you study, quiz yourself about what the passage says about you. Chances are you will discover verses and phrases that seem just right for your situation. God will use his Word to help you be sure you are loved, valued, and useful!

 TALK: How are you letting God's encouraging Word into your life so you can get hold of God's view of you?

 PRAY: *God, open our eyes to what you say about us in your Word.*

 ACT: Take some time alone with God to hear what he has to say about you.

17 Pinpointing Your Need

Bible Reading: Deuteronomy 4:16-20

Remember that the Lord rescued you . . . to become his own people and special possession; that is what you are today. Deuteronomy 4:20

No sooner had Samantha jumped into the beautician's chair than she started to rattle off all the wonders she wanted worked upon her appearance—eyebrows raised, ears shrunk, teeth whitened, slouch straightened. When Samantha inhaled before naming more imperfections she wanted fixed, her beautician jumped in to set the record straight. "Look, girl," she said, "there's three things you gotta know. Betty only works from the neck up. Betty only does hair and makeup. And Betty is a beautician—not a magician."

You don't have to pluck your eyebrows or lop off the point at the top of your ears to accomplish the most important change you could ever make to yourself—because the biggest change you could ever do to *you* is to realize your true identity as God's wildly loved, highly valued child.

God isn't a beautician—he's more concerned with our inside thoughts, beliefs, and attitudes than our outside looks. He isn't a magician—he doesn't snap his fingers and make everything instantly better. His wiser way is to change us little by little.

And here's a big hint at where he wants to work in you. Talk about this: Of the following three statements, which is toughest for you to accept?

(a) I am *lovable*. God loves me just as I am and wants me for his child.

(b) I am *valuable*. God would have sent Jesus to die for me even if I were the only person on earth.

(c) I am *useful*. God trusts me to reach out and help others see who he is.

Maybe you can say each of those truths with a smile brought on by the knowledge that God loves you so intensely. But if you're like most Christians, you maybe choke a bit when you try to say one or more of those statements.

Your feelings about those facts probably hint at the area where God wants to rearrange your thinking first—to work a major change that helps you see yourself as his truly beloved son or daughter.

Whatever your need, God wants to meet it. He wants you to know the truth about you: You *are* lovable . . . You *are* valuable . . . You *are* useful. God says so!

 TALK: Why do you think we sometimes have a tough time believing the good things God says about us? How are you letting God remake how you see yourself?

 PRAY: Talk to God about the area where you would most like to grow in understanding his view of you. Tell him if you need to feel lovable, valuable, or useful.

 ACT: Ask a family member to remind you of your toughest-to-believe truth once a day for the next week.

18 Sharing Your Story

Bible Reading: 1 Peter 2:9-12

You are a chosen people . . . that you may declare the praises of him who called you out of darkness into his wonderful light.
1 Peter 2:9, NIV

Brain sparks flew as everyone in Mrs. Thompson's Sunday school class responded to her challenge to think of ways to share their faith.

"I think we should paint 'Jesus loves you' on a billboard!"

"I want to get a loudspeaker on a corner and scream at people!"

"I'm going to go to my Little League game and hold up a John 3:16 banner!"

Mrs. Thompson listened. "Those ideas are all very creative," she said. "But how can you share your faith with the people you already know?"

Talk about it: What's the absolutely best way you can share your faith with a non-Christian friend? Got any great ideas?

All around us are people who don't know Jesus. We don't have to turn into fire-breathing preachers to make sure our friends have a firm understanding of God's truth. We just need two crucial things to help them come to know Jesus.

We need to know what to say. We can share our faith by using a simple step-by-step approach. One easy-to-understand way to present the good news about Jesus is using the booklet "Would You Like to Know God Personally?"

We need to know why we're sharing. This is the second important ingredient to presenting the faith well. We can share our faith by telling our own story.

Do you know how to explain to others how you became a Christian? You can

- *tell why you trusted Christ.* Maybe you're only nine, but why did you decide to trust Jesus? What would your life be like without him?
- *tell how you trusted Christ.* What did you pray? Who helped you know what to say?
- *tell what your life has been like since trusting Christ.* What does Christ mean to you now? How has he changed you? How has he helped you?

Our friends need to know the straightforward facts of faith so they can understand that being a Christian starts by trusting Jesus. And our friends also need to hear how faith has changed us. That's how they will understand why faith matters in day-to-day life—and for eternity!

 TALK: As a family, talk through the why, how, and what of salvation. You might even want to jot down some notes.

 PRAY: *Jesus, give us wisdom as we think about how to share the gospel with our friends.*

 ACT: Can you tell your salvation story in no more than eight sentences? Grab a sheet of paper and write a first draft.

19 Tell It Like It Is

Bible Reading: 1 Peter 3:13-17
If you are asked about your Christian hope, always be ready to explain it. 1 Peter 3:15

Telling God that you want to share your faith might excite you. Or it might make you scared to death. Perhaps you're afraid your friends will reject you. Or that you don't know enough. Or that you'll mess up an incredibly important message.

Not to worry. Let's think about some things you should say—or not. Vote "yea" or "nay" on whether you should slip these statements in when you share your faith:

(a) The reason you don't believe in Jesus is because you're really stupid.

(b) Being a Christian means you have to walk, talk, act, dress, and doodle Christian slogans all over your school notebooks just like me.

(c) My church is the only church any real Christian would go to.

(d) I could tell you about Jesus, but the thought of spending eternity with you in heaven makes me gag.

(e) Trusting Jesus will instantly take care of every problem in your life—including your bad breath.

Well, that covers a few things *not* to say.

Actually, sometimes when we get nervous, messed-up words slip from our lips. But we don't need to be nervous. Without being pushy or proud, we can be confident in talking about Jesus with people who don't know him. Here are some helpful tips.

1. *Get ready.* You don't need to memorize the Bible for God to use you to share your faith. Yet you can keep learning. And each time you share your faith, you'll know more for the next time.

2. *Don't feel threatened.* You are representing Christ, so he won't leave you dangling. When you discuss the gospel with your friends, God's power is at work in you.

3. *Don't argue.* Just share the gospel with your friend, quietly asking the Holy Spirit to guide you. Then let your caring attitude be what helps to convince your friend that your message is true.

4. *Don't be afraid of questions.* Your friend might have a million questions. If you can't answer a question, tell your friend you will find out more and give an answer at another time.

TALK: How can you prepare so you will be ready to share Christ when he gives you the opportunity? How can you work as a family to reach out together?

PRAY: Ask God for opportunities to share Christ with your friends.

ACT: Which one of those tips do you most need to put into practice? Talk to God and a wise Christian about it.

20 Do the Math

Bible Reading: 2 Timothy 2:1-7

Teach these great truths to trustworthy people who are able to pass them on to others. 2 Timothy 2:2

The task of telling the world about Jesus sounds, um, sort of big, doesn't it? It's enormous enough to make many Christians think, *I'd love to help tell the world about Jesus. It would be really great to make disciples of all the nations. But how much can I really do? After all, I'm only one person.*

Well, you *are* only one person. That much is true.

But the following tidbit might help you see the enormous difference one person can make. Consider this job offer. You'll get paid once a week. The first week's pay is only a penny, but your employer will double your salary every week as long as you continue working. It doesn't sound very profitable, does it? But you'd be a fool to pass it up. In just over six months, you'll be a millionaire. After only a year, your salary will have reached $22.5 *trillion!*

How can this be? The process starts with one tiny penny, but that single cent results in a fortune. It works because of the principle of *multiplication.*

That principle works just as well in the kingdom of God. God, of course, isn't handing out job contracts that will make us zillionaires. But he has an even better offer. God gives us the opportunity to partner with him in reaching the world with his Good News. And he's planning on using the strategy of *spiritual multiplication.*

Here's how it works: Suppose you and four friends—five of you—each share your faith with three people. Then God works in the hearts of those fifteen people so that they accept him. During the next year, you train the fifteen to share their faith with others. In the second year, the five of you and your fifteen trusted friends each lead three others to Christ.

Here's where the math goes ballistic. Suppose you and the people you train keep up that practice year after year. In ten years, more than half a million will have been brought to Christ. And in fifteen years you could reach the whole world!

That's what Paul meant when he told Timothy to teach the truths of the gospel to "trustworthy people." He aims for us to share Jesus with people—and then help them grow to the point that they too can share Jesus with others. Just like a single penny can result in millions of dollars, God's spiritual multiplication can create a worldwide awakening to the truth of Jesus Christ. So why not let it start with you?

 TALK: Think of someone who needs to know about Jesus. Is sharing what you know about him something you can do?

 PRAY: *Lord, help us to show your love to someone today.*

 ACT: Look for opportunities to talk with your friends about the differences Jesus has made in your life and how they can know Jesus too.

21 Helping Babies Grow Up

Bible Reading: 1 Thessalonians 2:8-12

We loved you so much that we gave you not only God's Good News but our own lives, too. 1 Thessalonians 2:8

Sheri had a newborn. It wasn't a human baby, but a raw egg she had to tote around for two weeks in a plastic butter tub lined with cotton balls. It was a school assignment designed to give her a taste of the responsibilities of parenthood.

Everywhere that Sheri went, her egg was sure to go.

Except the day she forgot it on the corner of the lunch table.

It took Sheri only moments to realize her egg was missing. When she raced back to her table, she found her raw egg scrambled on the floor.

It's an enormous burden to care for an egg as if it's a human baby. But you might have an even bigger responsibility: Do you know anyone who has just trusted Jesus? If you do, you can be sure that God wants to involve you in some part of the care of that baby Christian.

You don't need to bundle up all the baby Christians you know and lug them around with you. But new believers freshly born into God's family do need spiritual care and protection just like newborns need physical and emotional care.

So what can you do to care for the spiritual babies in your life?

First, *supply nourishment.* New Christians need to feed on God's Word to mature (see 1 Peter 2:2). Remind them what happened when they trusted Christ:

- When you trusted Christ, you became a child of God (John 1:12).
- Your sins were forgiven (1 John 1:9).
- Jesus Christ came into your life (Revelation 3:20).
- He will never leave you (Hebrews 13:5-8).
- Your old life is gone (2 Corinthians 5:17).
- You have received eternal life (John 5:24).

Second, *do some bonding.* Without hugs and cuddling, newborns don't develop. Just like babies need to bond to their parents, new Christians need to be surrounded by the love of other believers. Introduce them to Christian friends. Invite them to church. Welcome them into your Bible study or Sunday school class.

Does this all make sense now? God trusts you to nurture new Christians. Take up the responsibility—and don't leave them alone at the lunch table!

 TALK: How do you feel about the awesome fact that God trusts you to be a spiritual parent to new believers?

 PRAY: Ask God to equip you to meet the needs of new believers.

 ACT: Plan ways to help a new Christian in your life. If you don't know any, pray that you can do your part to help someone in your life trust Jesus.

22 Helping New Christians Get a Good Start

Bible Reading: 1 Peter 5:2-9
Care for the flock of God entrusted to you. 1 Peter 5:2

"The aposo-what?" a kid in the front row stammers.

"That's 'apostle,' stupid," Austin corrects from the back of the Sunday school class. "As in 'the apostle Paul.' An apostle is an official representative sent by God to preach the gospel and to teach churches, often in more than one location."

The kid in the front row and several other Sunday school newcomers swivel around to look at Austin, who settles back in his chair and shakes his head at how dumb the rest of the class is. They are spiritually clueless, he figures, and after years and years as a Sunday school regular, he's too cool for Sunday school.

More and more kids who come to Christ have little understanding of what the Bible is about. Learning the nitty-gritty of the faith from a kind, patient teacher—not someone like Austin—is one of their greatest needs. Believe it or not, God has a part for each of us to play in helping the new Christians in our life.

Maybe you want to be a *teacher*. You can pair up with an adult to start a small group for new Christians that meets once a week to learn and grow. Maybe you want to be an *inviter* who spreads the word and gets students to the study. Or maybe you see yourself as a day-to-day *partner* who aims just to be there for the new Christians in your world.

Whatever approach you take, here are four things you can do to help your friends who are new Christians grow—and grow yourself in the process:

Open up to each other. Talk about what's going on in your lives. Share what you see God doing and how you are growing.

Study the Bible together. Read verses that will help your friends get a handle on their faith. Show them how to read the Bible on their own, along with a devotional book like this one. Or share the things that God makes jump out of the Bible at you.

Answer questions together. Your friends might have loads of questions. Let them ask! If you don't know an answer, find out.

Pray together. This gives a chance to show firsthand *how to pray* and *what to pray about*. Make prayer a simple conversation with God about your thoughts, feelings, and needs.

More than anything, you need to be a Christian friend. Some new Christians have lost their old friends. So be there for them!

 TALK: How can you help kids who are new to the faith?

 PRAY: *God, thanks for giving us the Holy Spirit, who shows us how to help people who have just met you.*

 ACT: As a family, look for easy-to-read Bibles and fun devotional books that can help people who have just met him.

23 The Christian's No-Brainer

Bible Reading: Matthew 25:34-40

When you did it to one of the least of these my brothers and sisters, you were doing it to me! Matthew 25:40

I once spent a summer teaching at Arrowhead Springs, the former headquarters of Campus Crusade for Christ down in the foothills of the San Bernardino Mountains in southern California. During that summer, my family and I lived in Blue Jay, a little town up in the mountains beside beautiful Lake Arrowhead. So every day I drove down the mountain twice—once in the morning and again after lunch.

It's hot in the San Bernardino Valley during the summer, with temperatures often breaking the 100-degree mark. During my trips up and down the mountain, I often saw cars pulled over to the side of the steep, winding road to the summit—hoods open, steam belching from their radiators. It was soon obvious to me that my teaching for God was pretty hollow if I didn't do something to help the poor stranded motorists. All my talk about loving God was meaningless if I didn't show love for these people in need.

So I came up with a plan. I kept four large water jugs in my trunk. Whenever I came across an overheated car on my daily drive on the mountain, I pulled over and offered to fill the radiator with water. People were overjoyed at the offer and grateful for the help. Once the radiator was full, I offered a copy of my book *More Than a Carpenter* and talked to the motorists about Christ. It was one of the best summers of ministry I have ever experienced.

Love isn't an option for Christians. It's a command. God is love, and people born of God must express his love. Jesus said, "Your love for one another will prove to the world that you are my disciples" (John 13:35).

Love always goes two directions at once. When you love people in Christ's name, you're also loving God. Jesus taught that when you help anyone who needs love and care, you help him (see Matthew 25:34-40). And when you truly love God, you can't help but love people too. As John wrote, "If someone says, 'I love God,' but hates a Christian brother or sister, that person is a liar; for if we don't love people we can see, how can we love God, whom we have not seen? And God himself has commanded that we must love not only him but our Christian brothers and sisters, too" (1 John 4:20-21).

You can't get around it, you can't avoid it, you can't push it aside: Love is part of your life as a Christian!

 TALK: What obvious, practical thing can you do to share God's love with people? What loving thing is within your reach to do right now?

 PRAY: *God, open our eyes to the obvious opportunities right around us to show love.*

 ACT: Make a list of the three places you spend the most time each week: What one thing can you do in each place to show God's love?

24 Love in Two Directions

Bible Reading: Exodus 20:1-17

I am the Lord your God. . . . Do not worship any other gods besides me.
Exodus 20:2-3

Mrs. Taylor wears a permanent frown. That's a problem, because she is a Christian. So everyone who meets her thinks that knowing Jesus must make you a crab.

Talk about it: Have you ever met believers who are unkind? How does that make you feel about being a Christian?

You've maybe bumped into Christians who seem to have forgotten that God puts love in the center of what it means to follow him. It's not enough to claim we love God. Our task is to love in two directions: God *and* other people.

Jesus taught, "'You must love the Lord your God with all your heart, all your soul, and all your mind.' This is the first and greatest commandment. A second is equally important: 'Love your neighbor as yourself'" (Matthew 22:37-39). Everything we're supposed to do is summed up in these two commands. We love God with our whole self—that's "vertical love." And we love others as we love ourselves—that's "horizontal love."

The Ten Commandments in Exodus 20 are organized into the two directions of love. The first four commandments show what vertical love for God looks like:

1. You shall have no other gods before me.
2. You shall not worship idols.
3. You shall not misuse the name of the Lord your God.
4. Remember the Sabbath day by keeping it holy.

Then the next six commandments paint a picture of horizontal love for others:

5. Honor your father and your mother.
6. You shall not murder.
7. You shall not commit adultery.
8. You shall not steal.
9. You shall not give false testimony.
10. You shall not covet.

Loving God means we worship him and recognize his total greatness in everything we think, say, and do. And to love people means we treat them in a way that fits their incredible worth to God. That's nothing to be crabby about!

 TALK: God calls you to love in two directions—to love him and love others. How are you doing at each?

 PRAY: *God, increase in us our love both for you and for people.*

 ACT: Are you ever a crabby Christian? What do you want to do to change?

25 Whom Should I Love More?

Bible Reading: Luke 14:25-30

If you want to be my follower you must love me more than your own father and mother, wife and children, brothers and sisters—yes, more than your own life. Luke 14:26

When Norm was just sixteen years old and announced he had become a Christian, his mom and dad blew up. Not a little blowup, mind you. Norm's mother actually threatened to boot him out of the house unless he gave up his faith.

Norm was nose-to-nose with a crisis. Should he obey his parents and turn his back on God? Or should he put God first and disobey his parents? With God's help, Norm chose God, and his mother didn't carry out her threat. For years Norm faced ridicule and criticism from his parents. During those years he kept praying for them. And in time he saw both of them trust Christ as their Savior.

God commands you to love God and people. But there are times when you need to love God *more* than people.

Talk about it: What do you think it means to "love God more than people"? Can you think of any examples?

Jesus said, "If anyone comes to me and does not hate his father and mother, his wife and children, his brothers and sisters—yes, even his own life—he cannot be my disciple" (Luke 14:26, NIV). Jesus isn't saying you should dislike or disrespect your family members. He's using hyperbole—hyped-up language—to teach two things.

First, he wants you to know that your love for God is to be greater than your love for any person—even those closest to you. It's to be so great that in comparison, your love for humans doesn't even seem to exist.

Second, he wants you to know that sometimes you need to obey God rather than people.

Suppose your parents say "no way" to you signing up for your school's bungee-jumping club. Their order doesn't violate any of God's commands—so you need to obey. But what if your parents tell you to fib about your age to get a discount at the movies? Or a coach tells you to cheat? When people push you to do wrong, says Jesus, your job is to obey him instead of the people.

That's what it looks like to love God more than people. God wants you to have an enormous love for every person in your life. But he wants you to have a love for him that's even bigger!

 TALK: Say it in your own words: What does it mean to love God even more than you love people?

 PRAY: *God, give us the courage to obey you first, last, and always.*

 ACT: Are you letting your peers push you into obeying them—at the price of obeying God? What might God like you to change today?

26 When Authorities Clash

Bible Reading: Titus 3:1-2

Remind your people to submit to the government and its officers.
Titus 3:1

Check out these statements. Which slip out of your mouth easily?

"I'm so glad the police caught me throwing snowballs at cars!"

"I'm totally happy my parents figured out I've been shoveling all my stuff under my bed instead of actually cleaning my room."

"I'm truly grateful that I got caught swiping answers off the math whiz who sits next to me."

"I sure am glad my mom makes me eat brussels sprouts."

"I wish the principal would call me down to the office and give me detention more often."

Most of us squirm when someone in charge of our life lays down a rule we're forced to follow–or catches us doing what we shouldn't. But most days we probably also admit that authorities–people like police, principals, parents, and teachers–usually act for our good.

Take this example: When you were a tiny tyke, your parents knew it would be nuts to give you everything you wanted. You begged for cake and ice cream at every meal. You dug in the medicine cabinet. You refused to buckle up in the car. And maybe you insisted on playing with steak knives. Your parents didn't love you any less by saying no to all those requests and requiring that you bend to their wishes. Whether you understood it or not, they had your best interests at heart.

The Bible challenges you as a Christian to show love for leaders by submitting to their authority, whether that leader is the head of your home or the head of your country. Peter wrote, "For the Lord's sake, accept all authority–the king as head of state, and the officials he has appointed" (1 Peter 2:13).

God's command to obey authorities is not meant to make you miserable. Paul wrote, "'Honor your father and mother.' This is the first of the Ten Commandments that ends with a promise. And this is the promise: If you honor your father and mother, 'you will live a long life, full of blessing'" (Ephesians 6:2-3).

Doing us good is a promise God seems to fulfill not just when we obey parents, but whenever we submit to the authorities he puts in our life. Count on it!

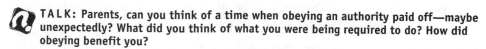 **TALK:** Parents, can you think of a time when obeying an authority paid off—maybe unexpectedly? What did you think of what you were being required to do? How did obeying benefit you?

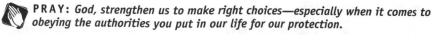 **PRAY:** *God, strengthen us to make right choices—especially when it comes to obeying the authorities you put in our life for our protection.*

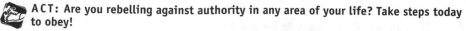 **ACT:** Are you rebelling against authority in any area of your life? Take steps today to obey!

27 Levels of Love

Bible Reading: Acts 5:26–29

We must obey God rather than human authority. Acts 5:29

Bekka and her mom are Christians, but her dad isn't. He's addicted to alcohol—and that made the summer after Bekka's sixth-grade year especially rough. As her dad saw several people at work lose their jobs, he panicked. Instead of working harder, he hid. When he drank too much in the evenings, he couldn't wake up the next morning for work. And his boss started to call the house asking for him.

While Bekka's mom was off at her own job, Bekka's dad told her to answer the phone and tell his boss he was on his way to work—even if he was still sound asleep.

Bekka knew it wasn't right to lie. She was smart enough to know it wasn't a kid's job to deal with a dad's boss. So what was she supposed to do?

That situation makes us ask a big question: Are we supposed to obey authorities no matter what?

If Bekka refused to obey her dad, it might look like she was shattering the fifth commandment, the one that says "Honor your father and mother" (Exodus 20:12).

She wasn't.

We're fortunate that we don't often have to choose between obeying a human authority and obeying God. But sometimes that's exactly the choice even Christian kids face—probably not with parents, but possibly with teachers, coaches, or even the government.

Bekka chose to be smart. She didn't think that "honor your father and mother" wasn't meant for her. She didn't say, "Forget it! My dad wants me to be a liar. He's a cheat. I don't ever have to listen to him again. In fact, I'm not obeying my parents anymore!" Because of the bad spot her dad placed her in, she had to choose to disobey in this one instance. But she worked hard to obey her parents in every other way.

Love doesn't mean you cave in to others' sinful wishes. It isn't going along with their ungodly plans. Love means you act for their best, and sometimes the biggest good you can do is to stand against their sin.

Your job as a Christian is to build a habit of respectfully obeying the authorities in your life. Yet you might face situations where your duty to obey human authorities clashes with your bigger duty to follow God—like the apostles who found they had to disobey Jewish authorities and declare, "We must obey God rather than human authority" (Acts 5:29). And be sure of this: Whenever you have to choose between love for God and love for people, love for God always wins!

 TALK: How can you respond when someone you're supposed to obey expects you to do something you shouldn't?

 PRAY: *Lord, help us love the people in our life completely—and love you supremely.*

 ACT: How would you help a friend like Bekka who's in a tough spot?

The Oil of Relationships

Bible Reading: Luke 7:36-50
A person who is forgiven little shows only little love. Luke 7:47

"Allison *said* she was sorry for blabbing my secret," Brooke fumed. "But it wasn't like she was actually sorry. She laughed and made a face like she thought I was stupid for being angry. And then she told some more people that afternoon."

Talk about it: What should Brooke do about her blabbermouthing buddy?

Brooke told Allison she was upset she had spread her secret, so she's talked first-hand to the person who wronged her—that's a great start. From now on Brooke would be smart to watch what she shares with Allison. And it might even be good for Brooke to take a break from their friendship.

But there's one more thing Brooke can do: She can *forgive.*

Why would she bother to forgive? I'll give you two good reasons.

Big Reason Number One: *Unforgiveness kills.*

It's simple: Anytime we store up grudges toward a person, that friendship dies. When people don't take time to confront and mend hurts, they rip apart relationships. They break up the closeness God wants for Christians to enjoy. They split families, friends, youth groups, and churches. And unforgiveness makes it tough to feel close to God.

Big Reason Number Two: *Forgiveness frees.*

Learning to forgive the people who wrong you is the only way your relationships will grow strong. Brooke found that Allison truly wasn't interested in treating her in a way that would build a strong friendship. But Brooke has found other friends with whom she can talk about mess-ups and move on. She and her friends have discovered that if they can love each other despite their faults—and even accept each other when they hurt one another—they can't help but become even better friends.

Forgiveness works like oil in relationships. It reduces friction and it allows people to get close to each other without overheating.

Without forgiveness, in fact, relationships freeze up like an engine a few quarts short on oil. If you don't sense a forgiving heart in someone, you won't ever be truly open to him or her. You know that an unforgiving person won't give you half a chance to develop a deep, lasting, and close relationship. And if *you* aren't a forgiving person—no matter how smart, talented, or downright good-looking you might be—you won't develop the close relationships you want.

Can you see it? Unforgiveness kills. But forgiveness frees.

 TALK: How skilled are you at forgiving—and receiving forgiveness?

 PRAY: *God, help us learn this crucial habit of forgiveness. We want our friendships and our relationships with one another to be strong and healthy.*

 ACT: Do you sense that you have a relationship in which you need to work on forgiveness? What's your plan?

Bible Reading: Psalm 103:8-14

[The Lord] has not punished us for all our sins, nor does he deal with us as we deserve. Psalm 103:10

When Molly arrived at school on Monday morning, Mrs. Spencer asked everyone to take a seat in the hall. After the bell rang, she said, "Someone broke into our school over the weekend. We're afraid that some of your things might be missing."

As soon as Mrs. Spencer unlocked the classroom door, Molly ran to her desk and flipped open the lid. Her school stuff was all a-jumble—but everything was there. Then she remembered she had used her camera last week for yearbook club. She had hidden it in her desk over the weekend. And now it was gone.

The camera was easily Molly's most treasured possession. She wasn't just sad. She was as mad as a honeybee come home to an empty hive.

If you've ever faced a loss like Molly's, you know that forgiving someone who hurts you is hard. And it's even harder if you aren't sure exactly what forgiveness is.

Check out these definitions. Forgiveness means

- to erase, to give up what is due
- to quit being resentful
- to wipe the slate clean, to release from a debt, to cancel punishment
- to give up all claims on the one who has hurt you and let go of the emotional consequences of that hurt

Forgiveness means more than mumbling "I forgive you." It involves letting go of your hurts. It includes putting aside all bitterness, giving up the right to get even—no matter how good it would feel to settle the score.

Besides that, forgiveness is an action. It doesn't let you wait for the person who hurt you to say, "I was wrong, will you forgive me?" Forgiving means you take the first step, just as Jesus reached out to you by dying for you while you were still a sinner (see Romans 5:8).

God wants you to forgive in the same way he forgives you. He doesn't forgive you because you deserve it, but as a free gift. Likewise, you don't forgive because the person who hurt you has earned it—by changing for the better, for example, or by begging for your forgiveness. You forgive simply because you want to show the same mercy Jesus showed you!

TALK: Say it in your own words: What is forgiveness? And another question: How easily do you forgive?

PRAY: *Christ, when people wrong us, help us to have your forgiving heart.*

ACT: Does forgiveness make sense to you? If not, pull out a Bible concordance, look up what the Bible says about forgiveness, and fill your mind with God's way of thinking.

30 Sundown Is Coming

Bible Reading: Matthew 6:9-15

If you forgive those who sin against you, your heavenly Father will forgive you. Matthew 6:14

Quiz time. Here's a list of people who have wronged you. Vote for the folks you are willing to forgive:

(a) The older brother who practices his batting swing in the middle of the backyard—and hits a grand slam into your forehead

(b) The friend who breaks the ceramic mug that won you first prize in your school's art fair

(c) The little sister who annoys you with her unending knock-knock jokes

(d) The kid at school who teased you on the playground two years, five months, and three days ago

Here's some big news: Forgiveness isn't just for people you feel like forgiving. God says to forgive *everyone who hurts you.* Say that again?

Yes, God calls you to forgive anyone who has angered, hurt, or offended you.

Knowing God's command to forgive, of course, doesn't make forgiveness any easier, especially when you feel like you've been walloped with a baseball bat.

As tough as forgiving can be, God doesn't intend it to take forever. In fact, he wants us to give or receive forgiveness *immediately.* In Ephesians 4:26 Paul wrote, "Don't let the sun go down while you are still angry." And Jesus said that when we realize someone has a grudge against us, we should go solve the problem right away—even if that realization dawns on us in the middle of worshiping him (see Matthew 5:23-25).

One caution: We can run to God for forgiveness as soon as we realize we've done wrong. We can decide in our heart to forgive the minute after someone wounds us. But when it comes to dealing with real people over really hot issues it's sometimes wise to let a situation simmer down for a few days before you go forgive or ask forgiveness. You'll both be more ready to reason.

Forgiveness cuts both ways. You might be able to think of a pile of people who have wronged you. But you wrong others too. Tape this phrase someplace you'll see it daily: "When I refuse to forgive, I am burning a bridge that someday I will need to cross." Be happy to forgive, because more often than you can imagine you are going to need forgiveness from someone else!

 TALK: Why is it good to forgive right away? What makes it hard?

 PRAY: Talk to God about people you need to forgive—or people you need to ask for forgiveness.

 ACT: Is there someone you need to forgive today? Do you need to ask someone to forgive you? Take care of it before sundown.

31 Phony Forgiveness

Bible Reading: Matthew 5:23-26

If you are . . . offering a sacrifice to God, and you suddenly remember that someone has something against you, . . . go and be reconciled to that person. Matthew 5:23-24

The fact that Greg and Brian were best friends since kindergarten didn't mean they never clashed. It had been three days since the boys had squabbled over cheating in a backyard baseball game, and their anger came out in a fierce fight. As the boys socked and shoved, Greg grabbed Brian's arm and twisted it behind his back. A moment later when the boys tumbled to the ground, they heard a snap. Brian screamed. His arm was broken.

Even the best of friends can have a lot to learn about forgiveness.

So far you've been hearing what forgiveness *is*. Real forgiveness imitates what God did for us. He took the first step, forgiving us freely and completely even while we were still sinners. But if you want to understand what forgiveness *is*, you also need to know what forgiveness *isn't*. So check out what a busted arm taught two boys:

Forgiveness isn't earned. Forgiveness doesn't wait for the other person to come and apologize. If either Greg or Brian had taken the first step and forgiven the other back when they were angry about their ball game, their fight probably wouldn't have happened.

Forgiveness isn't pretending a hurt never happened. The cast on Brian's arm and the pain he felt made it tough to forget how Greg had hurt him. The boys had a problem, and ignoring it wouldn't make it go away.

Forgiveness isn't a feeling. Stuck alone at home with a broken arm, Brian didn't feel much like forgiving. But once he forgave Greg—knowing he was doing what God wanted him to do—he felt better. Forgiveness always starts with a decision.

Forgiveness doesn't erase consequences. Even after Brian forgave him, Greg was still in a heap of trouble. The boys' parents made them take a time-out from playing together. And as long as Brian wore his cast, Greg helped in whatever ways he could to make Brian's life easier.

Phony forgiveness is no forgiveness at all. It helps neither us nor the people who hurt us. So make your forgiveness real. Think hard about what it is—and what it *isn't*. And put it into practice!

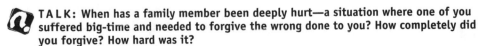

TALK: When has a family member been deeply hurt—a situation where one of you suffered big-time and needed to forgive the wrong done to you? How completely did you forgive? How hard was it?

PRAY: *God, we want to make forgiveness a habit in our life. Help us grow in putting it into practice.*

ACT: Talk to God about anyone you need to forgive but haven't because you misunderstood what forgiveness is and isn't.

1 Chasing the Wind

Bible Reading: Ecclesiastes 2:17-26

God gives wisdom, knowledge, and joy to those who please him.
Ecclesiastes 2:26

Amy thought she was prepared for school to start. She was going to do way better this year. But no. Little by little, week by week, subject by subject, and assignment by assignment, she falls behind until she almost crumbles under the load. "I can't take it anymore," she whines. "It's too much. I can't wait till school's out. "

Flash forward to the end of the school year. On the first day of vacation, Amy sleeps till noon. Two days later the words are out of her mouth before she can choke them back. "I'm bored!" Amy howls. "There's nothing to do around here."

Life isn't much fun if you just lie down in bed and collect belly-button lint. Without something big to be part of, you wilt.

You might be surprised that the best-known case of boredom in the history of humankind comes from the Bible. Solomon—the wisest guy on earth—wrote a whole book of the Bible to describe his lifelong quest for meaning. Ecclesiastes tells us all about his quest.

Right after Solomon became king, he asked God for wisdom. God granted his request. Solomon read, studied, looked around, and asked deep questions to find out what life was all about. His conclusion went something like this: "I have seen everything that is done under the sun. Look at it! It's all pointless. It's like trying to catch the wind" (see Ecclesiastes 1:14).

The king tried everything to find excitement. First he lived for *pleasure*. He surrounded himself with women and wild living. But he became bored.

So Solomon tried another route. Maybe he would find thrills by living for *pride*. He did things to make himself feel important. He stashed away cash. He undertook massive building projects. But even with success, he was still stuck in boredom.

"Oh, great," you might say. "If the smartest man who ever lived couldn't find his way out of boredom, what hope do I have?"

Thankfully, Solomon found the secret of excitement, a secret he shares with us. He wrote, "God gives wisdom, knowledge, and joy to those who please him" (2:26). The true path to adventure, says Solomon, is *living for God*.

Life becomes an adventure when you follow God because he's the one who invented adventure. So it's up to you. You can try to catch the wind and live in total boredom—or run straight to the One who holds your exciting future in his hands.

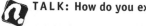 **TALK:** How do you expect to keep life exciting? Is your plan working?

 PRAY: *God, we want to find adventure and excitement by following you.*

 ACT: Are you stuffing your life full of things that give you excitement that won't last? Check your schedule. And chuck what you need to.

2 The Basics of Being Unbored

Bible Reading: Acts 20:32-35
My purpose is to give life in all its fullness. John 10:10

Here's your assignment: Bust boredom. Break loose from the ordinary. So take a vote: Which of these activities would send the most electric shiver up your spine?

(a) Going tandem bungee jumping with your mom
(b) Letting a world-champion rifle marksman shoot an apple off your head
(c) Going to a camp with experiences in skyboarding and cliff rappelling
(d) Doing barrel rolls at Mach three in the backseat of a fighter jet
(e) Visiting a nursing home to volunteer your time playing checkers with the elderly

How 'bout that last one, huh?

Talk about it: What do you think of that last choice?

None of us signed up for a boring, empty, purposeless life. We all would like to be stuffed from head to toe with the fullness Jesus promises in John 10:10. But here's the catch: We find that extreme excitement only when we put into practice the biblical principles that bring us true life.

Check out this astounding truth: The most fulfilled people in the world are those more concerned with giving than with getting.

The Bible consistently tells us it's more blessed to give than to receive. Despite that, a habit of selfishness still lives inside of us. It says, "Take care of yourself first." Listen to that lie, and life loses its zing. Yet if we can pull our attention off our own life and put it on others, we experience a brand of excitement we would never have expected. Like Jesus said, "If you try to keep your life for yourself, you will lose it. But if you give up your life for me, you will find true life" (Matthew 16:25).

Checkers might not be your favorite game. Senior citizens might not be your favorite part of the population. And nursing homes might not be your favorite place to visit. But finding a spot where you can serve others is the ultimate way to bust boredom. It's a strategy that works for all of us.

Living the life Jesus mapped out for us is the one lifelong answer to our weariness. In fact, no one who genuinely follows Jesus ever gets bored! If you're bored with life, Jesus wants to grab you by the hand and lead you into some way-better-than-bungee-jumping life experiences.

 TALK: What do you think of helping others as a way to bust boredom?

 PRAY: *Jesus, show us new ways to follow you and serve others. Help us find the excitement you have planned for us.*

 ACT: Decide on a new way to give your time and attention to others. It's your best bet for busting boredom!

3 Those Times When You Want to Disappear

Bible Reading: Hebrews 6:1

Let us go on instead and become mature in our understanding.
Hebrews 6:1

"I can't do it! I hate school!" Todd bellowed, slamming the front door behind him and throwing his book bag on the hall table. "I'm never going back to school again!"

"What's this all about?" Todd's dad asked.

"Oh, nothing," Todd answered glumly. "Except I'm so stupid I'll soon be going to third-grade math instead of fifth-grade with my classmates."

His dad made him sit down and explain why he was so frazzled. "I felt like a total idiot, Dad," he confessed. "We had a test today. It was brutal. And everyone finished before me."

So will Todd ever figure out how to divide fractions? Of course. And over the next weeks he will figure out that most of his classmates are just as nervous as he is—and feel just as stupid.

News flash: We all have moments when we feel as if we don't have what it takes to do something well. If you don't have those moments, you're either not trying very hard or you never try anything new!

Feeling unsure of yourself is normal. The real problem comes when you think you're the only one who ever feels frustrated. You need to ditch the thoughts that say you're dumber or slower or clumsier than everybody else. How would you respond if you heard a friend mumbling:

- "If people knew I can't _____, they wouldn't like me."
- "I'm the only one who gets nervous about _____."
- "I'm the only person who can't _____."

When you hear those words coming from someone else, they sound silly. When you say them about yourself, it's as if they're totally true.

Those feelings fuzz up your thinking so that you can't see how all people, young and old, have to cope with limitations. Those thoughts blind you to the fact that God and his people stand ready to help you. And they make you forget that the chance those statements are actually true is somewhere between slim and none.

When you feel like a failure, it's time to let God, your family, and good friends remind you how false those loser statements are. And it's time to remember that God and the people who love you accept you even when you struggle.

 TALK: Discuss how the people in your family can help one another remember that none of you are alone in your struggles.

 PRAY: *Jesus, thanks for being with us and for showing us how to encourage each other when things don't seem to be going so well for us.*

 ACT: The next time you see yourself as a loser, find a friend to talk sense into you!

4 The Gift That Keeps on Giving

Bible Reading: John 14:15-18
He is the Holy Spirit, who leads into all truth. John 14:17

It's done! Your spanking-new invention looks a lot like a Walkman, so you call it "Truthman." You clip the control box to your belt and slip the headphones over your ears. The rest of the world thinks you're listening to tunes. *But this is no CD player,* you think proudly. *This is one rockin' righteousness machine. In every situation it tells me through my headphones what's right and true.*

On your way to school you're about to cross the street against the "Don't Walk" sign when you hear a voice through the headphones: "Romans 13:1-2 says we should obey the laws of the land. This is God's way of protecting you from getting hurt." *Truthman works!* You decide to wait for the "Walk" sign.

Hustling through the crowded hall, you bump into another student. "Leper!" he snarls at you. Truthman reminds you, "You're no loser. John 1:12 says you are God's child." You feel an instant lift.

In social studies your teacher drops a pop quiz on you. No worry. You sit next to geography genius Lynn Brazil. As you glance toward Lynn's paper, Truthman says, "One of the Ten Commandments is 'Do not steal,' and that applies to quiz answers." You snap your eyes back to your paper.

Things don't work so well after lunch. During a basketball game in phys ed, your teammate fumbles the ball. With Truthman stashed on the sidelines, nothing stops you from blasting him. Later you drop Truthman. As an angry thought rumbles in your brain, all you hear is "Bleeble . . . zok . . . gooby . . . hazzit . . . snork." And when your mom asks if you have your homework done, Truthman's batteries are dead. You say "Almost, Mom" when you haven't even started. So much for your invention.

Having something like Truthman would be great—if it worked. But you already have something way better! It's the Holy Spirit living inside you. He helps you understand and apply God's truth to your everyday life. In fact, Jesus often calls the Holy Spirit the "Spirit of truth" (John 15:26).

Unlike Truthman, the Holy Spirit can't get lost, broken, or run out of batteries. He lives inside every believer—including you (see John 14:17). And you won't ever find the Holy Spirit on the sidelines, because Jesus said his gift "will never leave you" (John 14:16). Moment by moment, day by day, the Holy Spirit hangs to you tighter than headphones, ready to share God's truth with you.

 TALK: How do you respond when the Holy Spirit tries to teach you truth?

 PRAY: *God, thanks for giving us the Holy Spirit to teach us.*

 ACT: Let the Holy Spirit convince you that it's a good idea to put some truth in your head the old-fashioned way. Memorize a favorite verse today!

5 An Inside Job

Bible Reading: John 14:19-21

When I am raised to life again, you will know that I am in my Father, and you are in me, and I am in you. John 14:20

Tara wakes up in a great mood and dresses quickly. She and the Griffith family are spending the day at Dizzyland, their favorite amusement park. Bounding down the stairs to the kitchen, she chirps, "Hi, Mom. Beautiful day, isn't it?"

Mom turns and smiles. "Yes, it is, dear. I hope you have a wonderful time at the park. I'll be at work all day, but I should be home by the time you return." Tara gives Mom a hug, glad that she can always count on Mom to give her an encouraging word.

As Tara leaves her house, she runs into a police officer at the end of her driveway. "Hi, Officer Nelson," she says. "I'm going to Dizzyland today."

The officer gives her a thumbs-up signal. He tells her he wishes he could go with her, but he'll look forward to hearing about her day. Tara appreciates his interest and waves as he goes his way and she goes hers.

When Tara knocks on the front door at the Griffiths' house, Kyle answers. He tells her that his parents will be ready in a couple of minutes. He looks excited. "Let's go to the House of Monsters as soon as we get to Dizzyland," he says.

Tara starts to shiver, but she nods. She knows monsters aren't for real, so she doesn't have to be afraid of them. She also knows that Jesus is her Lord and Savior. He lives inside her and is stronger than any fake monster. Nothing can harm her.

Jesus told his disciples that he would be in them—not just *with* them, not just *beside* them, but *in* them (see John 14:20). Paul confirmed it. He wrote, "Christ lives in you" (Colossians 1:27).

"Hey, time out," you may say. "Yesterday you said it was the Holy Spirit living inside me. . . . Now you say it's Christ. Who is really living within me: the Holy Spirit or Christ?"

If you are a Christian, Jesus Christ and his Holy Spirit *both* live inside you. The Bible explains that the Spirit of God is the Spirit of Christ (see Romans 8:9). And the same Holy Spirit who lived inside Jesus lives in you to teach you, comfort you, and make you strong.

 TALK: Who are some of your closest family members and friends? What do you think about the fact that God is even closer to you than they are, living inside you and never leaving you?

 PRAY: *God, thanks that you are always close and available to us.*

 ACT: Spend some time praising the God who loves you so much he wants to live inside you.

6 Taking Your Spiritual Vitamins

Bible Reading: John 14:22-26

The Holy Spirit . . . will teach you everything and will remind you of everything I myself have told you. John 14:26

It's Saturday morning, and you are going to be baby-sitting two-year-old Justin Miller. You'll be taking care of the cute little guy from morning until night. So his mom is giving you instructions before she leaves for the day.

"Justin isn't a good eater," she explains. "When you feed him lunch and dinner, it doesn't matter if he finishes. Just serve him a good meal and let him eat as much as he wants. Then give him one of my homemade cookies."

"Are you serious?" you ask, amazed. "He gets a cookie, even if he doesn't finish?" Justin's mother says yes. You can't believe it. Your mom never gives you dessert unless every single pea and carrot vanish from your plate—and if you slip them to the dog, your only dessert is a double helping of peas and carrots.

You silently wish Mrs. Miller would adopt you.

At lunchtime you serve Justin chicken-noodle soup and carrot sticks. He slurps a little soup and eats half a carrot, then dumps the rest on the floor. You give him a cookie, and he eats the whole thing. At dinnertime you watch the same thing happen. A few bites of veggies, a lot of flying food, then a whole mouthful of cookie.

After Justin's mom pays you that evening, you find the courage to say, "Mrs. Miller, Justin shouldn't get a cookie if he doesn't eat his lunch or dinner. He's not getting enough vitamins."

"That's why he always gets dessert," Mrs. Miller says with a smile. "His daily vitamins are in the cookies."

The Holy Spirit is like that wise mom. His ministry is to keep you spiritually healthy by getting spiritual vitamins into you. He lovingly takes the truth you need and serves it up in a form you can digest.

You might be reading your Bible, for example, and it's whooshing way over your head. Then you read a verse and—*wham!*—something suddenly becomes clear to you. It's like God is right there saying, "Here's what this means in your life." Or you're listening to a Christian CD and a line of the lyrics nudges you to make a much needed change in your behavior. Or you're in a Bible study, and something your leader says helps you make an important decision.

God knows how to make sure you get the vitamins you need to keep you spiritually strong. And he does it without making you gag!

 TALK: Are you surprised that God is so wisely, lovingly committed to your growth? What does that tell you about him?

 PRAY: *God, thanks for teaching us truth in a way we can digest.*

 ACT: How are you going to let the Holy Spirit teach you today? Tell God you want to hear from him!

7 Rest in His Peace

Bible Reading: John 14:27-31

I am leaving you with a gift—peace of mind and heart. John 14:27

It's nighttime, only a few hours after Jesus was crucified and buried. The disciples are sitting around together, still in shock from the death of their beloved Master. The following conversation isn't in the Bible, but something like it might have happened.

"I can't believe we were just eating dinner with the Master," Bartholomew says, shaking his head. "It seems like only yesterday."

"That's because it *was* yesterday, Bart," Peter snorts.

"Oh yeah, I knew that," Bartholomew snaps.

Thaddaeus scratches his head. "The Master told us so many things last night during dinner. I wish I had listened better. What do you guys remember from last night around the table?"

Bartholomew says, "Well, I thought the meat was a little dry and—"

"We're not talking about what we *ate* for dinner, Bart," Peter cuts in. "We're talking about what the Master *said* during dinner."

"Ah . . . I knew that."

Thomas looks up. "What did the Master mean when he said he was going to send some kind of 'Holy Spirit'? I don't get it."

Philip speaks next. "He said this Holy Spirit would lead us into all truth. I'd sure like to know the truth about everything that has happened lately."

"The thing I remember most," Matthew puts in, "is the Master saying this Holy Spirit is *his* Spirit, and that he's going to be in us."

"Hey, guys, what if it's all true?" Simon wonders aloud. "What if the Master is really going to be inside us to show us what is true, teach us about the Father, and remind us of all the things he said to us? What could that mean to us?"

For several moments the men don't breathe. Then one of them says what they are all thinking: "Wow. We would have total peace—Jesus' peace."

Peter brightens up. "Hey, the Master talked about peace last night too."

"Right, he said he's leaving his peace with us," John remembers, "just like he is sending his Spirit to us."

"He said his peace is a gift," James interrupts, "just like the Spirit he is giving."

"Maybe they're connected," Bartholomew tries. "Maybe the Master's peace comes with the Master's Spirit."

"Bart, maybe you do have a brain," Peter says with a smile.

 TALK: Do you sense God's peace as you consider the Holy Spirit's presence and power in your life?

 PRAY: *God, thank you for the gift of your Spirit. Thank you for sending the Spirit to give us peace and teach us truth.*

 ACT: When you need wisdom or peace today, tell God that you are glad the Holy Spirit is at work inside you.

8 Who's Number One?

Bible Reading: Matthew 20:20-28

Whoever wants to be a leader among you must be your servant.
Matthew 20:26

Think about whether you'd like to become a leader like Ms. Rachel someday.

Ms. Rachel is a businessperson with an important position at the top of her company. She looks down on anyone she considers to be less important than her—which is basically everyone. When her assistant enters her office, Ms. Rachel barks her usual orders. "Get that stupid jerk Patterson in here. And tell Allison to—" She stops in midsentence, alarmed by the pained expression on her assistant's face.

The secretary says, "Your baby-sitter called. Danielle disappeared."

Ms. Rachel grabs her cell phone, dials the sitter, and fires questions as she races out of the office. She flings herself into her BMW, squeals onto the street, and speeds toward the sitter's house. *If anything happens to Danielle, I'll die.* She runs a red light. *What if I don't find her?* The thought terrifies her.

Near the sitter's house, she spots a crossing guard in the intersection just in time to slam on her brakes. Her fury erupts like a volcano. Mr. Richter, the old crossing guard, has been helping children cross the street for years, and Ms. Rachel has always looked down on him as an unimportant old man. And now, by forcing her to stop, he's wasted precious seconds.

Ms. Rachel opens her mouth to yell at him, then notices a child in his arms—Danielle! The old crossing guard had found Danielle at the park and was bringing her back to the sitter. Ms. Rachel swings open the door and runs hysterically to the man. She sweeps her three-year-old into her arms and hugs her, crying tears of joy and thankfulness. Ms. Rachel, the powerful executive, suddenly feels very small. And Mr. Richter, the old man she once looked down on, is very important.

Talk about it: What do you think of Ms. Rachel?

Ms. Rachel is an "egoist," a person who sees herself as the center of the universe. She puts her interests before those of everyone else, thinking, *Forget everybody else. As long as I get what I want out of life, I'll be happy.* But life doesn't work that way. Following that strategy can make people wealthy or powerful, but it also leaves them bitter and lonely.

Jesus taught that you and every other human being are immensely and equally important to God. Realizing the worth of everyone around you doesn't get in the way of your happiness. It makes happiness happen.

 TALK: What do you think of God—who sees all of us as valuable?

 PRAY: *God, help us treat everyone around us as people who are important to you.*

 ACT: Who have you looked down on in the past? What do you want to do today to show that person's value?

9 It's What's Inside That Counts

Bible Reading: 1 Samuel 16:7

People judge by outward appearance, but the Lord looks at a person's thoughts and intentions. 1 Samuel 16:7

Catherine is beautiful enough to grace the cover of a fashion magazine. She looks as comfortable decked out in diamonds and a black evening gown as the rest of us look grubbed out in a sweatshirt and jeans. Her elegance and charm fit right in at the parties of the rich and famous.

So why is she crawling around in a sewer?

In the old television series *Beauty and the Beast,* Catherine hangs out underground with Vincent the man-beast. It's an old story in a new setting. And the whole show revolves around one gigantic question: *What does she see in him?* A gorgeous woman in love with a half-man, half-lion who lives in abandoned subway tunnels—what's up with that?

So how can a beauty love a beast? Catherine is attracted to Vincent not *because* of how he looks, but *in spite* of it. She loves the guy under the lion's mane. She likes him for his kindness . . . and maybe for his marvelous voice too.

Talk about it: How does our world say we're supposed to look to qualify as beautiful? Why does Catherine's love for the beast seem so weird to us?

Lots of people buy the idea that looks are everything. Television, magazines, movies, and videos all tell us that people who lack the looks of supermodels are ugly.

That's ridiculous.

Christians don't have to be ugly. But we can be happy without looking like a girl in a skin-cleanser commercial or a guy selling a bodybuilding machine. There's far more to beauty than clear skin and bulging biceps. The greatest beauty more often comes from the inside. God chose David to be king of Israel not because of his looks or the bulk of his muscles, but because of the upright attitude of his heart.

Beauty as the world defines it often isn't a blessing. Being stunning on the outside is no guarantee you won't be filled with loneliness, insecurity, and unhappiness on the inside.

Truth is, if you think that the color of your hair or the brand of your clothes will bring you happiness, you're sure to be disappointed. Clothes can be cool, but they aren't as important as what you can't see in the mirror. God is thrilled with how he made your outsides. But he's even more thrilled to see your inner qualities shine.

 TALK: How are you trying to spot in yourself—and in others—a beauty that is more than skin deep?

 PRAY: *Lord, develop in us the inner attitudes that you find beautiful.*

 ACT: Look for ads on TV and in magazines that communicate the false idea that outward beauty is what really matters in life.

10 "Everybody" Isn't Always Everybody

Bible Reading: Daniel 1:6–15

Daniel made up his mind not to defile himself by eating the food and wine given to them by the king. Daniel 1:8

Nicholas bounded home from school with an invitation to ride his BMX on the cool bike trails winding through the woods on Robert's property. "I need to go now, Mom," he urged. "Can't you drive me? The guys are meeting right away."

"I've already said no, Nicholas," his mom repeated.

"Come on, Mom," Nicholas pleaded. "All the guys are going."

"It doesn't matter how many of your friends are going to be there. I don't want you at a friend's house—period—without an adult in the house."

Nicholas stewed in anger all afternoon and evening—until he talked to Robert on Monday. It turned out Trevor was the only guy whose parents let him go. And there was bigger news. Trevor had wiped out on his bike and broken his wrist. With no adult around to help, Robert had to call 911.

Nicholas had bought the common belief that "everybody's doing it." What a lie! Fewer people dive into off-limit activities than you might think.

- Everybody is *not* using tobacco. Surveys indicate that more than 70 percent of high school students don't smoke regularly.
- Everybody is *not* using alcohol. More than 50 percent of students surveyed said they had not used alcohol in the last thirty days. More than 20 percent have never tried it.
- Everybody is *not* doing drugs. Almost 50 percent of all American young people refuse illegal drugs all the way through to high school graduation.
- Everybody is *not* losing or outgrowing their faith in God. In a recent Barna Research Group study, 65 percent of youth said they want a close relationship with God.*

Students often use the lie that everybody's doing it to manipulate their friends and parents. Don't believe it! And even if everybody *was* doing it, you wouldn't have to. You can be like Daniel and his three friends. They didn't yield to the pressure to conform, and God blessed them as a result.

 TALK: How do you stay strong when people pressure you to conform?

 PRAY: *God, give us the courage to resist the line that "everyone is doing it."*

 ACT: Promise to catch each other—kids or adults—when you try to use the argument that "everyone is doing it."

---

*Josh McDowell and Bob Hostetler, *Beyond Belief to Convictions* (Wheaton, Ill.: Tyndale House, 2002), 7.

11 The Fun-Giver

Bible Reading: Proverbs 1:10-16
My child, if sinners entice you, turn your back on them! Proverbs 1:10

"Oh, sure it is," Troy sassed. "Following Jesus is a blast. Church sounds *soooo* exciting. And being good all the time? That has to be loads of fun."

Most of the kids Evan invited to church said yes. And lots of them agreed that church was a good place to be—and that following Jesus was great! But Troy had a whole other attitude. He assumed that the only people interested in obeying God's commands were mean old hags with their hair pulled back into too tight buns. Troy seemed to think that God's biggest goal for the universe was to zap the fun out of life.

Talk about it: When has someone tried to tell you that following God—or doing the right thing—steals away your fun?

Maybe someday Troy will change his mind. But God knows who the real fun-zappers are. Just ten short verses into the first chapter of Proverbs—the Bible's book of wisdom—we learn that *sinful people* are the folks who take the fun out of life.

You probably don't know anyone who actually makes a habit of beating up innocent people like the bloodthirsty bunch described in Proverbs 1. But you'll notice a close similarity to what all sinners say as they try to drag you into sin. Check these smooth lines:

- "Come and join us!"
- "No one is going to get hurt!"
- "Look at all the great stuff we'll get!"
- "We guarantee you'll have fun!"

Those sinners aren't too bright. Their fun ruins their own lives, and by setting out to destroy others they wind up destroying themselves. Like Proverbs 1:18 says, "They set an ambush for themselves; they booby-trap their own lives!" Psalm 73 tells how God handles people who think sin is the route to success: "Truly, you put them on a slippery path and send them sliding over the cliff to destruction" (verse 18).

That doesn't sound like much fun!

God speaks through Solomon to give you some clear advice when people try to tell you that sin is a smart idea: "My child, if sinners entice you, turn your back on them!" (Proverbs 1:10).

God isn't out to spoil your fun. His wisdom aims to show you the way to true fun. God isn't the fun-killer. He's the fun-giver.

 TALK: How do you know that God wants to give you a good life—not make your life miserable with his rules?

 PRAY: *God, thanks for putting up boundaries that guide us into a good life. You keep us safe and happy.*

 ACT: Do you have a friend who thinks God's goal is to zap fun from life? Share the good news of the truth about this with him or her!

12 Loving the Person in the Mirror

Bible Reading: Ephesians 5:29-30
No one hates his own body but lovingly cares for it, just as Christ cares for his body, which is the church. Ephesians 5:29

Alyssa is so wrapped up in herself that the rest of the world can slide by right under her nose, totally unnoticed. Take today, for example.

As Alyssa crosses the street to school, she steps into traffic without looking. Horns blare. Tires squeal. Multiple cars crash and bang and pile up on top of each other. *Did I hear something?* Alyssa asks herself.

As Alyssa charges through the front door of school, she knocks down an elderly school lunch lady. She stomps all over Mrs. Fudgebottom as she presses on to homeroom. "Those custodians really need to sweep better," she mumbles.

And as Alyssa fiddles with her hair at a mirror in her desk, her whole school is suddenly ablaze. Alarms wail. Students shriek. Only when a firefighter tosses Alyssa over his shoulder does she realize something might be amiss—with her hair, that is. "Put me down!" she yells. "I'm not finished!"

It's clear that Alyssa loves herself in a big way. But this might surprise you: Did you know that Jesus commands you to love yourself?

In Matthew 22:39 Jesus says you should "love your neighbor as yourself." He means that you should model your love for others after your love for yourself.

Wait a minute! you might be thinking. *I'm not supposed to love myself. Jesus said I should* deny *myself. Loving myself is bad.* But that's confusing a good thing (taking care of yourself) with a bad thing (being stuck on yourself).

As Christians our most basic job is to care for ourselves—to feed ourselves and guard ourselves from harm. We should look after ourselves mentally, physically, spiritually, and socially. And that loving respect we show for ourselves will teach us how we should love others. Jesus didn't say, "Love others *instead* of loving yourself." Jesus is saying something like this: "You already love yourself, and doing that in the right way is good. Now love others just like that."

God declares that you are lovable just because he made you. If you are his creation, you deserve care and respect. If God says you are lovable, then it's right to love yourself. Don't trash what God says is a treasure!

 TALK: What are some right ways you can love yourself?

 PRAY: *God, teach us to take care of ourselves—not to be selfish, but to have the right kind of self-love.*

 ACT: Lots of moms and dads are so busy caring for kids' needs that they never care for their own. Ask your parents how you can lend a hand—so they can find some time for themselves!

13 Looking Out for Number One

Bible Reading: Mark 12:28-34

I know that it is important to love [God] with all my heart and all my understanding and all my strength, and to love my neighbors as myself. Mark 12:33

True or false: At the start of all airplane flights, a cabin attendant

☐ True ☐ False   tells you where the plane is headed
☐ True ☐ False   points to the exits
☐ True ☐ False   explains how to buckle your seat belt
☐ True ☐ False   instructs you that "in the unlikely event of a sudden loss of cabin pressure, you should help your neighbor put on his or her oxygen mask—before you put on your own"

If you marked that last choice false, then you're a brilliant airplane passenger. Here's the rule: If the inside of the airplane suddenly runs short on air, your first job is to put on *your own* oxygen mask. *Then* you can help the people sitting around you. After all, if you're wheezing, you're not much good to anyone. Including yourself.

Self-love works the same way. Jesus told us to love others as we love ourselves (see Matthew 22:39) because the right kind of self-love equips us to love others.

- Physically: You buckle up in the car, refuse to abuse substances, and get enough sleep so you don't get grouchy.
- Mentally: You guard your mind by turning off negative TV programs, videos, music, and movies.
- Socially: You stay out of groups where you give in to doing wrong.
- Spiritually: You fill your heart with Scripture, make yourself accountable to others, and stand against Satan's attempts to discourage you.

Self-love means investing time and effort in our own growth so we are prepared to minister to others—because we can't give what we don't have. Only as we love and care for ourselves are we equipped to love and care for others as Christ commanded us.

If we do anything less than cautiously, wisely care for ourselves, we hurt both ourselves and others. We cheat ourselves out of the healthy love God expects us to show ourselves. And we won't have what it takes to serve others. God loves you too much to let you trash yourself!

 TALK: How can you wisely love yourself? How can you help others in your family take care of themselves?

 PRAY: *God, we're grateful that you think we're worth taking care of.*

 ACT: How are you cheating yourself of healthy self-love? Pick one area and set one goal for better caring for yourself.

14 Don't Overdo It—or Underdo It

Bible Reading: 1 Corinthians 12:14-27

All of you together are Christ's body, and each one of you is a separate and necessary part of it. 1 Corinthians 12:27

Suppose you and your kinfolk wander out to Billy Bob's Bovine Steak and Burger Barn for the Friday night all-you-can-eat special. Exactly how do you feel after you've bellied up to the buffet? Vote for your choice:

(a) I go home stuffed because I edge my way to the front of the line—and then I inhale every last bit of vittles I can find.

(b) I go home hungry because I take itty-bitty spoonfuls—even of my favorite foods. I'm scared to take more than a mouthful for fear that someone else might miss out.

(c) I go home comfortably full—and there's still plenty of food left for everyone else to eat when they saunter through later that night.

Did you know that you face the same three choices when it comes to showing yourself love? Think about it:

(a) You can love yourself so much that you leave nothing for anyone else in your world.

(b) You can skimp on loving yourself until you wither away.

(c) You can learn to rightly love your neighbor as you love yourself.

In 1 Corinthians 12 Paul said that as Christians we have something to share with each other that's even more vital than food. He explained that the Holy Spirit has built inside each of us gifts to serve others. Not only that, but he's equipped each of us with exactly the gifts he wants us to have. He's made us like a body—and each person is like a body part. Whether we have the abilities of an eye, an ear, or a foot, our goal is to appreciate, develop, and put into action all of the abilities God has built into us for the good of the rest of the body—the rest of our church family.

Can you see how that kind of self-love isn't selfish? If you love yourself too much, you'll keep your gift to yourself. If you love yourself too little, you won't believe you can be of any help to anyone. But when you love yourself rightly, you think enough of yourself to put your one-of-a-kind assortment of gifts to work for the good of others!

  TALK: Do you think you love yourself too much—or too little—or just right? How does loving yourself help you love others?

PRAY: *God, help us love ourselves just right—so that we use our gifts for the good of others!*

 ACT: Show yourself some respect: Use your gifts to make a difference in someone's life today!

15 How Can Anyone Love a Mess like This?

Bible Reading: 1 John 2:1-6

If you do sin, there is someone to plead for you before the Father. He is Jesus Christ, the one who pleases God completely. 1 John 2:1

"I'm no good at this. I can't help anyone," Miguel moaned to himself. Hours after the church Christmas play had ended, he was helping pack up the costumes. He thought volunteering to lend a hand was a good thing. Mr. Garcia didn't think so.

"You can't just bunch them up," Mr. Garcia barked. "They have to be folded."

Discouraged, Miguel moved to another pile of costumes and started sorting. Soon the angels' halos were mixed up with the shepherds' headgear. And when Miguel fumbled a ceramic baby Jesus and broke off his arm, Mr. Garcia huffed and threw up his hands. "Miguel Diaz, you're doing more harm than good," he said. "I think you should call your father for a ride home."

Miguel broke into tears as soon as he crawled in the car. He told his dad, "When I try to help, I just make a mess of things. I know I'm supposed to love others like I love myself, but I can't see anything about me worth loving."

Miguel's attempt to help turned into a mess. Has that ever happened to you? It usually happens to everyone now and then. And it may make you feel worthless.

But the reflection you see of yourself in the eyes of other people isn't always very accurate. Sure, it matters what others think about you. But what matters far more is that you get God's view of you. When you see yourself through the eyes of the God who loves you, then you realize you have nothing to feel inferior about!

The straightest route to a strong self-love is to soak in the scriptural truth about the true you in Christ. For example:

- You are loved by God and worth the death of his Son (see 1 John 4:10).
- You are a child of God (see John 1:12; Romans 8:14-15).
- You are Christ's friend (see John 15:15).
- You have God's Spirit living in you (see 1 Corinthians 3:16; 6:19).
- You are brand-new in Christ (see 2 Corinthians 5:17).
- You are righteous in Christ (see Ephesians 4:24).
- You are in the light, not in the darkness (see 1 Thessalonians 5:5).
- You are God's workmanship (see Ephesians 2:10).

The more thoroughly you absorb those truths about who you are in Christ, the more you'll be able to love yourself as God does, even when your efforts are less-than-perfect. Even when you mess up, those facts are true!

 TALK: What do you think of all those Bible facts about your identity in Christ?

 PRAY: *God, thank you that you still believe in us even when we fail.*

 ACT: Is there something you've given up on? Give it another try!

16 One-Sided Friendships

Bible Reading: Romans 15:1-4

We should please others. If we do what helps them, we will build them up in the Lord. Romans 15:2

Long before Clark started school, his parents discovered that he had a learning disability. Year by year Clark's teachers tutored him and poured themselves into keeping him on track with the rest of the class. Yet of all the people who have helped him, Clark's biggest encouragement has come from a classmate, Thomas.

At first Clark didn't know whether to trust Thomas. Clark knew firsthand what it was like to have friends who promise to help but then forget. Or who stop helping when others tease them about hanging out with "the stupid kid."

Sometimes our friends turn out to be less than perfect. You've probably uncovered a few people who weren't the true pals you believed they were.

We need to be on guard against at least four kinds of friends that are bound to leave us disappointed and frustrated.

- *Part-time friends.* Ted is a great buddy to Scott when they get one-on-one. But Ted ignores Scott—or slams him—when they're around a crowd. Some part-time friends are just the opposite—cozy when you're with a mob of people, ice-cold when you're alone.
- *Conditional friends.* Stacie treats friendship like bait, dangling a relationship in front of other girls to get them to do what she wants. She's your friend as long you cough up what she wants. As soon as you choke, the friendship sputters.
- *Careless friends.* Bethany blabs secrets, gossips, and breaks promises. It's tough to have much of a friendship with her because you never know where you stand.
- *Shallow friends.* Even when Simon's friends need some serious help, he cracks a joke. It's fine to chitchat and share activities with him, but it's doubtful you can expect much more.

Maybe you're in the middle of one of these types of friendships right now. So talk about it: Do you have friends and acquaintances who fit any of the above descriptions? Have you wound up discouraged, hurt, or lonely?

It's impossible to completely avoid less-than-perfect friends. Our job, however, is to be friends who are as true and as real as we know how to be.

 TALK: What does a true friend look like? What makes them so rare and special?

 PRAY: *God, help us to be true friends to the people around us.*

 ACT: Do you shows any signs of being a part-time, conditional, careless, or shallow friend? What one bad friendship trait do you want to work on changing?

17 Talking Deep

Bible Reading: Ephesians 4:25-29

Let everything you say be good and helpful, so that your words will be an encouragement to those who hear them. Ephesians 4:29

Brent loved the Wednesday night kids' club at church. He got into games like a maniac, memorized Bible verses faithfully, and paid close attention during Bible lessons.

Yet when the club leader said that the kids would break into small groups for a few minutes each week for a time called "Care and Share," Brent said, "No way." He didn't hide his disgust. "Girls gab," he argued. "Boys don't."

Maybe you think you can make real friendships without ever talking about solid stuff. But you might as well try to make friends with a wall. Friendships need talk-time to grow. The deeper you go into understanding one another's lives—talking about your feelings, favorites, and frights—the deeper your friendship grows.

Listen to these ways we can talk—going deeper step-by-step:

- *Level 1: Chitchat talk.* Your conversation starts and stops with "Dude, how's it going?" "Fine, how about you?" You never get beyond "Wassup?"
- *Level 2: Fact talk.* You swap information about shared interests—sports scores, clothing styles, school subjects, music groups, school events, etc. You talk about stuff "out there," not how you feel about it.
- *Level 3: Opinion talk.* You take facts a step deeper by sharing your thoughts and ideas about them. If you talk scores, you tell your favorite play of the game. If you discuss music, you share what you think about the lyrics of a song. You're getting closer to personal issues, but you're still basically playing it safe.

Here's where you head deeper. Do you ever get to these?

- *Level 4: Feelings talk.* You share how you *feel* about factual matters. "When that happened, I was really scared!" "This has been the loneliest week of my life." "Since Nate told that lie about me, I've been totally sad." You start to see what goes on inside each other.
- *Level 5: Gut talk.* You chat about your deepest feelings. You're completely open about your life.

We all need friends we trust so completely that we can be totally open about ourselves. It's the only way to go deep—whether you're a gal or a guy!

 TALK: How well do you share deeply with your friends? How would you like to grow in that area?

 PRAY: *Father, give us friends with whom we can share our deepest thoughts and feelings.*

 ACT: How do you talk as a family? Take time today to talk deep.

18 Who Are You Hanging With?

Bible Reading: Proverbs 4:10-16

Do not do as the wicked do or follow the path of evildoers. Avoid their haunts. Turn away and go somewhere else. Proverbs 4:14-15

"I was at this sleep-over with a whole bunch of girls," Abby explained. "It was at Jenna's house. I'm close friends with most of the girls, but there were a couple I didn't know well. It was about midnight when one of those girls said she wanted to go toilet-paper the house of a girl no one likes. Not many of us dared to go. But four girls went."

"Well, we had a sleep-over again a couple months later. Next time TPing didn't sound so bad. Pretty soon everyone was saying things like, 'Yeah, I hate her too. Let's go do it.'

"After a while you begin to feel the pressure. If a lot of your friends talk about doing something wrong, your conscience kind of goes to sleep, and it's tough to keep feeling it's wrong. After a while, you say, 'Sure. Why not?' so you do it!"

That's sharp insight—and it shows why we need to be careful who we hang out with. It's no huge news that the wrong friends can pull us into wrong behavior that can tear us away from our parents and Christian friends. When we wind up on the wrong side of right, we're going to feel some painful loneliness.

Talk about it: What can you do when you get caught in that kind of pressure-packed situation? How can you make choices that *prevent* that situation?

Peer pressure, of course, can also push you in the right way. It can be a huge help in living how God wants. As one guy said, "I know my friends have a great influence on who I am and also on what my values are. Godly friends can be a real source of encouragement when I'm struggling to do what's right." If you want the right kind of peer pressure, you need the right friends.

Those words you read from Proverbs contain two helpful pieces of advice. First, there is a clear warning on the danger of being caught in the *wrong* crowd. Sometimes you need to run from the wrong people, no matter how fun they seem. Then there is unbeatable encouragement on the worth of being with the *right* people. You need to hunt for like-minded people to hang with. Aim at friendships with people who share your sense of right and wrong.

Like it or not, you tend to become like the people you hang out with. So grab hold of God's wisdom. Make your closest friends the kind of people you want to be like!

 TALK: How are your friends shaping the person you are becoming? Who can you get closer to who will help pull you in the right direction?

 PRAY: *Lord, give us wisdom as we choose our friends. We want them to be people who help us follow you.*

 ACT: Be a great friend today. Encourage someone to choose to do the right thing.

19 Super Friend

Bible Reading: Proverbs 18:24

There are "friends" who destroy each other, but a real friend sticks closer than a brother. Proverbs 18:24

Becky feels ditched. She and Victoria were best friends all summer long. They bonded at softball camp. They had sleep-overs at each other's houses. For vacation Bible school they did up each other's hair in *fwangy* ponytails that sprang from their heads in every direction.

But once summer ended, their friendship plummeted like acorns off an oak tree in autumn. No matter where Becky and Victoria went—school, church, Girl Scouts, or just hanging around town—Victoria acted like she no longer knew who Becky was.

Not every human friend acts as mean as Victoria. If you've ever been dumped like Becky was, then you know how wonderful it is to have a friend you can depend on. As great as some human friendships get, however, we have one totally unique friendship that outshines and outlasts all the others. It's our friendship with Jesus Christ. He's promised to stay with us forever (see Matthew 28:20).

Talk about it: What makes Jesus the perfect friend? How is the friendship he offers different from friendship with any human friend or family member?

Check out these facts about your perfect friend:

Jesus is a *full-time* friend. He's always there for you. He doesn't treat you onc way when you're alone and another way when others are around.

Jesus is your *unconditional* friend. He always forgives when you fail him. He sticks with you no matter what happens in your life.

Jesus is your *dependable* friend. You don't need to fear him mocking you, ditching you, or spilling your secrets. And his promises are even more certain than the fact that the sun will rise tomorrow.

Jesus is your *deep* friend. He's never shallow or stupid. He wants a life-changing relationship with you. He treats you with love and respect when you open your heart to him. He shows intense, personal care for you!

When Jesus walked the earth, he wasn't stiff or stuffy. Ordinary people didn't cringe when he came around. You don't have to put on a superspiritual act to attract his attention. Just be yourself with him, and he will be himself with you.

In Jesus you have one great, faithful, unconditional friend. Cultivate your friendship with him every day—and you'll experience the kind of love that lasts forever.

 TALK: Have you made Jesus your best friend? How do you see that affecting your daily life?

 PRAY: *Jesus, make our friendship with you our best, most important friendship of all.*

 ACT: Do your friendships with people ever squeeze out time with Jesus? Wouldn't you like to spend some time with him today?

20 Bust Loose from Loneliness

Bible Reading: Colossians 3:12-15

You must clothe yourselves with tenderhearted mercy, kindness, humility, gentleness, and patience. Colossians 3:12

When Max graduated from elementary school and moved into middle school, his tight-knit group of buddies were scattered among more than two thousand other students. With all of his friends assigned to another team of students and teachers, he seldom saw them in the hallways, much less had the chance to share a class or eat lunch with them. His only hope of staying connected with his friends was finding time to play after school. Yet as his old friends chatted about their new experiences together, he felt more and more out of place. As weeks went by without finding any friends on his own team, Max started to feel like his loneliness was a lifetime sentence.

Even if you've never switched schools, you've maybe been in a bad spot where you felt like Max. You think, *I'll never have any real friends.* You feel, *I guess I just don't deserve having someone like me.*

You don't have to stay trapped. Even when you feel like you've been doomed to a life of solitary confinement, you can bust loose into a world of close friendships.

Talk about it: When have you felt lonely? What did you do to solve your situation?

The next time you're trapped in a friendless prison, take these tips:

Get honest. Take an honest look at your life. Are you doing anything that scares people away?

Get help. You don't have to sign up for charm lessons, but you can still rely on *someone* to show you the way. Max found that his older brother could give him kind, helpful feedback that helped him be a better friend. And his support helped Max know he wasn't facing the situation alone.

Get realistic. Trying to fit in with the popular crowd usually just makes you feel worse. Decide whether you're shopping for a friend or a status symbol!

Get friendly. Your job is less to *get* friends than to *be* a friend. Max decided to put his energy into befriending others and quit trying to convince everyone to like him.

Max found new friends when he looked for others who were on the outside looking in. It turned out the guys he thought were losers were just as unfairly left out as he was. His new friendships didn't happen overnight. But they happened because he took small, planned steps toward friendships.

 TALK: How are you doing in your friendships? How can you gain friends by being a friend?

 PRAY: *Jesus, help us be the kind of friend to others that you have been to us.*

 ACT: Almost everyone would like more friends. What one thing do you want to do today to be a better friend to someone?

21 Laying Down the Law about Love

Bible Reading: Deuteronomy 28:1-6

If you fully obey the Lord your God by keeping all the commands I am giving you today . . . you will be blessed wherever you go.
Deuteronomy 28:1, 6

Morgan had been putting off doing her chores all week. And when her parents told her they needed to be finished on Saturday morning—before she did anything else—she got sassy. Her parents calmly pointed out that if she wasn't available to help with chores that morning, they wouldn't be available in the afternoon to give her the ride she wanted to her friend's house.

Morgan didn't like that line of reasoning. She glared at her parents. And then she shouted, "If you really loved me, you would let me do what I want!"

Talk about it: When someone makes us follow rules, is that a good thing? How does requiring us to do what's right show us love?

You don't have to look hard to spot kids and teens who can't understand how rules and love can ever get along. They don't merely have a problem with parents or teachers laying down the law. They think that God must be a horrible guy to have handed us a book with so many commands. They figure one of two things:

(a) If God loves me, he won't hold me to any rules.
(b) If God has rules he expects me to follow, then he can't possibly love me.

Those folks have their facts mixed up. See, love is at the heart of the rules God makes. The introduction to the second commandment makes it clear right from the start: "I, the Lord your God, . . . lavish my love on those who love me and obey my commands" (Exodus 20:5-6).

When God gave the law, he said it was "for your own good" (Deuteronomy 10:13). Its purpose was to provide for and protect God's children. His goal in giving his law was to ensure our prosperity and joy and spare us from heartache and hurt.

All of God's rules show us love in another way. They are a sign of God's love because they tell us *how* to enjoy love. The whole point of the Ten Commandments and other Bible commands is to explain exactly what love looks like—and steer us clear of unloving ways of getting along.

Maybe the words of King David sum it up best. He had an incredible outlook on God's rules: "Oh, how I love your law! . . . I love your commands more than gold" (Psalm 119:97, 127). God gave us his lovable commands because he loves us!

 TALK: Isn't it great that God loves you enough to provide what you need to love him and others?

 PRAY: Express your thanks to God for his wise love.

 ACT: Spend some time today worshiping the God behind the Bible's commands.

22 Which Testament Is Number One?

Bible Reading: 1 John 2:7-11

I am not writing a new commandment, for it is an old one you have always had . . . to love one another. 1 John 2:7

Alexander's parents bought him a ruler with all the books of the Bible printed on it. At church camp he even learned a rap. But he still always got stuck somewhere after Obadiah. Worse yet, he couldn't figure out why that was so awful.

Talk about it: Does the front part of the Bible matter today?

Yes! Jesus said, "I did not come to abolish the law of Moses or the writings of the prophets. No, I came to fulfill them" (Matthew 5:17).

The Ten Commandments, for example, teach us loving things to do—and unloving things to avoid—in our relationships with God and others:

1. *Do not worship any other gods besides me* says your love for God should be pure—unrivaled by any person, thing, or idea.
2. *Do not make idols of any kind* says to focus your loving dedication to God on *him*—not on religious props or fake gods.
3. *Do not misuse the name of the Lord your God* says your loyalty to God includes respect for his person and his name.
4. *Remember to observe the Sabbath day by keeping it holy* says you should honor God by spending time weekly in worship and rest.
5. *Honor your father and mother* says to express love for your parents by respecting and obeying them.
6. *Do not murder* says you show your love for others through a huge regard for human life.
7. *Do not commit adultery* says to stay faithful and pure for your spouse or future spouse.
8. *Do not steal* says you care for others by respecting their possessions.
9. *Do not testify falsely against your neighbor* says you show love through honesty and truthfulness.
10. *Do not covet* says love for others should focus on what you can *give* to others instead of how you can *get* what belongs to them.

God doesn't want us guessing about what love looks like. He lovingly, clearly spells it out in his commands. We have an incredibly caring God!

 TALK: What good does the Old Testament do you?

 PRAY: *God, teach us right and wrong through your unchanging commands.*

 ACT: Memorize the books of the Old Testament or the Ten Commandments.

23 So Is Grace Good Enough or Not?

Bible Reading: Hebrews 10:1-10

The old system in the law of Moses was only a shadow of the things to come, not the reality of the good things Christ has done for us.
Hebrews 10:1

Kalli looked puzzled. With her forehead scrunched up and half of her upper lip raised, her whole face curled up in a big question mark. She wasn't the only one in her Sunday school class looking lost. "Some of this Old Testament stuff is really strange," she said to her teacher. "I mean, as Christians are we supposed to follow the Old Testament—or not?"

"Well, let's start with the really big difference," Mr. Swan suggested. "You've probably noticed that Christians don't follow the Old Testament practice of sacrificing animals to get right with God."

"Yeah," she said, nodding. "No one ever told me to bring a pet cow or pigeon to church—and leave it here. But why did God tell people to sacrifice animals? And if animals got people right with God in the Old Testament, why did Jesus have to die?"

Mr. Swan explained that in the Old Testament, people offered grain and birds and animals as acts of worship. A truly special sacrifice happened each year on the Day of Atonement (see Leviticus 23:28). Yet these sacrifices had to be repeated year after year, because they didn't fully cleanse people from their sin. Worshipers still felt guilty. They knew they needed something more.

Jesus was that "something more." When Jesus came to earth, he did away with the sacrifices of Old Testament faith by paying the penalty for our sins once and for all.

When Jesus died, he did for us what we couldn't do for ourselves. As Christians we trust in Jesus as God's payment for our sins. His death on the cross means we don't need to please God by trying to be perfect. Or by paying for our sins with our life. Or by shedding the blood of animals.

Sometimes as Christians we wish we could fast forward past the Old Testament and jump straight to Jesus. But the whole Old Testament was written for our instruction (see 1 Corinthians 10:11). And the sacrifices of Old Testament times were a picture of how Jesus would give his life to bring us forgiveness. God used hundreds of years of sacrifices to paint a picture of the awfulness of sin and humankind's deep need for a real Savior. He must think those are important lessons for us to learn!

 TALK: How was Jesus a better sacrifice than animals?

 PRAY: *God, we're grateful that your love for us never changes. Thanks for providing Jesus as the perfect and complete sacrifice for our sins.*

 ACT: Come up with a way to explain to a friend what Old Testament sacrifices have to do with what Jesus did for us.

24 A Little Rest and Relaxation

Bible Reading: Matthew 6:19-24
You cannot serve both God and money. Matthew 6:24

"Okay. I get the point that I can't toss out the front half of my Bible or the commands it contains," Kalli said. "But look at the Ten Commandments. A Christian friend and I had a big blowup about the fourth commandment—the one about 'keeping the Sabbath holy.' Does it mean that I'm sinning if I do homework on Sunday? Or if I make somebody else work because I eat out—or watch Sunday afternoon football? My friend said the Bible says we can't work or even do homework on Sundays."

Here's the first half of an answer. Christians today aren't required to follow the *Old Testament Sabbath law*. In fact, it's the only one of the Ten Commandments not repeated in the New Testament. Following that law would mean halting all work between sundown Friday and sundown Saturday. That's the Jewish Sabbath.

But here's the second half of the answer. The *moral principle behind the law* was kept by the early Christians who reserved the first day of the week—Sunday—for rest and worship (see Acts 20:7; 1 Corinthians 16:2; Revelation 1:10).

So glue those two parts together: You don't have to obey the Old Testament Sabbath law, but you should reserve one day each week for rest and worship (see Hebrews 10:25).

Sunday works because that's when most Christian church services are held. Christians who can't escape work on Sunday should take part of Sunday or another day for worship and rest. They can attend the Saturday evening services that many churches now have.

And that isn't just a good idea for grown-ups. If you're a student, school is your job. So God wants you to figure out how to keep homework from crowding out the time for worship and rest he wants to give you.

Now, you're probably sweating about those football players forced to work on Sundays because you want to crash on the couch in front of a good game. Well, you aren't sinning by watching ball games, running around in the yard, eating in a restaurant, or going shopping on Sunday. If the people serving you want to obey God, they will choose another day of the week for rest and worship. If they don't, that's their choice, not yours.

God wants you to experience a once-a-week special focus on him. He also wants rest for you. And that worship and rest is a gift to *you!*

 TALK: What do you think of a God who *wants* you to take time each week to rest and worship? Is that a loving gift or what?

 PRAY: *God, thanks that you love us so much you want us to rest and worship you.*

 ACT: What do you do as a family to make Sunday (or another day) a day of worship and rest?

25 Up Close and Personal

Bible Reading: James 4:7-10
Draw close to God, and God will draw close to you. James 4:8

So what do you want to do to get even closer to God than you are now?

(a) climb in an SR-71 Blackbird spy aircraft and soar to 80,000 feet
(b) climb Mt. Everest
(c) have stilts permanently welded to your legs

Just kidding. Getting close to God has nothing to do with getting *physically* closer to the heavens. Your goal is to get closer *relationally.* That's a great desire. In fact, just being interested in getting up close and personal with God is a step in the right direction.

Talk about it: What real attempts have you made to get close to God? What worked best? What didn't?

When you want to get close to God, here are three biggies to try:

First, think straight about God. There's not a shadow of doubt that God wants to be your incredibly close friend. Even more than you want to be near him, he wants to be near to you. So if you ever worry that God isn't interested in you, whack those thoughts right out of your head. They aren't from God. He loves you and will pull as close to you as you let him.

Second, spend time with God. That translates into the nitty-gritty activities of reading his Word and talking to him in prayer. So open his book. Tell him about your fears and hopes. Thank him for loving you and wanting to be your tight friend. Confess your sin and ask him to help you stay close to him by doing the things that please him.

Third, spend time with people who like to spend time with God. You pull close to God through worship—singing praises to God with other Christians, talking to him, thinking about him, remembering how much he loves you, recalling what Christ did for you, and gaining bonus insights into his Word by studying with other Christians.

Your key is found in James's simple words: "Draw close to God, and God will draw close to you" (James 4:8). With every step you take toward God, he takes a giant stride toward you. You can't get closer to God just by fitting a few "Christian" things into your life. But you can get closer to him by having a purpose-filled relationship with him and asking him to help you get to know him better!

 TALK: How are you trying to get close to God? Does anything need to change?

 PRAY: *God, thanks that you want to be our incredibly close friend.*

 ACT: What one thing do you want to do today to draw close to God?

26 No Lie

Bible Reading: Ephesians 4:25
> Put away all falsehood and "tell your neighbor the truth."
> Ephesians 4:25

Anthony was dumbfounded. *I thought Justin and I were friends,* his brain noodled. *If he doesn't want to play, he should just say so. This is the fourth time Justin has told me his aunt Beatrice died and he had to go to her funeral.*

Talk about it: Do you have friends who make excuses instead of telling you the truth? Or do they tell fibs to dodge things they don't want to do?

Justin could have told Anthony, "I don't want to play right now." Or he could have spoken honestly and said, "I don't want to play because you always mess up my room and don't help pick up, and I hate getting in trouble." Or he could have been totally blunt and blurted, "Look, last time you were here you ran over my dog with your bike and made my cat so nervous she lost all her hair five minutes after you were out the door. *Stop calling me!"*

Perhaps you can identify with Justin. If you have a friend like Anthony, you might wonder if it's okay to tell a little lie once in a while. But you might as well ask, "Is it okay to put your hand on a red-hot burner sometimes?" or "Is it okay to step in front of a roaring freight train sometimes?" or "Is it okay to drink rat poison sometimes?"

Telling the truth is one of those absolute, always-right kind of things to do. That's because God always tells the truth. It's never right or good to lie. Not even sometimes. Not even a little.

Telling the truth can be tough at times. But doing right is always right, even if it isn't always easy.

In the long run, doing your life God's way is better for you and everybody. Believe it or not, the people around you really want you to be truthful with them. If you tell the truth even when it's hard, people will think, *Wow!* Your friends, classmates, relatives, and neighbors will trust what you say.

Sure, there are some times you'll need to say, "I can't answer that." Or "I'd rather not say." Or you might need to just tell someone, "I really appreciate the gift," without explaining that you hate the color. Make it a personal rule always to speak the truth, but to speak it in love (see Ephesians 4:15). There's a good chance that your dedication to truth-telling will motivate others around you to be honest too.

 TALK: How are you doing as a truth-teller? How can you be honest and kind at the same time?

 PRAY: *God, you are always totally honest with us, yet you are also totally kind. Help us to speak as wisely as you do.*

 ACT: Maybe you feel lost on a trail of lies you've been telling for a long time. You can start being honest today!

27 Can the Garbage

Bible Reading: Philippians 4:8
Fix your thoughts on what is true and honorable and right.
Philippians 4:8

Boris, a big black horsefly, was starving. He buzzed around the outside of the house, banging up against the windows, looking for a hole to get in. He wanted to get inside so he could feast on scraps and crumbs lying around in the kitchen. But the house was locked up tight, and the famished horsefly was getting desperate.

As Boris circled the house again, he spied the garbage can in the backyard. Flying closer, his eyes bugged out with delight. On the grass next to the garbage can was a big hunk of moldy lunch meat that had been thrown away earlier in the day. Boris swooped down and started eating. It was delicious, so he stuffed himself. Even when he felt as if he couldn't eat any more, he still kept munching away.

When Boris tried to fly away, he was too bloated to get off the ground. He cranked his wings up to full speed, but he was still too heavy to get airborne. He needed some kind of a head start to launch him into the air. Looking around the yard, he spotted a lawn mower sitting on the sidewalk. He dragged himself heavily to the lawn mower and started climbing up the wheel to the engine. He trudged heavily up the long arm of the mower to the handle. He thought, *Now I can jump off and my wings can take over and fly me home.*

Boris got his wings buzzing as fast as he could and then stepped off into space. But he was still too heavy, and the chubby horsefly plummeted to the cement and exploded with a splat. Boris's final thought before impact was, *I should never fly off the handle when I'm full of baloney.*

Whoops.

As Boris proved, nothing good ever comes from filling up on garbage.

That's especially true of some of the garbage you might be tempted to put in your head. It's not wrong to watch television, listen to hit music, or watch videos. But God wants you to be wise about what you put into your mind through those media. There's a lot of garbage served up by the TV programs, videos, and music popular in our culture. And like Boris, those who feed on trash are likely to crash.

You know which media are no better for your mind than rotten meat or moldy bread is for your stomach. You wouldn't dine on a plate of garbage, so think about how important it is to be just as picky about what you watch and listen to!

 TALK: What are you putting into your head these days? Is it good for you?

 PRAY: *God, give us your wisdom as we think about the media we consume. Help us guard our minds.*

 ACT: Do you need to change the kind of media you consume? Act today!

28 Sucked into the Sewer

Bible Reading: James 1:12-16

Temptation comes from the lure of our own evil desires. James 1:14

"I think it sounds cool," Kara said in a hush. "I want to find out what it's like."

Janine knew Kara smoked. Last summer when Janine stayed at her cousin Kara's house, Kara showed her some cigarettes and started to light up. When Janine threatened to call her parents—and never do a sleep-over again—Kara promised she would never bring the cigarettes out again. Kara had kept her promise—so Janine never told her aunt and uncle or her own parents. But now Kara was talking about smoking pot.

Curiosity can be like a crocodile loose in the sewers of New York City. You hardly even know it's there. But then it suddenly climbs out of the drain, seizes you by the throat, and drags you down into the muck. And this beast isn't a figment of your imagination.

Curiosity can either be a blessing or a nightmare. There's a whole world of good things to be curious about. You can wonder what a career is like—and go explore. You can imagine what white-water rafting is like—and go try.

But often what we're most curious about are the things that God says are off-limits. God says they'll hurt us, but we don't believe him. God says they're out of bounds, but we spend time poking our nose through the fence, imagining what it would be like to take part.

That's when curiosity suddenly turns into temptation. James explains how it works. "Each one is tempted when, by his own evil desire, he is dragged away and enticed. Then, after desire has conceived, it gives birth to sin; and sin, when it is full-grown, gives birth to death" (James 1:14-15, NIV). As sure as allowing a crocodile to thrive in the sewer will turn you into a snack for a hungry reptile, letting wrong desires grow will snatch you into sin.

Follow these two tips when you catch yourself wanting what you shouldn't:

- *Deal with your curiosity immediately.* If it's a desire for something wrong, talk to God about it *before* it has a chance to grow big teeth.
- *Surround yourself with friends who share your values.* Promise each other that you'll talk sense into each other if your desires ever draw you into dangerous situations.

Your curiosity is one of God's greatest gifts to you. But be on your guard when your curiosity causes you to desire evil things. God wants better for you!

 TALK: How can curiosity pull you into places you shouldn't go? How can you fight against that?

 PRAY: *God, we want the right things. Ignite our desires for you and everything good.*

 ACT: Who can you talk to when the lure of doing wrong grows strong? Pair up with a friend who can help you guard your heart.

29 An Attitude of Gratitude

Bible Reading: Exodus 20:17

> *Do not covet your neighbor's house. Do not covet . . . anything else your neighbor owns. Exodus 20:17*

Shane has a professional-grade skateboard. Betsy has a rare show dog. Yoko has her own TV and phone. Francisco has a sound system loud enough to bust windows on a whole block. And Travis? He wants it all.

The crisis of wanting what everyone else has isn't new. And God knew all about overheated wants way back at the time when he first gave the Ten Commandments. In fact, he thought that dealing with desire was a topic big enough for its own commandment. It happens to be number ten.

All nine of the other commandments deal with *actions* toward God and people. The one dealing with desire gets at *attitude*—the stuff we want.

In the tenth commandment God tells us not to "covet." That's a weird little word. But it means having a big desire to possess something that belongs to somebody else. Coveting isn't just about liking a thing. It's being miserable because you don't have it. And being willing to do just about anything to get it.

God recognized all sorts of things that would drive us wild with desire—things we would covet. He listed houses and spouses, servants and animals, and the catch-all "anything else your neighbor owns."

You might not want a friend's house. (Well, maybe you do—the one with the swimming pool.) But your friends may have a lot of little things you want. And it doesn't matter whether the goods belong to your next-door neighbor or to Mr. Wal-Mart or Mr. Best Buy. If you're miserable with desire, you're coveting.

There's only one known cure for coveting. It's *contentment*. It's growing an attitude of gratitude for what you already have—whether that's a little or a lot.

Does that sound impossible? It's not.

Listen to how Paul managed to be happy no matter how much he had. He wrote, "I have learned how to get along happily whether I have much or little. I know how to live on almost nothing or with everything. I have learned the secret of living in every situation, whether it is with a full stomach or empty, with plenty or little" (Philippians 4:11-12). That's contentment.

Having lots of stuff might or might not be God's will for you. But being thankful is always in God's plan when you belong to Christ Jesus (see 1 Thessalonians 5:18). Do you have an attitude of gratitude?

 TALK: When have you wanted to get a good thing in a bad way? How can you encourage one another to lower your demands?

 PRAY: *God, we desire a lot of things. But we really want to desire only the things you want for us—in your way and in your timing.*

 ACT: Make a list of what you're thankful for! Post it where you can see it!

Find Friends to Help

Bible Reading: 2 Timothy 2:20-22

Run away from the evil young people like to do. 2 Timothy 2:22, NCV

You and your friends notice the new boy at your church's weeknight meeting for kids. But no one exactly rushes up to say hi. Actually, you stand in your circle ignoring him from across the room. You feel a twinge of conscience telling you to go talk to the boy, but you easily shake it off.

Which of the following thoughts might keep you from being friendly?

- ☐ *He can fend for himself. I had to when I came here.*
- ☐ *I'm a girl. The boys should talk to him.*
- ☐ *I'm a boy. The girls should talk to him.*
- ☐ *He looks like a dork.*
- ☐ *Someone else must have invited him. Not my worry.*

Face it: A couple of those excuses are iffy. Most are downright icky.

There's a good chance that after this episode of unfriendliness you'll feel more twinges—guilt, this time. On the way home you might feel bad for a while that the new boy couldn't bust into your circle. Maybe he was a fellow believer who really needed a friend that evening. Or maybe he was a kid who doesn't know Jesus—and now he's been blown off by Christians.

What you needed was a nudge to do the right thing at just the right moment. Now it's too late.

Talk about it: How could a friend determined to do the right thing have helped you in that situation?

The Bible tells you all about the kind of friends who could help. You can call these "2 Timothy 2:22 friends." The friends identified at the end of this verse help you ditch evil (run from it) and chase good (pursue and keep on pursuing friends who reflect God's good character). Wouldn't choosing good be a lot more fun with friends around to help you?

If you're looking for help to live like a Christian, then 2 Timothy 2:22 friends are the people you can count on to nudge you in the right direction. They'll help you show the attitudes and actions God says are best. Choices are still yours alone to make, but right friends can help you make right choices!

TALK: How could 2 Timothy 2:22 friends help you day to day? Do you have friends who help you make good choices, including your choice of additional friends? If not, how can you find some?

PRAY: *God, help us choose friends who will pull us closer to you. We want friends who can help us choose to do the right thing.*

ACT: Spend some time with your 2 Timothy 2:22 friends today. Or make a plan to find some!

1 The Greatest Job on Earth

Bible Reading: Mark 16:15-18

Go into all the world and preach the Good News to everyone, everywhere. Mark 16:15

For the last twenty minutes of each school day, Jeff serves as a student assistant to Mr. Rittmaster, the music teacher. Most days he helps with paperwork, straightens up the room, and totes messages around the building.

Late one afternoon Mr. Rittmaster called Jeff to his desk. In front of him was a pile of rubber-banded cash. A *big* pile.

"Jeff, I need you to do something important for me," he said as he slipped the bills into a manila envelope. "This is the $850 we took in at the music fest last night. I need you to take it to the office."

Jeff had never seen a wad of cash like that. His eyes widened as he nodded and took the envelope. On the way to the office, Jeff couldn't help but feel proud that Mr. Rittmaster had trusted him with the delivery. He grinned when he handed over the envelope and told the secretary what it was.

Talk about it: When has someone shown great trust in you—like asking for your help with an important task? How did it make you feel?

Chances are you liked being taken seriously. Most of us work our incredible best as a way of thanking a person who puts so much trust in us.

As Christians we've been given the most important job on earth. The God of the universe has an ultraimportant package. It's the message that salvation comes from Jesus alone. God wants the package carried to people all around the world. And guess who he intends to deliver it? Yep, it's you and me!

One of the last, clearest, and most important commands Jesus ever gave his disciples was to "go into all the world and preach the Good News to everyone, everywhere" (Mark 16:15; see also Matthew 28:18-20). This "great commission" isn't just a big task. The responsibility of sharing the truth about Jesus with the world is a big *gift*. It's a privilege that comes with the amazing promise that Jesus Christ will always be with us to help us complete the task.

Your all-powerful God could have found an endless number of ways to tell the world about his Son. He could have jotted it on the clouds for everyone to see. He could have covered the planet with angels shouting out the message of Christ. But instead he trusts the great message to us. Be glad to serve God. And be faithful to deliver the package!

 TALK: How does it make you feel that God has trusted you with the important message of his love and truth?

 PRAY: *Lord, thank you for trusting us to share the good news of your Son with others today.*

 ACT: How would you like to have a part in taking God's message to the whole world? Plan with your family how you can start.

2 Missionary in the Mirror

Bible Reading: 1 Corinthians 9:16

Preaching the Good News is not something I can boast about. I am compelled by God to do it. How terrible for me if I didn't do it! 1 Corinthians 9:16

Nora thought that missionaries were always out-of-style and out-of-touch—until she met Dan Barker, that is. One Sunday morning during a fall missions festival, Dan fired up the engine of his classic Harley-Davidson motorcycle. He roared his Hog up the center aisle of church to announce an interesting sermon that Sunday night. That evening, decked out in leather from head to toe, Dan told what it was like to talk about Jesus with bikers from Alaska to Argentina.

Nora suddenly realized that missionaries could be mighty cool.

Missionaries are ordinary people. But they do understand Christ's command to his followers to "go and make disciples of all the nations" (Matthew 28:19).

You became a missionary as soon as you trusted Christ to be your Savior. That doesn't mean you have to jump on the next flight to some place like "Ukarumpa." What it really means is that *wherever* you go and *whatever* you do, your words and actions help people understand better who Jesus is.

You might have a tough time seeing yourself as a missionary. You wonder if you're good, smart, or spiritual enough. But if you think that way, think again:

- *God gives you the power to do what he commands you to do.* The Holy Spirit lives inside you, so you have everything you need for the task.
- *God doesn't expect you to be perfect.* You are useful to God in spite of your faults and failures.
- *God doesn't give you the job of being a missionary all by yourself.* God plunked you down as just one part of a world of believers. The job belongs to all of us.
- *God brings the results.* It's not up to you to change anybody's heart or force anyone to trust in Christ. You share his message through your words and actions, and he takes responsibility for the results in people's lives.

You are sent by God to share the Good News of Jesus Christ wherever you go. And you are his chosen representative to your next-door neighbors, your classmates, and to people all over the world. What an awesome privilege!

 TALK: How does it feel to know that God has chosen you to be his representative?

 PRAY: *God, thanks for making us your representatives. Help us believe that we are up to the challenge!*

 ACT: Talk to someone today about what Christ has done in your life.

3 Do You Have a Target?

Bible Reading: 1 Corinthians 9:24-27

You also must run in such a way that you will win. 1 Corinthians 9:24

Picture this: You have a God's-eye view of your school, and you're looking down at yourself as you listen in total fascination to your favorite teacher. In fact, you're sitting atop the Hubble Space Telescope and you have the superhuge lens zoomed up close on you. Just you.

Now widen that shot.

Exactly how many students sit in your row?

Count them. Name them if you can.

How about in your classroom? How many students do you see?

Now pull your view out wider. How many people are in your grade?

And how many students are in your whole school?

Do you have a good guesstimate of each of those numbers? Parents, can you approximate how many people work with you?

Here's the point. God has an even better view than your superhuge zoom lens. And God's goal for evangelism is to reach everyone he can spot in a wide-angle shot of the whole world.

Reaching the world is a job he's given to the whole church—that's not a task you can tackle by yourself. You could easily get discouraged by the hugeness of that task, so you need to zero in on your part of the job.

Your efforts to share Jesus need to focus first on your inner circle—your friends, teammates, classmates, neighbors, and so on. And you can zero in further by asking this: Of all the people near you, who needs to know Jesus? Ask God to remind you of several people within your zoomed-in picture frame. Write down their names.

These are people you want to pray for. You can keep your list of names in a place where you are sure to see it often, and pray for these people daily.

These are people you want to surround with love. You can help people learn to trust you by spending time with them and being their friend.

And these are the people you want to share Christ with. You can watch for and create opportunities to share Christ with them, and invite them to respond.

Someone once said, "If you aim at nothing, you will surely hit it." You have the privilege of sharing Christ with your non-Christian friends. Do you want to know the secret to success? Zero in on your target and plan how to hit it!

 TALK: God had a plan to reach you with the Good News. What is your plan to reach the people in your zoomed-in zone?

 PRAY: *God, help us to be willing messengers who will share the Good News. Help us create a plan to reach people, just like you had a plan to zero in on us.*

 ACT: Talk with other Christians about how you can work together to spread the good news of Christ to your classmates, neighbors, and teammates.

4 After God Made You, He Broke the Mold

Bible Reading: Psalm 139:13-18

Thank you for making me so wonderfully complex! Psalm 139:14

Shelby was spooked. Minding her own business walking through the mall in her hometown, suddenly she saw her twin sister.

That wouldn't be so weird if Shelby *had* a twin sister.

Shelby's head spun. Maybe she and this look-alike girl had been separated at birth. Or maybe Shelby's parents had secretly cloned her. Or maybe a freak mutation had produced a girl who looked amazingly like her.

All right, all right. That was all made up! Truth is, you'll live your whole life and never run into anyone who matches you perfectly—inch for inch, pound for pound, nose to nose, ear to ear, hair to hair. Even "identical" twins display physical differences. And even if your *outsides* happen to look similar to someone else, no one can even begin to describe the differences on your *insides*. We have an obvious variety built into our brain. Our background creates even bigger differences. All of those things add up to make each of us a wildly unique person.

When it came to making you, God crafted you to be one-of-a-kind. Of the billions of people alive right now on Planet Earth, *no one* is just like you. You fill a place in God's perfect design. You might not know all the details of why God designed you exactly the way he did. But *he* knows. Even before you were born, he had every moment of your life already laid out.

Maybe you're brainy and wish you were good at sports instead. Or maybe you're quiet and would prefer to be the life of the party. Yet every quality has something valuable about it. So don't waste your life wishing you had someone else's hair, body, talents, or abilities. Every minute you focus on becoming someone else is time you're missing out on being you.

God is overjoyed by variety. So there's no way we should expect him to make people all alike. His love for our differences shows in the way he created us. Tall, short, fat, skinny. People who need glasses. People who like to grow beards. Brown eyes, blue eyes. People of all different skin tones and hair colors. God made them all.

God has given you special personality qualities and skills—things that make you *you!* Only when you appreciate those traits will you develop them to the fullest. And only when you put to use all the gifts God has given you will you be everything God planned for you to be!

 TALK: Think of the special qualities that God has given each member of your family. How can you each use those gifts to serve him?

 PRAY: *Lord, help us to value the unique qualities you have given each member of our family.*

 ACT: Show your appreciation for each family member's uniqueness today.

5 Thank God for Elbows!

Bible Reading: 1 Corinthians 12:1-7

A spiritual gift is given to each of us as a means of helping the entire church. 1 Corinthians 12:7

Chances are that when you think about the most important parts of your body, elbows don't even make your top-ten list. They don't keep you alive, like your heart. They don't give you the ability to reason, like your brain. They don't even help you hear or see or sniff.

Yet life would be rough without elbows. Stretch out your arms and imagine life without these joints. You couldn't fix your hair, brush your teeth, or aim your food anywhere near your mouth. You couldn't play the flute, French horn, or violin, though you could handle one or two low notes on a trombone. And you would look really stiff swinging a baseball bat or tossing a football.

Elbows aren't beautiful. But without them, life just wouldn't work very well.

Paul says that the body of Christ is made up of people with different spiritual gifts—special abilities for serving other believers and reaching out to non-Christians. The Bible promises that *you* possess one or more of these unique abilities. God wants you to use his gifts to express his love through you.

Spiritual gifts include many abilities, from preaching and teaching to giving, encouragement, and mercy. Maybe you're still trying to find out what your gift is. Or you're afraid that you might not have one at all. Don't worry. It's there, and God knows exactly what it is.

That's a truth you accept by faith—that is, God said it, so you can trust it's true even if you can't see right now exactly what your gift is. You can relax and enjoy knowing God has some special ability he's put inside you. And you can look forward to God bringing it to light as you learn how to share your life with others.

Here's the hitch: Some gifts seem way more important than others. But just as our forgotten elbows play an important part in the human body, every spiritual gift is needed in the body of Christ. One gift isn't any better than another, because "it is the same God who does the work through all of us" (1 Corinthians 12:6).

Your gifts make you significant not only to God, but to your whole world. You might think you're just an elbow. Yet whether you realize it or not, you are a needed part of God's plan. No one else can do the job God designed you to do!

 TALK: How have you used your talents and spiritual gifts to benefit others?

 PRAY: *God, help us to use our gifts to serve you—and to bless others.*

 ACT: Are you wondering how you can figure out your spiritual gift? Start by volunteering for a variety of service activities at your church. The things you enjoy and do well will give you a good clue about your spiritual gifts!

6 More Love than You Can Handle

Bible Reading: Jeremiah 31:1-6

I have loved you, my people, with an everlasting love. With unfailing love I have drawn you to myself. Jeremiah 31:3

Heather's friends tease her because her mom won't buy her the hottest jeans—even if they had the money. Jacob doesn't fit with his friends anymore because he didn't make the football team. And ever since Su-Jung refused to help her best friend cheat on her homework, her friend has made her feel like a real loser.

Talk about it: How have your friends let you down recently? How did you feel?

We've all been there. Just when we needed their love the most—well, if we were passing out grades, they would have flunked. Friendship is a great gift from God. But it can also hurt us too, because even the best of friends don't love us perfectly.

Have you ever noticed how people often require us to measure up to their expectations if we hope to keep them as our friends? They make us feel like we have to earn their love and acceptance by acting exactly how they want. Some expect us to keep up with the latest hairstyle or clothing trends to stay in the group. Others accept us only if we get good grades or do well at sports. Still others want us to act up before they accept us. If you think about it, we spend a lot of our life trying to live up to others' standards to earn their love.

That's what makes God's love so awesome. There isn't anything you *have* to do to gain his love and friendship. In fact, there's nothing you *can* do. His love is *unfailing* because he never fails you or lets you down. He loves you just the way you are. He will never leave you.

You never want to lose that kind of love. And the great news is that you never will, because God says that he loves you with an *everlasting* love. He will always love you no matter what!

You are significant to God, and it can never be otherwise. His acceptance of you never depends on your performance. Remember that God as your heavenly Father affirms you, loves you, and drenches you with significance. He loves you with all your special strengths and is there for you in your weaknesses. And when people let you down, remember that God is always with you, loving you just the same.

A God who loves this way is worthy of our affection and devotion. Enjoy his love, and thank him today!

  TALK: How is God's love different from that of other people around you?

PRAY: *God, help us not to worry about being just like other people so we can win their love. Thanks for loving and accepting us just the way we are.*

 ACT: Since God has shown you this kind of unfailing and everlasting love, how would you like to show love to a friend or family member today?

7 Is the Bible Holy or Holey?

Bible Reading: John 19:35

This report is from an eyewitness giving an accurate account; it is presented so that you also can believe. John 19:35

Jessica didn't know what to say. She sat in her front row desk in science class and listened as Mr. Miller blasted the Bible. He said that after centuries of scribes translating and copying the original text, there was no way to prove that the Bible we have today says what the authors first wrote. On top of that, he claimed that the Bible was filled with historical and scientific errors and couldn't be trusted.

Mr. Miller's words cut through Jessica. She had always believed the Bible was the Word of God, reliable in every way. But how could she disagree with her teacher?

Talk about it: Do you know people who don't believe that the Bible is true—and they think it's their duty to make you question it as well? How do you handle that?

Maybe your faith has been rattled by a teacher or friend who insists that the Bible is full of holes. But let's look at some of the facts about the Bible that Mr. Miller forgot to mention:

- The Bible was written over a period of sixteen hundred years by about forty different authors, yet the message is consistent throughout.
- Jewish scholars who copied the text of the Old Testament followed strict guidelines to ensure they copied everything exactly as it was.
- The events recorded in the New Testament—including Jesus' resurrection from the dead—have been confirmed by historical writings from the same time period.
- The Old and New Testaments are the most accurately preserved and widely proven documents of the ancient world.

It's true that the Bible contains some pretty unbelievable stories—miraculous things that can't be explained by science, such as Jesus raising Lazarus from the dead or feeding five thousand people from five loaves of bread and two fish. But as the book of Acts points out, the events recorded in the Bible "were not done in a corner" (Acts 26:26). In other words, many people saw them happen and testified that they were true.

The next time someone tries to convince you that the Bible is full of holes, tell him solid evidence confirms it is the true, accurate, and holy Word of God.

 TALK: What facts about the Bible help you believe it is true?

 PRAY: *God, show the truth of your Word to people who don't believe it. Thanks that we can rely on your accurate Word.*

 ACT: Do you have a friend who needs to hear these truths? Spend time asking God for wisdom in how you should pass along these facts—then make a plan to share!

8 Standing on the Promises of God

Bible Reading: Matthew 4:1-11

People need more than bread for their life; they must feed on every word of God. Matthew 4:4

The kitchen chair looked fine. But when Michael sat down to dinner, one of the chair's legs snapped in two. As he tumbled to the ground, Michael reached for the table. The only problem, however, was that he nabbed a corner of his place mat, which happened to be holding a tall glass of milk and a plate loaded with spaghetti. A little crack in the chair leg meant Michael wound up wearing his dinner. The chair just couldn't hold Michael's weight.

Some people think the Bible is just like that old chair with the broken leg. They figure it has some nice things to say about God and love and faith. But they suspect that under pressure the Bible will fall apart—that it can't stand up under the weight of hard questions.

Talk about it: What do you think? Is the Bible valuable only because it has a nice message, or is it the totally true Word of God? How do you know?

If we believe that Jesus is the Son of God—that he is true and all-knowing—then we should believe in what *he* taught about the Bible. Jesus himself said that "the Scriptures cannot be altered" (John 10:35). In Matthew 12:40, he related the experience of Jonah as fact, not fiction. Over and over he referred to the Scriptures in his teaching, and obviously regarded the teachings, historical details, and events of the Old Testament as accurate.

We see Jesus' attitude toward Scripture very clearly in the account of his temptation in the wilderness. Each time Satan hurled a question or temptation at Jesus, our Savior responded by quoting Scripture. Not only was he totally convinced that the Word of God is true, but he used it as a powerful weapon to defeat his enemy.

To Jesus, the Bible wasn't just a good book with inspiring stories. It was a reliable account of human history, a powerful picture of God's involvement in our life, and a dependable promise of God's faithfulness.

Proverbs 30:5 says that "every word of God proves true." You can be sure that the Bible is God's true and accurate message to people. It's not like an old chair that will crumble under the slightest amount of pressure. It's the solid truth of the Lord that will remain standing no matter what.

 TALK: How does Jesus' obvious faith in the Bible help you to believe that God's Word is trustworthy? Does it encourage you to trust in the Bible with all your heart?

 PRAY: *Lord, thanks for giving us a reliable message of your love and truth.*

 ACT: Jesus was able to recite Scripture so well because he had devoted his time to studying and learning it. Choose a Bible verse to think about and memorize today.

October

9 Details, Details

Bible Reading: 2 Peter 1:16-21

It was the Holy Spirit who moved the prophets to speak from God.
2 Peter 1:21

As Cody's family finished their dinner at the Golden Wok restaurant, a waitress passed out fortune cookies. Cody was excited about the cookie, but he was blown away by the small slip of paper inside. "You will experience great victory," it read.

"Mom, Dad, look at this," he said, showing his parents the message. "This must be talking about my baseball tournament this weekend. We're going to win!"

Cody's dad chuckled. "Son," he said, "of course we hope you'll win the tournament. But if you do, it certainly won't be because of this fortune cookie."

"What do you mean?" Cody asked.

"The fortunes they write are just fuzzy messages that could be true for almost anyone at any time. You can't stake your life on a fortune cookie."

"I'll tell you what you *can* take seriously," Cody's mother added. "The prophecies recorded in the Old Testament of the Bible were written hundreds of years before Jesus was born. They're the real deal."

Cody was interested. "Like what?"

"Like Jesus being born in Bethlehem," she said. "Micah predicted that. And Zechariah predicted that the Messiah would ride into Jerusalem on a donkey."

Cody's dad joined in. "*And* that he would be betrayed by a friend for thirty pieces of silver. And that his hands and feet would be pierced. The predictions by God's prophets all came true with 100 percent accuracy."

Cody's parents are right. Biblical prophecy makes one of the strongest arguments for the truth of God's Word. Consider this: Jesus Christ fulfilled *all* the prophecies about the Messiah that were recorded in the Old Testament. The chances of one man fulfilling forty-eight major prophecies, according to Peter Stoner in *Science Speaks,* is 1 in 10 to the 157th power. That's the number 10 followed by 157 zeroes. We can't even imagine a probability that small!

That tells us two important things about the reliability of the Bible. First, as Peter wrote, the Old Testament writers who predicted the Messiah weren't speaking on their own but were inspired by God. Second, because Jesus fulfilled the prophecies of the Messiah, we can trust that he was who he said he was—the Son of God.

God didn't want there to be any doubt in your mind that his Word is true, so he gave undeniable proof through historical evidence and biblical prophecy. Why? Because he loves you and wants you to trust him.

 TALK: How are biblical prophecies different from fortune cookies and horoscopes?

 PRAY: Praise God for giving you his true and reliable Word.

 ACT: Do you rely on false sources of information about the future, like horoscopes? Make a habit of going to God's dependable Word instead!

10 A Life Worth Watching

Bible Reading: 1 Peter 1:13-20

[God] paid for you with the precious lifeblood of Christ, the sinless, spotless Lamb of God. 1 Peter 1:19

Tears rolled down Kristin's cheeks as she closed her hymnal and stood to exit the church. As her family filed out of the pew at the end of her great-grandma's funeral service, she wondered how all the people who looked up to Grandma Nelson would get along without her.

Kristin's great-grandma came to America with her parents when she was even younger than Kristin. She couldn't speak a word of English, but she adapted to a new culture, married, and raised five children. She sent sons to war and buried a husband and a daughter. She arrived in poverty and always lived modestly. Through ninety-five years of life she relied on God's strength to bring her through every trial. She was the best example of love and obedience Kristin had ever seen.

When it comes to knowing and doing right, there is no substitute for a living, breathing, right-under-your-nose example.

But Jesus Christ does one better. No, you can't see him in person. But through the Bible you can read about him in action and witness his awesome acts as the ultimate example of doing right. Jesus not only taught the moral law of God, but unlike any other human being in your life, he also lived it to perfection.

The Bible leaves no doubt about the purity of Christ's life.

Peter said, "He never sinned, and he never deceived anyone" (1 Peter 2:22). He is "the sinless, spotless Lamb of God" (1:19).

Paul declared that Christ "never sinned" (2 Corinthians 5:21). He "faced all of the same temptations we do, yet he did not sin" (Hebrews 4:15).

John's first letter talks often about Christ's sinlessness: "There is no darkness in him at all" (1:5); "Jesus Christ, the one who pleases God completely" (2:1); "Christ is pure" (3:3); and "There is no sin in him" (3:5).

Pilate said, "I find nothing wrong with this man!" (Luke 23:4). Pilate's observation has been the verdict of history. Jesus lived a truly perfect life.

Even the best human examples of obedience and purity fail at times. Say thanks to God for the good examples you have in your family members, church leaders, and friends. But keep your main focus on the *perfect* example by filling your mind with the words and deeds of Jesus Christ, the Son of God.

 TALK: How do you feel to have such an awesomely perfect leader?

 PRAY: *Jesus, we're glad you blazed a trail for us, showing us the right way to live and love.*

 ACT: Did you know that *you* are an example for all of the people around you, just as Kristin's great-grandma was? Be faithful to God in your words and actions today so that others will be inspired by your life.

Bible Reading: Mark 10:46-52
When Jesus heard him, he stopped and said, "Tell him to come here."
Mark 10:49

Makoto knew there was going to be a new student in his class, but he had no idea this person would roll into the room in a wheelchair. Makoto had really never known anyone who was handicapped before, and he felt a little uncomfortable around Derrick. Apparently, so did the rest of his classmates, because the only person who even spoke to Derrick all morning was Mrs. Davis.

In the cafeteria that day, Makoto noticed that Derrick was eating all alone. The new kid glanced up at Makoto and his friends and made eye contact with Makoto.

"Hey, you guys," Makoto whispered to the group with him, "why don't we go sit with the new guy?" His friends rolled their eyes at him and asked if he was kidding, then took their lunch trays and walked to the far side of the room. Makoto just stood there, not sure if he wanted to pay the price of doing right.

Jesus was the perfect example of love. And one of the huge characteristics we see in him is that he loved everyone, no matter who they were, what they looked like, or what their problems were. Jesus loved everybody—even those not welcomed by the people around him. He ministered to blind beggars, dishonest tax gatherers, cruel Roman soldiers, and stuffy religious leaders. He was a friend to the wealthy and the poor, the educated and the uneducated, adults and little kids, those who believed in him, and even those who didn't. He surrounded himself with people of a variety of backgrounds, stories, and needs . . . and he loved them all.

Jesus loved everyone because he knew that all people are God's handiwork. As he looked into people's eyes and saw the creative touch of his Father, he acknowledged their value and worth.

Jesus said that other people would know Christians by the love we show for one another. Since God is our heavenly Father, we should be able to see, like Jesus did, his handiwork in everyone we meet. This doesn't mean that we will always like everybody or be best friends with everyone. But we can treat them all as valuable in the sight of God.

The next time you bump into someone different from you, focus on how God made that person according to his perfect plan to bring himself glory and honor. Get to know that person. Determine what makes him or her special. And dream of all the unique ways God can use that person. That's loving like Jesus loves.

 TALK: Is there someone you know who is in special need of love? How can you show Christ's love to this person?

 PRAY: *God, help us see value in everyone we meet, because you created them in your image.*

 ACT: Share God's love with a person in need this week—even if that person is very different from you.

12 The Love Pro

Bible Reading: John 15:9-13

I command you to love each other in the same way that I love you.
John 15:12

Here's a really tough question to vote on. Suppose you want to be a world-whipping soccer player. Who would you rather spend time with: *(a)* a professional horse-racing jockey? *(b)* a professional couch potato? or *(c)* a professional soccer player?

You chose *(c)*, right? Of course. The most excellent way to sharpen your soccer skills would be to spend time with the person who plays your sport to the highest level. It wouldn't make sense for you to study the example of anyone but a pro.

Many people claim to be experts on love. But if we really want to learn how to love, we've got to get close to the person who loved best. Jesus is "the love pro." He lived a perfect life of love here on earth, and when we follow his example we can't go wrong. So the important question is this: "How did Jesus love?"

You can't help but notice that Jesus' love is *sacrificial.* He gave of himself in a thousand everyday ways. And his giving never stopped.

After Jesus' cousin John the Baptist was killed by an evil ruler, for example, Jesus longed for some time alone. Yet when the crowds followed him, he didn't shoo them away. Out of compassion he stayed and ministered to them. He taught them, healed them, even fed a mob of more than five thousand men (see Matthew 14:13-21).

Just before Jesus was arrested in the Garden of Gethsemane, he was still giving. He healed the ear of one of the men who had come to arrest him. And in this agonizing and sorrowful time, Jesus took care to teach his disciples until the very end (see Matthew 26:50-54).

Jesus' death on the cross for us was the ultimate example of sacrificial love. As Jesus said, "The greatest love is shown when people lay down their lives for their friends" (John 15:13). Jesus gave his life willingly to rescue us, his people, from having to pay the price of our own sin—a price we could never have paid.

Amazingly, Jesus commanded us to love others in the same way he loves us. Most of us won't ever be in a position where we need to give up our life for our friends. But we can be sure God will put us in places where we will be asked to sacrifice our time, money, energy, comfort, and convenience.

It's not easy to love like "the love pro," but it's what real love is all about!

 TALK: What does sacrificial love mean? How can you show it to a friend or family member this week?

 PRAY: *Lord Jesus, thanks for loving us at all costs. Please help us love others like you do.*

 ACT: Think of a way you can imitate Jesus' sacrificial love today. And do it!

13 Tapping Into the Power of Love

Bible Reading: 1 Corinthians 13:1-13; Galatians 5:22-23

When the Holy Spirit controls our lives, he will produce this kind of fruit in us: love, joy, peace, patience, kindness, goodness, faithfulness, gentleness, and self-control. Galatians 5:22-23

Beautiful Hollywood couples claim they're in love—but their love rarely lasts.

TV commercials promise a car you can fall in love with—at least until next year's model catches your eye.

And *you* might be well-known for your affection for a certain frozen treat—whether you love to lock lips with a root-beer Popsicle, a low-fat raspberry yogurt, or a double scoop of death-by-chocolate ice cream.

Those are all everyday ways we use the word "love." But Christ's love goes far deeper. Over the past few days you've heard what Christ's love is like—and how you can demonstrate his love in all your relationships. In 1 Corinthians 13 the apostle Paul pulled all of this love-talk together in "the love chapter."

The love chapter helps us to learn more about Jesus Christ because love is perfectly wrapped up with his character. He is the ultimate example of love, so each of these qualities of love actually is also a trait of Christ's. Try reading verses 4-7 (NIV), replacing the word "love" with the name of Christ. See what new insight you can gain about Christ's character:

> *Christ* is patient, *Christ* is kind. *He* does not envy, *he* does not boast, *he* is not proud. *Christ* is not rude, *he* is not self-seeking, *he* is not easily angered, *he* keeps no record of wrongs. *Christ* does not delight in evil but rejoices with the truth. *Christ* always protects, always trusts, always hopes, always perseveres.

Nothing in the world compares to Christ's love! What's amazing is that God wants to place the love of Jesus Christ in *us*. In fact, if you are willing to allow God's Holy Spirit to flow through you to others, you can receive the power to love as Christ loved.

The Holy Spirit wants to live and love through you. The more you allow him to remake your attitudes and actions, the more his love will become your love. In fact, try reading 1 Corinthians 13:4-7 again. Only this time, put *your* name where it says "love." Do this with each member of your family, and spend some time praying that God will fill each of you with his love. His power working in you will make it possible for you to love others like Christ loves!

 TALK: Which quality of Jesus' love do you appreciate the most? Which is the hardest for you to show?

 PRAY: *Thank you, Lord Jesus, for your amazingly awesome love. Help us show your love to others, so they will see you in our life.*

 ACT: This week find a way to practice the quality of love you want to develop.

14 Beyond "Being There"

Bible Reading: 2 Corinthians 1:3-7

When others are troubled, we will be able to give them the same comfort God has given us. 2 Corinthians 1:4

When Cady came home from school, she immediately ran up to her room, flopped down on the bed, and burst into tears. Michelle had just told her she was moving away, and Cady's heart broke at the thought that she wouldn't see her best friend again.

Before long, Cady heard a soft knock. She lifted her head to see her big sister, Darby, standing at the door.

"What is it, sweetie?" Darby asked, as she came and put her arms around her. Cady just sobbed in her sister's arms and told her all about Michelle's news.

"I'm so sad for you," Darby said. "You and Michelle have so much fun together."

Cady wiped her tears and nodded. "She's my best friend," she said. "We tell each other everything."

"I'm sorry," Darby said as she hugged Cady again. "I'm sorry you have to go through this. It hurts me to know that you're hurting. I love you, and I'm here for you whenever you want to talk."

Do you know someone who has experienced a loss like Cady's? Maybe someone you know has lost a pet, faced a tough move, or even had a family member who died. Or it could be that you've experienced a loss yourself. It can really be hard.

Cady was fortunate to have someone in her life who understood that her greatest need at that painful moment was *comfort*. That sounds obvious, but comfort might not be what you think it is.

Comfort is *not* a "pep talk" urging you to hang in there, tough it out, or hold it together. It's not an explanation of why bad things happen or an attempt to convince you that you shouldn't be sad. It isn't even a bunch of positive words about God being in control or a promise that everything will be okay. In time all those things can be helpful, but they don't fill our pressing need for comfort.

One way God shares his comfort is through people. You receive comfort when you know you aren't suffering alone—when people feel sad with you and tell you they hurt with you. Paul said, "When others are happy, be happy with them. If they are sad, share their sorrow" (Romans 12:15).

When people you love are hurting, be a friend who comforts. Be with them in their time of hurt, and let them know that you hurt with them. And when you need comfort, it's okay to ask for it. It's how God wants to heal you when you hurt.

TALK: What does true comfort look like? What does comfort sound like?

PRAY: Ask God to help you show this kind of comfort to your family members and friends when they hurt.

ACT: Go show comfort to a hurting friend.

15 Working Your Way through the Pain

Bible Reading: Romans 8:26-30

We know that God causes everything to work together for the good of those who love God and are called according to his purpose for them. Romans 8:28

A month after Amy's dad died, her friends, who had been so sympathetic at first, didn't seem to care so much anymore. She was still a jumble of emotions when they started saying things like "It's time to move on," and "You have to think about other things," and even "Snap out of it!" Amy wondered what was wrong with her that she couldn't just shake the pain.

What no one explained to Amy was that when tragedy strikes so close to home, you can't escape a powerful emotion called *grief*. In fact, there's a pattern of grief most people go through. Grief can last weeks or months, but people often pass through five clear stages. Knowing these stages can help you or a friend understand the swirl of emotions that people experience when tragedy hits:

Often the first response to grief is *denial*. You can't believe such a terrible thing has really happened. One of the ways your mind tries to handle grief is to think, *No way. This isn't happening to me.*

The second stage of grief is *anger*. You start to ask, *Why did this happen?* When you don't find a good answer, you might lash out at people you think are responsible, at the person who died and left you alone, and even at yourself, thinking you are partly to blame.

The third stage of grief is *bargaining*. You want relief from this awful event. You promise you'll do anything for God if he will just fix the situation and make the pain go away.

Another stage of grief is *depression*. You realize you can't undo the tragedy. You feel overwhelmed with sadness—and maybe fear, anxiety, or loneliness.

The final stage of grief is *acceptance*. As time goes by, you start to accept the reality of your loss and begin to put life back together.

It's normal—and healthy—to experience the five stages of grief when you experience a sad event in your life. Some of those stages may come and go and come back again. There's nothing wrong with you or your powerful emotions. And in time your grief will give way to better feelings—a certainty that God loves you and is still in control of your world.

TALK: What are those stages of grief all about? Could you use that knowledge to help a hurting friend?

PRAY: *God, help us understand the swirl of emotions we feel when we face horrible hurt. Help us know how to help our hurting friends through their grief.*

ACT: You might not need this information today. But tuck those five stages of grief in your memory, because sooner or later you or a friend will face the powerful emotion of grief.

16 Help to Make It Through

Bible Reading: Galatians 6:1-5

Share each other's troubles and problems, and in this way obey the law of Christ. Galatians 6:2

"When my Grandma died, it's like I froze," Ryan admitted. "My homework wasn't getting done—especially a huge research paper for social studies. But Taylor got on the phone every night with me. He talked through the project little by little. We brainstormed a topic, talked about research sources, went to the library together to check out books, and came up with a list of questions to ask the teacher when I got stuck. Taylor even helped me get the right format for my footnotes. I couldn't have survived that semester without his help."

When you lose a loved one through death—or you face any other life-altering tragedy—you need more than just comfort to get through the pain.

Talk about it: What other kinds of help do hurting friends need?

Here's a big one. *Support.* It's another type of help you can offer friends who suffer. And it's a type of assistance many of us find easy to offer. So what's the difference between comfort and support? Check this out:

People supply *comfort* when they share your emotional pain.

People supply *support* when they help in practical ways.

Life doesn't stop after a tragedy. But the heavy emotions you feel often drain the energy you need to keep up. When you hurt, you usually need help for a while just to get normal tasks done. You need people to carry your burdens.

You might not like to admit you need help. But don't push away the support others offer. God put Galatians 6:2 in the Bible because he knows there are times we need the support of others. Whenever bad things happen, that's a time to let others do things for us—like helping with homework. It's one of God's great ideas for meeting our needs when we need it most.

So what if I need something and nobody steps up to help? *Ask for it.* There's nothing wrong with telling a trusted friend or a leader at church about our needs—and explaining exactly what kind of help we need.

God didn't design you to go through life's toughest moments alone. You can't survive without both comfort and support from others. After a while your needs won't seem as large as they do at first, but don't expect to dive back into life-as-usual right away. Let your friends and family care for you as long as you need it!

 **TALK:** How have you shared comfort and support with a hurting friend? How did it help?

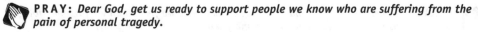 **PRAY:** *Dear God, get us ready to support people we know who are suffering from the pain of personal tragedy.*

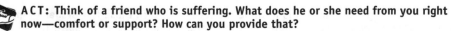 **ACT:** Think of a friend who is suffering. What does he or she need from you right now—comfort or support? How can you provide that?

17 Down but Not Out

Bible Reading: Genesis 37:18-28; 50:20
God turned into good what you meant for evil. Genesis 50:20

Joseph was in a bad spot. He had tight relationships with God and his father—a marvelous thing. Those special friendships, however, made his older brothers extremely jealous—a hazardous thing. His brothers were so jealous, in fact, that they thought about killing him. Instead, they came up with a cruel plan to sell Joseph into slavery and report to their father that he had been killed by wild animals. Not only was Joseph sold as a slave, but he wound up in an Egyptian prison for refusing to do wrong.

You might not have experienced exactly what Joseph did, but maybe you've been rejected by friends. Maybe you've been punished for something you didn't do or ridiculed for doing what was right.

Talk about it: When people have teased you or made you feel left out, did you wonder what God was doing while you were in pain? What did you expect him to do to make things right?

We can only guess what Joseph felt as he wasted away in a prison cell. But he didn't let his circumstances keep him from trusting in God and doing what was right. Why? Because he still believed that God was in control.

If you read Joseph's whole story, found in Genesis 37–50, you'll discover how God eventually sprang Joseph from prison and promoted him to a high position in the land. God had a special plan for Joseph that resulted in him saving a whole country from starvation. And in a unique twist, Joseph even got the chance to save the lives of his brothers.

Joseph's story proves how God unfailingly sticks with his people and turns even evil circumstances to our good. There's a phrase woven throughout Joseph's story that tells the key to his success: "The Lord was with Joseph." God is working out a master plan to bring himself honor—a plan that rolls together the positive happenings of life with the experiences that appear downright rotten.

None of us can escape being roughed up by others. But we can remember that when people poke us with evil, God will bring good out of the pain. Even when you feel ditched by others, God hasn't ditched you. He's right there with you. And he's in control.

 TALK: Talk about a time you suffered for doing the right thing. How did God show himself faithful to you? How was God honored through it?

 PRAY: *Lord, help us to trust that you're in control, even when things seem to be out of control. We know you are always there for us.*

 ACT: As you choose to do the right things today, remind yourself that God is with you—no matter what!

18 Happy Dependence Day!

Bible Reading: James 4:7-10
When you bow down before the Lord and admit your dependence on him, he will lift you up and give you honor. James 4:10

Most Americans can't let July 4 slide by without a celebration. The party isn't just about fireworks, hot dogs, or family togetherness while parked in a traffic jam on the way to the beach. It helps us remember the principles America stands for. And it's a salute to the day that our nation adopted the Declaration of Independence, announcing our freedom from Great Britain and the founding of a new form of government. That first Independence Day was a huge step for our country—but a lousy day for the king of England.

Do you realize, though, that there is something better than being *in*dependent? It's being *de*pendent on God.

You've probably never thought of throwing a Dependence Day party. Dependence is humbling, isn't it? We don't like to admit that we aren't able to do everything for ourselves.

God gives each of us strengths and gifts to serve him. But as soon as we try to serve him in our own strength, we are declaring independence—and that's exactly the opposite of what God wants. God wants us instead to admit a fact we find hard to force out of our mouth: Without his strength working through us, we are *weak*.

At the moment when Paul felt the most helpless in life, here's what the Lord told him: "My gracious favor is all you need. My power works best in your weakness." Then Paul added, "So now I am glad to boast about my weaknesses, so that the power of Christ may work through me" (2 Corinthians 12:9). Bragging about your weakness sounds like a weird way to gain power, but that's how God works!

As Christians we have all chosen to admit that we need God to save us. Trusting Christ means saying we could never earn his love and forgiveness by our own strength. But the next step God wants us to take is to admit we also totally need his help as we live the Christian life.

There are many things God made you to do well. But before you launch into life in your own strength, admit that you depend on God for his power and guidance in everything you do. Don't be frustrated or ashamed when you have to rely on God. You can celebrate your *de*pendence . . . every day of the year!

 TALK: Is it hard for you to admit you need help? Why?

 PRAY: *God, we want to rely on you in everything we do. Show your power through us as we live in dependence on you.*

 ACT: Give this dependence thing a shot. Try serving God today in a way you don't think you're good at—and ask him to fill you with power as you do!

19 Turn to the One Who Understands

Bible Reading: Philippians 4:10-14

I can do everything with the help of Christ who gives me the strength I need. Philippians 4:13

Bethany didn't know what was up. She was hanging out at home on a Friday night feeling more than a little bored, so she tried calling some of her friends. Oddly, none of the girls were home. She hadn't heard that anything special was going on. But it was like all of her friends had just vanished.

Bethany tried not to worry about it, but the next week at school one of the girls let it slip that they were all at Jasmine's house for a slumber party. Jasmine's mom told her she could invite five friends, and Bethany was the one who had been left out. She felt like she'd had a big red "L" painted on her forehead: *Loser.*

You're normal if you want to have friends and be liked. Like every other human being on earth, you have a built-in need to be important to others. And at times you are likely to face situations where you're left out. How you handle those painful times can either make you stronger or set you up for further hurt.

Talk about it: What do you think Jesus knows about rejection?

You've maybe never pictured Jesus Christ as a friend who knows all about rejection. Isaiah, however, described him this way: "He was despised and rejected—a man of sorrows, acquainted with bitterest grief. We turned our backs on him and looked the other way when he went by. He was despised, and we did not care" (Isaiah 53:3).

Can you feel a bit of what Jesus must have felt? We may see him as our Lord who was always worshiped and adored. In reality, many people rejected him—and still do! The religious leaders of his day accused him of horrible things—some even claimed that he was the devil! When Jesus was nailed to the cross, he endured mockery not only from the soldiers but from the heartless crowds. Some of those he loved the most turned their backs on him.

So when you feel rejected, ridiculed, or ignored by others, remember that your dear friend Jesus knows better than anyone what you are going through. He not only knows about the loneliness of rejection, he's the answer to it. He's right there with you, sharing your hurt and reaching out to encourage you. He's the one true friend who will never let you down. No matter how hurt you are, remember Christ is there to comfort your hurt—he really understands what you're going through!

 TALK: Is it hard to imagine that Jesus—the powerful Creator of the universe— understands and cares about what you're going through? Why or why not?

 PRAY: *Jesus, thanks for understanding, caring, and comforting us when we hurt.*

 ACT: Do you have feelings of rejection you want to tell Jesus about? Talk to him now—and pass on to a lonely friend the comfort he provides.

20 The Wisdom of "Foolish" Words

Bible Reading: 1 Corinthians 1:18-20

I know very well how foolish the message of the cross sounds to those who are on the road to destruction. 1 Corinthians 1:18

Jose couldn't wait to get to school that morning. He had to talk to Tony, the kid who sat next to him in homeroom.

"You should have been there!" Jose exclaimed.

"Been where?" Tony asked, shuffling books in his desk.

Jose explained. "My dad took me to the NASCAR race this weekend. It was so awesome! You should have seen the cars."

"I've seen cars," Tony said.

"No, you don't understand. These were awesome. When they revved their engines it was like you could feel it shake your bones. And they were so fast, you thought they were going to fly right off the track and land in the stands."

Tony shrugged. "They just go around and around. It sounds kind of stupid."

Jose's enthusiasm suddenly disappeared. "All I know is, it was cool," he said with a sigh. "If you had been there, you'd think so too."

Talk about it: Have you ever tried to explain an experience to someone—and he just didn't get it? How did you feel?

Frustrating, isn't it? It's so clear to you, but it might not make much sense to your friends who didn't experience it for themselves.

It can be that way when we talk to some people about Jesus. The Bible tells us to be ready to share our faith with anyone, but sometimes our explanation of Christ and what he has done in our life can sound weird. You share the startling news that Jesus is the Son of God, and some people blow you off. You tell someone that you have trusted Christ as your personal Savior, and she might laugh. You talk about something you learned in church or from reading the Bible, and they just don't get it.

That's what Paul was talking about. He said that the message of Christ—the very message that is so superpowerful to those who believe—sounds like foolishness to others.

But don't be discouraged. Go ahead and share with confidence, because you are telling about God's complete wisdom and truth. You never know how the Holy Spirit is using your words. After all, it's not up to you to change anyone's heart. So you can be faithful to talk about what God has done in your life, trusting he will use it to honor himself.

 TALK: How do people react when you talk about Jesus?

 PRAY: *Lord, help us to be good friends today. Use our words and kindness toward people as a way to open up their hearts to you.*

 ACT: Can you name three friends who need to trust Christ as their Savior? How can you let God use you to show them he wants a relationship with them?

21 Take It Away, Jesus

Bible Reading: 1 Corinthians 1:21-25
Christ is the mighty power of God and the wonderful wisdom of God.
1 Corinthians 1:24

There once was an old scientist who traveled from university to university delivering lectures on his field of expertise. After long weeks of travel, the scientist and Bob, his chauffeur, became friends.

The scientist tired of giving the same lecture over and over. So one day—knowing his chauffeur had heard his lecture so many times he had it memorized—the scientist asked Bob to give the lecture for him.

Bob gave it a whirl, and the lecture went off perfectly. No one knew that the "scientist" talking to the audience was the chauffeur and that the "chauffeur" sitting in the front row was actually the scientist. There was even a question-and-answer time, but Bob had heard the scientist answer the same questions so many times that he answered them all perfectly.

Then someone asked a new question—a question Bob couldn't answer on his own. "That's a great question," he said confidently, "but it has a simple answer. It's so simple, in fact, that even my chauffeur can answer it." Nodding toward the front row, he added, "Take it away, Bob."

Bob was wise not because of *what* he knew, but because of *whom* he knew. He knew the answers because he had hung around the scientist. And as long as the scientist was close by, Bob had nothing to worry about.

As a Christian, you might not look too wise to the non-Christians around you. When people toss you tough questions about God, you might not always have the answers. But isn't it encouraging to know that you have a close friend who *does* know all the answers? Not only that, but he *is* the answer. His name is Jesus Christ, and Paul calls him "the wonderful wisdom of God."

Just as Bob the chauffeur spent a lot of time with the scientist and learned from him, so you need to make time to learn from Jesus. That means reading the Bible and listening to your parents, pastor, or Sunday school teachers when they talk about the Lord.

Even if you don't always know how to answer the tough questions, you can know that Jesus is always with you. Just look his way and say, "Take it away, Jesus."

 TALK: Has someone ever asked you a question about Jesus you couldn't answer? How does it help you to know that *The Answer* is always with you?

 PRAY: *Lord, help us learn to know you better so that we can answer the questions our friends ask. Thanks that you always know the answers.*

 ACT: What one question about your faith stumps you the most? Spend some time digging for the answer!

22 The Futility of Hoop-Jumping

Bible Reading: 1 Corinthians 1:26-31

Remember, dear brothers and sisters, that few of you were wise in the world's eyes, or powerful, or wealthy when God called you.
1 Corinthians 1:26

Have you ever seen pro athletes from rival teams being interviewed before a big game? They come on camera all pumped, talking up their team—and trashing the other guys. "We have the strongest defense in the nation," they brag. "There's no way they're getting past us today."

Bragging is part of the game. But it's pointless. No matter what athletes say and no matter how sure they are of stomping the other team, the game is still won or lost on the field.

It's easy to laugh at sports figures who try to impress others with their triumphs. But Christians often fall into the trap of relying on all the good things we've done to win God's favor.

Take a vote: Which of these great deeds are good enough to impress God—and maybe get someone into heaven?

- I got straight A's on all my Sunday school report cards.
- I played the accordion in church every week for fifty years.
- I was a missionary. Check out the hydroelectric plant I built for Bosnia.
- Oh yeah? Look at my Swahili translation of the Old Testament.
- Every Sunday I walked ten elderly ladies to church through a blizzard when the snow was up to my throat. And it was uphill both ways.

Those words sound as ridiculous as athletes before a game, don't they? God doesn't accept us because of great things we do. We don't have to jump through any hoops to earn his love. Why? Because Jesus is the One who already won our acceptance with God. He was the one-and-only adequate sacrifice for our sins. That's why the Scriptures say, "The person who wishes to boast should boast only of what the Lord has done" (1 Corinthians 1:31).

We could never have earned our way into God's family, but he accepted us anyway. And someday when we're together in heaven, we will all proclaim that we are there because of the grace of God. He provided Jesus Christ for our salvation. And God will get all the glory.

 TALK: How does it make you feel to know that you don't have to jump through hoops to earn God's love?

 PRAY: *God, thanks for sending your Son so we can spend eternity with you.*

 ACT: Tell a friend the Good News that God is already impressed with us because of what Jesus did.

23 Being the Right Kind of Friend

Bible Reading: James 1:17-18

Whatever is good and perfect comes to us from God above. . . . He never changes or casts shifting shadows. James 1:17

Emily's fifth-grade class was in the middle of a math test when Mrs. Chen got called out into the hall. Emily noticed the teacher had left the room, but she quickly focused her brain back on the word problem she was working on.

"Psst, Emmy," she heard from behind her. She glanced over her shoulder and saw her friend Charlotte leaning forward trying to get her attention. "I'm stuck. What's the answer on number five?"

"Shhh," Emily whispered. "I can't help you. That would be cheating."

"Don't be a dork," Charlotte said. "You know I didn't get a chance to study last night."

Emily turned back to her own desk, and then she heard the words she dreaded to hear: "Come on, Emmy. If you're really my friend, you'll help me with this test."

Talk about it: Was Charlotte right? Does true friendship really mean you'll do whatever your friends ask, even when you know it's wrong? Why—or why not?

This can be a hard truth for some of your friends to hear: True friends don't always do what their friends want them to do.

So how do you know the right way to treat your friends?

Well, you can keep looking to God's standards for friendships. You don't have to wonder if his standards are true because they are based upon God himself—his character and nature. God's standards of right and wrong are true at all times in all places for all people. The standards don't change because your friends think they should.

Sometimes that might mean you can't do what your friends want. But there's good news: When God says something is right, you can count on it to bring his good into your life—sometimes later, often sooner.

Next time you have a question about how to be a true friend, look to God's Word. You will discover that honesty is always right in your friendships because God is a true God—who is always honest. Friendship based on being honest and truthful is always right even if you lose a "friend" or two in the process. And when you let God be the model for your friendships, you'll be sure to make friendships that last.

 TALK: Why would you want to handle your friendships according to God's standards of right and wrong?

 PRAY: *Lord, help us not to give in when our friends want things that aren't what you want. Help us encourage them to seek God's best in their lives.*

 ACT: Have certain friends been causing you to give up your standards—getting you to do things you know are wrong? How are you going to break that bad habit today?

24 Soaring above the Storm

Bible Reading: Isaiah 40:25-31

Those who wait on the Lord will find new strength. They will fly high on wings like eagles. They will run and not grow weary. They will walk and not faint. Isaiah 40:31

Terry just got a D on his report card. Carlos was cut from the team. Shannon was back-stabbed by a friend. Situations like these can be heartbreaking. And for some the pain goes even deeper—like Melinda, whose mom and dad are going through a divorce. Or Suzanne, whose best friend was killed last month in a car accident. Or Corey, who was just diagnosed with a rare form of cancer.

Have you ever noticed that no one escapes hard times? Some of those times are life-and-death situations. Others are just frustrations or setbacks. But without exception, they all cause agonizing pain. They make us feel like our world is caving in. And at times like these there is nothing we need more than an eye-popping look at who God is. Think about this wonderful description in Isaiah 40:

- *God is all-powerful.* He created all of the universe—from the intricate design of the tiniest cell to the massive grandeur of the vast heavens. Nothing is too big or too difficult for him. Nothing is too tiny for his attention.
- *God is entirely loving.* Since God created all the stars and calls each burning ball of gas by name, how do you think God feels about you, his child created in his image? Jesus answered that question: "Look at the birds," he said. "They don't need to plant or harvest or put food in barns because your heavenly Father feeds them. And you are far more valuable to him than they are" (Matthew 6:26). God loves you more than you can even imagine.
- *God gives strength to the weak.* You might feel bogged down and beat up by difficult circumstances in your life. But you can put your trust in the Lord and not give up. He sees your needs and will give you strength to keep going—even to run, take flight, and soar high above the pressures of life.

Ponder what it means that God is *both* all-powerful and all-loving. If he were mighty but didn't love, we would spend our life fearing his anger and judgment. If he were loving but weak, he couldn't help us through our trials. The God we serve is both strong and kind, and that's why we can trust in him!

 TALK: What stormy situation have you faced in your life lately? Has God promised to give you strength to go through it?

 PRAY: *We praise you, God, because you love us enough to help us through our difficulties. And you are powerful enough to do it.*

 ACT: Build your trust in God today by memorizing Isaiah 40:31. And share that encouraging word with a friend.

25 Divorce Is a Dirty Word

Bible Reading: Mark 10:1-10

Since they are no longer two but one, let no one separate them, for God has joined them together. Mark 10:8-9

Mike and Jessica were both high school students when they met in the supermarket where they worked as clerks. They started to date and fell madly in love. They married before graduation and before their first anniversary Jessica gave birth to an adorable baby. But during their second year, Mike and Jessica fell out of love almost as quickly as they had fallen in. They ended their Cinderella romance with a divorce.

Most of us know some couples—acquaintances, neighbors, friends, maybe even parents—who have become victims of the divorce epidemic that rages in our culture. Sadly—and for a variety of reasons—divorce happens among Christians too. Divorce is a topic many Christians argue about today.

Divorce was a hot issue in Bible times too. The Old Testament referred to a man divorcing his wife if he "discovers something about her that is *shameful"* (emphasis added, Deuteronomy 24:1).

By the time Jesus arrived on the scene, there were two wildly different views of divorce among the Jews.

The Pharisees—the hard-nosed sticklers for detail—said "shameful" only meant "unfaithfulness." A husband could divorce his wife only if she ran off with another man. The second view said "shameful" meant *anything* that displeased a husband. A man could divorce his wife for any mistake—like torching his toast at breakfast or losing a sock in the clothes dryer!

When the Pharisees pushed Jesus to say what he thought about divorce, they were hunting for a reason to get rid of him. But Jesus dodged the trap. He didn't take sides. Instead, he let them know that in God's view of marriage, divorce is a dirty word. Jesus repeated God's first words on marriage: "A man leaves his father and mother and is joined to his wife, and the two are united into one" (Genesis 2:24). In God's original design for marriage, husband and wife were glued together into one unbreakable unit. Period. Divorce wasn't even in God's vocabulary.

Divorce at best is a last resort, the final option after all other attempts to resolve conflicts, solve incompatibility, and heal offenses have been tried and retried but have failed.

No one ever gets married planning to get divorced. But your best option is to fix in your mind right now that you someday want a marriage that will last a lifetime.

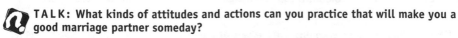 TALK: What kinds of attitudes and actions can you practice that will make you a good marriage partner someday?

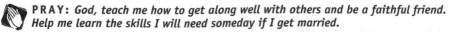 PRAY: *God, teach me how to get along well with others and be a faithful friend. Help me learn the skills I will need someday if I get married.*

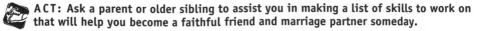 ACT: Ask a parent or older sibling to assist you in making a list of skills to work on that will help you become a faithful friend and marriage partner someday.

26 God's Version of Superglue

Bible Reading: Genesis 2:18-25

A man leaves his father and mother and is joined to his wife, and the two are united into one. Genesis 2:24

There's an incredible secret you need to know about married love. And you're old enough to know all about it. Ready? Here it is: If you want to have a long-lasting, love-filled marriage someday, you need one special ingredient: superglue.

You might be thinking, *Whoa! God wants me and my spouse to glue our eyebrows together so we'll always see eye-to-eye?*

Not exactly. God has a deeper kind of glue. Genesis 2:24 commands a man to be glued to his wife. That's what "joined" means. When husband and wife are glued together with God's superglue, they become one in a marriage that will last.

Falling in love—the emotional side of love—is a lot like the glue stick you have in your desk at school. It isn't strong enough to hold a marriage together. Even in the best relationships, feelings come and go. They don't make an unbreakable bond or a lifelong marriage.

But there's another kind of glue. It's like an industrial-strength adhesive. It's the only stuff that holds a marriage together. It's the superglue of *commitment.*

Oh, you're thinking, *you mean having a marriage ceremony.* No! Saying "I do" in front of a minister and signing a marriage license are part of it, but commitment is way deeper than that. Commitment means choosing daily to give yourself to your partner—and then the two of you giving yourselves to God as one. That kind of glue welds people together with such power that they can endure all the pressing, pulling, stretching, and twisting that life inflicts on them.

Someday your prince or princess will probably come along. You'll see fireworks explode in the sky. You'll hear guitars rock when he or she speaks. And you'll swear that you're in heaven whenever you're with that special person. That's the falling-in-love thing, and it's a beautiful experience. But putting a marriage together with that feeling alone is like trying to hold two bricks together with paste. You'll be ready to get serious about marriage only when you pop this important question: "Am I ready to glue myself to this person for keeps?"

When you and your loved one share the bond of commitment to God and to each other, the fireworks and guitars won't disappear. They just won't be as important as the superglue.

 TALK: What kind of glue are you counting on to keep your marriage together someday?

 PRAY: *God, teach us each day for the rest of our lives what true, loving commitment looks like.*

 ACT: Write a note to say thanks to the people who show you what the superglue of married commitment looks like.

27 What's So Funny?

Bible Reading: Ephesians 5:4

Obscene stories, foolish talk, and coarse jokes—these are not for you. Instead, let there be thankfulness to God. Ephesians 5:4

So have you learned any good jokes in the locker room—or at a slumber party? Do you have any you'd like to share right now—during family devotions? Maybe not.

You probably know firsthand how quickly guy-talk and girl-talk and even guy-girl talk can slide into the category of rudely crude. You've maybe heard some jokes that were hysterically funny—but that sizzled your ears.

Talk about it: Is it okay for the same mouth that says "I love Jesus" to also say "Did you hear the one about . . ."? Why—or why not?

Maybe you wonder what the fuss is about. Then answer this: If dirty jokes are no big deal, why don't you run home to tell them to your mom? If you won't share your most comic material with Mom, it's good to understand why. Fact is, crude humor makes us think our bodies are dirty . . . that it's okay to make fun of the opposite sex . . . and that bodies that grow up at different speeds and shapes are somehow defective.

The apostle Paul nailed down three kinds of things better left unsaid:

Obscene stories. That's an easy one. It's "filthy language," like rolling in the mud by making sin into a joke.

Foolish talk. Dirty jokes are usually about things you have no clue about—often to give the idea that you do. Paul literally called it "the talk of morons."

Coarse jokes. Those are the ones about your fabulous body parts—or your body functions—or the body parts and body functions of someone else.

As believers in a pure and holy God, "these are not for you." Here's another way to say that: Those words are "out of place" (NIV) and don't meet God's requirements.

So what's better? Thankfulness!

What does that have to do with anything? It doesn't mean you insert into conversations a "Praise Jesus!" where previously you would have told a foul-smelling joke. It does mean you have better things to talk about.

And that's because you have better things inside of you. Jesus said that "The mouth speaks the things that are in the heart" (Matthew 12:34, NCV).

Are "obscene stories, foolish talk, and coarse jokes" all that you have inside you? Of course not! God is remaking you from the inside out. So let your speech show off what he's doing in you!

 TALK: How can you do a U-turn on a conversation that's gone dirty? What are some better things to talk about?

 PRAY: *God, you've given us clean hearts. Help us to have clean mouths.*

 ACT: If you have some bad habits in your speech, ask a Christian friend to help you monitor your mouth and clean it up.

28 Loving People . . . Honestly

Bible Reading: Ephesians 4:14-16

We will hold to the truth in love, becoming more and more in every way like Christ, who is the head of his body, the church. Ephesians 4:15

Talk about it: Suppose you spotted a friend asleep in the middle of the street and a car was approaching. What would you do?

No question, right? You would run to the middle of the road and shake your friend awake—even if you had to slap him or splash a soda in his face. You would point to the oncoming car. You would grab him by the hand and run for safety.

That one was easy. But sometimes we see our friends making poor choices— choices that in the long run can be just as destructive as waking up in the middle of a road to meet an oncoming car face-first. Maybe you have friends in the habit of lying, stealing, or disobeying their parents. Or perhaps you know someone interested in smoking or even doing drugs. You know what you *should* say and what you *want* to say. But it's a little harder to spit out the words, isn't it?

Once again, since Jesus was the perfect example of love, let's look at how he loved people in tough situations.

The Bible tells us about a time when religious leaders dragged to Jesus a woman who had been caught sinning. Jesus didn't trash the woman for her sin, but neither did he ignore her wrongdoing. He kindly told her to "go and sin no more" (John 8:11).

Another time, Jesus met a Samaritan woman—a foreigner most Jewish people wouldn't have talked to. He knew she was living a sinful lifestyle. Once again, Jesus didn't put her down, but neither did he let her sin slide by. He lovingly helped her see that he was the only one who could truly meet her needs (see John 4:4-26).

Jesus even confronted Peter, one of his best friends in the world, when Peter stood in the way of God's purposes (see Matthew 16:21-23). And again, Jesus didn't attack Peter, but he didn't ignore his mistake.

Jesus spoke the truth to these people because he loved them. He knew they weren't living in a way that was pleasing to God, and he wanted them to experience God's best in life. He showed how truth and love can go hand in hand.

True love is honest because it seeks God's best in the lives of people we love. It's hard to see our friends making poor choices—choices that keep them from God's best and eventually bring them great harm. But Jesus has given us the perfect picture of how to help them. Follow his example. Be honest with your friends. It's the most loving thing to do.

 TALK: Why is it sometimes hard to tell your friends the truth when they are making harmful choices?

 PRAY: *God, give us strength and wisdom to speak the truth in love.*

 ACT: Do you have a friend who is getting into harmful behavior? Talk with a mature Christian about ways you can lovingly speak truth to your friend.

29 Love No Matter What

Bible Reading: Romans 5:6-11

When we were utterly helpless, Christ came at just the right time and died for us sinners. Romans 5:6

Chris and Phil were lifelong chums, friends since meeting at the playground wading pool when they were two years old. They had never even had a fight—until eighth grade, that is, when Andrew Patterson walked into their lives. Andrew's family had moved to their town from out of state at the beginning of the school year. One Saturday when Chris told Phil he would meet him at the roller-skating rink the way he always did, he was shocked. Andrew had already asked Phil to meet *him* there. And Phil had said yes!

So will Chris still be friends with Phil, or will he yell, "You dirty rat!" and never talk to him again? The answer depends on whether or not Chris has learned how to love like Jesus loved—unconditionally—no strings attached.

Jesus knows what it means to be let down and rejected by friends. When Jesus was arrested, "all the disciples deserted him and fled" (Matthew 26:56). Even Peter, who insisted he would never turn his back on the Lord, triple-denied him while Jesus stood trial.

Jesus could have resented his friends for walking away when he needed them most. But he forgave them. When he rose from the dead, he appeared to these same disciples and trusted them to do his work throughout the world. He even spent extra time with Peter, strengthening him for the enormous task ahead of him (see John 21:15-19).

Jesus' love also extended to the men who killed him. As he hung, nailed to the cross after a brutal beating by Roman soldiers, Jesus prayed, "Father, forgive these people, because they don't know what they are doing" (Luke 23:34).

And Jesus' unconditional love even extends to us. Paul wrote that we were "helpless" (Romans 5:6), that we were "still sinners" (verse 8), and that we were "enemies" (verse 10) of the Lord because of our sin. Even at our worst, Jesus Christ loved us and gave his life for us so that we could be "made right in God's sight" (verse 9). Because of his unconditional love, we can say with Paul, "Now we can rejoice in our wonderful new relationship with God—all because of what our Lord Jesus Christ has done for us in making us friends of God" (verse 11).

Aren't you glad you have a friend like Jesus? Let his unconditional love be your model in all your relationships with friends and family!

 TALK: Under what conditions is it hard to love someone? How would Jesus respond in those situations?

 PRAY: *Lord, we're so grateful to you for loving us unconditionally. Help us to show that kind of love to everyone around us.*

 ACT: Show some of Jesus' no-strings-attached love today to someone who has wronged you.

30 Claim It and Enjoy It!

Bible Reading: Hebrews 10:11-14

Our High Priest offered himself to God as one sacrifice for sins, good for all time. Hebrews 10:12

Trish told Angela a secret. Guess what? Angela told someone else. Ever since then, Angela has felt like a traitor, a two-timer, especially since Trish found out about it. Now every morning on the school bus, Angela apologizes to Trish.

Finally Trish stopped her. "Angela," she said, "I've already forgiven you."

"But I want to make sure that we're still friends," she insisted.

"Of course we are," Trish said. "I need you to believe that I've forgiven you."

Just like in our human relationships, some Christians have a hard time believing God has really forgiven their sins. They imagine God keeps a record of all our sins, waiting for the day when he will bring them up again and use them against us.

To experience the freedom of God's forgiveness, take these steps:

1. *Remember that God loves you unconditionally.* You are God's special child. He paid a high price for your salvation from sin—the death of his one and only Son. When you accept God's gift of salvation, you receive his forgiveness and become his own child. Sometimes you still disobey God, and you grieve him (see Ephesians 4:30). Sure, he might discipline you when you sin. But he does that out of love as well, because he wants you to stay close to him and experience his best (see Hebrews 12:5-12).

2. *Confess your sin.* At times we all disobey God because of our sin nature (see Romans 7:20-25). According to God's Word, the solution begins with confession (see 1 John 1:9). To confess means to agree with God that your disobedience is sin. God already is totally aware of your sinful attitudes and actions, but he wants you to admit it—to humble yourself before him and experience his saying "I forgive you."

3. *Claim God's forgiveness.* Christ has already forgiven you once and for all through his death on the cross (see Hebrews 10:12-14; 1 Peter 3:18). But to turn from your sin and start down the right path, it's important that you admit your need for forgiveness and accept the forgiveness that is already yours.

Claiming forgiveness is like discovering a treasure that's buried in your own backyard. God's loving forgiveness is already yours. Unearth it and enjoy it!

 TALK: Is it harder to accept God's forgiveness for some sins than for others? Why or why not?

 PRAY: *Father, help us to confess our sins and move on in the light of your love and forgiveness.*

 ACT: Do you still struggle with believing you are forgiven? Talk to a mature Christian about how you feel.

31 Are You Sure You're Sure?

Bible Reading: 2 Timothy 1:9-14

I know the one in whom I trust, and I am sure that he is able to guard what I have entrusted to him until the day of his return.
2 Timothy 1:12

Night after night little Ricky was scared to crawl into bed. He struggled to go to sleep as spooky thoughts kept him wide-awake. He saw creepy shapes float across the ceiling. He feared that monsters hid in the dark shadows of his closet. He thought he could hear big-fanged creatures munch on the dust bunnies under his bed.

Believe it or not, some of us are haunted by some even scarier spiritual questions. We might wonder, *Am I really saved? Has anything in my life really changed? If I'm a Christian, then why don't I feel any different?* We might think, *Maybe I'm not really a Christian. Maybe I didn't do it right.*

Talk about it: Do you ever worry that you really aren't a Christian?

For Satan, the enemy of your soul, every day is Halloween. Satan is always on the job, trying to scare the truth out of you and make you doubt your salvation—the fact that you really belong to God.

Doubts are common. But a Christian doesn't have to feel saved in order to be saved, any more than a millionaire has to feel rich in order to be rich.

In 2 Timothy 1:12 Paul said some awesome things in some interesting ways. He said that "I know the one in whom I trust," not just "what I trust." He also said, "I am sure that he is able to guard what I have entrusted to him." Paul wasn't just putting his faith in facts, but in a dependable friend. He was trusting the God who had proven himself worth trusting.

When you wonder whether you really are a Christian, read Isaiah 12:2 aloud several times: "God has come to save me. I will trust in him and not be afraid. The Lord God is my strength and my song; he has become my salvation." Then pray this Scripture-based prayer aloud:

Father, you are the one who saves me. Help me to trust and not be afraid. You give me strength and make me sing. Help me draw near to you with a sincere heart and a sure faith. Grab hold of my heart and give me sure knowledge that the gospel is true. Thank you for your promise that I belong to you—today and forever. In the name of Jesus I pray. Amen. (See Isaiah 12:2; 1 Thessalonians 1:5; Hebrews 10:22.)

 TALK: Do you ever wonder if you are really saved? Spend some time looking up the additional Bible passages listed above.

 PRAY: *God, thank you that we can trust our life to you—now and forever!*

 ACT: Write out the prayer above. Put it where you can see it often until God's assurance takes hold in your heart.

1
Close Your Eyes
to Blind Faith

Bible Reading: John 8:31-32
You will know the truth, and the truth will set you free. John 8:32

You're trying to tell a friend about Jesus when she starts to sound like a college professor. "So," she says with a creepy voice and one eyebrow raised, "can you prove with 100 percent certainty that Jesus rose from the dead?"

You're not sure where your friend suddenly got the jumbo-sized brain and smart-sounding question. Your answer comes out in a mousy squeak. "Umm, no."

Some people call our Christian belief in Jesus' resurrection a "blind faith." That's a belief accepted without any proof. Or they slam our faith with nasty labels like "ignorant," "irrational," or "unreasonable." Those are all big words that more or less mean the same thing as "dumb." If someone puts you down this way, you're probably left feeling red-faced. Odd. Stupid. Defeated.

Some people figure that if a truth can't be proven with 100 percent certainty, it's useless or untrue. If Jesus' resurrection or his claim to be the Son of God can't be proven with 100 percent certainty, they say, then the Christian faith isn't worth believing.

That's a myth. Few things can be proven with 100 percent certainty.

In a court of law, for example, a jury can never be 100 percent sure that someone committed a crime. But the jury weighs *the evidence* to declare that someone is guilty—or not—beyond a reasonable doubt.

In the same way, your belief that Jesus is God can't be proven with 100 percent sureness. But that doesn't mean it's stupid to believe the Christian faith. The apostle John wrote, "Jesus' disciples saw him do many other miraculous signs besides the ones recorded in this book" (John 20:30). Jesus, in other words, did many other things that demonstrated that he was the Son of God. The evidence the Bible provides doesn't include everything Jesus said or did, but what it does tell us is enough to form a well-grounded belief. John wrote in the next verse, "These are written so that you may believe that Jesus is the Messiah, the Son of God, and that by believing in him you will have life" (verse 31).

Your belief in Jesus is plenty smart. Blaise Pascal—a famous French mathematician, philosopher, and scientist—said that there is enough evidence for the Christian faith to convince anyone not already set against it. But there isn't enough evidence to bring anyone into God's kingdom who doesn't want to come.

 TALK: Answer in your own words: Why is it *not* foolish to believe in Jesus?

 PRAY: *Jesus, give us opportunities to share with our friends the truth about who you are and what you've done for us.*

 ACT: Is there a question about your faith that puzzles you? Ask a more mature Christian for help digging for the answer.

2 Believing Isn't Rocket Science

Bible Reading: Matthew 28:1-7

He isn't here! He has been raised from the dead, just as he said would happen. Matthew 28:6

A man and a woman wearing lab coats enter a laboratory. She holds a clipboard and pencil, and he clasps a small white rectangular object. The man puts the white object in a small glass tank filled with water. It bobs to the surface. The woman makes a note on her clipboard. The man again pushes the object to the bottom of the tank. It again bobs to the surface. The woman writes.

After performing the event over and over, the scientists come to a stunning conclusion: Ivory soap floats. It has been proven scientifically.

True or false: A science experiment is the only way to prove if a fact is true.

That's absolutely false. The scientific method is a great tool for getting smart, but it isn't the only way to prove something.

If science experiments were the only way to get at truth, then you wouldn't be able to prove that Abraham Lincoln was ever president of the United States. But just because Honest Abe's presidency can't be proven in a laboratory doesn't mean that it didn't happen. It *can* be proven with a different kind of evidence.

It's the kind of proof offered every day in law courts around the world, and it's the only kind of proof that applies to events in history. So how could you prove that Abraham Lincoln was president? You would provide evidence.

If you could find eyewitnesses, you would interview them. That's "oral testimony." You would gather copies of letters that Lincoln wrote, newspapers that reported on him, and books about him. That's "written testimony." You would offer exhibits of items such as his pocket watch, photographs of him and his birthplace, even his sugar bowl. That's "physical testimony." With that mountain of evidence, nobody has a problem believing in Abraham Lincoln.

That's called the "evidential" or "historical" method of proof, and it's how we can prove the resurrection of Christ. We can't gather any *oral* evidence, because no one is still alive from the first century. But we have the *written* evidence of the disciples in the Bible and the *physical* evidence of the empty tomb.

Your faith in Christ isn't blind. It's not stupid. The life and ministry of Jesus, his miracles, and his resurrection can be proven—and they have been. You can be sure of your faith—by the evidence!

 TALK: How would you respond to someone who said you can't prove the truth of the Christian faith?

 PRAY: *God, thanks for giving us a faith that we can be sure about.*

 ACT: Quiz each other later today or tomorrow: What three kinds of testimony count in the "evidential" method of proof?

3 A Difference That Counts

Bible Reading: 1 Corinthians 6:11

Now your sins have been washed away, and you have been set apart for God. 1 Corinthians 6:11

Suppose you're chatting with a non-Christian about Jesus. You think you're getting your point across with your gentle and ultrawise persuasion—until you get bopped over the head with this line: "Well," your friend smirks, "people who are dead stay that way. They don't rise from the dead."

You can't make Jesus rise again in a laboratory. But you can point to the Bible for evidence of the empty tomb. Along with that, you can supply an additional sign of life: the change that happens to people when they trust Jesus.

Talk about it: Do you think that the changed lives of Christians prove anything about the truth of what we believe?

Suppose you are a non-Christian. You have a friend who one day says, "You know, a year ago I trusted Jesus. He's totally changed my life. I used to scream at my parents. I always trash-talked my little sister. I was totally selfish. I'm not perfect, but I'm not that way anymore. Having a relationship with Jesus has made me a different person. And he's given me a peace and love and joy I never experienced before."

Would you believe her?

It's hard to argue with your friend if her life backs up what she says—if you can spot real change. But what if she's some weird spiritual mutant? What if she's the only one whose life has been changed by this Jesus guy?

Well, your friend isn't alone. Countless others have experienced the same awesome changes by turning their lives over to Christ. They don't claim that merely reading a book changed them. They don't say that a creepy encounter with aliens has left them altered forever. And none of them claim that their new power comes from inside themselves. They talk about one cause for their peace, joy, and victory over sin. It's Jesus Christ and his resurrection power.

When we want to prove that the resurrection of Jesus Christ actually happened, we can point to a difference obvious in millions of people from every walk of life and all nations of the world. And the change can be traced to one source—their relationship with the living Jesus Christ. That's evidence that your friend isn't selling you some crazy story. She's sharing a persuasive fact.

Your experience of Jesus is more than wishful thinking. You've met the risen Savior. And he's made a real difference in your life!

 TALK: When a non-Christian looks at you, what can that person see that points to God at work in your life?

 PRAY: *Dear God, change us so our friends can see your power at work. Make our life a convincing display of the power that raised Christ from the dead.*

 ACT: Explain to a friend some of the differences Christ has made in your life.

Bible Reading: John 20:24-29
Don't be faithless any longer. Believe! John 20:27

Not many people have nice things to say about the disciple Thomas.

After Jesus rose from the dead and appeared to the disciples behind closed doors, Thomas wasn't with them. So when the disciples told Thomas that Jesus was alive, he didn't believe them. "I won't believe it," he said, "unless I see the nail wounds in his hands, put my fingers into them, and place my hand into the wound in his side" (John 20:25). When Jesus later appeared to Thomas, the Lord took him up on his offer. He said, "Put your finger here and see my hands. Put your hand into the wound in my side. Don't be faithless any longer. Believe!" (verse 27).

Talk about it: What do you think of Thomas? Is he a model for our faith—or would it have been better to leave his story out of the Bible?

Okay, so Thomas wasn't as bad as Judas, the guy who betrayed Jesus. He might not even have been as awful as Peter, who denied the Lord three times. But of all the disciples—the twelve guys closest to Jesus during his three years of teaching and preaching—Thomas is usually lumped among the bad boys.

Many people put Thomas down because of his doubt. But they forget one fact: None of the other disciples believed until they, too, had seen evidence of the Resurrection. Everyone else had already seen Jesus' hands and side. What's more, Jesus didn't say to Thomas, "You were a really bad disciple for doubting me." Instead, he showed his disciple the evidence and *then* said, "Stop doubting." And finally, when Thomas did see the evidence, he uttered one of the loudest confessions of faith in history, calling Jesus "my Lord and my God!" (verse 28).

For some reason we think that doubt is totally bad. "*Real* Christians don't doubt," we say. That's a myth.

Doubt is actually the starting point of faith. In the Bible's original language of Greek, the meaning of "doubter" is "inquirer." An "inquirer" is someone inquiring, asking, or hunting for answers. Sure, there are dishonest doubts people use to distract others from trusting Jesus. Yet there are honest questions about faith.

You can learn these lessons from an honest doubter named Thomas: Doubt is natural. It's okay to be honest about your doubts. And if you're truly looking for answers, your doubts should be replaced by faith when Jesus shows you the truth.

Jesus doesn't want you to hide your doubts from him. He loves you. He even understands your questions.

 TALK: What doubts keep you from following Jesus totally?

 PRAY: *God, when it's hard to trust you, show us more of yourself and help us believe.*

 ACT: Do you have any friends who doubt God? What can you tell them about doubt?

5 Who Knows You?

Bible Reading: Psalm 91:1-12
He orders his angels to protect you wherever you go. Psalm 91:11

Trevor couldn't wait to reach middle school. He could finally take Tech Ed. He imagined that his first class project would be to put a loft in his bedroom. His next would be to build a house-sized half-pipe for backyard skateboarding. And his crowning achievement would be to erect an Olympic-sized ski jump on the empty lot behind his school.

Trevor was totally disappointed when he learned that Tech Ed class only lasted forty-five minutes. He was wildly discouraged when his teacher said his first assignment was to make a little knickknack for home, picking from a half dozen designs for napkin holders, recipe boxes, and dresser organizers. But Trevor doubled over in dismay when he received his project back. The grading sheet attached by the teacher screamed "F." At the top of the sheet was scrawled a question: "What is it?"

If you're looking at someone's thingamabob school project and you can't figure out what it is, there's only one place to find out. You ask its creator.

So if you're trying hard to figure out who *you* really are, who should you ask? The One who made you, of course. God is the One who knows exactly who you are.

So how exactly does God see you?

First, *God sees you as eternally lovable*. He is your Father. He created you in his own image (see Genesis 1:26-27). You are the best expression of his creative genius. In response to your faith in Christ, he welcomed you into his family as his child (see John 1:12-13). God loves you so much that he appointed his angels to watch over you (see Psalm 91:11-12).

Second, *God sees you as infinitely valuable*. At the Cross God declared to everyone listening that you are worth the gift of Jesus Christ, his dearly loved Son. If you ever put a price tag on yourself, it would have to read "JESUS!" because it was the price of Jesus' life that God paid to save you (see 1 Peter 1:18-19).

Third, *God sees you as thoroughly capable*. Paul boasted, "I can do everything with the help of Christ who gives me the strength I need" (Philippians 4:13). God trusts you so much that he left you on earth to complete the ministry Jesus began. He's given you the job of leading people back to him (see 2 Corinthians 5:20).

If you want a clear view of your true identity, you need to see yourself as God sees you—no more and no less. You're lovable, valuable, and capable. No doubt about it, that's what you are!

 TALK: Have you ever felt like a messed-up school project? Who do you listen to when you want to know who you really are?

 PRAY: *Father, help us to see ourselves as you see us—with your true view.*

 ACT: Tell a friend what it means to be lovable, valuable, and capable.

6 Switch On the Light

Bible Reading: Ephesians 5:8-14

Though your hearts were once full of darkness, now you are full of light from the Lord. Ephesians 5:8

Picture yourself strolling through a portrait art gallery. The room lights are on, but the spotlights that usually shine on the various paintings are off.

With the room lights on, you can see the portrait frames. You might even be able to make out some of the faces in the portraits. But only when the spotlights are flipped on and an intense light beams down on each painting can you see all the details—the facial expressions, the skin tones, the eye colors. Only when the spotlights are on can you see the people as the artists intended you to see them.

God shines his light on you—a light that shows who he created you to be. But before you see yourself clearly, you need to know how to turn on the lights.

You get light from three places:

Jesus Christ is your first source of light. John said that Jesus "gives light to everyone" (John 1:4). Jesus called himself the light of the world (see John 8:12). You flip on this light when you enter into a personal relationship with Christ. As your friendship grows deeper through the time you spend with Jesus in prayer, you see even more clearly that you are loved, valued, and competent.

God's Word, the Bible, is another source of the light. David wrote, "Your word is a lamp to my feet and a light for my path" (Psalm 119:105, NIV). The more you open your mind and heart to the Word of God, the more light you enjoy.

Other believers are a source of God's light. Jesus told his followers, "You are the light of the world" (Matthew 5:14). Being friends with God's Son, the Light, fills you with light. As you and your Christian friends share the light of the Son of God and the Word of God with one another, you grow in your understanding of who you are. That's a huge reason the Bible tells us, "Let us not neglect our meeting together, as some people do, but encourage and warn each other" (Hebrews 10:25).

God wants you to know how he shines his light into your life so you can see yourself clearly for who you are—lovable, valuable, and capable. When you stick tight to Jesus, open your Bible, and grow close to other Christians, God's light will shine into your life. Go ahead—flip the switch!

 TALK: Do you want to see more clearly who you are in God's eyes? How does he help you get into the light?

 PRAY: *God, flood us with your light as we read your Word and grow in our friendships with you and your people.*

 ACT: Pick a good habit to work on—talking with God, reading the Word, or spending time with Christian friends.

7 Who's Blocking the Light?

Bible Reading: 1 Thessalonians 5:5-6

You are all children of the light and of the day. 1 Thessalonians 5:5

Mara's big brother, Brent, was proud of his classic 1967 Mustang convertible. But he didn't keep it clean, so a friend wrote "Wash me" on it and scratched the paint with his fingernail. Brent yelled at his friend for scratching the car.

On the way home from work one day, a passing truck threw a sheet of mud across Brent's windshield. It should have been no big deal—except that Brent had let his car run out of wiper fluid. As Brent tried to steer his car, the road was invisible through the mud-smeared windshield. He accidentally swerved across the centerline into oncoming traffic. He was very fortunate that no cars were coming, because he could easily have had a head-on collision.

Sometimes other people are like that mud-splashing truck. You're motoring through life and suddenly an enemy smears you. Or your friends are like the car-scratching guy. They may scratch you with their words until it really hurts. Sometimes the pain even comes from someone close to you:

- A family member treats you like you're worthless.
- A friend avoids you, ignores you, harasses you, or ridicules you.
- A classmate calls you names like "loser," "numb-brain," or "clod."

That kind of mud blocks God's light from your life. God sees you as lovable, valuable, and capable, but the more mud people splash, the harder it is for you to see God's truth about who you are. When you feel hurt, you're likely to fling mud at everyone around you. Or run off the road.

If you have difficulty seeing yourself as lovable, valuable, and capable, it might be because God's truth is being blocked from your view by people who cover up the truth of your true identity. Could that be happening to you? Ask yourself

- Do the people I hang out with the most see me as God does?
- Do my best friends reinforce what the Bible says about me?
- Do these people reflect Jesus' love for me?

If the closest people in your life keep flinging mud your way, you will have a tough time seeing through the slop to get God's view of you. But making sure you have the right people in your life is like filling up on God's kind of wiper fluid. It's what you need to clear away the smears.

 TALK: Do your close friends see you as God sees you? Is it time to get some new friends?

 PRAY: *God, help us pick the right friends so your light floods our life.*

 ACT: Stop yourself today if you fling mud at people—if you say or do anything that communicates that they are less than lovable, valuable, and capable.

8 For Such a Worm As I

Bible Reading: Psalm 86:11-17

You, O Lord, are a merciful and gracious God, slow to get angry, full of unfailing love and truth. Psalm 86:15

Joanna's view of herself couldn't creep any lower. Listen to her talk: "I'm even worse than a worm," she says. "A worm can crawl underground and hide without leaving a trail. I'm more like the ugly slugs on my patio. Everywhere they go, they leave this horrible trail of slime behind them. That's what I'm like. I mess up everything wherever I go."

That's a sad self-image! It's doubly sad because Joanna is a Christian. She's clueless about her true identity. She isn't a worm or a slug. She makes mistakes—like we all do—but she certainly doesn't "mess up everything" wherever she goes.

If you are a believer who isn't convinced of your true identity as God's beloved, valued, competent child, the results in your life can be dismal:

- Tyrone has a fearful, always-in-the-dumps view of his world.
- Felicia sees new or unexpected situations as suffocating threats.
- Mitch takes total blame for all of his difficulties.
- Chelsea puts on a tough shell to scare people out of her life.
- Sammi can't trust anyone who treats her nicely.
- David has a tough time accepting compliments from others.
- Lisa feels like her world is closing in on her, crushing her.

When you let one of those ugly views of yourself control your thinking, you let life push you around. You don't try to change or challenge your world.

But when you're confident that God sees you as lovable, valuable, and capable, you greet tough situations as opportunities to trust Christ to pull you through. You rely on God to give you power to help you change your surroundings for the better. You let other people into your life as partners who help carry your burdens. And you know that God's plan is to do great things through you—and that you will accomplish significant things for eternity.

You might have moments when you think like Joanna. That's when you can be sure that God understands exactly how you feel—and that he loves you completely. He is a compassionate God. He knows that you sometimes feel like a slug, but he also knows this truth: You are far better than slime!

 TALK: What does it mean to you that God is compassionate? How could letting God's compassion touch you remake your life?

 PRAY: *God, thank you for your compassion. Thank you for having a great view of each of us.*

 ACT: Help the people in your family spot when they see themselves as anything less than lovable, valuable, or capable. Remind them that they're way better than slugs!

9 Turn On the Love Light

Bible Reading: 1 John 4:16-21

> *God is love, and all who live in love live in God, and God lives in them.*
> *1 John 4:16*

Toby hadn't meant to wreck anything. But during a game of hide-and-seek at Nolan's house he spotted a big woven basket Nolan's parents had picked up years ago on a trip to Africa. He knew it was one of their prized possessions—which meant Nolan would never look for him inside it.

Toby climbed in and pulled the basket's lid down on top of himself, but as he sat in the dark he realized that hiding in the basket wasn't such a great idea. As he clambered out of the basket before Nolan walked in, his leg broke through the old reeds, ripping a gaping hole. He pulled free, put the top back on, and darted to another hiding spot.

Toby isn't sure if Nolan's parents know who destroyed their basket. And even though Nolan is his best friend, Toby feels too ashamed to ever go to his house again.

Shame is the feeling that tells us we've messed up so badly that no one could ever love us again. It's what made Toby stay away from Nolan's house, because he didn't want to run into his best friend's parents—or be reminded of his unlovableness.

Ripping the basket didn't make Toby suddenly unlovable, but he wasn't seeing himself clearly. While shame is a feeling that hits all of us from time to time, some kids live their whole life in shame, haunted by the horrible feeling that they're too bad for anyone to ever love. "No way can God love me," they might say. "I know what I have done. He puts up with me because I've accepted Christ as my Savior. But he won't ever love me as his child."

Whether our shame is a short-term emotion or a long-term problem, the solution is the same: God wants us to come into the light, letting his truth shine on us and show us who we really are.

God doesn't bring us into the light to show off our faults. He wants us to see ourselves as he does. Sure, we might spot failures we need to confess. But we can rest peacefully in God's presence because we are sure that his forgiveness covers whatever we've done. And we can bask in the Son-shine as we realize we are his lovable, valuable, and capable children.

Do you feel like hiding? There's no better relief than coming into the light.

 TALK: Have you made it a habit to hide your failings from God or people because you fear they won't love you anymore? How can you let the light in?

 PRAY: *God, we all do things we are ashamed of. Help us walk in your light by being honest and receiving forgiveness from you and others.*

 ACT: When you fail today, don't let yourself begin to feel shame. Step into God's light right away by confessing your sins—and letting others see you for who you are.

10 Is Anybody Interested in Me?

Bible Reading: John 1:10-14

The Word became human and lived here on earth among us. He was full of unfailing love and faithfulness. John 1:14

Even before Katrina was born she was destined to be a model and an actress. She was six months old when her mother, Joyce, moved them to California and signed her with a modeling agency to do baby-product commercials. The little girl's childhood was packed with modeling contests, dancing and acting classes, and commercial auditions. Joyce was determined her daughter would have the perfect looks of a Hollywood star. Every piece of food Katrina ate was okayed by her mother. Every minute of her demanding fitness routines was charted and analyzed. Every hair on Katrina's head was always in place.

The night Katrina graduated from a private school in Los Angeles, she disappeared from the all-night country-club celebration. Months later she was found in a shelter for homeless teens in Baltimore, a dirty and scared runaway.

Joyce bought Katrina a plane ticket home. "Look at your hair, your skin," Joyce cried as she saw her daughter. "You have ruined your life."

"No, Mother," Katrina shot back. "I ruined *your* life. I never had a life, not until I left home. You made me into a Barbie doll. I was your toy. I only mattered to you when I was posing or performing. Well, your Barbie doll has grown up now, Mother, and you can't play with me anymore."

Katrina stayed in Los Angeles, where a former classmate invited her to attend a small church. Even though the church members didn't know about Katrina's past, she had difficulty accepting their kindness. She had the same distrust for God, thinking he couldn't possibly be interested in her.

Talk about it: How do you feel when people are interested in the things that interest you? How do you feel when people ignore you?

If people don't pay attention to you—who you are and what *you* love to do, you feel like trash. But when people enter *your* world and show interest in the things that interest *you*, you feel like the treasure you are. The good news is that God loved you enough to enter your world. He came from heaven to earth to be part of your human struggles and to die for your sins. He is totally interested in you—and he always will be!

 TALK: How have the people around you shown interest in your world? How has God proven his interest in you?

 PRAY: *God, sometimes we feel like we have to fit a mold made by other people. Thank you for being interested in us just the way we are.*

 ACT: Show interest in a hobby or activity of a friend you've ignored or put down in the past. Report back on how your friend reacts to your attention.

11 You Can Do It

Bible Reading: Hosea 2:20

I will be faithful to you and make you mine, and you will finally know me as Lord. Hosea 2:20

Remember Joanna? She's the girl who saw herself as a slug. (See November 8.)

When you understand Joanna's background, it's no surprise she feels like she messes up everything she does. Joanna's stepfather, Buck, was a hard worker who pushed Joanna to be the best at everything she tried. His favorite way of getting Joanna to try harder was humiliation. If Joanna didn't make an all-out effort, Buck made fun of her. Over the years he gave Joanna nicknames like Dummy, Stupid, Clumsy, Tubby, and Numbhead. The more he ripped into Joanna, the more frazzled she felt and the more mistakes she made.

With all those ugly messages burned into her brain, Joanna grew up with an I-can't-do-anything-right attitude. Under pressure to succeed, she failed to keep her first job. Now she has kept a low-stress, low-pay job for ten years, but her performance would earn her a C-minus or a D back at school. She can't see herself for who she really is, a person loved by God no matter how much she accomplishes.

Talk about it: How do people wind up hurt and handicapped like Joanna? What could have helped her feel capable?

As family and friends, we have the chance to give each other some essential ingredients that can keep us from feeling like slugs. Here are three ways we can help each other:

Give encouragement. When people are always criticized, blamed, or embarrassed for what they do, their confidence and motivation are shaken. Why try if they always fail? Encouragement helps others feel capable.

Give practical support. Everyone needs burden-bearers who come alongside and share the weight of a difficult task or trial. God doesn't plan for any of us to depend only on ourselves.

Show appreciation. None of us are 100 percent good at everything we try. Some people even struggle at tasks the rest of us think are easy. But everyone has a trait or talent worth appreciating—things like effort, helpfulness, positive attitude, determination, or willingness to try.

Families and friends can make or break us as we grow up. God invites us to give each other the encouragement, support, and appreciation we need to feel confident in every step of life. Get to it!

 TALK: How can we treat each other in ways that make us feel capable? What three ingredients are important?

 PRAY: *God, fill us with confidence. You make us capable.*

 ACT: Help someone feel capable today. Show a friend or family member some encouragement, support, or appreciation.

12 Howdy, Neighbor

Bible Reading: Luke 10:25-37

"You must love the Lord your God with all your heart, all your soul, all your strength, and all your mind." And, "Love your neighbor as yourself." Luke 10:27

Travis and Kyle walked home from school together almost every day, stopping at the MinuteMart to buy sodas. After Travis finished his drink, he usually tossed the empty paper cup on someone's lawn—unless he was in front of the Cooks' house. Kyle couldn't figure out why Travis wouldn't trash the Cooks' lawn. He finally asked, "How come you throw your cups on anybody's lawn but the Cooks'?"

"Because," Travis answered, "we're supposed to love our neighbors, and the Cooks are my next-door neighbors. The other people aren't my neighbors, so I don't care if I leave trash in their yards."

Huh?

Travis sounds like he's rather confused. Jesus made it clear that the command to love your neighbor isn't just about the people who actually live next door. God wants you to love *all* your neighbors because *he* loves all your neighbors.

When Jesus was asked, "Who is my neighbor?" he told the parable of the Good Samaritan, who showed love toward a man mugged by robbers (see Luke 10:29-37). The story shows that neighbors aren't just people who have the same education, income, ethnic heritage, or zip code as you do. Neighbors are *people in need*—whoever and wherever they may be. Neighbors are all people everywhere, because everyone needs to be loved.

Jesus' command for us to love everyone wasn't new. Way back in the Old Testament Moses wrote down into law God's words, "Love your neighbor as yourself" (Leviticus 19:18). God commanded Israel to show loving concern not only for those of their own kind, but also for the poor and strangers (Leviticus 19:9-10). God's invitation runs through the Old Testament: "Love people—all people—like I do."

In the New Testament, God's love is offered to all people. Christ died for the whole world (see John 3:16), and God plans for us to share the good news of salvation with "all the nations" (Matthew 28:19). He commands us to "do good to everyone" (Galatians 6:10).

So if you want to love like God, don't limit your love to people like you—or people you like. Jesus left no one out of his command to love. He instructed, "Love your enemies. Do good to those who hate you. Pray for the happiness of those who curse you. Pray for those who hurt you" (Luke 6:27-28). You get to love all people just as Jesus does, because everyone is your neighbor!

 TALK: How wide does God's love stretch? How can you enlarge your love?

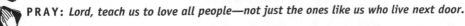 **PRAY:** *Lord, teach us to love all people—not just the ones like us who live next door.*

ACT: Make a plan to show love today to someone who isn't like you.

13 All in the Family

Bible Reading: 1 Timothy 5:3-8

Those who won't care for their own relatives . . . have denied what we believe. Such people are worse than unbelievers. 1 Timothy 5:8

"Hey, Travis," Kyle said as the two walked home from school again, "has it ever occurred to you that Jesus' command to love your neighbor really means to love everybody—not just the people who live next door?"

"Wow!" Travis exclaimed. "I guess I can't go to the movie with you tonight."

"Why not?"

"I have to get to bed early and get my sleep," Travis explained, "because I have six billion neighbors to love!"

Travis is getting the message, but he's still confused.

Yes, Jesus wants you to love everybody, but you can't show your love in specific ways to *everybody.* You don't have enough time, energy, or resources to care for every person on the planet. That's why you need to figure out where to start.

Talk about it: When your goal is to love, where should you begin?

God wants us to start with the people closest to us. Then we can work our way out to the whole world "whenever we have the opportunity" (Galatians 6:10).

Here are two big ones:

Yourself. Believe it or not, your first love responsibility is yourself. If you don't provide for your basic needs and protect yourself from hurtful influences, you won't have much love to give others. Without the right self-love—taking care of your mental, emotional, spiritual, and social growth—you'll run out of gas when you try to love the other people God has called you to love.

Your family. Next to loving yourself, your next biggest job is loving your own family. As Paul wrote, "Those who won't care for their own relatives, especially those living in the same household, have denied what we believe. Such people are worse than unbelievers" (1 Timothy 5:8). People all need help, encouragement, prayer, and comfort from others. God says your energy to meet those needs should go to your parents, brothers, and sisters first. Caring for extended family members, such as grandparents, aunts, and uncles, comes in a close second (see 1 Timothy 5:16).

Do you ever wonder what God means when he says "Love your neighbor"? God intends your first love commitment to be to those closest to you—people who need you—and that's your family. God wants you to love everyone. But loving everyone starts at home!

 TALK: Does God's command to love everyone seem like more than you can handle? What are some things you can do to start loving the people closest to you?

 PRAY: *Lord, we want people to see you in us. Teach us to love the people closest to us.*

 ACT: Do one jumbo loving thing for a family member today. Make it a surprise!

14 Let the Love Flow Out

Bible Reading: 1 John 3:14-17

If anyone has enough money to live well and sees a brother or sister in need and refuses to help—how can God's love be in that person?
1 John 3:17

It wasn't until a few days after her mom came home from having heart surgery that a truth tiptoed through Amanda's brain. With her mom recovering for the next couple of months, things wouldn't magically get done around their apartment. So Amanda pitched in and made cooking and cleaning part of her daily routine.

The evening before Amanda's mom started back to work, she took Amanda out to dinner. "I couldn't have made it after my surgery without you," she said. "I have something for you that I hope will always remind you of how well you took care of both of us." Her mom made Amanda close her eyes and hold out her hands. When Amanda opened her eyes she found a delicate gold necklace.

Right then another truth tiptoed through Amanda's brain. Amanda suddenly understood how cool it was to truly help people—not to get a gift, but to see the real difference she could make. And she realized lots more people could use her help!

Think about this: Let's assume you're figuring out what it means to love yourself and that you've got your family covered. Now what?

Loving people is like aiming at a big bull's-eye. The inner circle is loving yourself and your family. Here's your next circle: loving other Christians.

Maybe you haven't thought of your Christian friends as folks needing your special attention. But Paul urged, "Whenever we have the opportunity, we should do good to everyone, *especially to our Christian brothers and sisters* (Galatians 6:10, emphasis added). God wants you to love the believers with whom you spend time worshiping, learning, serving, and fellowshipping. Your care can extend to missionaries and even to Christians you won't likely ever meet—believers in other churches, cities, and countries.

But there's one more circle to think about: all those neighbors you are to love as you love yourself. This huge ring includes everyone, from the folks next door to your classmates to remote tribes in faraway countries you can't even name. Whoever and wherever they are, you get to love them.

Like a pebble tossed into a pond, the big splash of your love will be at the center, to those nearest you—family and fellow believers. But as you love, a wave ripples outward to needy unbelievers all around you.

 TALK: How does your love for others spread to all three rings?

 PRAY: *God, show us how we can spread your love to every person with whom we have contact.*

 ACT: Make a plan as a family to show God's love to someone in that outermost ring.

15 Both Soup and Salvation

Bible Reading: James 2:14-18

Faith that doesn't show itself by good deeds is no faith at all—it is dead and useless. James 2:17

"Fixing houses?" Ethan frowned as he looked at the brochure for the family mission trip offered by his church. "How could a fixed-up house help someone learn to love Jesus? If I'm not knocking on doors to talk to people about Jesus from dawn till dusk, it's not a mission trip."

You know you're supposed to love other people. That's a big fact of your Christian faith. But *how* are you supposed to love?

Many Christians think the only part of people we should care about is their soul—the part that will live forever. Their only concern is to make sure people are on their way to heaven. God wants us to do more.

God made people. And he wants us to love the people of our world in all the ways they need love. In Jesus' parable about the Good Samaritan, that kind helper didn't preach to the wounded man. He patched up his wounds and took him to an inn to be cared for. Jesus didn't just talk to people about spiritual bread to fill their spiritual hunger for God (see John 6:35). He also gave them physical bread for their physical hunger (see John 6:5-11).

Talk about this: Suppose you get a chance to work in a poor neighborhood, presenting a church service and then serving a hot meal to the homeless. Which activity is more loving—sharing "soup" (or whatever is on the dinner menu) or offering "salvation" (through the music and Bible message your group presents)?

Is that your final answer? Here's the correct response: *They are equally loving activities because each shows love by meeting genuine needs.*

Food, clothing, and shelter alone don't bring people into the kingdom of God. People also need to hear about Christ and trust him as Savior and Lord. But it's tough for people to listen to a Bible lesson when their stomachs are growling with hunger or their bodies are aching from disease.

Taking care of physical needs often flings wide the door for us to meet spiritual needs. Besides that, the world is watching us. Non-Christians aren't impressed by our passion to introduce people to Jesus if we neglect painfully obvious physical needs.

Every Christian has the privilege of showing love to the whole person—soul and body—because those parts are equally valuable to God!

 TALK: How does meeting people's practical needs help them see Jesus in us?

 PRAY: *Father in heaven, help us to see people as whole creatures—and give us strength to meet both physical and spiritual needs.*

 ACT: Think of a person in your life who needs God's love. What kind, everyday things could you do for them to demonstrate God's love?

16 When Sin Gets in the Way

Bible Reading: John 8:1-11

"Neither do I condemn you," Jesus declared. "Go now and leave your life of sin." John 8:11, NIV

"I know we're supposed to love people just as they are," Gabriella said. "But what about Christians who are walking away from God? I have a friend who's doing some really stupid stuff. It started when her older brother began drinking and doing drugs. I'm not sure if she's into that yet, but all she wants to do is hang out with her brother and his friends. At school it's like she hardly knows me. She doesn't come to church anymore. I don't even want to know what she is doing. How can I love her?"

Good question. Love sees the hurt that people cause themselves when they disobey God. And love tries to protect people from harm. So the loving thing to do for Christians who run away from God is to lovingly confront them about their bad behavior—with the goal of protecting them from the consequences of doing wrong.

Suppose you have Christian friends who are starting to hang with the wrong crowd. They need someone to lovingly say, "The Bible makes it clear that what you do with those people is wrong. I hate to see you hurt yourself and others. You need to break off those friendships." Your friends might not want to hear those words, but you have their best interests at heart. You don't want to pretend evil behavior doesn't exist. You want to do what you can to keep your friends from getting hurt.

But you can imagine how most people will react to that kind of honesty. That's why this approach is called "tough love." It risks friendship in order to turn Christian friends away from sin. The people you confront might not listen to you, and they might walk away from you for a while—or for good. Your job, though, is to do your best to persuade them. How they respond is between them and God.

And in the meantime you can keep loving them the way Christ loves by

- meeting their needs for friendship
- looking for ways to be a positive influence and encouragement
- doing kind things you would do for anyone else
- praying that God will give you opportunities that will help your friends ditch sin and turn to Christ

When friends sin, you aren't helping them by ignoring their behavior in order to spare their feelings or to stay friends. You have an incredible opportunity to be honest and show the tough love they really need.

 TALK: What's the best way you can love a Christian who is trying hard to ditch God?

 PRAY: *God, give us wisdom when it's tough to know exactly how to love.*

 ACT: Do you know any Christians who aren't walking close to God? Make a plan as a family to show love to them.

17 Big Problems

Bible Reading: Colossians 4:2-6

Let your conversation be gracious and effective so that you will have the right answer for everyone. Colossians 4:6

Maggie's dad walked softly down the stairs to the family room where Maggie and her mom were both reading on the couch. "Andrew finally fell asleep," he sighed.

Maggie nervously cleared her throat. Her parents turned to look at her.

"What's up?" her dad asked.

Maggie said, "I'm really worried about a friend."

"Who is it?" her mom asked.

"Do you remember Brenda Dunnigan? She was in my kindergarten class. She's in my language class this year. She's acting strange."

"Is Brenda in some kind of trouble?" her dad asked.

Maggie started to cry. "I don't know for sure. But I know her situation at home is really awful. I wonder if she's thinking about running away."

There are some problems that are far too big to deal with on your own.

Maybe, like Maggie, you've noticed behavior in a friend that disturbs you. Maybe you saw something. Or heard something. Or just suspect something. Things like

- long stretches of sadness
- out-of-control anger
- a lot of talk about death
- misuse of drugs, alcohol, or other substances
- signs of physical or sexual abuse
- threats to hurt teachers, classmates, or anyone else

Even if you can't quite figure out what's wrong with your friend, you can't shrug off your concern. Whenever a friend might be facing one of those big dangers, you *must* talk with an adult you trust about the problem. You can bring up your concern to your parents, teacher, school counselor or principal, or pastor. That's not being a tattletale. You might be the only person who can get your friend help. And you aren't accusing your friend of anything. You're just raising a concern to an adult who can decide if a problem is real—and how to deal with it.

If you ever think something might be hugely wrong in a friend's life, it's time to do something to help. Speak up! Immediately!

 TALK: What situations that your friends might face would you *always* tell an adult about?

 PRAY: *Jesus, show us how to help our hurting friends. We want to point to you as the solution to their problems.*

 ACT: Agree as a family to talk about problems that are too big for one person to handle.

18 Turning the Dark Clouds Away

Bible Reading: 1 Thessalonians 3:1-8

We sent him to strengthen you, to encourage you in your faith, and to keep you from becoming disturbed by the troubles you were going through. 1 Thessalonians 3:2-3

You had a terrible day. You're totally down. You failed a quiz, tripped and tossed your tray across the lunchroom, and forgot that wear-your-clothes-backwards day was *tomorrow*, not today. You feel like crawling into a deep hole.

So answer this: What would you like your friends to do?

(a) Yell "Bye-bye, Bozo!" as you head out from school.

(b) Promise to listen to your sob story next month when they aren't so busy.

(c) Ding your doorbell every ten minutes to remind you how stupid you are.

You would dig further down into your hole if your buddies tried any of those tactics on you. So whenever you notice a friend is down, you have the chance to act better. You can treat them the way you want to be treated. Try these ideas:

Show concern. Luis found that the first step to helping his hurting friend was letting himself feel the same hurt. Feeling for his friend kicked him into action.

Be available. Matt found that more than anything, his hurting friend needed his T-I-M-E.

Make the first move. Renee figured out that calling her friend first—just to say hi, even when they weren't planning something—made her friend feel wanted.

Pray. Brian took a bold leap when he asked his friend how he could pray for him. Besides inviting God to help, Brian sent a loud message to his friend: He cared.

Remind your friend he matters to God. Kaitlin noticed that her friend wasn't exactly remembering her great worth to God. So she reminded her that God thinks she's lovable, valuable, and capable. Even non-Christian friends are created in God's image—and are people for whom Christ died.

Talk. Lots of kids who feel down say they can't talk to their parents about their problems, hurts, and decisions. Kim let his friend talk about his problems. But Kim also invited his friend over to his house so he could open up to Kim's parents if he wanted to.

When someone you care about feels down-and-out, the most important thing you can share is *you.* Take those tips, use them, and you'll build a caring relationship that will help your friend feel less alone!

 TALK: What's the best thing you can offer a friend who feels down in the dumps?

 PRAY: *Lord, help each of us to be a loving and sensitive friend to those around us who are hurting.*

 ACT: Think of a friend who is hurting. Work on a plan to help your friend feel less alone.

19 Everybody Is a Priceless Treasure

Bible Reading: Romans 8:15-17

His Holy Spirit speaks to us deep in our hearts and tells us that we are God's children. Romans 8:16

Imagine that you have a bunch of friends who are poor. Now imagine that you are wealthy enough to be able to put money into your friends' bank accounts—money that helps to make a better life possible.

You may or may not have friends whose families struggle financially. But you do have people around you who severely lack a sense of belonging. They have nothing that tells them they matter, and they feel they have nothing awesome to offer the world. You have it within your power to give them something that will remake their lives. You won't be putting in the kind of treasure that clanks like cash or flutters like a dollar bill. But you *are* able to give something even more valuable. You can pass on to them the truth about who they are as God's children.

You can offer your friends three rich biblical truths:

God says you're lovable. Like everyone else, your friends need to know they belong to someone. John 1:12 tells us that when we received Christ, we became children of God. So how can you say that to a friend? Try "God loves you so much he made you his daughter [or son]." Or "We're both in God's family. Because of Jesus, you're my sister [or brother] forever."

God says you're valuable. God loved us "while we were still sinners" (Romans 5:8). Your friends may question how much they're worth as persons. Their great worth is proven by the fact that their loving God allowed Jesus Christ, his sinless Son, to die for their sins. You might say, "Even if you were the only person on earth, God would have sent his Son to die for you."

God wants you to know you're useful. Paul wasn't bragging when he said, "I can do everything with the help of Christ who gives me the strength I need" (Philippians 4:13). He saw in himself what God sees in all of us: He was empowered by the Holy Spirit to serve God and others. You could say to your friend, "God gave you the ability to _____. It's really cool."

Sometimes it's easier to write these things than to say them out loud. But do you understand the importance of helping your friends see themselves through God's eyes? The more your friends realize they are lovable, valuable, and capable, the richer the life they will lead—all because you gave them huge gifts of biblical truths!

 TALK: What good will it do your friends to hear these truths?

 PRAY: Ask God for wise ways to communicate his truths to a hurting friend.

 ACT: Who do you want to share these biblical truths with? What are you going to say?

Bible Reading: Mark 10:32-45

Whoever wants to be a leader among you must be your servant.
Mark 10:43

As Jesus was walking with his disciples toward Jerusalem, two of them—James and John, the sons of Zebedee—let their imaginations run wild. Jesus had clearly laid out what was ahead for him in Jerusalem: rebuke, torture, and death. But James and John thought Jesus would supernaturally drive out the Romans from Jerusalem. In their minds, Jesus and his followers would soon rule Palestine.

The Zebedee brothers were so sure their fantasy would come true that they decided to apply early for the top two jobs in Jesus' new government. "'We want to sit in places of honor next to you,' they said, 'one at your right and the other at your left'" (Mark 10:37). They were clueless about Jesus' prediction of his coming suffering.

Jesus more or less asked them, "Are you two ready to go through everything I will go through?" (see verse 38). He was thinking about his upcoming trial, beatings, and death on the cross.

"Oh yes," they replied confidently.

Then Jesus saw years into the future and told them they would experience what he would experience (see verse 39). The Master knew that James would be rejected and killed for his stand as Christ's disciple (see Acts 12:2) and that John would be rejected and sent to live at an island prison (see Revelation 1:9). Each would indeed go through suffering similar to what Jesus would soon face.

Like James and John, some Christians have the wrong picture of what it means to follow Jesus. "What am I going to gain from being a Christian?" they ask eagerly. They have a tough time accepting the message that the Christian life isn't a smooth-sailing, hassle-free, magic-carpet ride to heaven. We don't get to live the life of a king—at least not here on earth.

If anybody should have lived on earth like a king, it was Jesus. But we live the life of servants, just like Jesus did. So we don't ask what we can *get* from being a Christian—even though the Bible promises us that the rewards and blessings of following Christ are endless. This is the question we *should* ask: "What can I *give* as a servant of God and of people?"

James and John Zebedee became great not by obtaining high positions in a government set up by Jesus, but by serving Jesus Christ and his church selflessly. They eventually realized that *giving*—not *getting*—is the heart of the Christian life!

 TALK: What kind of greatness do you expect in God's kingdom?

 PRAY: *Jesus, we want to serve you unselfishly today.*

 ACT: Imitate your Savior today. Do an unexpected act of service!

21 Mercy, Mercy

Bible Reading: Mark 10:46-52
"What do you want me to do for you?" Jesus asked. Mark 10:51

Here is a report of what happened in Jericho one day, based on what Scripture tells us. (We added the part about the mayor.)

City leaders, Jesus, and a big crowd listen to the mayor of Jericho as they jostle one another through the gate on the road to Jerusalem. "And so we want to express our thanks to you, Jesus, for your brief visit—"

A rustling at the back of the crowd interrupts the speaker. "Jesus, Son of David," a man yells, "have mercy on me!"

"Shut up, you blind fool," one of the important men growls over his shoulder.

The mayor looks at Jesus nervously and continues, "We want to thank—"

"Jesus, Son of David, have mercy on me!" This time the voice from outside the circle is loud and demanding.

"Hush, old beggar!" several people join in harshly. But Jesus is visibly moved by the plea. He calls the blind beggar named Bartimaeus forward and heals him.

What caused Jesus to turn his attention away from the crowd to a persistent, blind beggar? Maybe it was the man's cry for mercy. "Mercy" is compassion that causes a person to provide relief for someone in misery. A "merciful" person is someone who feels the hurts of others and relieves those hurts.

Groups like the Red Cross show mercy with huge, organized programs. But we can show mercy in simple acts like comforting and bandaging a littler brother or sister who has skinned a knee. Or listening to a friend's problems. Or helping out a parent whose workload is overwhelming.

God said about himself, "I am the Lord, the merciful and gracious God" (Exodus 34:6). And Moses said about God, "The Lord your God is merciful" (Deuteronomy 4:31). Since Jesus was God in a human body, it's no surprise that mercy was one of the major characteristics of his earthly ministry. His heart of mercy was moved by the suffering of people—and his power allowed him to heal and free people from their hurts.

There's no pain, fear, or loneliness that Jesus doesn't understand. When you come to him crying, "Master, I need help," Christ answers you with compassion. Sometimes you spot his kind deeds when he supernaturally fixes someone's body, like he did for Bartimaeus. Other times you spot him through the caring of a Christian friend. Jesus had a whole bunch of mercy for poor Bartimaeus, and God has the same great mercy in store for you when you run to him for help.

 TALK: In what area of life do you need God's mercy? Have you cried out to him for help?

 PRAY: Tell God today about your deepest needs—and trust him to meet them.

 ACT: Be like Jesus today. Show a friend or family member a heap of heavenly mercy!

22 Give till It Helps

Bible Reading: Mark 12:41-44

They gave a tiny part of their surplus, but she, poor as she is, has given everything she has. Mark 12:44

Esther was old enough to be a grandma, but she had never married or had children. She lived alone in a tiny house. In public she was so shy that she was often overlooked, yet she was a faithful Christian who rarely missed a service at her small church. Whenever the pastor or his wife or children had a birthday, Esther quietly presented them with a birthday card and a gift of money. The children received two or three dollars, and the pastor and his wife always found ten or twenty dollars in their cards. When the pastor's family took a vacation, Esther always gave them another card with money tucked inside.

The pastor eventually moved to another town. Years later he learned that Esther had become ill and died. Then came some amazing news. Esther had been living on a total of $150 per month—almost nothing! One of the most generous persons in the church had barely enough to buy food and clothes. But she gave to others as if she were wealthy, just like the poor widow in Mark did.

Talk about it: Can you think of times you wanted to give but didn't think you had enough? What does Esther's example teach you?

The New Testament shows us a major principle about giving. You could call it the "open-hand policy," and it's everywhere you look. Luke says it this way, "If you give, you will receive. Your gift will return to you in full measure, pressed down, shaken together to make room for more" (Luke 6:38).

There are two main points to the open-hand policy:

Give whatever you have to whoever needs it. If a friend at church is too broke to go to Bible camp, you can open your piggy bank and slide him the seven bucks you were saving. Or if a family in the community loses everything they own in a fire, you can give part of your wardrobe to a kid in the family who is your size.

Trust God to give to you when you give generously to others. "Oh, good," you might be thinking, "I want to give more so I can get more." That's not exactly what Luke 6 means. When you give without *thought* of a payback—and especially without *planning* on a payback—then God will gladly surprise you by pouring his gifts and blessings into your life.

You don't have to be rich to be an openhanded giver. It just takes practice.

 TALK: How has God been generous to you? What are you doing to be an openhanded giver?

 PRAY: *God, help us to be as generous with others as you have been with us.*

 ACT: Pull out a dollar or two and ask God to show you where that money can do more good than in your pocket. Then stand back and let God amaze you at how rewarding it can be to be an openhanded giver!

November

23 My Tribute

Bible Reading: Mark 14:1-11

Why are you bothering her? She has done a beautiful thing to me.
Mark 14:6, NIV

Brother Sun, Sister Moon is a movie about St. Francis of Assisi. Francis was ready to inherit his father's business and live in comfort and ease. But after he trusted in Christ, the young man grew uncomfortable with his wealth because of the poverty all around him. Since Christ gave up the treasures of heaven to become the Savior, Francis reasoned, he should do the same. He walked away from his father's wealth and lived in poverty as he ministered to the poor.

In Mark 14 you catch a glimpse of two individuals. One, like St. Francis, thought no gift was too great to honor Christ. The other had a crazed craving for money that led him to turn in Christ to his enemies for a few pieces of silver.

Two days before the Last Supper, a woman visited Jesus and poured expensive perfume over his head, an act of loving recognition of Jesus as her Lord and King.

"What a waste!" some disciples mumbled. "We could have sold that bottle and helped a lot of poor people with the money."

Not a bad idea, really. But there's a time to help the needy, and there's a time to show respect for Jesus, our Lord and King. Jesus appreciated this woman's splashy gift.

Then there's Judas, whose greed greased the way to his downfall. He led the grumbling about the bottle of perfume. John tells the truth about Judas: "Not that he cared for the poor—he was a thief who was in charge of the disciples' funds, and he often took some for his own use" (John 12:6). The chief priests recognized Judas's love of money and paid him to turn Jesus over to them (see Mark 14:11).

So how can you show honor to Christ the King like that generous woman did? After all, Jesus isn't here in the flesh. Yet here's one great way: Pay tribute to Christ by blessing someone who *is* here in the flesh. Try these suggestions:

- Buy your pastor or youth leader a gift—a book, CD, jewelry, gift certificate.
- Donate to charity in thanks for Christ being your King.
- Make a sacrificial contribution to your church's building fund.
- Find out what your best friend has always wanted and give a surprise gift.

"Tribute gifts" mean even more if you give them anonymously. It's a way to keep your focus on the real purpose of giving—honoring Christ. He will know what you have done, and it's a way to declare Jesus is Lord of everything you own.

 TALK: How can you give generously in a way that honors Jesus?

 PRAY: *Lord, build in us hearts that are grateful for everything you have given us—and hearts that recognize your greatness.*

 ACT: Make a plan as a family to give a tribute gift.

24 Liar, Lunatic, or Lord?

Bible Reading: Matthew 16:13-19
You are the Messiah, the Son of the living God. Matthew 16:16

"You're so stupid," Sean laughed. "Heather, how can you believe all that Bible stuff? Jesus might have been a good person, but he wasn't God."

Heather's mouth dropped open. She and Sean attended a Christian school together. Heather wanted to object, but she fumbled for words.

"I know," Sean said. "You're wondering how they ever let me into Heritage Academy. I know all the right answers. I'm just not sure I believe them."

Sean isn't the first person to have had doubts like that. He's not even the first person who grew up in a Christian home and went to a Christian school to question his faith. But there's a problem. Jesus claimed to be God—period.

But let's try out Sean's point of view for a second. If Jesus wasn't God, what was he? There are only three choices:

First option: *Maybe Jesus was a liar.* Jesus said he was God. But suppose he knew he wasn't. That would make him the biggest liar who ever lived. He told others to be honest even while he taught and lived a huge lie.

The possibility that Jesus was lying, however, doesn't fit what we know about him or the results of his life. Whenever people have discovered who Jesus is, lives have been changed for the good. Someone who lived like Jesus lived, taught, and died couldn't have been a phony.

Second option: *Maybe Jesus was a lunatic.* If someone told you he was God, you would think he was crazy—like someone who claims to be Santa Claus. But Jesus didn't show any of the symptoms that go hand in hand with being mentally unglued. Jesus stayed calm when his enemies attacked. He spoke some of the wisest words ever recorded. Jesus Christ was no crazy man.

Third option: *Jesus is Lord.* If our Savior isn't a liar or a lunatic, he is who he claimed to be—the Son of God.

Jesus is either a liar, a lunatic, or the Lord God. You have to make the choice. But you have help to make the right choice—the Bible. This provides the historically trustworthy record of Christ's rising from the dead. Providing you with solid reasons to believe is a huge reason God gave you the Bible. As John wrote, "These are written so that you may believe that Jesus is the Messiah, the Son of God, and that by believing in him you will have life" (John 20:31).

 TALK: So who do you think Christ is—liar, lunatic, or Lord? Why believe that?

 PRAY: *Jesus, you are Lord. We want to honor and worship you with our praises.*

 ACT: Talk through the three options for who Jesus was until you can explain them in your own words. How do you know Jesus is Lord—the Son of God—who is in charge of everything?

25 Eyewitness News

Bible Reading: 1 John 1:1-4

*We saw him with our own eyes and touched him with our own hands.
He is Jesus Christ, the Word of life. 1 John 1:1*

For centuries, some of the brainiest people have attacked Christianity as ridiculous. Problem is, many have ignored or tried to explain away the biggest proof of our faith—the resurrection of Jesus. But the historical evidence just can't be ignored. The facts of the empty tomb are as powerful today as they were two thousand years ago.

Here are some of the facts:

1. Jesus of Nazareth—a Jewish prophet who claimed to be the Savior written about in the Jewish Scriptures—was arrested, judged a political criminal, and executed by Roman crucifixion.
2. Three days after Christ's death and burial, some women who went to his tomb discovered that his body was gone.
3. In the following days the disciples of Jesus claimed that God had raised him from the dead and that he had appeared to them at various times before ascending into heaven.
4. From that core of early disciples, the message of Jesus Christ spread throughout the Roman Empire and has continued to change people's lives down through the centuries.

So did the Resurrection really happen? There are only two possible answers to that question. The resurrection of Jesus Christ was either the world's most wicked hoax—or the most astonishing fact in human history.

If the accounts of the resurrection of Jesus were not true, they could easily have been disproved in the early days of Christianity. The New Testament descriptions of the Resurrection spread while the men and women who witnessed the events were still alive. If the accounts were not true, those people could easily have spoken up. And if the writers of the Bible books of Matthew, Mark, Luke, and John made up the story of the Resurrection, their report never would have lasted past the first century. These books were based on facts everyone knew. And even people who hated Jesus and wanted to disprove the Resurrection couldn't deny what everybody else knew to be fact: the tomb was empty and Christ was alive.

None of us has seen the empty tomb or the risen Christ, but we have the reliable, time-honored testimony of the New Testament writers. Christ is risen!

 TALK: How would you answer a non-Christian friend who said Jesus didn't really rise from the dead?

 PRAY: Pray for a friend who doesn't believe the truth of the Resurrection.

 ACT: Who can you explain this truth to? Share the powerful evidence that Jesus is alive!

26 You Can't Get Around the Empty Tomb

Bible Reading: Acts 1:1-5

During the forty days after his crucifixion, he appeared to the apostles from time to time and proved to them in many ways that he was actually alive. Acts 1:3

For forty days after his crucifixion, Jesus let his disciples see him. He gave the world living proof that he had actually come back to life. Despite that evidence, some folks still argue that Jesus never really rose from the dead. They think he's still stuck in a grave, as gone as the day he died on the cross.

Suppose you lived back in Bible times and you really despised everything Jesus stood for. You totally hated his teachings. You disliked this wonder-worker from Nazareth so much that you wanted to prove his disciples went to the wrong tomb on Easter morning. You wanted people to think that instead of going to the tomb where Jesus had been buried, his followers went to an empty one.

To disprove the Resurrection, all you would have needed was one necessary piece of evidence. If you knew that Jesus was actually dead and his disciples were just directionally challenged, you would only have needed to pop open the right tomb and point to the dead body. That—of course—didn't happen.

The other excuses people offer for the empty tomb aren't any better.

Some insist that the disciples stole the body of Christ. But a handful of disciples would have been easily chased away by the elite Roman troops guarding the tomb.

Still others believe that Jesus didn't really die on the cross—that he was just unconscious from exhaustion and lack of blood, and he regained consciousness in the cool tomb. But the idea that a whipped, wounded, and weakened Christ could bust loose from a tomb sealed with a two-ton stone—that's laughable.

Those are silly stories.

Here's the real scoop: Three days after Jesus was crucified, his tomb was empty. The followers of Jesus saw him alive from the dead. He appeared to them over a period of forty days, offering them many certain proofs that no one could deny. Paul reported that Jesus even appeared to more than five hundred of his followers at one time, most of whom were still alive when Paul wrote and could back up or boo his report.

Christians believe Jesus was raised from the dead by the supernatural power of God, and Jesus offered solid proof of his bodily resurrection. It might be tough to believe that a man could rise from the dead, but the problems of not believing are even tougher.

 TALK: That's the evidence. The verdict? Jesus Christ actually rose from the dead, and he lives today. Are you letting him live in you today?

 PRAY: *Jesus, we want your resurrection power to fill us up today. Be our Lord and take charge of our life.*

 ACT: Talk with a non-Christian friend about how it's harder *not* to believe Jesus rose from the dead than to believe he did.

27 To the Death

Bible Reading: Philippians 3:7-11

I have discarded everything else, counting it all as garbage, so that I may have Christ and become one with him. Philippians 3:8-9

As his wide receiver flies into the air and pulls down the football in a one-handed grab, the coach of the home team leaps just as high in celebration of the game-winning touchdown. An instant later the coach of the visiting team shouts for an instant-replay review of the catch. So an official trots to the sideline and peers into a monitor. The fans hush. The players hold their breath. An announcement echoes over the loudspeaker. Like it or not, the touchdown stands.

Instant replay lets you see a sports play all over again. That won't work with the events of history. But there's still a reliable way to figure out the facts. You dig into the testimony of eyewitnesses.

A real eye-popping picture of Christ's resurrection comes from the lives of the early Christians—the people alive when it happened.

Talk about this: What would early Christians have gained by making up a false story about Jesus rising from the dead? What would they have lost?

For decades after Jesus died on the cross, life looked grim for those who claimed to be his followers. Authorities used every imaginable method to stop them from talking. The early Christians were beaten. Stoned to death. Thrown to lions. Tortured. Even nailed to crosses.

The early Christians didn't react like we would expect. They didn't say, "Hey, we were just kidding about that Jesus dude. He's still dead." Instead, they gave their lives as proof of their total confidence in the truth of their message.

Some people say the disciples must have made up the story about the Resurrection. But if the Resurrection were a made-up story, don't you think at least one of the twelve disciples would have admitted the so-called lie for which some of the apostles were beheaded or stoned or crucified? Or what about the dozens of Christ followers who refused to crumble under torture? Or the thousands of first-century believers who were thrown to the lions for refusing to stop believing in Christ? If the Resurrection were a lie, somebody would have cracked, spilled the truth, sold out, and blown their cover-up plot.

Nothing less than the truth—the real-life appearances of the resurrected Christ—could have caused these people to maintain to the death that Jesus is alive and that he is Lord. Are you glad for their faithfulness—so that you can know the truth?

 TALK: Do you think the disciples would have died for a lie? Why or why not?

 PRAY: *Jesus, help us experience the Resurrection power that kept the early Christians faithful to you until the end.*

 ACT: Log on to www.opendoorsusa.org to find out about Christians who still suffer for their faith today.

28 Is It Good for You?

Bible Reading: Deuteronomy 10:12-13

What does the Lord your God require of you? He requires you . . . to obey the Lord's commands and laws that I am giving you today for your own good. Deuteronomy 10:12-13

"How was church?" asked Andrew's dad.

"Awful!" Andrew said, sounding frustrated. That was a surprise. Andrew always liked his Bible-study group. "Dana taught the study tonight."

That was a clue. Dana was the one adult leader Andrew didn't like. To be honest, he drove Andrew nuts. This leader seemed immature for someone in his twenties.

"I've always thought Dana was so mean," Andrew went on. "Now I understand why. He talked tonight about how his dad beat him up when he was little, and how both his parents are still alcoholics."

Andrew's dad cringed. "That's really hard stuff to go through–and to hear about," he said. "That must be why he doesn't always know how to work well with kids, don't you think?"

"Yeah, that's what he said. I feel sorry for him. It's like he doesn't know any better. And he's working really hard to change. What I'm mad about is that now I don't have a reason to dislike him. Would it be okay if I hated him just a little bit?"

When it comes to following Jesus, many Christians have one question running through their minds: *How bad can I be and still be okay with God?* Most kids want someone to step up, draw a bold line, and say, "Okay, everything up to here is fine. But if you go past this point, you're out of God's will." It sounds nice and simple, but it doesn't work that way.

Get this: Wondering how much you can get away with misses the whole point of being God's child.

God didn't send his Old Testament people wandering in the desert for nothing. When he first set them free from slavery in Egypt, they thought his goal was to kill them off (see Exodus 14:11). They couldn't believe he would help them conquer the Promised Land (see Numbers 13). They didn't trust God–they didn't believe that he really wanted their good. They needed retraining. So God sent them for a time-out in the desert where they could think about two simple truths: "Obey me only" and "My commands are for your good."

If something you want to do is "only a little bad," then you're missing the point. It's clearly not *the best.* And God wants better for you than that!

 TALK: What do you think about your God—who doesn't want you to get away with something "just a little bad"? Is that loving—or what?

 PRAY: *God, thanks for loving us and for giving us your good commands. Help us to want your best—always and completely.*

 ACT: Remind yourself why God gave his commands—and what response God wants from you. Memorize today's Bible passage!

29 Out with the Bad, In with the Good

Bible Reading: Ephesians 4:17-24

Throw off your old evil nature and your former way of life, which is rotten through and through, full of lust and deception. Instead, there must be a spiritual renewal of your thoughts and attitudes.
Ephesians 4:22-23

If Marissa had a buck for every time she had counted to ten when she felt like bopping someone in the nose, she would be running neck and neck with Bill Gates for richest person in the world. With the threat of getting kicked out of school hanging over her head, she decided to steer clear of fistfights. Keeping her conflicts down to screaming matches, she figured, was a worthy goal. She still wanted to be bad—just not as bad as she'd been.

Talk about it: What's the best way to get rid of an ugly habit in your life?

Take a tip from the chemistry kit on your toy shelf. What's the best way to force gas out of a test tube? If you answered, "Pour liquid into the test tube," you're right. The liquid pushes out the gas because they both can't occupy the same space.

There's a similar principle for dealing with bad habits. You don't get rid of them by replacing them with habits that are a little less bad. You replace bad with good. And the way to do that is by changing how you think.

If you want to inject good thoughts, you can do it by memorizing Scripture. God's Word forces out unhealthy thoughts by stuffing your brain full of the best thoughts.

Start by memorizing a Bible verse each week. Here are some great places to begin: Psalm 51:10; Psalm 119:9, 11; Romans 12:1-2; 1 Corinthians 10:13; Philippians 4:8.

Memorize each verse word for word. Find a Bible translation that's easy to understand, then write the verse on a small card you can keep in your pocket.

Meditate on the verse. Ask yourself what the verse means. Think about the verse throughout your day.

Apply the verse to your life. Complete the statement: "As a result of this verse, I will . . ."

Review. Go over the new verse every day for two months, then once a week.

The best way you can keep Bible verses fresh in your mind is to respond in some way to what you've memorized. Whenever you're tempted to go back to an ugly habit, pull out one of your memory verses, review it, and go over it in your mind until the good thoughts force out the bad thoughts.

 TALK: Say it in your own words: How does the Bible help you break bad habits?

 PRAY: *God, remake us to think like you through the Scriptures we memorize.*

 ACT: Make a plan to slowly but surely get your brain full of God's best thoughts.

30 A Way Out

Bible Reading: 1 Corinthians 10:12-13

When you are tempted, he will show you a way out so that you will not give in to it. 1 Corinthians 10:13

Bekka has a potty-mouth. It's not hard to figure out that she inherited her unhealthy habit from her dad, who would be guaranteed to win a gold medal if cussing were an Olympic sport. A friend told Bekka that when she was tempted to let fly a streak of swearwords, she should pray about it. "But telling me to pray about not swearing is like telling me not to think of a purple elephant," she moaned. "I just think about it more. Just praying about the bad thing I want to do doesn't seem to help."

Bekka is right. The pressure to fall back into bad habits is strong. Chances are you feel forces all around you pushing you to do anything but what God desires.

Memorizing the Bible remakes your mind. Prayer taps you into the power of God. But you also need some specific strategies for dealing with temptation. Try out these "escape routes" from sin:

Decide ahead of time to do what's right. Don't wait until pressure hits to pick between right and wrong. At the moment you're tempted, doing bad always looks better. (That's what makes it a temptation!)

Steer clear of bad situations. If you're driving a car, it's not safe to swerve toward an exit at the last second. In the same way, it's not safe to put yourself in a place where you might quickly get into a jam. If you see temptation approaching, get yourself in a safe spot *now.*

Pick friends who pull you in the right direction. Hang out with people who have the same beliefs you have. Get involved in groups that support your right choices.

Seek the wisdom of others. Scripture says you can gain much wisdom from the experience of others. Talking with parents, pastors, or youth leaders can help you sort out your choices.

Break off harmful relationships. If you are getting pressured or giving in to pressure from someone, backing off from that relationship or ending it relieves the pressure.

Bolt. Be honest about your weakness. If you think you can't handle a situation, make a fast, strategic exit by heading for the door.

Pray. While you're at it, don't forget to pray. Ask God for help, because none of these other strategies will work unless you realize you really do need God's power. Use prayer as your first step in avoiding temptation—and use it all along the way.

 TALK: What pressures to do wrong do you face right now? How can you use these strategies to do what's right?

 PRAY: Spend time talking to God about the pressures you face.

 ACT: Think of a temptation you often face. Write down three escape routes you can use to steer clear of wrong. Put your note where you'll see it!

1

How to Get <u>There</u> from <u>Here</u>

Bible Reading: Psalm 119:57-64
I pondered the direction of my life, and I turned to follow your statutes.
Psalm 119:59

It's hard to have any sympathy for these goofballs:

Famed pirate historian Dr. Chester Doubloons stumbled onto a map to a sunken Spanish ship loaded with gold. After tucking the map into a safe, Doubloons set out on a quest to get rich. But after sixteen years, he's still searching the Caribbean for signs of the buried treasure.

Girl genius Lotta Graymatter graduated from college and entered law school at age twelve. But in seven years of law school, Ms. Graymatter has failed every class she has taken. "Law books are so heavy and they don't have pictures," Lotta explained to her family. "I'll just have to become a lawyer my own way."

With his dying breaths, a scientist dictated to his assistant, Sinus Naselmeister, a formula to cure the common cold. After typing the formula into his computer, Naselmeister shut down the machine and began experimenting. His best medicine so far is a cough syrup that tastes so bad even lab rats won't take it.

You can't find a sunken galleon full of gold if the treasure map is locked in a safe. You can't become a lawyer if you don't read the textbooks. And you can't develop a cure for the common cold if the formula is rotting on your hard drive.

No one is that dumb—but some folks come close. It seems like plenty of Christians make the same mistake our three weird friends made. We want to find God's direction for our life, but we overlook the most obvious guidance device God has provided: the Bible. It's our map to God's treasures for our life. It's our textbook for wisdom and understanding. It's our formula for dealing with problems. If we don't turn to the Bible for direction, we're worse off than those three dunces rolled together.

Last July we talked about God's *universal will* and his *specific will*. God's *universal* will is for everyone in the universe, and it's clear beyond any doubt because it is spelled out in his Word. It covers the commands that apply to everyone. God's *specific* will includes details just for you.

God has good in store for you. He said in the Old Testament, "For I know the plans I have for you. . . . They are plans for good and not for disaster, to give you a future and a hope" (Jeremiah 29:11). But the only way you'll discover those good plans is if you follow his directions!

 TALK: Isn't it great that God loves you enough to give you all the direction you need for your life? How does knowing that make you feel?

 PRAY: *God, thanks for guiding us through your Word.*

 ACT: Do you have a tough decision to make right now—big or small? What does God's Word have to say about it?

2 Finding Your Way One Step at a Time

Bible Reading: Psalm 119:105-112
Your word is a lamp for my feet and a light for my path.
Psalm 119:105

Some of us would give a whole lot to be Gary Hobson, the character played by actor Kyle Chandler on the TV drama *Early Edition*. Hobson is a quiet guy who becomes a hero after reading the news of the future in his newspaper. Week after week, Hobson prevents life-threatening tragedies because he knows about them hours before they happen, thanks to the mysterious "early edition" left on his doorstep.

Think of the advantages of knowing the future.

- You could study for all those surprise quizzes in school.
- You could steel yourself ahead of time to look thrilled when your grandparents give you a CD of Wayne Newton's greatest hits for your birthday.
- You would have prior warning when someone is about to tell a hilarious joke at mealtime that makes you laugh and squirt milk out your nose.

Wouldn't you like to know in advance the details of God's specific will for the major matters of your life? Your life would be a whole lot less complicated if you knew now where you'll go to college, what you'll do for a career, which lucky person you'll marry, even where and when you'll retire and expire. Don't you wish that God, who actually *does* know the future, would let you in on just a little of it?

In his loving wisdom, God chooses to keep the future hidden. He chooses instead to reveal his specific will for your life one day at a time, one step at a time.

God has a plan for showing you his specific will. The critical first step to discerning his step-by-step direction for your life is getting into his *Word*. A second step is *prayer*. Go ahead and ask for his wisdom. A third step is the *counsel* of mature believers. Getting wisdom from others keeps you from rushed or immature decisions. And a fourth step is *circumstances*. That's when you watch for God to open and close doors in your life.

God doesn't hide knowledge of your future from you to be mean. He's holding back information that would be too much for you to handle. And as he leads you step-by-step through life, it's also his tender way of holding you close.

 TALK: What would you think of God if he had left you to find your way in the world alone?

 PRAY: *God, in all the areas of life where we need to make decisions, thank you for giving us direction.*

 ACT: Do you have friends or family who are looking for God's guidance? Steer them toward *God's Will, God's Best,* a book on discovering God's will by Josh McDowell and Kevin Johnson.

3 Don't Ever Buy a Compass That Points South

Bible Reading: Psalm 119:33-40

Turn my eyes from worthless things, and give me life through your word. Psalm 119:37

Even though God is the one source of total smarts in the universe, there are still plenty of unwise ways people look for direction. They don't depend on God. They even dabble in dark stuff. This story will show you what I mean.

The audience goes crazy with applause as the emcee glides to center stage. "Welcome to the annual Compass Awards show for the Home Guidance Network," he says. "Ladies and gentlemen, the Home Guidance Network provides programming to help the public find direction for their lives. Tonight we will honor the best of these programs with the coveted Compass Award.

"This year's first nominee is the ever popular program *Do What I Do,* where rich, famous, and successful people tell how they live so our viewers can copy them.

"Our second nominee is the warm and wonderful program *If You Can't Trust Your Friends, Who Can You Trust?* where viewers are encouraged to direct their lives solely on the advice of their friends.

"Next is the Monday night runaway hit *Keeping Up with the Culture.* This knockout show tells us that if we guide our life by what we see on TV, in the movies, and in other media, we will find success.

"Our fourth nominee is the spirited program *Direction from the Dark Side.* This show highlights occult practices, from horoscopes to tarot cards to psychics to palm readers—all practices by which people make important decisions.

"And our final nominee is the Thursday night drama, *As My Feelings Turn,* the show that says, 'If it feels right for you, it probably is right for you.'"

The host produces a large, sealed envelope and begins to tear it open. "And the winner of this year's Compass Award is—"

Wait a minute! There's no such thing as a Home Guidance Network—and if there were, who really cares which of these "programs" would win? *They'd all be worthless!* The practices they'd preach—copying the lifestyles of famous people, depending on your friends to tell you what to do, doing what the culture does, seeking occult insights, or following your feelings—aren't God's way to provide direction for your life.

God, who created you and loves you, has a better way to direct your life. Are you relying on his Word—or on these wacko ways that can't provide you with the wisdom you need?

 TALK: Say it in your own words: What are some of the wrong ways people look for guidance?

 PRAY: *God, we want you to guide our life.*

 ACT: Have you or any of your friends ever relied on worthless methods for guidance? Talk to God about it.

4 Getting the Word on Tough Choices

Bible Reading: Psalm 119:97-104
Your commands make me wiser than my enemies, for your commands are my constant guide. Psalm 119:98

You've barely settled into your seat when your teacher drops a bomb: "Class, I need to record who completed last week's reading assignment. I'm sending around a sheet of paper. Sign it, then put yes or no. I will grade you accordingly."

Way to go, dog brain! you ding yourself. *I should have finished reading the book on Friday instead of goofing off after school. I'm toast.*

Panic sets in. The Fruitsie Hoopsies you sucked down for breakfast churn in your stomach. The sheet of paper is getting closer. *Hey, I read more than half of those pages. I could write yes,* you tell yourself. *And I know how the story ends, so that's like reading it all. Besides, I read more than most of the kids who signed yes.*

The paper suddenly lands on your desk. You sign your name, then hesitate over the space where you must write either yes or no. What will it be?

Talk about it: What would you do if you were faced with that decision? How would you decide what to do?

We face choices like that every day. Sure, choosing between right and wrong is a no-brainer if the choice is between stealing a CD or saving up to buy one. But how can we make the call when the line between right and wrong looks fuzzy?

God's commands are vital to getting the wisdom and guidance you need for puzzling decisions. And one way to put God's Word to work in your tough choices is a process you can remember as the four Cs. Here's how it works.

C-1: Consider the choice. Every decision is an opportunity to pick God's will or your own way. What exactly is the choice you need to make?

C-2: Compare it to God. Are there any clear Bible commands that tell you what to do in this situation? Any principles? Does God's character tell you anything about what you should do: What is God like? What would he do?

C-3: Commit to God's way. Decide to do what God and his Word show you to do. No exceptions. No excuses. Make the commitment and stick to it.

C-4: Count on God's protection and provision. God's care doesn't mean everything is going to be rosy. But living God's way brings ample spiritual blessings, like freedom from guilt and God's blessing on your life.

The next time you feel puzzled about right and wrong, remember the four Cs. And you can be clear on what God wants you to do!

 TALK: What decisions about right and wrong have you faced lately? Do your choices stand up to the four-C test?

 PRAY: *God, thanks for the sure guidance of your Word.*

 ACT: Get together with a friend to talk about tough choices you face. And put your choices to the four-C test.

5 Rare Book

Bible Reading: Psalm 119:137-144

Your promises have been thoroughly tested; that is why I love them so much. Psalm 119:140

After five years of school with the exact same twenty-two kids in her small-town class, Aubrey jumped when she saw a new face at the desk next to hers. Gem, along with her parents and older brother, had moved straight from Asia.

It didn't take Aubrey long to invite Gem to the Christmas program at her church. Aubrey explained that she would be playing Mary, the mother of Jesus.

"Thank you very much for the invitation," Gem said politely. "My family is Buddhist. I don't know much about Jesus."

Aubrey explained that she could learn about Jesus in the Bible. "I have never read the Bible," Gem said. "Do you find it helpful?"

During the last few days you've seen why the Bible is our guide for making right choices. But that fact is only half of why reading the Bible is worthwhile. The Bible isn't just our road map for life. It's a map we can trust.

We believe the Bible is worth trusting because of some significant facts:

- *Unity.* The Bible was written over a period of 1,500 years by more than 40 authors (kings, peasants, fishermen, poets, and statesmen), on three different continents (Asia, Africa, and Europe), in three different languages (Hebrew, Aramaic, and Greek). Yet the Bible speaks with amazing unity on hundreds of controversial subjects. No other book can claim that!
- *Circulation.* With more than 2.5 billion copies in print, the Bible is by far the world's all-time best-seller. No other book can claim that!
- *Translation.* The Bible has been translated in part or in whole into more than 1,600 languages. It is available in the languages and dialects of 95 percent of the earth's people. No other book can claim that!
- *Survival.* From the ancient world, very few manuscripts have survived. But 24,633 New Testament manuscripts have survived to now. No other book can claim that!

All together, these are facts that are true *only* of the Bible. They don't prove that the Bible is *true,* but they prove that the Bible is *unique.* That's the first step toward understanding that the Bible is *reliable.*

So why has this book landed in your hands? Because its Author loves you and wants you to have the guidance you need for a successful and rewarding life.

 TALK: What do you think of how God lovingly produced and protected his Word?

 PRAY: *God, thanks for giving us your unique, utterly reliable Word.*

 ACT: Practice what you would say to explain the uniqueness of the Bible to a non-Christian friend. Then go do it!

6 Are You Buckling under the Pressure?

Bible Reading: Romans 15:5-7
Accept each other just as Christ has accepted you. Romans 15:7

School starts in ten minutes, so you figure it's time to roll out of bed and get ready. You look in your closet and pull out the shirt, pants, belt, socks, and shoes you're sure your gang of friends will wear. You scurry into the bathroom. There you spray two cans of mousse into your hair before parting it just above your left ear and raking it all over to the other side of your head. You glance in the mirror. *Perfect.* But as you sprint for the school bus another thought shoots through your brain: *Why am I dressed this way? I look stupid!*

Maybe your parents still pick most of your clothes. If not, you probably dress the way you do because of your peers—that crowd of youth your age who make up your everyday world. Have you ever noticed that they're the same people who try to tell you what words to use, who to hang out with, and what attitudes to hold?

Talk about this and take a guess: Back in the 1950s, what do you think were the biggest influences in a young person's life? And what are the biggest influences now?

Back in the 1950s, youth took their cues from *parents.* Next came *teachers,* then *peers.* Nowadays *peers* rank first, followed by *parents* and then *media* like music, TV, radio, and the whole on-line world. It's not that peer pressure didn't exist when people like your grandparents were kids. But it wasn't so intense.

You might have great friends who push you toward God's best. But if your peers are pushing you the wrong way, you want to take some of the pressure out of those peer relationships.

Here's how.

Know it or not, your big job is to get a handle on God's deep love for you. Peer pressure is powerful because you and every human being alive has a built-in, God-given need to be loved and accepted. God plans to be the first to meet that need for you, because without being certain of his love for you as his chosen child, you'll try hard—too hard—to fit in with your friends. The more unsure you are of God's love, the more sure it is that you'll be swayed by the opinions of your friends.

Feeling accepted by friends is important.

But Jesus Christ, the Son of God, accepts you totally. Make his opinion of you the one that matters!

 TALK: How has pressure from your peers shaped your life this week? Are you okay with that? Is God?

 PRAY: *God, thanks for accepting us always. Help us grow more and more certain of your deep love for us.*

 ACT: You might feel driven today to act in a wrong way that wins the acceptance of your peers. That's the time to tell God thanks for accepting you totally.

7 Getting Away with Evil

Bible Reading: Psalm 73:1-11

My feet were slipping, and I was almost gone. For I envied the proud when I saw them prosper despite their wickedness. Psalm 73:2-3

Not only is Tabitha the sneakiest girl in the sixth grade, she's also the biggest—a head taller than everyone else in her class. Everyone knows she bullies kids on the playground. But everyone is way too scared to speak up. They know that the last kid who told on her wound up bumped and bruised at the bottom of a staircase.

Talk about it: Take turns filling in the blanks in this sentence: "I, [your name], watch [someone else's name] get away with [something wrong] all the time, and nothing ever happens."

Psalm 73 doesn't say exactly what was bugging Asaph when he wrote this sad song. It's clear, however, that he and a horde of other people were watching some bad dudes get away with monstrous evil. As Asaph and the rest of the crowds witnessed these events, they uttered some stomach-turning words: "Does God realize what is going on?" They might as well have yelled, "Get a clue, God! Where are you?"

If you've ever watched someone get away with evil—and you have—you can guess how Asaph ended up feeling. Right after the verses you read, he asked himself, "Was it for nothing that I kept my heart pure and kept myself from doing wrong? All I get is trouble all day long" (verses 13-14).

Asaph figured he did right—and got squat for his efforts. But that's when God came to his rescue, doing two vital things:

God helped Asaph understand where evildoers wind up. Evildoers won't do evil forever. "You put them on a slippery path," Asaph said, "and send them sliding over the cliff to destruction. In an instant they are destroyed" (verses 18-19).

God pulled Asaph tight. When Asaph recognized God's awesome power and protection, he said, "You are holding my right hand. . . . My spirit may grow weak, but God remains the strength of my heart; he is mine forever. . . . How good it is to be near God! I have made the Sovereign Lord my shelter" (verses 23, 26, 28).

Those are points repeated throughout the Bible. The next time you watch someone get away with what seems like unstoppable evil, try this New Testament promise. "So the Lord knows how to save those who serve him when troubles come. He will hold evil people and punish them, while waiting for the Judgment Day" (2 Peter 2:9, NCV).

How do you like them apples?

 TALK: How would you answer someone who says people always get away with their sins?

 PRAY: *God, help us know how we can stop evil. Help us to know you are with us even when we feel helpless against it.*

 ACT: Read all of Psalm 73 to get more of God's great words on this subject!

8 Under Control or Out of Control?

Bible Reading: Proverbs 23:29-35

Don't be drunk with wine, because that will ruin your life. Instead, let the Holy Spirit fill and control you. Ephesians 5:18

As much as Jon likes the friends he's had since kindergarten, they haven't been very kind lately. About the time they got into junior high, his friends all started experimenting with alcohol. And these days all they care about is saying things like

- "So why don't you go drinking with us?"
- "You're such a baby."
- "Come on, there's no harm in a little brew. You might like it."

You might not even know anyone who drinks right now. But when people ride you hard because you don't drink, what are you going to say to make them back off?

You can start by saying it's not fear that keeps you from drinking. It's brains.

Proverbs 22:3 says, "A prudent person foresees the danger ahead and takes precautions; the simpleton goes blindly on and suffers the consequences."

Do you know the consequences that people who drink stumble into? According to recent statistics:

- Alcoholism causes health problems in one out of every thirteen American adults.
- Alcoholism affects more than 10 million people, costs 150 billion dollars, and is blamed for more than 100,000 deaths annually.
- Alcohol is involved in more than 50 percent of deaths by motor vehicle and fire and more than 30 percent of murders and suicides.
- Alcohol contributes to death in some cancers and to many other diseases.

And there are more ill effects. *Physically,* alcohol can damage your liver, stress your heart, and take away your memory. *Emotionally,* it can create anxiety, cause embarrassment from stupid behavior, and lead to family hassles. *Spiritually,* it destroys your freedom by limiting your ability to make right decisions.

People might tell you someday that you'd be a whole lot more fun if you would drink. But if you really want to pep up your personality, try Ephesians 5:18 instead. Filling up with power from the Holy Spirit will cause you to act differently. You can't predict what alcohol will do to you. But you can be sure how the Holy Spirit will make you act—just like Jesus.

 TALK: How are you going to react when people tease you about not drinking?

 PRAY: *God, help us to look in the right places for fun and fulfillment. Help us remember the dangers of alcohol when people make drinking sound fun.*

 ACT: What's your family plan for handling the pressures of alcohol abuse—pressures that can start as early as elementary school?

How to Turn to the Right

Bible Reading: Deuteronomy 10:12-13

What does the Lord your God require of you? . . . To obey the Lord's commands and laws that I am giving you today for your own good. Deuteronomy 10:12-13

"Gather around, ladies and gentlemen, and feast your eyes on this magnificent bottle of pills. Just one capsule a day and you will automatically and flawlessly know the difference between right and wrong. That's right—one capsule a day and you'll never make a bad choice again. Who will be the first to pay one hundred dollars and take home this bottle of miracle pills?"

How hard would it be to part with a mere hundred dollars to make sure you made the right choice in every decision of life? Not very. Whenever you couldn't tell if something was right or wrong, you'd just pop a pill.

Well, there's no such wonder drug. But there are some questions you can ask yourself that will help you make the right choice:

The Personal Test: Will doing that thing bring me closer to Jesus?
The Practical Test: Will doing it bring good results?
The Social Test: Will doing it help others be more like Jesus?
The Universal Test: What would the world be like if everyone did it?
The Scripture Test: Does the Bible clearly label it wrong?
The Stewardship Test: Is it a waste of God's talents invested in me?
The Missionary Test: Will doing it help others see Jesus in me?
The Character Test: Will it make my character stronger?
The Publicity Test: Would I want my friends to know about it?
The Common-Sense Test: Does it show everyday smarts?
The Family Test: Will it make my family look bad?

God put you here on Planet Earth and released you to experience life at its best. But that's why he made certain things off-limits. He knows everything isn't good for you. He knows there are places in life where you can fall down and get hurt, and he doesn't relish the idea of scraping you up off the pavement.

So let God guide you in your choices by helping you choose what is right. He isn't down on your fun at all. He wants you to have a whole lot of it—but without even a hint of regret. The limits he puts in your life are to protect you!

 TALK: Do you believe that God is looking out for what's good for you? What evidence do you see?

 PRAY: Say thanks to God for his plan to protect you from harm and provide for your best.

 ACT: Are you wondering if some activity is right or wrong? Put it to these tests!

10 Trapped in the Middle

Bible Reading: Romans 7:18-25

Who will free me from this life that is dominated by sin? Thank God! The answer is in Jesus Christ our Lord. Romans 7:24-25

Fernando sat on the family-room floor with his nose just a foot from the TV. He had heard that his favorite ballplayer had trusted Christ, and there he was, telling his story. After years of doing drugs after every game and chasing women in every city he played in, he had trusted Jesus. God had set him free from his old life, and he had been a totally different person for more than a year. He felt ready to tell his story to the world.

When you hear how wild ballplayers and drug addicts and prison convicts come to believe in Jesus, you probably figure your story is too boring to interest anyone. After all, you don't have the gory past of a ballplayer gone bad. You didn't belong to the Mafia and break the thumbs of hundreds of people.

Actually, *not* having a gory personal story is a great thing. And you still have an exciting story to tell. Here's why.

There's a fact you might not know: *Before you trusted Christ, you were a slave.* That's right. You weren't a bad-news, big-league ballplayer whose life of sin splashed you on the front page of the newspaper. Yet sin held you prisoner. You wanted to speak kindly, but you spewed meanness. You knew you should love, but you showed hate. You were powerless to do good, because badness kept you tied up.

That's what the Bible means when it says you were the hopeless victim of your "sinful nature." The apostle Paul described it like this: "Sin rules me as if I were its slave. . . . When I want to do good, evil is there with me" (Romans 7:14, 21, NCV).

And here's another fact that's just as true about you: *When you trusted Christ, you were freed from slavery.* When you came to Jesus, God began a process of changing you. You probably didn't need to kick cocaine. But have you stopped kicking your sister? You probably didn't throw baseball bats at umpires. But have you seen an improvement in your bad mouth?

When you know Jesus, sin has lost its grip on you. As Paul said: "You are not ruled by your sinful selves" (Romans 8:9, NCV).

Being freed from sin doesn't mean you *automatically* do good but that you become *able* to do what's right. You can obey God happily. That's exciting! And that's something you can share.

 TALK: What would you tell someone who asked you about the pros and cons of being a Christian?

 PRAY: *God, thanks for bringing us to you. And help us to eagerly share the story of how you set us free.*

 ACT: Explain to a non-Christian friend what your life is like because Jesus has set you free!

11 Growing Up God's Way

Bible Reading: 1 Peter 5:5-7

Humble yourselves under the mighty power of God, and in his good time he will honor you. 1 Peter 5:6

"I believe in Christ," Trent admits, "but he doesn't have a lot to do with my life. I'm really busy. I've got football. And my parents make me play trumpet and sing in the choir at church. But what I really like is skateboarding—and snowboarding. It's not like I don't *want* to read the Bible to find out how God can matter in my life—but I don't have *time.* I've noticed that God never seems as close as other people say he is. I know that he cares for me, though, so when I hit a big problem, I pray hard then."

With every year that passes, your parents, teachers, and other adults in your life give you freedom to fling yourself into more and more big stuff. But growing up isn't a chance to grab that freedom and run. It's a chance to follow God on your own.

Talk about it: If growing up means getting more freedom, why would you want to surrender that freedom by letting the Lord lead your life?

Here's why following God is so great.

For starters, life can be a struggle when you call the shots. When you take control of your life, you lack the joy that should be yours as a Christian. Your anxiety can soar sky-high. Peace is in short supply because you're solving all your problems by yourself. You don't have much power over temptation, and you might get more discouraged than you want to admit.

But think about what happens when you let God lead you. God makes you brave. He sees everything in your present situation and in your entire future, so he can show you how to live your whole life. While walking without God bogs you down, God promises to lift you up.

The passage you read tells the first step in letting God lead your life. You humble yourself before God and allow him to direct how you live, play, and serve. First Peter 5:5 in the New International Version says to "clothe yourselves with humility." This refers to a slave putting on an apron before serving. Our job is to imitate our Lord, who put a towel around himself and served his disciples (see John 13:4-17).

How do you "clothe yourself with humility"? By admitting you need God's power in every bit of life. You admit you need God's brains. You admit you need God's love. You make time for God and his purposes—and you admit you need every kind of help he can give you!

 TALK: How are you doing in your relationship with God? What's the next step you can take to grow closer?

 PRAY: Tell God you want to get closer to him.

 ACT: Make a list of the pros and cons of being a Christian. If your con list is longer and more impressive than your pro list, chat with a mature Christian for more ideas on the great points of following Jesus!

12 Tap Into Your Power Source

Bible Reading: Ephesians 3:14-19

I pray that from his glorious, unlimited resources he will give you mighty inner strength through his Holy Spirit. Ephesians 3:16

Do you think of yourself as a disciple? "Not me," you might answer. "It's too cold where I live to wear sandals. I gag at the smell of fish. And wearing bathrobes all day long is really out of style where we live."

Know it or not, if you have chosen to follow Christ, you already are a modern-day disciple. It has nothing to do with wearing flip-flops or a bathrobe. It's all about letting God work in and through you just like he's worked in and through his disciples for the past two thousand years.

There's a lot to learn about being a disciple. What is lesson number one? It's discovering exactly how God works in you by his Spirit.

When you became a Christian, God's Spirit entered your life (check that out in Romans 8:9 and 1 Corinthians 3:16). How? Because the Holy Spirit is God, he is omnipresent. That means he can be everywhere at once. But being all-present isn't merely like having a McDonald's on every corner. God comes and lives *inside* you and every other Christian around the world at the same time.

And the Holy Spirit living in us is how God remakes our life.

- He teaches us how to understand the Bible (see John 14:26).
- He makes us courageous and puts the words in our mouth that we need in order to share Christ with others (see Acts 1:8).
- He builds in us the qualities that make each of us a winner in our relationship with God and others. Those qualities—love, joy, peace, patience, kindness, goodness, faithfulness, gentleness, and self-control—are so much a sign of the Spirit's work that the Bible calls them "the fruit of the Spirit" (see Galatians 5:22-23).

So will you feel different when you're overflowing with God's Spirit? Not necessarily. Being filled with the Spirit isn't so much about feelings as it is about facts. God fills you because he promised in his Word that he would. That's a fact! Feelings come and go. The biggest signs of God's control in your life are the power and fruit of the Spirit you experience.

And count on this: As God strengthens you through his Spirit in your inner being, you'll get the power you need to live your Christian faith from God's Spirit.

TALK: How do you feel about the fact that God wants to come and fill you up with his Spirit? Is that a cool power source or what?

PRAY: Pray today for the Spirit's power in your life.

ACT: Ask a mature Christian how the Holy Spirit can work in your daily life and faith.

13 Fill 'Er Up at the Soda Fountain

Bible Reading: Ephesians 5:15-20
Let the Holy Spirit fill and control you. Ephesians 5:18

The basics of tapping into the Holy Spirit's power for your daily life aren't all that different from filling a cup with soda at your favorite fast-food place. In case you aren't clear on the technique, there are three crucial things to do: (1) make sure the cup is in the right spot; (2) check that the lid is off; and (3) once you push the button and the flow starts, be ready for some mighty fizz.

God designed you to be filled and led by the Holy Spirit. Just like you need to follow those three steps to top off your drink, you need three simple steps to get more of the Spirit into your life.

1. Get in the right spot by confessing your sin (see 1 John 1:9). The Holy Spirit can't fill and lead you when you choose to live far from God. Whenever you realize that you've disobeyed God, admit that what you did was wrong. Give thanks that forgiveness is yours because Christ paid for your sin through his death on the cross.
2. Get the lid off by believing that God will fill you and lead you by his Spirit. What do you need to do to be filled with the Holy Spirit? First, give every area of your life to God (see Romans 12:1-2). Say, "God, it's yours— my hobbies, sports, friends, school, desires, all of it." Ask God to be your boss in each area. Then ask the Holy Spirit to fill you. The Holy Spirit is a free gift, yours for the asking. As you tell God you want to be filled, God promises to answer (see 1 John 5:14-15).
3. Keep the power bubbles a-fizzin' by walking in the Spirit. Getting filled isn't a one-shot deal. Just because you trust God to fill you with his Spirit doesn't mean you'll never blow it through lack of faith or disobedience. When you blow it, confess your sin on the spot and turn back to God.

Bonus: God gives free refills! Ask him again to fill you, and trust him to do it. Then boost your faith through prayer and studying God's Word (see Romans 10:17). Yes, you have to be ready for spiritual conflict with the world, the flesh, and Satan. But if you respond to the conflict by relying on God's Spirit working in you and through you, you will conquer. Get yourself in the right spot. Get the lid off. Then get set for God to fill you to overflowing!

 TALK: Got those three steps down? Which step does God want you to take to let his Spirit fill your life?

 PRAY: *God, we want so much for your Spirit to fill us. Give us all we need to walk close to you through life.*

 ACT: Make a poster with those three Spirit-fill-me-up steps. Put it where you'll see it!

14 Filling Up the Train to Heaven

Bible Reading: 2 Peter 3:9-16

The Lord . . . does not want anyone to perish, so he is giving more time for everyone to repent. 2 Peter 3:9

When Megan hears that God wants her to have a healthy self-image, she wants to wiggle away. "I'm really not interested in hearing how special God thinks I am," she protests. "I *don't* want to see myself that way. People who focus on themselves end up totally selfish. I can't see how thinking about myself helps me glorify God and show the world how great *he* is."

Talk about it: Is Megan right or wrong? Does knowing that God thinks you're special make you a spoiled brat?

Pssst. I have to disagree with Megan. God wants you to see yourself like he sees you—lovable, valuable, and capable.

But why would God want you to think that way? Is it just to make you feel warm and fuzzy? Could he possibly want to feed your selfish side? No and double no. God wants you totally convinced that you are lovable, valuable, and capable because he has a gargantuan reason for fixing your faulty self-image. He has work for you to do.

You might not realize that you're God's gift to the world. But you didn't really think God just put us here to take up space, did you? He could have zoomed us straight to heaven the moment we trusted Christ. The fact that he chooses to have us hang around on earth even after we belong to him proves that we have a real reason for being here.

So what's our purpose in life? I like how one young guy answered that question. "My purpose in life," he said with fire in his eyes, "is to go to heaven and take as many people with me as I can."

I hope you have the same burning desire to be part of God's big plan to rescue the world. When you are sure that God created everyone in his image and sent Christ to die for everyone, you want to share his love with others. And when you realize that you too are lovable, valuable, and capable, suddenly you give your time to help with God's work from a heart jammed with the love of Jesus.

You may say, "If the whole reason I'm here is to lead people to Jesus, then I'm a rotten failure. Hardly anyone—no, make that *no one*—has come to Christ because of me." That might be true. But it's also likely to be true that as you keep growing, a bunch of people are on their way to trusting Christ because of who you are in Christ and how you love them!

 TALK: Say it in your own words: How does having a healthy self-image *not* make you a selfish person? How does it help you love others?

 PRAY: *Lord, we want to reach out and tell the world of your love.*

 ACT: Since God has given you this important job, what bold step can you take today to talk about Jesus?

Bible Reading: Matthew 5:13–16

Let your good deeds shine out for all to see. Matthew 5:16

Whoa—tell people about Jesus? you might think. *Don't I have to be a pastor or missionary to be able to talk about Christ? I mean, I need to know more about the Bible. And besides, I'd have to be way more mature. Nobody listens to kids my size. And here's the biggest problem: I do all sorts of stuff wrong. I have to get my act together before I can talk about Christ. Why, just yesterday my brother spouted off and I popped him in the nose.*

The *I'm-not-good-enough* fear might not be the only misguided attitude that could keep you from speaking up about Jesus. Some people have the *I'm-going-to-get-blasted* fear. They expect ugly reactions if they tell others about Christ, so they clam up. Others have the *I-can't-do-this-no-way-no-how* fear. They expect their tongues to knot up if they mention Jesus, so they zip their lips.

You know that your self-esteem is crucial to how you relate to God. But knowing that you're lovable, valuable, and capable also has everything to do with being confident you can be part of God's exciting work in your world.

If you think you aren't "good enough" to witness for Christ, get a grip on God's love for you. The more you see yourself as God does—accepted, forgiven, created in his image—the less you will let your blemishes be a barrier to sharing what you know about Jesus. If God had to wait for you to totally mature before he sent you out to share the gospel, he'd have to wait until you get to heaven!

If you fear the negative reactions you might face as you witness, get hold of your worth to God. Worrying too much what others think about you can mean you have a low view of your true worth to God. What are you afraid of? Even if everyone refuses to listen to you, you are still valued by the King of the universe!

If you worry about saying the wrong thing when you witness, trust that God will make you capable. If you fear stumbling over your words, you're saying to God, "You sure botched things up when you created me, because I'm not any good at this. And in my case practice won't make perfect."

Witnessing doesn't begin with what you say or how well you say it. It starts with knowing who you are in Christ. You are God's beloved child—unique and useful to him just the way you are.

 TALK: Do any of those fears keep you from speaking up about Christ? Is there anything about the way you see yourself that you need to let God fix?

 PRAY: *God, we want to share our faith the best we know how—and we'll leave the results to you.*

 ACT: If you've always been scared to share your faith, talk with a mature Christian about how you can overcome your fears.

16 For Goodness' Sake

Bible Reading: Galatians 6:7-10
Don't get tired of doing what is good. Galatians 6:9

Ten-year-old Jessica dives outside as soon as it snows to shovel the sidewalk and driveway of the widow next door. She does this to be kind, not because her neighbor pays her—because she can't afford to.

Twelve-year-old Michael is required to be a reading tutor for second-graders. It's a class requirement, but it means a lot more. He's seen the skills of a couple students he tutors really pop. All of a sudden they can read!

Are you looking for a first-class way to share Christ with the world? There's a simple way to start that probably won't make you squirm with nervousness: *Do good to others.*

All through the Bible we can spot instructions to do for others what is right and good:

- "If we do what helps [others], we will build them up in the Lord" (Romans 15:2).
- "Whenever we have the opportunity, we should do good to everyone, especially to our Christian brothers and sisters" (Galatians 6:10).
- "Never tire of doing what is right" (2 Thessalonians 3:13, NIV).
- "Let us not become weary in doing good" (Galatians 6:9, NIV).

When we do good things for other people, they get the chance to see the Savior in us.

Just because you're working for someone else doesn't mean you can go at it halfheartedly. People see God acting through us when we do *good.* They also see God in us when we jump on every situation as an opportunity to do our *best.* Paul challenged the Galatian Christians, for example, "Be sure to do what you should, for then you will enjoy the personal satisfaction of having done your work well, and you won't need to compare yourself to anyone else" (Galatians 6:4). Doing your best for others peels people's eyes off of you and lets people see God in your actions.

And here's a truth to rely on: When you use your gifts, talents, and abilities with the power of the Holy Spirit, it doesn't matter how people respond in the short run. God will make the most of your hard work and wholehearted service to draw people to himself!

 TALK: How can you share your faith through good deeds toward others?

 PRAY: *God, open our eyes to the opportunities all around us to do good for others.*

 ACT: Make a plan as a family to do a good deed today for someone who doesn't know Jesus!

17 What's Love Got to Do with It?

Bible Reading: 1 Corinthians 13:1-13
Love is patient and kind. 1 Corinthians 13:4

You be the judge: Are the people who make these statements megaconfused about the meaning of true love?

"I love my new outfit."
"I love that new band, the Brain-dead Tsetse Flies."
"I love how my dog flies through the air when I throw him a Frisbee."

Looking at that list you might get the idea that love could mean any sort of affection for just about anything. So what in the world do people mean when they say they *love* something or someone? What is true love anyway?

Hearing humans talk about true love can get pretty confusing. But one look at the Bible shows that God doesn't have any problem defining true love.

Let's start with what true love *isn't*.

True love as the Bible defines it isn't just about feelings. It isn't merely a strong emotion or attraction. In fact, love as it is described in the Bible isn't based on sight, looks, romance, or warm fuzzy feelings. You might be thrilled beyond words to do math problems until your eyes sag shut. But you might want to come up with another word besides "love" to describe that crazed emotion!

Just because real biblical love isn't about feelings doesn't mean that it will make you miserable. It produces strong feelings. But our feelings come and go like the wind, depending on our mood. So true love is something more.

If that's what true love *isn't*, here's what true love *is*.

- Love is spelled G-I-V-E. It is always giving.
- Love shows respect for one another.
- Love has no conditions for acceptance.
- Love is realistic. It doesn't live in a dream world.
- Love takes responsibility for its loved one.
- Love is demonstrated in a sustained commitment.
- Love never stops growing.

The more we understand what God's Word has to say about true love, the more love we'll have to share.

 TALK: So how do your attitudes and expectations of love measure up to this biblical definition of love?

 PRAY: *God, teach me to love—to really love as you defined it.*

 ACT: Muzzle your mouth—at least for today—when you use "love" to mean something less than true love!

18 Don't Settle for Anything Less

Bible Reading: 1 John 4:7-12

Anyone who does not love does not know God—for God is love.
1 John 4:8

Ask some elderly friends or relatives if they ever heard that old song about crushes and marriage going together like a horse and carriage. They will tell you it's love—not crushes—and marriage that go together like a horse and carriage. But in everyday life, loads of people get the two mixed up. So what's the difference?

Crushes are when girls get googly-eyed at boys. It's when boys punch girls in the arm. Maybe you wouldn't mistake those gushy feelings for true love. But look at some of the huge differences between crushes and true love:

Crush	True Love
Starts and stops suddenly	Grows over time
Stays shallow	Goes deep
Up and down feelings	Steady commitment
In love with love	In love with a person
Breaks up when irritated	Doesn't panic over problems
Focuses on looks	Focuses on character
Takes	Gives
My feelings	Other's needs
Self-centered	Self-controlled
Physical attraction first	Emotional and spiritual attraction first
Expects to find happiness	Expects to work at happiness
Asks, "How am I doing?"	Asks, "How are you doing?"
Accepts if other is good enough	Accepts unconditionally
Thinks the other person is perfect	Sees strengths and weaknesses
Avoids problems	Works through problems

That's a heap of difference! Crushes go away. But true love lasts. Even if a guy-girl friendship doesn't end in marriage, true love still keeps on loving.

Do those characteristics of true love remind you of someone? They should, because they reflect the characteristics of God's love for you. You are the object of that selfless, unconditional love every day. And when you start to live out those traits in your human relationships, you mirror God's love.

 TALK: Answer in your own words: What's the difference between crushes and true love?

 PRAY: *God, help us to express true love to the people we care about.*

 ACT: You've probably seen boy-girl crushes. Maybe you've felt pressured to have a boyfriend or girlfriend. Do you need some one-on-one chat time with Mom or Dad about that?

19 Loving God's Temple

Bible Reading: 1 Corinthians 6:19-20
You must honor God with your body. 1 Corinthians 6:20

Derek's mom stares slack-jawed, startled by the word that just erupted from her five-year-old's mouth. "Honey, do you know what that word means?"

Derek shyly shakes his head no.

"Well, it's the name for a boy's body part," Mom says, "but it's not a very nice name. You know the name the doctor uses, right? Let's stick to that."

God had a wonderful idea when he made people. He didn't make our soul to float in thin air. He tucked it into a body. He made some parts private. And the body he gave us deserves total respect.

Ephesians 5:29 says that "No one hates his own body but lovingly cares for it." Problem is, some people have a messed-up love for their body. They might go without food or get into piercing and cutting. Others abuse drugs, overeat, never get off the couch, or indulge themselves in pleasure in a million other ways.

God has a better plan for your body.

The apostle Paul had a big question for the people in Corinth. "Don't you know that your body is the temple of the Holy Spirit, who lives in you and was given to you by God?" (1 Corinthians 6:19). If your body is God's temple, he said, then you should use it for God's glory. And that's where total respect comes in. Here are three respect-filled facts to remember:

Your body has to last a long time. As a kid you have the chance to take care of your body now before it turns to flab—or before your teeth fall out. And to enjoy your hair while you have it!

Your body belongs to you. No one has the right to hurt your body. No one has a reason to touch the parts covered up by your swimsuit—unless it's a doctor making sure you're healthy or a parent helping you get clean.

Your body belongs to your future husband or wife. You've no doubt noticed there's a difference between boys and girls. God built you that way, and he designed you to enjoy being close to your spouse. One incredibly important way you can love your body is to play by God's rules when it comes to guy-girl relationships.

God made your body to give you all kinds of good feelings. But he made you to enjoy them in a way that doesn't hurt you or others. That's loving your body like God intended. And that's how you bring glory to him!

 TALK: Do you know people who abuse their body—by neglecting it or overindulging it? What happens to them in the long run?

 PRAY: *God, thanks for giving us our body. It is a wonderful gift from you.*

 ACT: How do you want to love your body today?

20 No Strings Attached

Bible Reading: John 3:16-21

God so loved the world that he gave his only Son, so that everyone who believes in him will not perish but have eternal life. John 3:16

"You can go in and see your dad now," a nurse told Little Matt. As he entered the hospital room, he stared with wide eyes at his father lying in the big bed. Big Matt was surrounded by big tubes and little TV screens.

Dad looked like he was sleeping, but his eyes flickered open when his son walked in. "Hi, Matty," he said, smiling. He tried to reach out to his son, but a needle stuck in his hand made it a struggle to move.

Little Matt gently took Big Matt's hand. He knew his dad wasn't sick. Dad had just done something unbelievable for his brother Ben, Little Matt's uncle. When Uncle Ben's kidneys quit working, Dad gave up one of his, letting doctors remove it from his body and transplant it into Ben's. His dad had saved his uncle's life.

Some gifts are so big and so good that there is no hope of ever paying them back . . . like a dad who donates an organ to his brother . . . a police officer who dies to save a child . . . a Savior who dies for the sins of the world.

Those are gifts given with no strings attached. But lots of the so-called love we get in life falls short of that incredible care.

Much love is an "I love you *if . . .*" or "I love you *because . . .*" kind of love. It says "I love you *if* you behave well" or "I love you *if* you act or dress a certain way" or "I love you *if* you disappear and don't bug me." Or it says "I love you *because* you are so beautiful" or "I love you *because* you make me laugh." That's love we have to earn by being the right person, doing the right thing, or having the right stuff. This *"if"* and *"because"* love is *conditional* love.

"I love you, *period"* is the kind of love we're all looking for. It comes with no conditions. It sticks around whether we deserve it or not. It says "I love you no matter what you might be like deep inside. I love you no matter what might change about you. I love you no matter what you can or can't do for me." "Love, *period"* gives without demanding anything in return. "Love, *period"* is unconditional.

That's the kind of love Big Matt had for his brother. And it's the great love God has for you, the one that prompted him to give his Son, Jesus, to die for your sins. There's no way you can earn this type of love, nor can you lose it. It arrives with no strings attached!

 TALK: In what ways can you love the people around you with a "love, *period"* kind of love?

 PRAY: Tell God thanks for his unconditional love and ask him to fill you with his love for others.

 ACT: Show a friend some "love, *period"* love today!

21 The Right Stuff

Bible Reading: Hebrews 13:4

> *Give honor to marriage, and remain faithful to one another in marriage.*
> *Hebrews 13:4*

Jeremy cried as he watched Julie's dad steer the heavy rental truck down the street. With shoulders heaving, he sobbed as Julie and her mom followed in the family van. The one perfect woman for Jeremy had just moved out of his life. Life as he knew it was over. He would never love again. Tough break for a second-grader.

You might never have thought about your own marriage. But it probably crosses the minds of your dad and mom once in a while. Maybe they're already praying that God will lead you to the right husband or wife someday. Scary!

You still might think the opposite sex has icky germs. Or you might be looking out the corner of your eye and kind of liking the boy or girl who sits kitty-corner from you at school. You never know when the magic moment will strike when you suddenly realize that guys—or gals—are God's greatest invention ever.

Wherever you're at, there's one key principle that works all along the way: *Never date someone who wouldn't make a fantastic mate.*

So what does "fantastic" look like? It might not be the gorgeous girl who wins the Teen Miss contest. Or the muscled guy who leads his high school football squad to a state championship. Here are two tips for picking top choices:

Tip 1: *God wants you to pick someone you love.* Don't bother chasing a person just because that's who everyone else likes. Find someone who fits you. Then limit your choice to people with whom you can share the love described in 1 Corinthians 13:4-8. When you spot someone you think you like, put your potential relationship to that test. Yep, it's a tough test. Go ahead and cross off your list everyone who doesn't pass!

Tip 2: *God wants you to pick someone who follows him like you do.* Second Corinthians 6:14 (NCV) says, "You are not the same as those who do not believe. So do not join yourselves to them. Good and bad do not belong together. Light and darkness cannot share together." The right date—and mate—will never be someone who doesn't follow Jesus enthusiastically. So don't aim your heart at non-Christians!

You can act on that principle right now by making up your mind *today* to always seek God's best choice for you. He has a great plan. Don't ever settle for second best—not in whom you like, not in whom you date, not in whom you marry.

 TALK: How is your heart? Is it set on seeking God's best—both now and later?

 PRAY: It's not too early to pray about marriage. Ask God today to lead you to the right person—but not for a whole bunch of years!

 ACT: Will you make one commitment today—to talk openly with your parents about guys or girls you think you could love? Your family can help you start learning how to make God's best choice.

22 Lemonade Boy

Bible Reading: Matthew 6:19-21

Don't store up treasures here on earth. . . . Store your treasures in heaven. Matthew 6:19-20

Evan's story all starts with lemonade stands. Not just *one* lemonade stand, mind you, but a whole chain of lemonade stands.

Evan loved the *whirrr-king-ka-chink* noise of his automated coin-counting bank. And one summer when the sun blazed hot and all the people of his hometown were suffering mightily in the heat, he struck on an idea. A money gusher of an idea. On the main street corner of his beloved hometown, Evan built a lemonade stand. With everyone in the town a-sweltering in the heat, he sold lemonade by the barrel. Because his lemonade was so good and the sun so hot, he could charge premium prices. And he did.

But Evan was just getting warmed up. Soon he opened other lemonade stands in the suburbs. He signed up other kids to dispense the lemonade while he mixed the juice, hauled it to the stands, and ran home with the profits. Pretty soon he was the undisputed lemonade king of Smellyfoot, South Dakota.

Evan was helping people by quenching their thirst, but he wasn't thinking much about that. All he cared about was the garage full of stuff he'd bought with his money. Not that he enjoyed any of it all that much. All that mattered to Evan was getting *more*.

Talk about it: Are you ever like Evan? Do you ever just want more and more?

It's normal to want great stuff. The secret is wanting the *best* stuff.

Like Evan, it's easy to think that the best stuff you could have are *things* like CDs, clothes, cars, video games, sports gear, computer equipment, and more. But have you ever pondered where that stuff will be just a year from now? The clothes will be out of style, the electronics obsolete, and the video games a total bore. And a few years after that, everything will be dust.

If stuff is all you can show for your hard work, you won't have much to show. But you have the chance to make a wiser choice—to invest your time and efforts in treasures that will last beyond the next couple of years.

The treasures that will last forever are the close, loving connections we make with people—the kind that result in them trusting Christ and growing as his disciples. Those are treasures that will never lose their value or become out-of-date. And that's an investment opportunity too good to pass up!

 TALK: How can you invest your time in treasures that will last?

 PRAY: *Lord, help us wisely invest our life in things that matter for eternity.*

 ACT: What changes do you need to make to the way you are investing your time? Invest some time and energy in a friend today!

23 What's So Funny about Money?

Bible Reading: Matthew 6:22-24
You cannot serve both God and money. Matthew 6:24

Did you hear about Fred and Frank, the two bungling counterfeiters? These dimwits printed a pile of funny money, only this phony currency was *really* phony. Instead of printing $20, $50, or $100 bills, they printed thousands of $18 bills.

"How are we going to spend our money?" Fred said to Frank. "Everybody around here knows that our $18 bills are fakes."

"I have an idea," said Frank. "Let's haul the money way out in the backwoods. Maybe people there will change some of our bills for real money."

So Fred and Frank took a sack of phony money and started driving far back into the hills, first on a highway, then on a country road, then on a dusty dirt road. After several hours, they drove up to an old, broken-down general store. "These people won't think twice about changing an $18 bill," Fred and Frank agreed.

They walked into the store and approached the old clerk behind the counter. "Would you be able to make change for us today?" said Fred.

"I reckon I will," said the store clerk. "What do you need?"

Frank answered, "Well, can you change this $18 bill?"

"Sure enough," the store clerk said, reaching for the bill.

Fred turned to Frank and winked. Their plan seemed to be working.

"By the way," said the store clerk, "which kind of bills would you like in return— two nines or three sixes?"

If money is always at the center of your life, you will have more problems than Fred and Frank.

Money is funny. The more you get, the more you want. But Jesus put it all on the line: You can't serve both God and money. When money controls your life, you want to grab and hoard and spend everything on yourself. When God controls your life, you are happy to share.

For Christians, money is a tool to help others. That doesn't mean you need to give away everything you have. It just means you don't let your desire to stuff yourself with stuff run out of control.

If the only thing dancing in your head right now is the swarm of presents you want to *get* this Christmas, you might be serving the wrong master—money. Let God change your heart as you think about all you can *give* at this giving time of the year!

 TALK: What is dancing in your thoughts right now—giving or getting?

 PRAY: *Father, build in us the kind of giving heart that you have—the one that was so selfless that you sent your Son to earth.*

 ACT: Stop and think today about the gifts you're giving this Christmas. Do you need to do any last-minute shopping or present making?

Bible Reading: Luke 2:1-7
She gave birth to her first child, a son. Luke 2:7

Do you really know the Christmas story? Test your knowledge by circling the correct response to each of the following items of Nativity trivia. Check your answers at the bottom of the page.

1. Joseph's ancestors came from
   a) Bethlehem   b) Nazareth   c) New Jersey
   d) none of the above

2. True or false: Mary and Joseph were married when Jesus was born.

3. A manger is a
   a) stable for domestic animals   b) wooden hay storage bin
   c) feeding trough   d) barn

4. Who told Mary and Joseph to go to Bethlehem in the first place?
   a) Caesar Augustus   b) an angel in a dream
   c) an old friend   d) a travel agent

5. Who saw the "star in the east"?
   a) shepherds   b) kings   c) queens
   d) none of the above

6. The wise men found Jesus in a
   a) stable   b) manger   c) Holiday Inn   d) house

The most important thing about the Christmas story isn't your mastery of Nativity trivia. At the center of Christmas is the birth of Jesus. Think about it: The God who made heaven and earth—the God who made you—came to earth in the form of a human baby born to a poor couple. God, who is spirit, became a human just like you.

And God did all of that because he loves you and wants to be friends with you. The greatest gift God ever gave you was himself—in the form of his Son. The greatest gift you can ever give him is yourself—so you can enjoy the friendship God wants to have with you.

 TALK: How are you going to give yourself to God in thanks for all that he has given you?

 PRAY: *God, we want to give ourselves to you. Show us how!*

 ACT: Spend some time today with God—worshiping the One who came into your world to know you!

Answers:
1-a (Luke 2:3-4); 2-False, they were only engaged, but Jesus was God's Son, not Joseph's (Luke 2:5); 3-c; 4-a (Luke 2:1); 5-d, the Bible calls them "wise men" (Matthew 2:1); 6-d (Matthew 2:11).

25 Peace on Earth!

Bible Reading: Luke 2:8-14

Glory to God in the highest heaven, and peace on earth to all whom God favors. Luke 2:14

You've probably sung each of the following Christmas songs below—except that the titles have been changed just to tweak your brains. See if you can figure out the real titles—the first one, for example, is "Deck the Halls."

1. Decorate the interior passageways
2. Listen, the heavenly messengers produce musical sounds
3. The Christmas preceding all others
4. Move toward me, entire group of those who are loyal in their belief
5. Expectation of arrival to populated area by mythical, masculine perennial gift giver
6. The first person plural of a trio of Far Eastern heads of state
7. Small masculine master of percussion instrument
8. Yuletide celebration colored with a color that is no color
9. Happy Yuletide desired for the second person singular or plural by us
10. Nocturnal time span of total quietness

There was no mixed-up message when the angels sang, "Peace on earth." They brought joyful news: Jesus Christ is the Prince of Peace!

Jesus came to bring peace to your world. He wants to bring peace to you. And no person and no thing can provide the peace Jesus promises. His peace starts with the inner peace of trusting him and letting his peace rule your life.

As you grow in Jesus' peace, you become a peacemaker just like him. When your family isn't getting along at home, are you an agent for peace or do you make things worse? When your little brother starts bugging you, do you try to calm him or do you bug him just as badly? When your friends are acting hurtful or gossipy—and you are the victim—do you look for ways to work things out?

The peace Jesus provided—that you can experience today—is what Christmas is all about. So spread God's peace. That's a birthday present Jesus will appreciate.

 TALK: How will you share the peace of Jesus today?

 PRAY: *Jesus, you brought real peace to our world. Make us peacemakers too.*

 ACT: Make a plan to spread God's peace to the world around you.

Answers:
1. "Deck the Halls"; 2. "Hark, the Herald Angels Sing"; 3. "The First Noel"; 4. "O Come, All Ye Faithful"; 5. "Santa Claus Is Coming to Town"; 6. "We Three Kings of Orient Are"; 7. "The Little Drummer Boy"; 8. "White Christmas"; 9. "We Wish You a Merry Christmas"; 10. "Silent Night"

26 The Gifts That Really Count

Bible Reading: Matthew 6:25-33

Your heavenly Father . . . will give you all you need from day to day if you live for him and make the Kingdom of God your primary concern. Matthew 6:32-33

This year you played it smart. You wanted to make sure everything you received was the right size and color, so your Christmas list was short and sweet:

- a gift certificate to my favorite clothing store
- a gift certificate to my favorite music store
- a gift certificate to my favorite computer and software store
- a gift certificate to my favorite video store
- a five-pound box of money

But as you sit surveying your opened gifts, you are seriously depressed. All your hopes and dreams for Christmas have turned into a nightmare.

Your dad gave you a complete bowling outfit—ball, bag, shoes, and two brightly colored bowling shirts. You don't even bowl.

Your mom bought you a cello and a series of instructional videos. But you're tone deaf.

Your little brother gave you his pet frog. He cried when you opened the jar he wrapped it in two weeks ago because old Froggy was dead.

Your grandmother gave you another pair of polka-dotted flannel pajamas—your sixth pair in six years—which are two sizes too small.

Your dear Uncle Smedley gave you a year's subscription to *Exceptional Student Magazine* and promised you a dime for every A you get this year.

Okay, maybe it wasn't that bad. But you probably didn't get everything you wanted for Christmas, did you? We all have to deal with unmet expectations.

But God has a gift for you that you won't want to return. In Matthew 6:25-33 God promised to provide everything you *need* for the coming year. It might be difficult to admit you can survive without that five-pound box of money, but somehow you'll make it. In the meantime, God knows your real needs—spiritual, relational, emotional, and material—even those you aren't aware of. And he loves you so much that he will make sure you never lack those things. You job is to keep living for him and watching him fill your life with his absolute best.

 TALK: What kind of gifts are you looking for God to give you? Are you looking for his best?

 PRAY: Talk to God about your disappointments about stuff—and set your heart on things that count.

 ACT: Are you angry because you didn't get enough for Christmas? Talk to God about it and trust him to always meet your *real* needs.

27 Why Pray When You Can Worry?

Bible Reading: Matthew 6:34
> *Don't worry about tomorrow, for tomorrow will bring its own worries.*
> *Matthew 6:34*

As you think about the upcoming year, are you worried about what might happen? Will money become worthless, sending people back to swapping cows and chickens? Will chunks from a meteor shower land in your backyard? Might a new ice age freeze your eyelids shut or global warming turn your pizza to liquid?

Enough happy thoughts. You can worry all you want about those things, but it won't do you any good. Just look at what two wise people say about worry:

- Worry never robs tomorrow of its sorrow, it only saps today of its joy. *Leo Buscaglia*
- Don't worry about the world coming to an end today. It's already tomorrow in Australia. *Charles Schultz*

The best word about worry, of course, comes from Jesus. His instruction? "Don't." Paul echoed that thought in Philippians 4:6: "Don't worry about anything; instead pray about everything. Tell God what you need, and thank him for all he has done." The apostle Peter added, "Give all your worries and cares to God, for he cares about what happens to you" (1 Peter 5:7).

Sure, there will be plenty of things about next year you won't like—natural disasters, world tension, community strife, rumbles with friends or parents or your piano teacher, or maybe the serious illness of someone you care about. God never promised you a life without problems.

When bad, scary things come up, do you feel a sudden knot of worry in the pit of your stomach? That knot is your reminder that it's time to pray. Whenever you feel yourself wound tight with worry, don't let it paralyze you. Instead let it *prayer*-alyze you. Rush your concern to God in prayer. Tell him straight up how you feel. Fill him in on the people or situations that worry you. Give him the details and invite him to take control of them and you. Keep praying until your worry settles down. And when your nervousness comes back, pray again . . . and again . . . and again.

When you interpret worry as a natural nudge to pray, whatever problems you face won't be so scary. You'll take them as opportunities for God to work as you hand them over to him in prayer.

 TALK: What worries you most about the next few days? the next month? the next year?

 PRAY: Take some time to give all your concerns to God, because he cares for you.

 ACT: Pray for and with a friend who is weighed down by big worries.

Time to Settle In

Bible Reading: John 15:1-4
Remain in me, and I will remain in you. John 15:4

Here we go again, Jared thought with disgust. He had become way too good at packing up his room for a move. His family hadn't ever stayed in one place for more than three years, and this time they didn't even come close to that record. Jared had hoped that this was the time they would stay put. He had made good friends, his family had found a fantastic church, and everything seemed to be humming along.

But then he heard the words he dreaded: "I've been transferred again."

"You'll love Madera!" his mom had said.

Madera! The steamy central valley of California didn't sound exciting in the least. Jared had heard summers were so hot you could fry an egg on the sidewalk! But all he could say to his mom was, "What choice do I have?"

Even though Jared struggled year after year through painful family moves, he learned an important lesson. Here's something he wrote in his journal shortly after arriving in Madera.

Here I am again, Lord—a new place, surrounded by strange things and unknown people. I miss my friends and my life back home. I wonder if this new place will ever seem like home. I wonder if I'll ever be able to really settle in here.

At least I have you, Lord. At least I know that wherever I go, whether it's Madera or Montana or the remote jungles of Madagascar, you are still with me. You have made your home in me. You have settled in, and you're not going to be transferred and leave me alone. And I have made my home in you. Wherever I go, we will be together. Thank you, Jesus, for that promise.

Jared had discovered an amazing truth we need to know too. Jesus makes his home in us, and he wants us to make our home in him. In Revelation 3:20, Jesus issued this invitation: "Look! Here I stand at the door and knock. If you hear me calling and open the door, I will come in, and we will share a meal as friends."

You might move from place to place. Your friendships might change from year to year. All sorts of changes might make your life tomorrow look radically different from your life today. But one fact is sure: Jesus will never leave you. He is totally at home in you, and he invites you to be at home in him.

 TALK: What difference does it make to you that Jesus will never leave you, no matter what changes today brings?

 PRAY: *Jesus, thank you for being our closest friend—and for never leaving us alone.*

 ACT: Do you have a friend who doesn't know Jesus? How can you introduce your human friend to the best heavenly friend he or she can ever have?

29 "I Want to Be like Mike"

Bible Reading: John 15:5-8

Apart from me you can do nothing. John 15:5

Once upon a time a huge sports-drink company ran an ad campaign encouraging people to "be like Mike," as in NBA basketball legend Michael Jordan. The phrase "I want to be like Mike" was everywhere. Kids said it. Adults sang it. And the ads made it look like all you had to do to be totally popular, talented, and wealthy like Michael Jordan was swig this sports drink.

Every push of the TV remote buttons bombards you with pleas to be like Mike or Garth or Cindy or Gwyneth or somebody else big. Splash on this cologne, dial that long-distance number, slip into these boxers and—*shazzam!*—you will be a celebrity.

Talk about it: Can we ever be like those people in the ads? How do we get to be like someone?

Unless you know someone personally, you'll never really know what he's like—and if you don't know what that person is like, you can never really be like him! If you want to be like Mike, you have to get to know the real Mike—not the Mike you spot in TV ads. You have to spend time with him, get thrashed in hoops going one-on-one against him, and let him whisper in your ear the brand of sports drink he actually drinks. You have to know Mike to be like Mike.

Just like that, to get to be like Jesus you have to know him personally. If you want to have Christ's character, you have to get to know the real Jesus Christ so well that what he is like makes a difference in your life. Jesus said it best: "Apart from me you can do nothing."

So how can you get to know Jesus Christ up close and personal? You can listen to what other people say about him, but is that enough? Not really, because you are only hearing how *they* know him. Just listening to your pastor or parents or Sunday school teacher tell you about Christ isn't enough. You have to go further. You have to go one-on-one with Jesus.

Other people can't get close to God for you. They can't read, study, memorize, and meditate on the Word of God for you. They can't make time for you to talk with Jesus.

It's your choice—and challenge—to get to know him. But when you do, a cool thing happens: You become like Jesus!

 TALK: Aren't you glad that Jesus, the Son of God, wants to get to know you one-on-one? What can you do in the upcoming year to keep getting to know Jesus personally?

 PRAY: *Jesus, thanks for the invitation to get to know you up close and personal.*

 ACT: Make plans to spend time with Jesus this week—and in the new year.

30 "If It Weren't for Emily . . ."

Bible Reading: John 15:9-13

I command you to love each other in the same way that I love you.
John 15:12

"Nice outfit, Karen," a classmate said with a smirk. "What did your mother do with the other half of her old curtains? Did she sew an outfit for your brother?"

Emily couldn't help but hear. She knew Karen was just getting her daily dose of verbal cruelty from her classmates. Karen didn't exactly have what it takes to be popular. She was quiet, shy—and totally brainy. She lived in the library. She wouldn't know a gym if she wandered into one and went *splat* on the floor. And her style of dress was, well, decades behind the times. Any girl who called her a friend risked becoming a social reject like her, so no one did.

The next Sunday Emily heard this passage in church: "If we don't love people we can see, how can we love God, whom we have not seen?" (1 John 4:20). For a couple of days all that Emily could think about was Karen—and that Bible verse—and she knew what Jesus wanted her to do. As her fellow students stared and snickered, Emily sat down with Karen at lunch.

Emily stayed close friends with Karen through high school, even when it cost her other friends. By the end of high school, brainy Karen had the best grades in her class. Quite an honor—except it meant speaking at graduation. As Karen stood on the stage at the ceremony, she did her best to thank her parents and her teachers for their support. Then she choked. As Emily watched her friend break into tears, she stepped up to stand at Karen's side.

Holding her friend's hand, Karen continued. "Most of all, I want to thank Emily. When I was at my lowest point—rejected and embarrassed—she showed me what it means to be a friend. If it weren't for Emily, I wouldn't be here today."

Loving others as Christ loves us can be costly. But think about the price Jesus paid to love us. He left the glory and splendor of heaven. He came to earth, where people made fun of him, rejected him, beat him, and spit upon him—then he hung on a cross. Loving us was far from comfortable for him. It cost him everything.

Jesus wants us to pass on the awesome love he has given us. Each person you meet is worth the price of loving. And when you love like Jesus loves, you never know what kind of great friends you might make.

 TALK: How can you love people whom the world doesn't love? What will it cost you? Are you willing to pay that price?

 PRAY: *God, teach us how to love others like you love us.*

 ACT: Can you think of someone in your world who reminds you of Karen? How can you befriend that person?

31
What Do You Want to Be When You Grow Up?

Bible Reading: John 15:14-16
I appointed you to go and produce fruit that will last. John 15:16

Meet Drew, the swimmer. Drew joined her first swim team in third grade and never looked back. She won nearly every event she entered—freestyle, butterfly, breast-stroke, and relays. In high school, she won titles at state and junior national competitions. Two years into a brilliant college career, she qualified for the Olympic team. Next summer Drew will compete in her first Olympics.

Meet Pete, the Christian. Pete loves to sing, act, and perform. In high school he won the starring role in several plays and musicals. He was also the lead performer in his church's drama ministry. Everyone who knows Pete expects to see him in the movies someday. He was offered a full scholarship to a well-known acting school in New York. But he turned it down to attend missionary-training school. In six months he will be traveling to the Philippines on an evangelistic drama team.

Talk about it: What do you want to accomplish right now? How about when you're in high school? Or after?

Two students, two totally different goals. For Drew, personal achievement is the focus of her life. Everything centers on excelling and winning. Pete is different. He also has special skills, high goals, and notable achievements. But unlike Drew, Pete's accomplishments don't define Pete. He isn't Pete the actor or Pete the musician; he is Pete the Christian who acts and sings. To Pete, serving Christ is bigger and better than his personal goals. He sees his gifts and talents as ways to serve Christ, and his choices confirm his beliefs.

No matter what your skills and talents, the first job God gives you is to use your gifts to "produce fruit that will last." In the Bible, fruit stands for both your inner character and the impact you make on your world. Pete's first goal is to be the person Christ wants him to be so his life will bring others to Christ. He knows fame and fortune won't last forever, but people who trust Christ through the witness of his character and message will.

So does that mean that a Christian can't grow up to be an Olympic athlete or Broadway actor? Absolutely not. Just don't let your identity be defined by these pursuits. If you have trusted Christ, you are a Christian first, last, and always. Be focused on God's goals for your life. Then go do your best at anything and everything he's gifted you to be.

 TALK: How can you use your talents and skills to glorify God?

 PRAY: *God, we want to put you first in everything we do. Help us focus first on your purposes for our life.*

 ACT: Make a plan as a family to keep doing devotions after today!

Index of Bible Readings
of the Day

Index of Verses of the Day

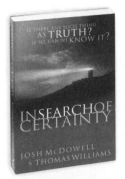

BE CONVINCED OF WHY YOU BELIEVE

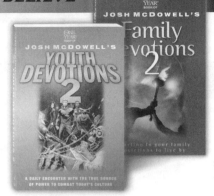

Josh McDowell's Youth Devotions 2
Josh McDowell's Family Devotions 2
to Youth/Families

"We are not fighting against people made of flesh and blood, but against the evil rulers and authorities of the unseen world . . ." (Ephesians 6:12, NLT). More than ever our young people need a spiritual defense. This second installment of Josh's best-selling youth and family devotions offer 365 daily devotional encounters with the true Power Source to strengthen your family spiritually and provide your young people with a resource that will help them combat today's culture. *Josh McDowell's Youth Devotions 2* 0-8423-4096-3
Josh McDowell's Family Devotions 2 0-8423-5625-8

The Deceivers **Book to Youth**

Written in the popular NovelPlus format, this book combines the adventures of Sarah Milford and Ryan Ortiz and their search for meaning, along with Josh's insights found in sections called "The Inside Story."

In dramatic fashion *The Deceivers* explains that unless Christ is who he claims to be—the true Son of God—then his offer to redeem us and provide meaning to life can't be real. This book presents not only the compelling evidence for the deity of Christ but also how God's plan is to transform us into a new creature with an intimate relationship with him. *The Deceivers* 0-8423-7969-X

Children Demand a Verdict **Book to Children**

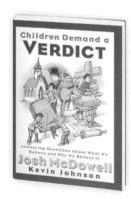

Children need clear and direct answers to their questions about God, the Bible, sin, death, etc. Directed to children ages 7–11, this question-and-answer book tackles 77 tough issues with clarity and relevance, questions such as: Why did God make people? How do we know Jesus was God? How could God write a book? Is the Bible always right? Are parts of the Bible make-believe? Why did Jesus die? Did Jesus really come back to life? Does God always forgive me? Why do people die? Will I come back to life like Jesus? *Children Demand a Verdict* 0-8423-7971-1

BE COMMITTED TO WHAT YOU BELIEVE

Video Series for Adult Groups

This 5-part interactive video series features Josh McDowell sharing how your young people have adopted distorted beliefs about God, truth, and reality and what you as adults can do about it. Step by step he explains how to lead your kids to know "why we believe what we believe" and how that is truly relevant to their everyday lives. This series provides the perfect launch for your group to build the true foundation of Christianity in the lives of the family, beginning with adults.

The series includes 5 video sessions of approximately 25 minutes each, a comprehensive Leader's Guide with reproducible handouts, the *Beyond Belief to Convictions* book, and a complimentary copy of *The Deceivers* NovelPlus book. (Also available on DVD.)
Belief Matters Video Series 0-8423-8018-3

Video Series for Youth Groups

Combining a powerful message, compelling video illustrations, and captivating group activities, this series will enable you to lead your students to this convincing conclusion: the ways of the world do not produce true meaning in life—only Christ as the true Son of God can transform our "dead lives" into a dynamic and meaningful life in relationship with him. Josh and Ron have created this interactive series to incite a revolution—a revolution to transform your young people into a generation of sacrificial and passionate followers of Christ. As a foundational building block of Christianity this series offers overwhelming evidence that Christ is the Messiah and challenges each student to commit totally to him.

The series includes 5 dramatic video illustrations, Leader's Guide of teaching lessons with reproducible handouts for group activities, and *The Deceivers* NovelPlus book. (Also available on DVD.) ***The Revolt Video Series*** 0-8423-8016-7

BE CHANGED BY WHO YOU BELIEVE

Workbook for Adult Groups

Combining interactive group discussion with daily activities, this workbook helps you overcome the distorted views of Christ and biblical truth held by most children and youth today. It will help you lead them to a fresh encounter with the "God who is passionate about his relationship with you" (Exodus 34:14, NLT). The daily activities reveal a credible, real, and relevant Christ you can share with each family member.

The workbook study provides 8 solid group teaching sessions for the weekly at-home assignments to model the message before others. *Belief Matters Workbook* Wkbk: 0-8423-8010-8 Ld. Gd: 0-8423-8011-6

Workbook for Youth Groups

When your students reject the world's counterfeit way of life, what will life in Christ really be like for them? This 8-session course helps each of your students realize that new life in Christ is about transformation, about belonging to Christ and one another in his Body, about knowing who they really are, and about living out their mission in life.

The Revolt Workbook is an 8-session youth group interactive course followed up with students engaging in two daily exercises per week. This study is the perfect follow-up to the companion *Revolt Video Series*. *The Revolt Workbook* Wkbk: 0-8423-7978-9 Ld. Gd: 0-8423-7979-7

Workbook for Children's Groups

To raise up the next generation of committed followers of Christ, we must start when they are young. These workbooks for children grades 1–3 and grades 4–6 present the foundational truth of why Christ came to earth. Written in simple terms, they lead your children to realize why doing wrong has separated them from God and why only Christ can bring them into a close family relationship with God.

In 8 fun-filled sessions, your children will learn why Christ is the true way and all other ways are false. These sessions lead children to a loving encounter with the "God who is passionate about his relationship with [them]" (Exodus 34:14, NLT).
True or False Workbook Younger Wkbk: 0-8423-8012-4 Older Wkbk: 0-8423-8013-2 Ld. Gd: 0-8423-8014-0

**Contact your Christian Supplier to obtain these resources
and begin the revolution in your home, church, and community.**